Donated by
Joseph and Diane Bast
to The Heartland Institute
2015

LABOR RELATIONS AND PUBLIC POLICY SERIES

No. 27

PREVAILING WAGE LEGISLATION:

THE DAVIS-BACON ACT, STATE "LITTLE DAVIS-BACON" ACTS, THE WALSH-HEALEY ACT, AND THE SERVICE CONTRACT ACT

by

ARMAND J. THIEBLOT, JR.

with a major contribution on the Service Contract Act by

BEVERLY H. BURNS, ESQ.

INDUSTRIAL RESEARCH UNIT
The Wharton School
Vance Hall
University of Pennsylvania
Philadelphia, Pennsylvania 19104-6358

Copyright © 1986 by the Trustees of the University of Pennsylvania
Library of Congress Catalog Card Number 85-081948
MANUFACTURED IN THE UNITED STATES OF AMERICA
ISBN: 0-89546-055-6
ISSN: 0075-7470

Foreword

In 1968, the Industrial Research Unit inaugurated its Labor Relations and Public Policy Series as a means of examining issues and stimulating discussions in the complex and controversial areas of collective bargaining and the regulation of labor-management disputes. Thus far, twenty-nine monographs have been published in this series. Eleven of these deal with various policies and procedures of the National Labor Relations Board. The other eighteen cover such significant issues as collective bargaining in the 1970s; welfare and strikes; opening the skilled construction trades to blacks; the Davis-Bacon Act; the labor-management situation in urban school systems; old age, handicapped, and Vietnam-era antidiscrimination legislation; the impact of the Occupational Safety and Health Act; the Landrum-Griffin Act; the effects of the AT&T-EEO consent decree; unions' rights to company information; employee relations and regulation; operating during strikes; union violence and the law; the impact of antitrust legislation on employee relations; deregulation and union losses in trucking; and comparable worth theory and practice.

This study, *Prevailing Wage Legislation: The Davis-Bacon Act, State "Little Davis-Bacon" Acts, the Walsh-Healey Act, and the Service Contract Act,* No. 27 in the series, marks the first overall study of these laws, most of which date back to the Great Depression. The Walsh-Healey Act of 1936 has been virtually moribund since 1964 when adverse court decisions ended its wage setting procedures. Since then the Occupational Safety and Health Act (OSHA) has assumed Walsh-Healey's functions in this important area, and just this year, legislation eliminated the Walsh-Healey requirement that government contractors pay time and one-half for work over eight hours in one day which is, of course, over and above the requirement for overtime after forty hours per week as legislated under the Fair Labor Standards Act of 1938, as amended, and under most state minimum wage laws. Truly the Walsh-Healey Act is an anachronism that should be repealed.

The largest section of this study concerns the Davis-Bacon Act and similar state laws. The oldest of such legislation setting so-called prevailing wage laws, these acts cover government-financed construction. They remained largely the private preserve of the construction industry, and particularly the AFL-CIO building trades unions, until the early 1970s when three important developments occurred: union construction wages inflated rapidly; the nonunion, or open shop, segment of the industry grew rapidly (today an estimated 70 percent of construction dollar volume is open shop); and Professor Armand J. Thieblot, Jr., wrote his initial study of the Davis-Bacon Act, which the Wharton Industrial Research Unit published in 1975. Dr. Thieblot, who resigned from his academic position in 1983, to pursue his writing and business career, also wrote shorter studies of state "Little Davis-Bacon" acts before turning to this larger work. There is no question that his pioneer work has provided the factual basis for the ensuing debate concerning the efficacy of such legislation which this current study shows has taken place even since 1975, and which has resulted in vastly increased knowledge of these laws by legislators and by the public. Dr. Thieblot's studies of prevailing wage laws are but part of his contributions to public policy issues. His other works, all published by the Wharton Industrial Research Unit, include *Negro Employment in Finance* (1970), *Welfare and Strikes* (1972), and *Union Violence: The Record and the Response by Courts, Legislatures, and the NLRB* (1983). Dr. Thieblot received the Master of Business Administration and Doctor of Philosophy degrees from the Wharton School, University of Pennsylvania. Chapter IV, examining state "Little Davis-Bacon" acts, was originally published in the *Government Union Review,* Vol. 4, No. 4 (Fall, 1983), and is reprinted here, after revision and updating, with the permission of the editors of this review.

The newest, and one of the least known prevailing wage laws, the Service Contract Act of 1965, purports to cover and to protect low-wage employees, but can also be extended to the affluent service employee. The basic research on this law and its administration was conducted by Beverly Hall Burns, Esq., member of the Detroit law firm, Miller, Canfield, Paddock & Stone. At the time during which the research was performed, she was on the faculty of Glassboro State College, Glassboro, New Jersey. Her original contribution appeared in the *Villanova Law Review,* Volume 29, No. 2 (1983–84). We are grateful to the editors of this review for permission to reproduce the bulk of the article, which was commissioned as part of this study.

Many persons assisted in this study. Interviews of state "little Davis-Bacon" acts across the country were conducted by Philip W. Northrup. Numerous administrative matters for the project were ably handled by the Industrial Research Unit's office manager, Ms. Marthenia A. Perrin. My secretary, Ms. Geraldine M. Fanelli, took care of regular communications with Dr. Thieblot.

Foreword

Initial support for the research was provided by the Carthage Foundation through the courtesy and interest of its treasurer, Mr. Richard M. Larry. Subsequent support for the Davis-Bacon and "Little Davis-Bacon" sectors was provided by the Public Service Research Foundation, courtesy of its chief executive, David Y. Denholm, and its former editor, George C. Bevel. This Foundation also provided a regular clipping file that was most helpful in keeping up with fast moving developments, especially at the state level. Publication costs were paid for by the Public Service Research Foundation grant, supplemented by support from the Industrial Research Unit's industry Research Advisory Group, the Gulf Oil Foundation, the Rollin M. Gerstacker Foundation, and the Mobile Oil Company.

As in all works published by the Industrial Research Unit, the author is solely responsible for the research and for all opinions expressed, which should not be attributed to the grantors or to the University of Pennsylvania.

HERBERT R. NORTHRUP, *Director*
Industrial Research Unit
The Wharton School
University of Pennsylvania

Philadelphia
September 1985

TABLE OF CONTENTS

	PAGE
FOREWORD	iii

CHAPTER

I. INTRODUCTION TO PREVAILING WAGE LAWS 1

    Purpose of and Support for Prevailing Wage Laws.... 3

        Competitive Bidding and Labor Costs................. 3
        Union Support 4
        Policy Considerations 5
        Summary 8

    Organization of the Study................................ 8

II. THE PREVAILING WAGE CONCEPT 11

    Origin of the Prevailing Wage Concept 12

        Mirror of Reality 13
        Problems with Defining Prevailing.................... 14

    Failure of the Prevailing Concept........................ 16

        Not a Statistical Parameter............................ 17
        Further Problems...................................... 18

    Summary.. 19

III. THE DAVIS-BACON ACT................................... 21

    Domain of Davis-Bacon.................................. 21

        Disproportionate Impact............................... 22
        Increasing Interest in Repeal 22

    Purpose of this Chapter 24

    History of the Davis-Bacon Act 25

        The Prevailing Wage Concept........................ 25
        State Precursors to the Federal Act.................. 27
        Congressional Activities 27
        Rationale for the Act.................................. 29

The Original Act... 31
The Current Davis-Bacon Law.......................... 33
Inclusion in Other Laws.................................. 35
Related Statutes.. 36
Coverage of the Davis-Bacon Act..................... 38

Administration and Its Problems......................... 40

Defining Prevailing.. 40
Comparison with Walsh-Healey Administration..... 43
Post-War Complications 44
Mechanics of Administration 47

Challenges to Davis-Bacon Administration............. 52

Comptroller General's Authority....................... 53
Comptroller General's Activities....................... 54
Comptroller General's Challenge...................... 54
Operating Patterns.. 57
Classification of Workers 61
Surveys 62
Similar Construction 63
Site of the Work... 64
Importation of Wage Rates............................. 66
Emphasis on Union Rates............................... 68
Sample Size and Other Survey Problems............. 71
Problems and Opportunities for Error................ 73

Defense of Davis-Bacon Administration................. 77

GAO Report Restated.................................... 77
Response of the Department of Labor 78
Other Defenses of Davis-Bacon Administration...... 83

Administrative Changes..................................... 84

1982 Proposals 84
Implications of the Changes............................ 89

Summary of Administrative Impact...................... 91

Economic Impact of Davis-Bacon......................... 93

Costs Based on Wage Differential Estimates......... 94
Direct Analysis of Project Costs 104

	Survey of Contractors...............................	107
	Econometric Analyses..............................	108
	Summary of Cost Estimates........................	113
Productivity and Related Matters......................		113
	Management Incentive Argument..................	114
	Productivity Argument	114
	Measures of Productivity Effect	116
	Summary of Cost-Related Questions	119
Policy Considerations..................................		120
	Original Purpose—Stated Rationale of the Act.....	120
	Imputed Purpose of the Act.......................	122
	Other Policy Issues................................	124
	Test of the Impact of Repeal......................	128
Summary and Recommendations		129
	Alternatives Short of Repeal......................	130
	Summary	135
IV. STATE PREVAILING WAGE LAWS.........................		137
History and Overview of State Prevailing Wage Laws		138
	Characteristics of the State Prevailing Wage Laws	140
	Contract Threshold.................................	142
	Local and Public Agency Contracts	144
	Federal-State Overlap.............................	145
	Establishment of Prevailing Rates	145
Individual State Laws: Summary, Analysis, and Present Legislative and Judicial Activity..............		150
	Alabama	150
	Alaska...	151
	Arizona	154
	Arkansas...	156
	California..	157
	Colorado	159
	Connecticut..	160
	Delaware...	161
	District of Columbia...............................	162

Florida	163
Georgia	164
Hawaii	164
Idaho	165
Illinois	167
Indiana	168
Iowa	169
Kansas	169
Kentucky	171
Louisiana	172
Maine	173
Maryland	174
Massachusetts	175
Michigan	177
Minnesota	178
Mississippi	179
Missouri	179
Montana	180
Nebraska	181
Nevada	182
New Hampshire	184
New Jersey	184
New Mexico	186
New York	186
North Carolina	189
North Dakota	190
Ohio	190
Oklahoma	191
Oregon	192
Pennsylvania	193
Rhode Island	194
South Carolina	195
South Dakota	195
Tennessee	195
Texas	196
Utah	197
Vermont	198
Virginia	198
Washington	198
West Virginia	199
Wisconsin	199
Wyoming	200

Table of Contents xi

      Summary and Evaluation of the Prevailing Wage Laws 201

          Summary of Recent Legislative Activity 201
          Ranking of the State Laws 202
          Conclusion 204

V. THE WALSH-HEALEY PUBLIC CONTRACTS ACT 207

      History and Development of the Walsh-Healey Act ... 207

          Enactment and Goals of the Walsh-Healey Act 209
          The Walsh-Healey Act in Its Original Form 210

      Walsh-Healey Administration 217

          Rate Setting 218
          Defining Prevailing 219
          The Locality Issue 223
          End of Wage Determinations Under Walsh-Healey 225

      Current Status of the Walsh-Healey Act 227

VI. THE SERVICE CONTRACT ACT 229

      History and Overview of the Service Contract Act 230

          Other Possible Rationales 232

      The Act in Its Original Form 235

      The 1972 Amendments 237

      The 1976 Amendments 239

      Problems with Administration and Interpretation of the Act 240

          The Locality Issue 240
          Legal Reaction to the Locality Question 244
          Summary, Locality Issue 248
          Contract and Employee Classification Issues 249
          Legal Reaction to the Classification Question 250
          Continuing Problems with Classification 251
          Summary of the Classification Issue 253

The Successor Contractor Issue....................... 254
Legal Reaction to the Successorship Question 255
Summary of Successorship Question 257
Administrative and Other Questions.................. 258
Other 1985 Rule Changes 261

1983 General Accounting Office Recommendations ... 262

Costs of the Act 263

Conclusions and Recommendations 265

    Providing Wage Protection for Unskilled, Low-Paid
      Service Workers...................................... 265
    Prevent Wage Busting and Maintain the Quality
      Level of Work 266
    Geographic Balance and Protection of Local Contractors from Itinerants............................ 268
    Other Rationales: Government as Model Employer,
      Protection of Government Workers, Encouragement of Labor Unions.............................. 269
    Recommendations 269

VII. CONCLUSION 271

Review... 271

Recommendations.. 272

INDEX 275

CHAPTER I

Introduction to Prevailing Wage Laws

This study reviews all of the prevailing wage laws of the United States affecting private employers. At the federal level, there are three such laws: the Davis-Bacon Act, which applies to the construction industry; the Walsh-Healey Public Contracts Act, which applies to employers in manufacturing and supply industries; and the O'Hara-McNamara Services Act (Service Contract Act), which applies to suppliers of personal and business services. Additionally, there are thirty-five prevailing wage laws at the state level and a few more at the local government level.[1] These last are "public works" laws and therefore apply principally to the construction industry, although in a few cases they extend to related groups such as trucking or material supply, and in even fewer cases to groups completely unrelated to construction, such as meatcutting, janitorial services, or printing.

In general, the prevailing wage laws require contractors performing covered work to maintain minimum rates of pay for certain of their employees. Their name derives from the fact that the minimum rates of pay they require are not fixed by legislation or regulation, but are set with respect to wage rates determined by the secretary of labor—or by a designated administrator in the case of the state and local laws—to be the wage rates that prevail for similar workers performing similar work on projects of a similar nature in the locality where the contracted work is to be performed.

---

[1] In addition to these, there is a larger number of prevailing wage laws used by municipal or county governments to set wage rates for civil service employees by fixing them with respect to privately employed individuals doing similar work in the community. They are not covered here because of the special nature of that employment relationship, and because the fundamental concepts underlying them are entirely different. The municipal civil service prevailing wage laws are a special case of the economic arguments concerning comparable worth. As to whether they result in higher wages for municipal service employees, the results are mixed. One recent study [Hirsch and Rufolo, *Effects of Prevailing Wage Laws on Municipal Government Wages*, 13 J. Urb. Econ. 112–26 (1983)] suggested that regardless of the statistical outcome, the threat of such laws causes municipal wages to increase, because government employers would rather overpay than submit to the restrictions and limitations on flexibility that such laws entail.

1

Although the requirements of these laws are simple, the process of establishing prevailing rates is neither easy nor sure; and although the laws would seem to make few impositions on government contractors, their impact can range from modest to severe. The three federal laws, although administered by the same agency, use three different methods for establishing prevailing rates; and the state laws add further variations. As a result, even if the same raw wage data were surveyed for the different laws, various rates could be selected as prevailing. Depending on the circumstances, the rate chosen might be the survey's minimum rate, a median or modal rate, or the union rate; additionally, a mean or average rate might be calculated from survey data and selected as prevailing, even though no individual in the survey was actually paid that rate; finally, some other rate might be selected, such as the federal minimum wage or a new union rate that had been negotiated but not yet paid. The amount of a prevailing rate could be the same as the federal minimum wage rate, or could be as much as five times greater than the federal minimum wage, depending on the particular situation.

The rate set by a prevailing wage law could impose minimal requirements on all contractors—as under the Walsh-Healey Act, for example, which has not set rates any higher than the federal minimum wage since 1964—or could affect different contractors in different ways. Under the Davis-Bacon Act, for example, although a union contractor might feel little effect other than from the requirement to submit wage reports and other paperwork, a low-wage, nonunion contractor might find it necessary to increase wage rates substantially and alter hiring practices or work assignments from those that would customarily be used on private contracts. Such a nonunion contractor would not only suffer the effects of disruption to normal practices, but would also lose the competitive advantage that the lower wages and greater flexibility of nonunion operation would otherwise allow.

Finally, the overall impact of the prevailing rate requirement is to increase the cost to the government of purchasing materials, services, and public works by substantial amounts over what they would cost in the open market. It is estimated, for example, that the Davis-Bacon Act may add $1 billion per year to the cost of federal buildings and other public works,[2] and the Service Contract Act may add as much as $500 million to the cost of services purchased by the federal government.[3] In addition, to the degree that

---

[2] See Chapter IV, *infra.*
[3] See Chapter VI, *infra.*

Introduction 3

the prevailing wage laws require payment of wage rates that are above the normal market rates, they tend to move the market higher, thus spreading inflated rates for government work into the private sector.

PURPOSE OF AND SUPPORT FOR PREVAILING WAGE LAWS

Prevailing wage laws have been under increasing pressure in recent years. The first half of 1985, for example, saw regulatory reform of the Davis-Bacon and Service Contract Acts, the final evisceration of the Walsh-Healey Act, and the repeal of three state prevailing wage laws. Nevertheless, strong residual support exists for prevailing wage laws; some of which may derive from a misunderstanding of the economic precepts attached to the prevailing wage laws because of their application as part of the system of government procurement. Because these precepts are common to all of the prevailing wage laws and are central to the laws' intended purposes, they will be considered here before proceeding to a discussion of the concept of prevailing and the analysis of the individual laws.

Competitive Bidding and Labor Costs

The prevailing wage laws all relate to government procurement of goods and services from the private sector. Since it is a duty of democratic governments to ensure that their procurement systems are free from favoritism or special privilege, under normal circumstances contractors are selected in open competition, based on their ability to supply or provide particular needs at lowest cost. With few exceptions, procurement systems are designed to award government contracts to the competitor who submits the lowest bid. This has led some observers to note that firms seeking government contracts must "competitively underbid" one another to produce the low bid necessary to obtain the work.

Given the limited number of options, labor costs loom large in the mix of input factors that can be controlled, and it is the specter of firms chopping wage rates to achieve low bids that provides the impetus for the prevailing wage laws. One important rationale for the laws, therefore, is that they are intended to shield employees of firms engaged in government contracting from the impact of competition on wage rates.

Union Support

There can be little doubt that the prevailing wage laws are closely related to the union movement, and that this support was also at least partially responsible for their enactment. As early as 1920, Sidney and Beatrice Webb attributed the adoption of British prevailing wage regulation to trade unions,[4] and unions were and are the principal proponents of prevailing wage laws in this country. This is true despite the fact that union members are rarely the direct beneficiaries of any super-minimum wage rates established, since collectively bargained rates provide the upper bound which may be equalled but is rarely exceeded by prevailing rates. The indirect benefits to union members, however, are substantial. Prevailing wages eliminate the economic penalties imposed on firms by unionization, making unionized firms more competitive in bidding for government work, and therefore lower employer resistance to unionization or to increased collectively bargained wage rates.

For these and perhaps other reasons, the principal spokesmen for prevailing wage laws have been union leaders, chiefly from the construction trades, since the Davis-Bacon Act, which covers construction work, is the most important of the prevailing wage laws. Thus, Robert Georgine, president of the Building and Construction Trades Department of the AFL-CIO, arguing for continuation of the Davis-Bacon Act despite its documented costs and administrative problems, gives the fundamental justification for all the prevailing wage laws:

> [The] conclusion [by the General Accounting Office] that the Davis-Bacon Act is unnecessary overlooks the fundamental principle which is the justification for all prevailing wage legislation.... The principle is that the price of labor should not become an element in the competition for Government construction wages and costs. It is this principle which must be addressed in any discussion of the continued need for the Davis-Bacon Act.[5]

Since the principles are the same for all government contracting, the arguments extend to the Walsh-Healey and Service Contract Acts as well. Because government contracts are awarded to the lowest bidder, protective legislation is deemed essential to prevent

---

[4] S. WEBB & B. WEBB, HISTORY OF TRADE UNIONISM (Longmans, Green, 1920 ed.) at 398-99.

[5] Statement of Robert A. Georgine, President, Building and Construction Trades Department, AFL-CIO, to the House Committee on Education and Labor, in Oversight Hearings on the Davis-Bacon Act, 96th Cong. 1st Sess., June 14, 1979, at 202, quoted in Reynolds, *Understanding Political Pricing of Labor Services: The Davis-Bacon Act* 3 J. LAB. RESEARCH 295-309 (1982) at 301.

Introduction 5

"cutthroat competition based on wage cutting" that would "undermine hard won local labor standards and permit unscrupulous wage-cutting employers to monopolize the construction industry."[6]

At first glance, Georgine's arguments (stripped of invective) appear to be a valid representation of reality, and seem to provide a watertight economic rationale for prevailing wage laws or some similar protective measure, provided that one is willing to grant the basic premise that government contracting should be independent of the price of labor. Furthermore, these arguments have undoubtedly been persuasive to legislators and others not directly connected with the labor movement. Former Secretary of Labor Ray Marshall, for example, felt that repeal of Davis-Bacon would "cause low wages to be transferred from one place to another," and would create "wage-busting" as employers sought to competitively underbid one another for government contracts.[7]

Policy Considerations

The degree to which government can and should protect the wage rates of its contractors from the consequences of competition is a policy question, which involves normative judgments about the proper role of government in the private employment relationship. There can be no definitive answer to such a question. Nevertheless, there are several factors that must be considered in evaluating the validity of prevailing wage laws for this purpose. The argument of the proponents may be fairly represented by the following synopsis. Government contracts are awarded to the lowest bidder, creating competition among contractors. In this competition, low-wage contractors are favored. To achieve low wages, contractors will cut wage rates or replace existing workers with low-rate workers from elsewhere. The government should not allow this to happen in the contracting of its own business, and therefore protective wage laws are necessary, regardless of their cost. Four counterarguments, not intended as comprehensive, are presented below.

Inconsistent Application. Arguing that protection of the type offered by prevailing wage laws is necessary is inconsistent, because many employees of government contractors are not provided with, and have never been offered, such protection. Clerical and supervisory employees of construction contractors do not receive any

---
[6] *Id.*
[7] Statement of Ray Marshall, Secretary of Labor, to the House Committee on Education and Labor, in Oversight Hearings on the Davis-Bacon Act, 96th Cong. 1st Sess., June 14, 1979, quoted in Reynolds, *Understanding Political Pricing of Labor Services,* at 301.

wage protection, for example, nor (since 1964) do any employees of government contractors performing manufacturing or supply contracts. Many types of service contractor's employees are excluded from coverage by the Service Contract Act, and in addition, a substantial proportion of covered service contracts are issued without prevailing wage specifications.

Furthermore, only direct labor is covered. In an incisive analysis by Professor Morgan Reynolds, this is deemed a glaring inconsistency in the arguments supporting Davis-Bacon (and by extension, the other prevailing wage laws). Reynolds notes that prevailing wage laws extend their coverage only to the approximately 30 percent of construction costs that are direct labor, neglecting the fact that the main ingredient in value-added for the intermediate goods purchased by contractors from materials suppliers is also labor expense, and that this labor is unprotected:

> An advocate of Davis-Bacon who concedes the virtues of competitive contracting must claim either (a) that it is all right for competition to determine pricing and labor costs for the other goods and services supplied to the construction industry but not for the labor services supplied to the construction industry or (b) that the labor and materials used by the suppliers to produce output for the construction industry also should enjoy the benefits of stability and higher productivity from prices set by Department of Labor administrators. Statement (a) is a plea for special privilege, and (b) is a plea to virtually abolish nonpolitical pricing throughout the economy. As Edward Chamberlin (1958) has said, "It is fundamental to distinguish between the labor market and the product market, but it is also common to place far too much emphasis on the distinction."[8]

Unreasonable Fears. The perceived need for wage protection is based on unreasonable fears that competition produces low wage rates. First, procurement of goods by competitive bid and selection of the lowest cost bidder is by no means a procedure uniquely employed by governments. A large proportion of private purchasing is carried out on the same basis, either formally, as in a solicited bid system, or informally, as when advertised prices are used. To the claim that the government system is more rigid and inflexible, forcing government to rely on price alone as a discriminator, one can respond that bid specifications can be varied, as can qualifications for inclusion on approved bidders lists. Therefore, proponents of prevailing wage legislation must argue either that all wage rates are debased by competition (in which case prevailing wage laws reflecting existing wage standards on private employment

---

[8] Reynolds, *Understanding Political Pricing of Labor Services,* at 304.

Introduction 7

would not improve them) or that wage rates are debased only by competition for government work, which is impossible.

Second, the argument assumes that employers are able to unilaterally control wage rates, without regard for market factors. This is positively untrue for unionized employers and employers of minimum-wage labor, and is at variance with the experience of most employers. It assumes that employers have monopsonistic control over labor services, which Professor Reynolds characterizes as "absurd."[9] He notes:

> Businesses purchase a tremendous variety of goods and services and allegedly collude or systematically depress the prices of labor services only, not the prices of other inputs. Presumably, some businessmen would be better off redirecting their energies to depressing prices of nonlabor inputs, yet we hear nothing about monopsony power over prices in other input markets. It is a baseless, threadbare idea, without substantiating evidence, kept alive by constant reiteration by unionists. Mobility on both sides of the market for construction labor is extremely high, ease of entry is very high, and there are large numbers of participants on both sides of the market. Eighty percent of construction activity is not covered by Davis-Bacon because it is privately financed; 1930s wage rates do not prevail there nor have construction wages in Florida collapsed since the repeal of the state version of the Davis-Bacon Act.[10]

Overlooked Economics. The usual laws of economics seem to be overlooked by proponents of prevailing wage laws who argue that government contracting causes wage rates to fall. Government purchase of goods and services represents increased demand for those goods and services, which causes increased demand for labor to produce them. Since supply is not affected, elementary economics suggests that the price of labor will tend to rise.

Ineffective Solution. During the Great Depression, when two of the three federal prevailing wage laws and many of the state laws came into being, it was easy to document that wage levels (and also profit, rents, and interest rates) were depressed, and it was also easy to ascribe these conditions to failures of the price market system, which might be curable by government-administered pricing. Without dealing with the broader question, it should be noted that with respect to government contractors' wage rates, existence of prevailing wage laws had no discernable effect during the Depression. In 1931, as depressed demand was lowering wage rates, increasing unemployment, and causing the other problems that the framers of the Davis-Bacon Act sought to alleviate with a prevailing

---

[9] *Id.* at 302.
[10] *Id.* at 302-3.

wage law, the same conditions were being experienced in Canada, England, France, and elsewhere. Yet in England a prevailing wage law had been in effect since 1891 (which required collectively bargained rates after 1907), in France since 1899, and in Canada since 1900. Clearly, whatever the problems of the Depression, they were greater than could be solved by a prevailing wage law.

Summary

These arguments support the thesis that the absence of prevailing wage laws would not cause wage exploitation by government contractors, and raise serious doubts that the laws are needed for the purposes expressed by their proponents. Consideration of the mechanics of the laws and their costs therefore becomes even more important in evaluating whether they continue to play a viable role in the nation's economy.

ORGANIZATION OF THE STUDY

It is fair to question not only why the prevailing wage laws exist, but also the methods that they use to achieve their purposes, their effectiveness, and their costs. One of the few common denominators of the laws is that despite differences in application, all rely on prevailing rates to provide a mechanism for establishing wage floors. Chapter II addresses the concept of prevailing and illustrates the difficulties administrators have had in defining and implementing it under the various prevailing wage statutes.

Chapter III covers the Davis-Bacon Act, which is the most significant and costly of the prevailing wage laws, even though its application is more limited than that of either the Walsh-Healey Act or the Service Contract Act. In general terms, the scope of Davis-Bacon is limited to contractors engaged in the construction or repair of buildings or other public works in which the federal government has a financial interest. The number of such contractors and the dollar amount of such contracts are less than the corresponding figures for supply and materials purchases covered by Walsh-Healey or for the purchase of services covered by the Service Contract Act. Because of the manner in which Davis-Bacon has been administered, however, its costs, estimated to be on the order of $1 billion a year, are more than twice those estimated for the Service Contract Act and many times those of Walsh-Healey. The implementing regulations of the Davis-Bacon Act were modified in 1985 and, in the opinion of many, improved. Nevertheless, the Davis-

Bacon Act is likely to remain the most intrusive of the prevailing wage laws.

Chapter IV reviews the characteristics and recent legislative history of the state "little Davis-Bacon" acts. In the mid-1970s, forty-two states (including the District of Columbia) had active prevailing wage laws. In 1979, however, Florida repealed its statute, and six other states have followed suit as of mid-1985. As a result, the total number of active state-level laws has shrunk to thirty-five. The majority of these laws are more restrictive in operation than the Davis-Bacon Act, and are therefore subject to an even greater degree to the same problems that plague the federal statute.

Chapter V covers the Walsh-Healey Act. Although Walsh-Healey is of potentially greater significance than Davis-Bacon because it applies to a much broader industrial and spending base, it has never had the impact of Davis-Bacon. Issuance of new wage rate determinations under Walsh-Healey stopped in 1964. After that time, its main effect was reduced to a requirement mandating daily overtime pay, and therefore prohibiting flextime scheduling. Even this requirement was repealed in 1985, so Walsh-Healey no longer has a legislative purpose to serve. The law remains of interest principally because of the contrasts it offers to the experiences provided by the similarly intentioned Davis-Bacon Act.

Chapter VI covers the Service Contract Act (1964), which is the most junior of the federal prevailing wage laws by thirty years. The Service Contract Act has generally been neglected by academic and other researchers, and has not been subjected to the scrutiny it deserves. Despite major amendments in 1972 and 1976 that generally expanded coverage, and regulatory reforms in 1985 that attempted to limit it, the act continues to suffer from inconsistency of purpose and uneven application.

Conclusions and recommendations with respect to each of the prevailing wage laws are contained in the relevant chapters. In addition, a few brief concluding remarks are found in the final chapter, Chapter VII.

CHAPTER II

The Prevailing Wage Concept

The three principal prevailing wage acts of the United States, the Davis-Bacon Act, the Walsh-Healey Public Contracts Act, and the O'Hara-McNamara Services Act (the Service Contract Act), share completely only two characteristics. All three apply as part of the government procurement process to provide a wage floor for employees of contractors doing business with the federal government, and all three use prevailing wages to establish that floor.

The fact that the laws are part of the governmental procurement process may affect their quality of administration and the need for administrative accountability to legislatures or the public because, in a sense, compliance with the laws is voluntary. Only government contractors must comply with prevailing wage laws, and no one is required to be a government contractor. If a potential contractor does not like the idea of paying prevailing wages; if he thinks the wage rates specified for his contract are wrong; if the stipulations and reporting requirements are burdensome; or if he has any other objections to the process, the contractor can avoid the problem by refraining from bidding for the work. Setting aside for the moment the fact that many firms cannot make such a decision without cutting themselves off from a substantial portion of their natural market, there is some validity in this reasoning. Certainly, the prevailing wage laws would be administered differently, and would have been subject to closer scrutiny and more frequent court challenge, if they were applied to a broader base.

Specifically, there are two areas of major impact. First, because the wage determination review process is limited to parties that have standing, it has been difficult for contractors' associations or other concerned groups to challenge even the accuracy of a specific rate determination within the Department of Labor, much less the process by which rates are determined or the philosophy underlying that process in the courts.[1] Second, because the Department of Labor

---

[1] Although this statement is true for the Davis-Bacon Act, the Service Contract Act, and most of the state prevailing wage laws, as will be discussed in Chapter IV *infra*, it is less so for the Walsh-Healey Act. As a result of an amendment made to that act in 1952, wage determinations under Walsh-Healey must be made "on the

11

does not have to defend itself against outside scrutiny or follow legal precedents from earlier cases, it has had the freedom to adopt "workable" compromises in both individual prevailing rate decisions and in the administrative procedures and definition on which they are based. Therefore, to a higher degree than is true for other, less "voluntary" labor laws (such as the Fair Labor Standards Act), definitions, procedures, and determinations under the prevailing wage laws have been arbitrary, changeable, and of questionable accuracy. Nowhere is this more apparent than in the fundamental question pertaining to the other factor common to all of these laws: What is a prevailing wage?

ORIGIN OF THE PREVAILING WAGE CONCEPT

All of the prevailing wage laws require government contractors to pay their employees doing government work some variation of wages determined by the secretary of labor (or designated administrator, in the case of the state laws) to be prevailing for employees providing similar services in the locality where the work is to be performed. But what is a prevailing wage? What process is to be followed by the secretary in making his determination? How is he to identify or choose from among all the wage rates that might already exist in a locality the one that is prevailing? The answers to these questions are vital to understanding both the development of the prevailing wage laws and the challenges to them in recent years by academics and others who are not directly involved with contracting or with the federal procurement process. Before addressing them, a brief examination of how and why the concept of prevailing wages originally developed is appropriate.

The details of how the prevailing wage concept came to be adopted in each of the laws will be discussed more fully in later chapters. But to summarize: 1) the concept was used in Davis-Bacon in 1931 because prior to the New Deal, Congress felt that the Supreme Court would not accept obvious federal interference in the private contract between employers and employees, and a statutory minimum wage was held to be such interference; 2) it was incorporated into Walsh-Healey in 1936 because the industry-by-industry negotiated minimum wages of the National Industrial Recovery Act had

---

record," and follow standard evidentiary procedures. Following this amendment, a case [Wirtz v. Baldor Electric, 337 F.2d 518 (D.C. Cir. 1964)] was successfully brought in 1964 which, although it did not challenge the rate-making process or the underlying philosophy of the Walsh-Healey Act, resulted in curtailment of rates issued under this act that were higher than those required by the Fair Labor Standards Act (the federal minimum wage).

just been struck down as unconstitutional, whereas the prevailing rates used in Davis-Bacon had not; and 3) it was adopted by the Service Contract Act in 1965 because this act was thought of as no more than an extension to another group of employees of the prevailing wage concepts already elaborated in Davis-Bacon and Walsh-Healey.

Mirror of Reality

The animating idea behind the choice of prevailing wages, as opposed to statutory or mandatory wages, is both simple and attractive. The argument made in the testimony taken at the time the acts were introduced, and frequently repeated in later hearings, is that the prevailing wage laws would act as a sort of mirror of existing wage conditions in a community.

It was intended that, by finding the wage rates that already prevailed in a community and reflecting them back in the form of mandatory minimum rates on government contracts, no disruption would occur in those existing wage rates, and the outside influence of government would be limited to ensuring that whatever community standards existed before a new government job was begun would continue thereafter. Thus, employees on government contracts could be assured that their wages would not be depressed below customary levels by competition among employers for government work, and that they would not be subject to losing their jobs to outsiders from low-wage areas who might be willing to come into the community and work for less than the local standards.

In the original conception of prevailing wage rates, the only apparent failing was the possibility that if local standards were too low, the prevailing wage law would not allow them to be arbitrarily increased to an acceptable level, as a minimum wage law would be able to do. But with this failing aside, not only the government, but also spokesmen for both labor and industry, generally expressed satisfaction with the idea of determining existing standards and reflecting them back as required wage rates on government contract work. In this way, wages would be eliminated as a factor in competition, and existing wage standards in a community would be preserved.

Furthermore, the elegant simplicity of the concept meant that it could be easily complied with by the employers to whom it pertained. As first envisioned and as embodied in the original Davis-Bacon Act of 1931 (that is, before the amendments of 1935) and in many of the early state prevailing wage laws, all an employer had to do was to pay "such rates as are generally found" in the locality where the work was to be done, and he would be in compliance.

Problems with Defining Prevailing

It is truly surprising that so few of those who were actively engaged in sponsoring or supporting the prevailing wage laws anticipated any problem with developing or implementing the concept of prevailing. Questions were raised concerning the propriety of laws that would impose any wage requirement or that would remove labor from the package of costs that bidders were supposed to minimize in order to win government contracts, but the early testimony fails to express any concern over problems that might arise in identification or determination of the prevailing rate in a community, and ignores the fact that in some cases such a rate might not even exist.

In all three of the major prevailing wage laws, Congress was content to delegate the problem of defining prevailing to the secretary of labor, along with the mechanical problems of determining and issuing the rate and ensuring compliance with it. All gave the secretary wide latitude, by specifying that whatever he determined was the prevailing rate would be the required rate of pay, but none gave further guidance or provided definitions.[2] Surprisingly—and this is not well known since the prevailing wage laws are typically studied separately—the secretary of labor adopted three entirely different ways, with many more subvariations, of defining prevailing in the context of these three laws.

Administrative Definitions. For administering the Davis-Bacon Act between 1935 and 1985, the secretary defined prevailing as the rate paid to at least a 30 percent plurality of the individuals in the designated class, but if no such plurality existed, then it was to be the weighted average of all of the rates paid in the class. This was called the 30-percent rule. In 1985, it was modified to be a 50-percent rule. For administering the Walsh-Healey Act, no explicit formula was developed, but the determination went through several variations. Between 1936 and 1947, no defined method existed; each rate was handled individually, by a panel until 1942, and subsequently by Department of Labor personnel; between 1947 and 1959, the

---

[2] The flexibility accorded the secretary of labor is not total, although the boundries are only inferential. The secretary is to *determine* the rate prevailing in the locality and require it to be paid, so presumably he must at least examine the existing rate structure and then draw what conclusions he will from it. Putatively, therefore, he could not use a table of random numbers or arbitrarily adopt the union rate without first conducting some sort of survey.

basic method apparently shifted to choosing as the prevailing minimum the rate that would require fewer than 10 percent of the firms in the industry to raise their rates; after 1959, it was taken as some variation of the minimum rate paid any covered employee by a statistically determined median plant, arranged by size or wage rate. For administering the Service Contract Act, the secretary has taken the median rate of all covered employees by class, while reserving the option of giving "due consideration" to federal civil service rates and other factors.

It is important to note that these methods are all alternative administrative attempts to define prevailing in some workable way. The various state prevailing wage laws add many further variations to that same end. Some take as prevailing the currently established union rate. Others use the modal rate (the rate that occurs with greatest frequency); the median rate (the rate that falls in the middle when all of the rates are arrayed by increasing amount); the average rate (the sum of all rates divided by the number of different rates); the weighted average rate (the sum of all rates multiplied by the number of employees receiving each, divided by the number of employees); the plurality rate that occurs at the 50, 40, or 30 percent level; the average of the rates paid by the highest 50 percent of firms arrayed by size; or "the rate that is generally paid," whatever that might be. Again, these alternatives are not intended to produce different results: all are attempting to provide a definition that identifies the same rate—that is, the rate that the framers of the legislation envisioned as the prevailing rate in the community.

Obviously, unless we are willing to declare all but one of these definitions invalid, the concept of prevailing is a very cloudy one that is not easily defined. But if this is the case, how could Congress (and the various state legislatures) pass laws that are so thoroughly incapable of being implemented according to any objective standard of fairness? Under the charitable view that Congress would not, in fact, do such a thing knowingly, the problem that has caused the confusion with these laws for so many years must lie elsewhere.

Intuitive Definition. The answer is that the concept of prevailing—like the related concepts of "predominant" or "generally current"—is both subjective and qualitative. In many situations, intuition alone is sufficient to determine whether the characteristic applies, provided that the outcome is obvious. Thus one can speak easily of the "prevailing winds from the west," the "prevailing fashion in neckties," or the "prevailing mores of today's youth," without precision, but also without the fear of being misunderstood.

Congress relied on this intuitive definition of prevailing when including the concept in Davis-Bacon and other wage laws, and did not think to question what might happen if situations arose where the outcome was not obvious. (Early applications would not have raised the question, because at that time the range of wages for skilled or unskilled work was small and wage rates tended to cluster around even numbers like 40 cents an hour, or $5 a day, or $18 a week.) Therefore, Congress had no reason to doubt the administrators' ability to identify or readily recognize the prevailing rate for any job in a community. Thus, the fundamental problem with applying the concept of prevailing to wages may have been disguised by the consensus that there was no problem.

FAILURE OF THE PREVAILING CONCEPT

The failure of the prevailing concept lies in this fact that it is inherently qualitative and limited in application, because there is no statistically valid logic to support an outcome when that outcome is not intuitively obvious. Thus, as applied to wage rates, it is a concept that works easily and intuitively only when an obvious preponderance of rates are the same. In other situations, it can be made to work mechanically (although not logically) with the help of statistics, but there are also times when it is totally inapplicable. This is probably best illustrated with a contrived example. Envision two large piles of balls, one red and the other green. Shown a mixture of 90 balls from the red pile and 10 from the green, most people could intuitively identify red as the predominant, or prevailing, color of the mixture because the answer is obvious. If the mixture contained 60 balls from one pile and 40 from the other, a casual glance might not be sufficient to identify the prevailing color, because the result is less obvious. At least some of the people would resort to counting the balls, but they are making an implicit assumption that the prevailing color is the modal one, that is, the one that occurs most frequently. And if the mixture contained 50 balls from each pile, no degree of perception or level of analysis would allow the determination to be made.

As the mixtures become more complicated, the degree of difficulty in making determinations increases and the logic becomes more prolix. For example, if shown a mixture of 100 balls consisting of 90 of various shades of red and 10 of the identical shade of green and asked to say which color prevailed, one would intuitively say red, but a statistical analysis, after careful sorting, would indicate green. A logic can be constructed to support or challenge either answer.

Prevailing Wage Concept 17

Not a Statistical Parameter

A closely related problem is that the prevailing concept is not in itself a statistical parameter, nor is it measurable by a statistical parameter. It is not a measure of central tendency, like the median, mean, simple average, or weighted average. It is implicitly a single point rather than a range or area. The parameter it is closest to—though not the same as—is the mode.

The mode is not a measure of central tendency except for normal, bell-shaped distributions. In a list of numbers, the number that occurs most frequently is called the mode, even if it occurs only slightly more frequently than others. The concept of prevailing is similar, but intuitively would seem to require a stronger showing and a more obvious result. The mode and the prevailing concept do share one problem. Assume the following list of digits: 2, 2, 5, 8, 8. For this list, although the measures of central tendency can be calculated (simple average, median, and mean all equal 5), there is no modal digit, and no logical or mathematical way of determining which digit is the prevailing one.

Another contrived example is perhaps the strongest way to illustrate the failings of prevailing as a statistical parameter (or as defined in terms of statistical parameters) for administering the prevailing wage laws. Consider the following series of digits representing wage rates: 1, 1, 1, 7, 7, 8, 8, 9, 9. For this list:

1. The median (middle) rate is 7. This is the rate which would be taken as prevailing by the Service Contract Act, absent other complications.
2. The simple average is the sum of the digits divided by the number of different digits. The different digits are 1, 7, 8, and 9, so the simple average is $(1 + 7 + 8 + 9)/4 = 6.25$. This is the rate that would be taken as prevailing by the Tennessee and Kentucky state prevailing wage laws.
3. The mean (or weighted average) is the sum of the different digits weighted by the number of times each digit appears, divided by the total number of digits. The mean is therefore $[(3 \times 1) + 2(7 + 8 + 9)]/9 = 5.67$. This would be the prevailing rate under the Walsh-Healey Act if the numbers represented the minimum wages paid by different firms and the firms were all the same size. It would also be taken as prevailing by the Davis-Bacon Act under the new 50-percent rule.
4. The mode is the digit which appears most frequently. In this list, it is 1. It is the rate that, in this case, appears with a 30 percent plurality, so it is the rate that would be taken as

prevailing under Davis-Bacon's old 30-percent rule, still used by a number of state prevailing wage laws.

In this case, therefore, depending on which of these actually used definitions of prevailing is applied, the prevailing rate is 7, 6.25, 5.67, or 1. None of the formulas or the standard statistical measures find a prevailing rate greater than 7, and two find rates that are paid to no individual. What is the actual prevailing rate? One might argue that since two-thirds of the digits in the list are either 7s, 8s, or 9s, the actual prevailing rate is "somewhere around 8," or "somewhere between 7 and 9," and certainly somewhere above 7. But this is arguing from an intuitive base, and there is no guidance from the concept of prevailing or the science of statistics for determining it.

Further Problems

The concept of the prevailing wage was adopted so that existing rates in a locality could be reflected back on government work to be constructed in that area. But because the rates found by the secretary of labor (by whatever formula or means) are reflected back as the minimum that can be paid, they have the effect of increasing the wage levels on government work in almost all cases, and therefore the cost of such work. All of the statistical methods of calculating prevailing rates, exclusive of the state laws that arbitrarily adopt union rates, are either a measure of central tendency or some variation of a mode. Regardless of the method, the rates so determined are applied as minimum rates. Employers can pay employees more than these rates, but not less.

Central Tendency Rates. If measures of central tendency are used to select the prevailing rate, then a figure from somewhere in the middle of the range of rates found in a locality will become the minimum rate applicable on the new contract work. It is axiomatic that when a previous middle rate becomes the new minimum rate, the new middle rate is going to be higher in all cases, except for the trivial case in which all rates are the same.

Consider a free-market labor force of only four individuals in a locality, whose hourly rates are represented by the digits 1, 2, 3, and 4. If a prevailing wage law based on a simple average were to be overlaid on this market, the prevailing rate determined by the rules would be the average of the four rates, which is 2.5. When applied, this average rate would become the minimum, and employers could pay more, but not less. Therefore, the wages paid in the locality would now be 2.5, 2.5, 3, and 4. In the next calculation of prevailing rates in the locality, the average of these—now 3—would be the new minimum, and the next average would be the average of 3, 3, 3, and 4, which calculates to 3.25. Thus, in two iterations, without introducing any other cost factors such as spillover or general price inflation, the average rate would increase from 2.5 to 3.25.

This is, to be sure, a highly contrived example, and is not intended to be representative of the effect that any central-tendency prevailing wage law would necessarily have in practice. But the mathematical principles are universal, and indicate the trend that any such central-tendency law would follow.

Modal Rates. Modal rates, whether pure or taken at the 30, 40, or 50 percent plurality, are not middle rates, and so do not automatically tend to increase wage rates under government contracts, but they do share three problems. First, they always increase minimum wages in the locality unless the modal rate chosen happens to be the federal minimum wage. Second, they tend to favor union rates—generally the highest rates in any given locality—because other than the federal minimum wage, only union rates are likely to be identical to the penny and paid to any substantial number of employees. In the construction industry, for example, even in situations where nonunion contractors might predominate over union contractors in total number of employees, it would be unlikely for employees of the nonunion firms to be paid the same rate to the penny since there is no coordinating mechanism similar to the union contract for setting the scale of wages. In a modal calculation, rates are interpreted as different even if they are only slightly different. Finally, in application, low prevailing rate determinations have relatively little impact, but high ones tend to be perpetuated because, as discussed above, employers can pay more but not less than the rates determined to be prevailing.

SUMMARY

Subsequent chapters will detail the problems associated with the specific prevailing wage laws. The purpose here was to point out that all of the prevailing wage laws suffer from inherent problems, and to demonstrate that all of the laws share two specific failings. First, they are based on a subjective principle that is inherently impossible to apply objectively, fairly, and equitably. Even with the best of intentions and perfect data sources, the results of prevailing rate determinations, in many if not most cases, will be the imposition of arbitrary super-minimum wage levels. And when intentions and data sources are beset by real-world problems, the arbitrariness of the result becomes compounded and even capricious. Second, in application, except in a few cases where the existing rates in a locality are all the same or where the prevailing rate determined is the same as the federal minimum wage, the prevailing wage laws all necessarily increase the government's cost of contracted goods over what similar work would cost on the open market, even to a buyer of much smaller size than a government. Thus, not only do the state and federal governments deny themselves the economies that would normally be associated with large scale purchases, they reverse them.

These two points alone may not provide sufficient grounds for repealing all of the prevailing wage laws because the laws may provide secondary benefits or other advantages despite their inherent problems. But they should provide motivation for examining such benefits critically and evaluating whether they are worth the cost. If so, and if they are not already duplicated by existing legislation, the next question must be, given the arbitrariness and flaws built into the prevailing wage concept, whether new and different laws might not provide a better way to achieve the same benefits.

CHAPTER III

The Davis-Bacon Act

The Davis-Bacon Act is the prevailing wage law for the construction industry. Because of the nature and size of that industry, the amount of government-sponsored building construction, and the fact that the Davis-Bacon Act was the first of the prevailing wage laws at the federal level, it has been an influential piece of legislation in the government procurement system. Furthermore, because of the wage-setting mechanisms of the law, it has had a profound impact on wage scales within the industry, as well as on the level of construction wages compared with those in other industries.

DOMAIN OF DAVIS-BACON

To give a sense of scale to the domain of the Davis-Bacon Act, in 1984, federal, state, and local governments spent more than $54 billion for construction of buildings, highways, military facilities, sewer systems, conservation projects, water supply facilities, and other public works[1]—about 20 percent of the aggregate total of all construction spending in the country. Although not all public construction was directly subject to the Davis-Bacon Act (the federal government's direct share was about $11.5 billion),[2] Davis-Bacon rates spread through most of the public construction sector as a result of adoption of the federal rates by a number of the state prevailing wage laws and because they apply to many joint federal-state projects and projects which involve federal aid, grants, or guarantees. Curiously, no one in or out of government is able to say with precision how much total public construction is actually covered by the Davis-Bacon Act, but most independent analysts in the past few years have put the figure between $30 and $40 billion.

In a typical year, the Department of Labor (DOL) might issue more than 15,000 new or revised rate determinations, each one covering from about 12 to more than 100 different job classifications.

---

[1] U.S. DEPARTMENT OF COMMERCE, SURVEY OF CURRENT BUSINESS S-7 (April 1985)
[2] Estimated from 1983 figures presented in U.S. DEPARTMENT OF COMMERCE, BUREAU OF CENSUS, CONSTRUCTION REPORTS C30-84-1, "Value of New Construction Put in Place," Table 1 p. 3 (1984).

These determinations set the minimum wages payable to employees on a substantial proportion of the 600,000 prime contracts and subcontracts awarded annually for public construction projects. Perhaps 1 million of the 3.8 million construction workers in the U.S. labor force were employed on these projects in 1977.[3]

Disproportionate Impact

These are huge figures, but they are small compared with the equivalent costs for government purchases of goods (paper clips, tanks, machine screws, desks, computers, etc.) and services (janitorial maintenance, guarding, laundering, computer programing, etc.) other than construction. These purchases are covered by prevailing wage laws also—the former by the Walsh-Healey Act, and the latter by the Service Contract Act. There are no equivalent state-level laws for these acts, so that the relevant expenditures are those at the federal level.

In 1984, federal purchases of durable goods totalled $74.3 billion, and spending for services (exclusive of compensation of employees) exceeded $70.7 billion. Therefore, the total amount purchased in each of these areas that would be subject to prevailing wage legislation is approximately double that of construction. The number of employees in these industries is also several times that of construction. Nevertheless, the other prevailing wage laws have nowhere near the impact that Davis-Bacon has on industrial structure, wage rates, or the level of prices paid for goods and services by the government when compared with that paid by private parties.

Since all three laws were intended to achieve the same purposes, it becomes an interesting question as to why the impact of Davis-Bacon, dealing with a single industry and covering wage rates of annual contracts of around $35 billion, is so much greater than that of the Walsh-Healey or the Service Contract Act, each of which spans many industries and covers about twice the amount of purchasing. This is one of the questions that will concern us in this chapter.

Increasing Interest in Repeal

In the introduction to my 1975 study of the Davis-Bacon Act, I wrote that the act was "an obscure piece of legislation,"[4] which, although it had a significant impact on government construction

---

[3] U.S. GENERAL ACCOUNTING OFFICE, THE DAVIS-BACON ACT SHOULD BE REPEALED 3 (1979).

[4] A.J. THIEBLOT, JR., THE DAVIS-BACON ACT 1 (1975).

spending and wage rates in the construction industry in general, had not been much protested or much studied. Since that time it has been both. Starting in the mid to late 1970s, a large number of evaluations appeared, providing employment for a substantial cadre of econometricians and other analysts. Most of the studies focused on the general coverage of the act and its administration; evaluated one or another aspect of its impact on construction wage rates, costs to the government, industrial structure, or inflation; or challenged the contentions of other studies.

In addition to the formal academic and economic evaluations, there has also been a great deal of testimonial evidence presented in court cases and in various senatorial and congressional hearings by contractors, union representatives, and others who deal with the law on a day-to-day basis. Additionally, special interest groups, both in favor of and opposed to the law, have issued what seems an unending stream of position papers, press releases, and other communications of their views. Finally several reports have been issued by congressional or other government organizations, including the General Accounting Office (GAO) and the Congressional Research Service. Over the past ten years, the dearth of analyses of the Davis-Bacon Act has become a glut.

The overwhelming majority of these presentations, with the obvious exception of the position papers of the organized labor groups and their supporters, find little to love in the Davis-Bacon Act. In one way or another, they find it expensive, inflationary, unnecessary, restrictive, or generally harmful both to the government's budgets and to the structure and development of the construction industry. Most feel that it is an outmoded child of the Great Depression, providing a cure for which there is no problem in modern times, and many recommend its repeal.

The case against Davis-Bacon has been structured by a wide range of experts and associations from several spheres of activities—union and nonunion contracting, large and small business, academia, government, farm and rural, politics, and journalism, among others—who seem to have little in common except that they have studied the Davis-Bacon Act and found it wanting. Although there are, of course, countervailing opinions about the worth of Davis-Bacon in many or all of the groups represented (whose individual positions are evaluated below) the preponderance of credible evidence from this diverse group of experts is definitely opposed to Davis-Bacon and the prevailing wage concept. Read objectively, it builds a strong case.

These various interest groups have been pressuring Congress to do something about Davis-Bacon since the early 1970s. Additionally, seven states have repealed their state "little Davis-Bacon" acts since 1979, a development which cannot have gone unnoticed in Congress. Furthermore, the administration and Senate that have been in office since 1980 are, at least superficially, less likely to be sympathetic to Davis-Bacon.[5] Nevertheless, none of the thirty or so bills for repeal or restriction introduced to Congress over the past several years has been successful.[6] The only changes made to the act have come at the administrative level within the Department of Labor.

This raises the second interesting question about Davis-Bacon. Why has the case against it not been more persuasive? As one observer noted recently, "The Davis-Bacon Act has been studied and studied some more, but it has not yet been studied to death."[7] Why not?

PURPOSE OF THIS CHAPTER

Unless one is willing to concede that Davis-Bacon remains in effect against all logic solely because of the political power of organized labor, there must be some reason why its adherents in Congress continue to support it, or why they fear the consequences of its repeal. The purpose of this chapter is to look for such reasons and, where appropriate, to evaluate them and formulate responses and recommendations. We shall also evaluate some of the reasons for the great influence of the Davis-Bacon Act when compared with

---

[5] Although he had expressed philosophical opposition to the Davis-Bacon Act, Reagan announced when campaigning for the presidency in 1980 that he would not actively seek its repeal. He reiterated and remained true to that promise during his first term in office, contenting himself with seeking the administrative changes first proposed in 1981, most of which finally went into effect in early 1985. Consideration of whether or not to repeal the act, however, lies with Congress rather than the administration.

[6] At the time this chapter was being written, the full Senate left standing by a tie vote an amendment by Sen. Phil Gramm (R.Tex.) to a Defense Department bill that would remove about 95 percent of the Pentagon's construction contracts from the purview of Davis-Bacon. The specific provisions would have set a new contract threshold at $1 million on defense contract construction and would have legislated the 50 percent plurality for establishing the prevailing rate, which, as is explained later in the text of this chapter, is established administratively rather than by law. Although the measure did not survive challenges within the House, and although it was not an amendment to the Davis-Bacon Act itself, it was significant in that for the first time in the act's 54-year history, the Senate voted to dilute its requirements. [*Senate Tie Would Cut Wage Law Protection,* Washington Times, June 5, 1985]

[7] Reynolds, *Understanding Political Pricing of Labor Services: The Davis-Bacon Act* 3 J. LAB. RESEARCH 307 (Summer, 1982).

the other federal prevailing wage laws, but will leave the majority of that analysis to the later chapters on the Walsh-Healey and Service Contract acts.

The major issues making up the cases for and against Davis-Bacon will be reviewed, as well as the likely impact of the administrative changes that became effective in 1985. Additionally, because the recently developed literature is a specialist's literature, even though there is much more of it now than there was ten years ago, it would be unfair to suppose that nonspecialists were familiar with it or with the details of the Davis-Bacon Act itself. Therefore, a brief overview of the history of the act and a summary of its administrative organization will also be formulated. These sections can be skimmed over by persons who are already familiar with Davis-Bacon.

HISTORY OF THE DAVIS-BACON ACT

The Davis-Bacon Act was the first federal wage law to apply to nongovernment workers. Its concept was under active consideration by various congresses for several years before it was passed in 1931. Fourteen earlier bills embracing prevailing wages for federal construction projects had been introduced to Congress beginning in 1927, a period of general prosperity.[8] The Davis-Bacon Act, therefore, is an early example of federal involvement in social and labor legislation which, in its original form, reflected the economic conditions and social attitudes of the 1920s rather than, as is now generally supposed, the exigencies of the Depression or the activism of the New Deal. On the other hand, it is unlikely that the 1931 Davis-Bacon bill would have met with any greater success than its predecessors if the Depression had not been in full sway. Therefore, although a child of the Depression, the Davis-Bacon Act owes its philosophy to an earlier era.

The Prevailing Wage Concept

The concept of prevailing wages is one of neutrality. It supposes that in any given locality a scale of wages suitable to local conditions and acceptable to local workmen develops through private agreement between employers and employees, which scale should be protected from the impact of competition among employers for government contracts that go to the lowest bidder. It supposes that if the existing local scale of wages were the one required to be paid

---

[8] Schulman, *The Case Against the Davis-Bacon Act*, 4 GOV'T UNION REV. 23 (1983).

on government contracts, local standards would be unaffected, and the impact of government purchasing would be eliminated.

In adopting the prevailing wage concept, the Davis-Bacon Act was not taking a very aggressive position. Many observers in that period felt that the free market could not be trusted to produce wage scales allowing an acceptable standard of living in various sections of the country, and that there should be a wage floor, a minimum wage, imposed regionally via the federal procurement process. The prevailing wage concept, they argued, would simply perpetuate deficiencies. But Congress did not have a free hand in choosing a wage policy. It felt compelled to respect limitations with regard to how far government could intrude into what, in 1931, was still considered to be the *private* contract between employers and employees. It seems clear that one of the reasons that Davis-Bacon adopted the prevailing wage concept was because prevailing wages offered a less stringent requirement than a set wage, including a mandated minimum rate.[9]

At that time, which was still before the changes brought by the New Deal and the packing of the Supreme Court, any undue social activism by the Congress was likely to be restrained by the Court.[10] Federal welfare or labor laws were almost always modest in their requirements, seeking an approach that would be acceptable to the country and accepted by the Court. Often, the course followed was to key federal legislation to laws already in effect at the state level, as was done with unemployment insurance and workmen's compensation, or to impose modest requirements that would change existing structures as little as possible. This was the case with Davis-Bacon.

Another reason for favoring a prevailing wage over a minimum wage was that labor leaders preferred it. They were afraid that if government had the power to set any specific wage rates in private employment relationships, that power could be used punitively as well as supportively to control labor and possibly harm the union movement.[11] Thus they favored an approach which would allow their privately won gains to be consolidated without exposing them

---

[9] If this was the view of Congress, it was undoubtedly an accurate one. The National Industrial Recovery Act, passed in 1933, was struck down in 1935 by the Supreme Court principally because it required various industries to pay their employees minimum wages, even though the wages were set by cooperative agreement between the industries and the government.

[10] For a telling example of the degree of frustration some members of Congress felt in trying to get the Supreme Court to accept the new social activism of the mid-1930s, see Ch. V, *infra,* note 5.

[11] HOUSE EDUCATION AND LABOR COMM., LEGISLATIVE HISTORY OF THE DAVIS-BACON ACT, Committee print, 87th Cong., 2d Sess. 2 (1962).

to the risk of arbitrary debasement by an administration unsympathetic to labor.

State Precursors to the Federal Act

The first public works laws in the country were passed at the state level.[12] Kansas enacted such a law in 1891 with the main purpose of closing loopholes in the state's then-new eight-hour law by prohibiting contractors from scaling down wages as well as hours when the shorter workday was mandated. Similar laws followed in New York (1897), Oklahoma (1909), Idaho (1911), Arizona (1912), New Jersey (1913), Massachusetts (1914), and Nebraska (1923).

These laws were applied to state contractors because of the voluntary aspects of the contractual relationship. No one was required to be a government contractor. Furthermore, the contractual relationship allowed the states to be surrogate "model employers," and encourage the spread of whatever practices they introduced to other employers by the good example provided. At heart, these were work hour laws or fair labor standards acts rather than prevailing wage laws. Their emphasis was on such things as mandating that payments be made to employees on a regular basis (usually once a week), or that wages be paid in cash or in full. They did, however, sometimes mention prevailing rates, and thus established a precedent for that concept when Congress took up the question of public works.

Congressional Activities

The first congressional hearings on maintaining local labor standards on construction were held in 1889, shortly after the Kansas Act was passed, but no legislation resulted.[13] During the 1920s, when upwards of eight state acts were already in place, renewed interest in the possibility of federal legislation led to hearings that were conducted in 1927, 1928, and again in 1930, but nothing came of them.

As late as January 10, 1931, the comptroller general under the Hoover administration expressed his opinion that a minimum or prevailing wage rate law for employees on federal contracts would "remove from competitive bidding ... an important element of cost and tend to defeat the purpose of the [procurement] statute" to

---

[12] For detailed coverage of the current state public works laws, most of which have evolved into state prevailing wage laws, see Ch. IV, *infra*.

[13] Price, *A Review of the Application of the Davis-Bacon Act*, 14 LAB. L. J. 614 (July 1963).

acquire goods or services at the lowest price "after full and free competitive bidding."[14]

This was a cogent argument. It said, in effect, that since labor is a major element in construction, removing it from competition defeats the notion that government procurement policy assures the purchase of goods and services at the lowest cost. But then as now, efficiency in contracting could be subordinated to social purpose: first, the "accept the lowest bid" policy of federal procurement could be and was neglected in many individual procurements where speed, technological merit, or the exigencies of wartime required it; and second, the policy was, after all, just a policy, and certainly could be modified by the same assembly that established it.[15]

Impetus of the Depression. The actual purpose of prevailing wage legislation can safely be characterized as that of protecting local wage scales from the consequences of competitive pressures on contractors to submit the low bid. This is neither a prounion nor an antiunion position. Organized labor and contractors' associations both favored the prevailing rate concept. Others worried, however, that such a limitation on employer flexibility was clearly anticompetitive; and the proposal came during an era when the evils of trusts, monopolies, and restraints of trade were well known and had formed the basis of public policy for a generation.

In 1931, the Depression was in full swing and the economy was near its most severe level of contraction. Pressures on the administration and Congress to do something were great. Work was scarce, creating an oversupply of labor and the resultant low wage rates. Workers displaced from their industrial or agricultural jobs looked for work where they could find it, even if it meant going on the road. Many sought jobs in construction, already a mobile industry, and were willing to take them at almost any wage, thus driving down the already meager pay rates. Before the Depression, $3.50 to $4.00 a day was a common wage in construction. By 1931, qualified construction workers were willing to accept $2.00 a day or less, and felt lucky to get it.[16]

---

[14] HOUSE EDUCATION AND LABOR COMM., *supra* note 11, at 2.

[15] Brozen, "The Davis-Bacon Act: How to Load the Dice Against Yourself," cited in U.S. Cong., Senate, Banking, Housing, and Urban Affairs Committee, *Improved Technology and Removal of Prevailing Wage Requirements in Federally Assisted Housing: Hearings Before the Subcommittee of Housing and Urban Affairs,* 92d Cong., 2d Sess. 398 (June 20–23, 1972).

[16] It is sometimes difficult to adjust the relative wage figures from past eras to those of the present time. The wage rates mentioned for the construction industry were certainly meager, but prices were also low. With careful shopping, a week's groceries could be had for $5, and houses could be rented for $25 a month. Managerial and experienced technical employees, such as engineers, commanded salaries on the

Furthermore, the private construction industry, like almost all others, had shriveled to a shadow of its former self, leaving the industry highly dependent on public contracts.[17] Post offices, veterans hospitals, and such provided the majority of construction projects available. For these reasons, despite the comptroller general's opinion that a prevailing wage law would be contrary to public policy, a new bill for a prevailing wage statute was formulated. Introduced simultaneously in both houses by two Republicans, Pennsylvania Senator James J. Davis, and New York Representative Robert L. Bacon, the bills set off a new round of hearings.

Development of a Specific Rationale. The depressed economy and the conditions of the construction industry offered the possibility of a new rationale for a prevailing wage requirement on federal contracts. At the time of these hearings, a new veterans hospital was being constructed in Congressman Bacon's home district in New York. A number of the contractors in his district had bid for this work, but were unable to compete effectively against an outside firm which, by importing laborers from the even-more-depressed South, was able to undercut the bids of the local firms.

Rationale for the Act

Congressman Bacon thus set both the rationale for the act and the tone for the new hearings, blaming "certain itinerant, irresponsible contractors, with itinerant, cheap, bootleg labor,"[18] for denying local labor and local contractors a fair opportunity to participate in the federal building program. Protection of local contractors and local labor from the predations of outsiders (rather than from each other) thus became the major *stated* philosophical underpinning of the prevailing wage concept and the Davis-Bacon Act, and remains one to this day. One might note the following points:

   1. This rationale for the act was a late addendum. Protection from itinerant outsiders was not part of the argumentation

---

order of $28 a week ($5.60 a day) during the Depression, and even by the beginning of World War II, average shop wages in a typical manufacturing plant were $.40 to $.50 and hour ($3.20 to $4.00 a day).

[17] Between 1929 and 1933, the dollar value of new construction declined steadily from about $10.8 billion to $2.9 billion; construction employment fell from 1.5 million workers to 800,000 workers; publicly financed construction rose from less than one-quarter of the total to more than one-half of it. [Cited in GENERAL ACCOUNTING OFFICE, *supra* note 3, at 8.]

[18] U.S. Cong., House, floor debate, "Rates of Wages for Laborers and Mechanics on Public Buildings of the United States," motion to pass S. 5904, Feb. 28, 1931, passed, 71st Cong., 3d Sess. 74 CONG. REC. at 6510 (1931).

for the earlier state acts, or for the federal prevailing wage bills introduced during the 1920s.

2. It was a "Jim Crow" position, motivated by fears of job loss to blacks. One of the supporters of the bill testified as to the employees of one of the itinerant contractors, calling them "cheap colored labor," and noting with implied horror that "it is labor of that sort that is in competition with white labor throughout the country."[19]

3. The itinerant contractor issue may have been a smoke screen to cloud the true purpose of the bill as a measure designed to bolster the status of the union movement. One opponent in the original hearings charged that the bill would have had no chance of passage had it not been demanded by organized labor.[20]

4. Whether real or not, the fear of itinerant contractors was overstated. On public construction projects tabulated at the time of the hearings, such itinerant workers as were employed worked mostly on a few projects undertaken in remote communities where the local labor force was small.[21]

---

[19] *Id.* at 6513, statement of Congressman Allgood. Some supporters of Davis-Bacon feel that too much emphasis has been placed on this reference by Congressman Allgood, since it is the only time that such a sentiment occurs in the recorded hearings leading up to the passage of the act. To the contrary, protectionism of this sort has always been a part—though perhaps not a critically important part—of prevailing wage laws. In July 1985, for example, in vetoing a measure that would otherwise have repealed Louisiana's state prevailing wage law, the governor supported his actions by calling the prevailing wage law in the state "the only process by which [Mexican and other aliens being employed in local construction work] can be identified and remedial actions taken by administrative enforcement." [*Prevailing Wage Repeal Fails in Louisiana*, 31 CONSTRUCTION LAB. REP., 485–86 (July 3, 1985)] The personna may be different, but the argument that "they're taking our jobs away" is the same.

[20] *Id.* at 6508–09, statement of Congressman Blanton.

[21] It is interesting to note that at the time of the survey, towards the end of 1930, on the 26 federal construction projects studied throughout the country, there were employed 1,724 men, of whom 1,356 were locals and 368 were nonlocals (21 percent), including 34 aliens. More than half of all of the nonlocal workers tabulated were employed on four projects located in the remote areas of Boise, Idaho; Fargo, North Dakota; Tucson, Arizona; and Juneau, Alaska. No outsiders worked on projects in such places as Brooklyn, Milwaukee, New Orleans, San Francisco, or Seattle. [CONG. REC., *supra* note 18, at 6505.] From this it is reasonable to conclude that the propensity to use outsiders was inversely related to the size of the local construction labor force. No information was presented on the wage rates of locals compared with nonlocals, or of wage rates on projects which had or did not have significant numbers of nonlocals, so no conclusions are possible in this area. If such information had been available, however, and supported the contention that nonlocals were low-rate itinerants, it is surprising that such information was not presented in support of the case for passing the act.

The Original Act

Despite these problems, the prevailing wage bill was reported out. Amendments which might have delayed its passage were rejected, and it was passed under suspension of the rules as an emergency measure.[22] The original act was brief and apparently deliberately vague, in an attempt to match the wording of some of the predecessor state laws which had generally proved to be noncontroversial in application.[23] It provided:

> That every *contract in excess of $5,000* in amount, *to which the United States* or the District of Columbia *is a party*, which requires or involves the employment of laborers or mechanics in the *construction, alteration, and/or repair* of any *public buildings* of the United States or the District of Columbia within the geographical limits of the States of the Union or the District of Columbia, shall *contain a provision* to the effect that *the rate of wages* for all laborers and mechanics employed by the contractor or any subcontractor on the public buildings covered by the contract shall be *not less than the prevailing rate of wages* for *work of a similar nature in the city, town, village, or other civil division of the State* in which the public buildings are located, or in the District of Columbia if the public buildings are located there, and a further provision that *in case any dispute arises* as to what are the prevailing rates of wages for work of a similar nature applicable to the contract which cannot be adjusted by the contracting officer, the matter *shall be referred to the Secretary of Labor for determination* and his decision thereon shall be conclusive on all parties to the contract: **Provided,** That in case of national emergency the President is authorized to suspend the provisions of this Act.[24]

A reading of the Davis-Bacon Act in its original form reveals that it was entirely a prevailing wage law rather than a fair labor standards law. It contains only two points of substance: 1) that a provision for prevailing rates be included in contracts for constructing public buildings, and 2) that the level of individual rates would be postdetermined, since they would be set by the secretary of labor only after disputes arose. Apparently, this seemed innocuous enough to President Hoover, for despite the recent opinions of his comptroller general, he signed the bill into law.

Flaws in the Original Act. The vagueness of the new law caused problems almost immediately. Labor objected because the law

---

[22] *See id.* at 6508.

[23] The original Kansas Act had been declared unconstitutional by that state's Supreme Court, but the same concepts had been picked up by other state legislatures, and the Kansas experience was attributed to reactionaries on the judiciary. [See Ch. IV, *infra*.]

[24] Davis-Bacon Act, ch. 411, § 1, 46 Stat. 1494 (1931). [Current version at 40 U.S.C. § 276a (1982).]

lacked any mechanisms for either policing or enforcement. Without such controls, unscrupulous contractors could simply ignore the legislation, especially since there was also no mechanism established for disclosure of the wage requirement to the workmen to whom it would apply. Contractors objected because wages were not predetermined. As a result, contractors had to be aware of the possibility that the secretary of labor could intervene after a contract had been let and require that higher wages be paid than those on which they had based their bids. This opened up a new element of risk in bidding for government work which they did not feel they should have to assume. Administrators objected because the law lacked an objective standard against which to measure wage rates. The concept of prevailing is a subjective one, so some definition was required to translate it into a measurable basis for action. No such definition was included.

New hearings were called for almost immediately after the law went into effect. As is typical in such situations, these hearings concentrated on enforcement problems and left the tough definitional problems unresolved.

Amendments to the Original Act. Various provisions for enforcement and for posting of wage rates were provided by executive order of President Hoover in early 1932,[25] but bickering continued. It culminated in amendments passed by Congress in the spring of 1932 calling for predetermination of prevailing wages, coverage of public works as well as public buildings, and stronger enforcement, including a variety of fines. This President Hoover vetoed, principally because he saw in the wage predetermination issue the beginnings of a major new federal data collection and dissemination problem.[26] His secretary of labor commented that the bill was "obscure and complex and would be impractical of administration," and that with such obscurities and complexities, the results "could only be dissatisfaction, endless controversy in enforcement, and great increase in expense to the taxpayer."[27]

A 1933 investigation of racketeering by the Senate Committee on Commerce and hearings by the Senate Subcommittee on Education and Labor uncovered the means used by a few unscrupulous con-

---

[25] Herbert Hoover, "Executive Order Stipulations for Payment of Prevailing Rate of Wages in Public Building Contracts," 574. MONTHLY CATALOGUE 535 (Jan. 1932).

[26] Herbert Hoover, "Memorandum Upon Senate Bill 3847" (Sen. Doc. 134), 1 July 1932, cited in GENERAL ACCOUNTING OFFICE, *supra* note 3, at 122.

[27] *Id,* attached memorandum of secretary of labor. Since almost all characteristics of the vetoed bill were repeated in the amendments made subsequently in 1935, the secretary's comments could have applied to them with equal vigor and equal foresight.

tractors to avoid paying prevailing rates. The disclosures led to the Copeland (Anti-Kickback) and False Statements Acts of 1934.[28] The hearings also gave renewed impetus to resurrecting the 1932 Davis-Bacon Act amendments and adding to them. Somewhat modified, the amendments were reported out again in 1935. The new administration, with new views on the role of government in labor relations, approved of the amendments. They passed both houses of Congress without debate or roll-call and were signed into law by President Roosevelt on August 30, 1935.[29]

The Current Davis-Bacon Law

The 1935 amendments were a substitution for the 1931 act and became the basic Davis-Bacon Act which is still current. The major changes included: 1) predetermination and posting of wages; 2) modification to include "public buildings or public works" rather than just public buildings, so as to cover levees, dams, and other heavy construction projects; 3) extension to cover painting and decorating as part of "construction, alteration, or repair"; 4) reduction of the contract threshold from $5,000 to $2,000, apparently because painting and decorating contracts tended to be small; 5) a requirement that payments to workers be made weekly and in full; and 6) several enforcement provisions, including set-asides, contract terminations, blacklisting, and right to recovery actions by employees. The essence of the new law is as follows:

> (a) The advertised specifications for every contract in excess of $2,000, to which the United States or the District of Columbia is a party, for construction, alteration, and/or repair, including painting and decorating, of public buildings or public works of the United States or the District of Columbia within the geographic limits of the States of the Union, or the District of Columbia, and which requires or involves the employment of mechanics and/or laborers shall contain a provision stating the minimum wages to be paid various classes of laborers and mechanics which *shall be based upon the wages that*

---

[28] Some of the paperwork requirements of these acts as they apply to Davis-Bacon jobs are particularly burdensome to smaller contractors, and seem to be of little if any use to the government in enforcement. This issue will be discussed later in the chapter, but it is interesting to note that the most recent bill introduced to amend Davis-Bacon (H.R. 472, 1985) has as one of its principle features eliminating the weekly wage reports currently required and substituting one report at the beginning and another at the end of the contract. It is also interesting to note that despite the amount of attention paid to the possibilities of kickbacks, there have been few if any cases involving convictions under the Copeland Anti-Kickback Act. [A.F. HINTZE, ASSOCIATED GENERAL CONTRACTORS DAVIS-BACON HANDBOOK 63 (1976). This may be because the law is exceptionally effective, but it is more likely that changing economic climates and employer-employee relationships since 1935 have rendered it obsolete.

[29] Act of Aug. 30, 1935, ch. 825, 49 Stat. 1011 (1935).

> *will be determined by the Secretary of Labor to be prevailing* for the *corresponding classes of laborers and mechanics* employed on *projects of a character similar* to the contract work in the *city, town, village, or other civil subdivision* of the state, in which the work is to be performed, or in the District of Columbia if the work is to be performed there;...[30]

The most troublesome of the modifications has obviously been the predetermination of wages. So long as the application of the law was vague, the consequences of not being able to identify, determine, or define prevailing wages were not serious.[31] But if the rates must be predetermined, then someone must accept the responsibility for establishing a definition for the statistically indeterminate concept of prevailing. The legislation and its amendments did not define this concept, so the duty fell by default to the secretary of labor. The decisions of the secretary in this regard and the problems they have caused will be covered later in the chapter.

Since the 1935 amendments, almost all of the changes have been made at the administrative level by the Department of Labor or by contracting officers rather than in Congress. There have been few additional changes to the Davis-Bacon law. The only additional amendments of substance came in 1964, when fringe benefits, including medical or hospital care, workmen's compensation, unemployment benefits, pensions, vacation pay, and "other bona fide fringe benefits . . . not required by other Federal, State, or local law" were added to the prevailing wage concept.[32]

Proponents of these amendments had argued successfully that fringe benefits had become so prevalent and so large that not including them in the prevailing wage destroyed the effectiveness of the law and gave an unfair competitive advantage to nonunion firms, which did not necessarily pay them. Identification of prevailing fringe benefits in an area is presumably determined in the same fashion as it is for prevailing wages; and contractors' obli-

---

[30] Davis-Bacon Act, 40 U.S.C. § 276a(a) (1982). (Emphasis added.)

[31] The Nebraska state prevailing wage law is the only surviving example of a prevailing wage law constructed on original principals of prevailing, as meaning apparently, a wage rate not obviously lower than the lowest rates offered in the local community for similar work and for which individuals were willing to work. (All of the other early state acts were modified to follow the federal Davis-Bacon Act example. The similar constructs of the Walsh-Healey Act, Ch. V, *infra*, were successively defined to be more statistical, and therefore more troublesome, before the wage portion of the act was made moribund by a court decision in 1964.) By remaining vague in application as well as in design, the Nebraska act has stirred little controversy over the years, but has remained an available weapon to weed out the kinds of low-wage gypsy contractors the drafters of Davis-Bacon feared.

[32] Act of July 2, 1964, Pub. L. No. 88–349, 78 Stat. 238 (1965).

gations to pay them can be satisfied by payments in kind or by cash payments as a supplement to the basic hourly rate of pay.[33]

The rationale successfully proposed for adding fringe benefit coverage represents a significant shift in the positioning of Davis-Bacon as public policy. Fringe benefits were not added to the prevailing wage concept in order to protect local wage standards from competitive pressures, or to keep itinerant contractors out of the local construction market. They were added to eliminate an area of competitive advantage enjoyed by nonunion firms. This is the first open public expression of a new agenda for Davis-Bacon, that of promoting unionism in the construction industry by shielding unionized firms from the consequences of their higher labor costs. This may or may not have been one of the original purposes of Davis-Bacon, but it had certainly become an important or even the preeminent one by the 1960s. As will be explained below, it was reflected in administration of the law as well as in amendments.

Inclusion in Other Laws

The Davis-Bacon Act was brought to substantially its present form by the amendments of 1935, but not to its present extent. It was an act to require payment of a prevailing wage (and prevailing fringe benefits after 1964) to laborers and mechanics on projects over $2,000 *"to which the U.S. or the District of Columbia is a party,* for construction, alteration and/or repair, including painting and decorating, of public buildings or public works of the U.S. or District of Columbia."[34] Extension of the concept of prevailing wages to other industries occurred with the introduction of the Walsh-Healey Act in 1935 and the O'Hara-McNamara Services Act (Service Contract Act) in 1965, which will be discussed below in Chapters V and VI.

Of greater significance in terms of the impact of coverage, however, has been the inclusion of Davis-Bacon requirements in public

---

[33] This has the curious effect of sometimes making it more expensive for open shop firms than for union ones on Davis-Bacon contracts performed under union rate determinations, because in the process of cashing out fringe benefits and adding them to the base rate, unemployment and FICA taxes apply to the higher wage amount. One representative sample showed the wage costs for a nonunion firm to be 3 percent higher than for a union firm at the same wage rate and fringe benefit amounts. [*How Trust Fund Contributions Affect Payroll Taxes*, ENGINEERING NEWS-REC., August 18, 1983, cited in H.R. NORTHRUP, OPEN SHOP CONSTRUCTION REVISITED. 339 (1984)]. It is fortunate, however, that Congress decided to allow cashing out of fringe benefits. The New York State prevailing wage law does not, but requires payment of such benefits in kind. This has the effect of substantially prohibiting nonunion firms from working on state projects because of the much higher costs for such benefits when purchased for small groups or for individuals. (See Ch. IV, *infra.*)

[34] Davis-Bacon, 40 U.S.C. §276a(a) (1982).

works construction in which the federal government is *not* a direct party but rather provides aid (grants, matching funds, guarantees, or the like) to federal agencies or for state or local projects. The 1935 act, for example, did not cover construction projects for the Public Roads Administration, the United States Housing Authority, the Rural Electrification Administration, or the Public Works Administration, contracts for all of which were classified as federal-aid contracts rather than contracts to which the United States was an actual party.[35]

But as time went by, compliance with Davis-Bacon provisions was added to these acts and a great many more. A study for the Congressional Research Service in 1978 estimated that the dollar amount of coverage for the federally assisted programs was larger than that for the federal government's direct purchases.[36] Extension to such programs began in 1937 with the U.S. Housing Act of that year. By 1960, the number of aid programs covered had grown to eight, including the Federal-Aid Highway Act of 1956; it then leaped upwards during the activist years beginning with the 89th Congress, reaching a total of sixty-two by 1972 and seventy-seven by 1977.[37] Many of these are acts to assist in the development of housing, highways, or other areas where construction would logically be expected; but others have a much less obvious connection to construction, which has trapped a few unwary contractors.[38]

Related Statutes

There are three additional statutes which, although not directly associated with the Davis-Bacon Act, are nevertheless related to it. The first of these is the Miller Act of 1935,[39] which provides that contractors performing construction work directly under Davis-Bacon must be covered by a performance bond and a payment bond to protect the government against financial loss resulting from a contractor's failure to perform, and to protect persons supplying

---

[35] Dadian, *Comparison of Davis-Bacon and Walsh-Healey Acts*, MONTHLY LAB. REV. 124 (July 1941).

[36] Joseph F. Fulton, *The Davis-Bacon Act: History, Administration, Pro and Con Arguments, and Congressional Proposals*, CONG. RESEARCH SERV., (LOC) Report No. 78-161 E, at 4 (1978).

[37] GENERAL ACCOUNTING OFFICE, *supra* note 3, at 125-30.

[38] Some of these, for example, might be the National Foundation on the Arts and Humanities Act of 1965, the Heart Disease, Cancer and Stroke Amendments of 1965, the Education Amendments of 1972, the Domestic Volunteer Service Act of 1973, the Indian Self-Determination and Education Assistance Act (1974), or the Developmentally Disabled Assistance and Bill of Rights Act (1975).

[39] 40 U.S.C. §270a (1982).

The Davis-Bacon Act

labor and materials to such a contractor from nonpayment.[40] The Miller Act applies only to direct federal construction, but federally assisted construction work that is subject to Davis-Bacon is also subject to similar bonding requirements.

The second related act is the Fair Labor Standards Act, which was passed in 1938,[41] seven years after the first introduction of Davis-Bacon. This act provided the country's first statutory minimum wage (25 cents an hour) and established an overtime rate of one-and-one-half times the regular hourly rate for employees working more than a certain maximum number of hours in a week. The wage provisions of this act extended only to nonexempt employees who were engaged in interstate commerce or in the production of goods for interstate commerce. Construction workers were not originally covered, but many were brought under the act when it was amended in 1961.[42]

The third related act is the Contract Work Hours and Safety Standards Act of 1962.[43] This act brought contract work under the time-and-one-half provisions of the Fair Labor Standards Act, and further required that the overtime rate be paid for work in excess of eight hours a day, as well as for work in excess of forty hours a week.[44] It has been a troublesome act for those employers who might like to consider the flexibility of, for example, four ten-hour days constituting a normal workweek.[45] In 1985, the Senate considered

---

[40] Since 1978, when the contract threshold for the Miller Act was changed, the coverage of the two acts has been slightly different. Although Congress has consistently declined to contemplate raising the threshold of the Davis-Bacon Act from the $2,000 level established in 1935; it was willing to raise the Miller Act threshold from $2,000 to $25,000. In raising the Miller Act threshold, the rationale seemed to be that very small contracts tend to be done by small contractors, who have difficulty getting bonded, and should be spared that problem in the interest of opening up such contracts to freer competition. Since small contractors also have difficulty coping with the wage and reporting requirements of Davis-Bacon, it would seem reasonable to apply the same logic to raising the Davis-Bacon threshold, but Congress has not seen fit to do so.

[41] 29 U.S.C. §§201–219 (1982).

[42] Since it is a fair interpretation of the arguments leading to the establishment of the prevailing wage requirement of the Davis-Bacon Act that prevailing wages rather than statutory minimums were selected because they were a less intrusive and more readily acceptable alternative, it must be concluded that they were still thought of as such in 1938 when the Fair Labor Standards Act was passed, else Congress could easily have included construction workers on federal projects among those to be covered by the minimum wage. It is unfortunate that Congress chose not to do so, for coverage of employees by the "tougher" statutory minimum would have rendered Davis-Bacon more obviously obsolete.

[43] 40 U.S.C. §§327–333 (1982).

[44] The Walsh-Healey Act also requires time-and-one-half pay after eight hours' work per day on all federal contracts which total $10,000 or more. [*See* Ch. VI, *infra.*]

[45] Union contracts in the construction trades are often more restrictive than the

the special work hour provisions of the Contract Work Hours and Safety Standards Act, along with similar ones of the Walsh-Healey Act. Citing the desirability of increased flexibility in scheduling, as well as a Congressional Budget Office estimate that eliminating these provisions could lead to annual savings of $550 million, the Senate overwhelmingly expressed its "sense of the Senate" that these provisions be dropped.[46] This resolution was carried through into separate bills introduced in committees of both houses of Congress, but before they were reported out, another situation arose which made them unnecessary.

In preparing the defense authorization bill for fiscal 1986, the Senate had left standing an amendment that would have exempted military construction contracts of $1 million or less from the prevailing wage requirements of the Davis-Bacon Act.[47] The final House bill passed did not contain this measure, so a House-Senate conference became necessary. At the conference, Senate conferees agreed to drop the Davis-Bacon modification, but only in exchange for the House conferees agreeing to accept an amendment adopting the language of the Senate version of the Walsh-Healey reform bill that had been approved by the Senate Labor and Human Resources Committee on July 17, 1985.[48] That bill amended the Walsh-Healey Act to permit employees of *all* federal contractors, not just defense contractors, to work any combination of hours in a 40-hour week without overtime pay.[49] Thus, it appears that the operative daily overtime provisions of the Contract Work Hours and Safety Standards Act no longer apply after January 1, 1986.

Coverage of the Davis-Bacon Act

About $265 billion was spent on new construction in calendar year 1983. Of this, approximately $214 billion was performed on privately financed projects, generally without the protection of the

---

statutory requirements for overtime. About 10 percent of union contracts, for example, set thirty-five rather than forty hours as the straight-time week, and a larger proportion require double time as the overtime rate for week-end or holiday work. [*See* NORTHRUP, *supra* note 34, at 516–17.] As a result of these and similar provisions, even in the event of a prevailing rate determination at the union scale, open shop contractors may have a cost advantage over their union counterparts, because Davis-Bacon follows statutory rather than prevailing provisions for overtime.

[46] Senate Concurrent Resolution 32, May 1985, in *Senate Passes Walsh-Healey Resolution*, GOV'T UNION CRITIQUE 2 (May 31, 1985).

[47] *See* Ch. III, *supra*, at note 3.

[48] S. 1105 99th Cong., 1st Sess. (1985).

[49] *House-Senate Conferees Drop Davis-Bacon, Add Walsh-Healey Amendments to Defense Bill*, 145 DAILY LAB. REP. A-10 (July 29, 1985).

Davis-Bacon Act or state prevailing wage laws.[50] The balance (about $50 billion) was performed on projects financed by various levels of government, the majority of which was covered by some sort of prevailing wage requirement. These figures represent spending for new construction. In addition, there was also spending for reconstruction, repair, and maintenance work which, although it tends to be on smaller projects, is probably split in about the same ratio between public and private work. No precise estimates are available as to the total amount of construction work directly or indirectly affected by the wage rate determinations of the secretary of labor under Davis-Bacon, because, among other reasons, a number of the state prevailing wage laws key on the Davis-Bacon rates, some of which preempt Davis-Bacon rates while others defer to them on joint federal-state projects. As a ball-park estimate, about $35 to $40 billion of new construction and reconstruction each year is probably done under Davis-Bacon rates.[51]

The total amount of construction work (public and private) can vary considerably from year to year. Between 1982 and 1983, for example, total new construction increased by approximately $32 billion even though 1983 was still considered to be depressed by the building recession that had begun in 1979. The amount of public construction in 1983, however, remained about the same as it had been in the previous year, and was down by about 10 percent from the 1980 peak of $55 billion. The reasons for this have to do with the fact that demand for public construction follows different economic stimuli than does private work. Public construction is sometimes undertaken to serve as a countercyclical balance to market forces that otherwise depress demand in the private sector, for example, in times of high interest rates. The public proportion of construction expenditures has remained remarkably static in recent years, varying from a high of about 24 percent in 1980 to a low of

---

[50] Figures in this section are taken directly or derived from U.S. Department of Commerce, Bureau of Census, CONSTRUCTION REPORTS C30-84-1, VALUE OF NEW CONSTRUCTION PUT IN PLACE, Table 1 (1984), cited in NORTHRUP, supra note 34, at 5. In some circumstances, privately financed construction may be subject to prevailing wage requirements if, for example, the facilities are specially constructed with the intention of leasing them to government occupants.

[51] The Congressional Research Service estimated that the amount of construction subject to the Davis-Bacon requirement was $27 billion in 1975, $29 billion in 1976, and $34 billion in 1977, Fulton, supra note 37, at 4. The Congressional Budget Office estimated the amount at $53 billion in 1981 [CONGRESSIONAL BUDGET OFFICE, MODIFYING THE DAVIS-BACON ACT: IMPLICATIONS FOR THE LABOR MARKET AND THE FEDERAL BUDGET (July 1983) at ix], but it appears likely that the CBO may have used the figure for all publicly financed construction, which would involve a substantial amount of work at the state and local levels (schools, for example) that is not subject to the Davis-Bacon requirements.

19 percent in 1983. Generally speaking, public construction is about one-fifth of the total.[52]

The GAO estimated in 1979 that Davis-Bacon provisions were attached to approximately 600,000 prime and subcontracts each year, that the majority of contractors to whom they applied were small businesses, and that about one million construction workers were paid wage rates set by the act.[53] These numbers, whose order of magnitude has not changed for 1985, give some insight into the extent of application of the prevailing wage concept.

ADMINISTRATION AND ITS PROBLEMS

As amended in 1935, the Davis-Bacon Act required that advertised specifications for public works contracts over $2,000 contain a provision stating the minimum wages to be paid various classes of laborers and mechanics. It did not specify what these rates were, but specified that they would be based upon the wages "determined by the Secretary of Labor to be prevailing for the corresponding classes of laborers and mechanics employed on projects of a character similar to the contract work in the city, town, village, or other civil subdivision of the State in which the work is to be performed."[54]

Congress gave no further definitions or guidelines to the secretary of labor as to how to fulfill his charge, leaving it up to him to determine such matters as: 1) what is a corresponding class of laborer or mechanic; 2) what is a project of similar character; 3) what geographic extent should be taken as the civil subdivision of the state. More important, it passed on to the secretary the task of wrestling with the most significant problem of the Davis-Bacon Act, how to define and give substance to the term *prevailing*.

Defining Prevailing

The lack of a satisfactory and generally acceptable definition of prevailing is the cross that all of the prevailing wage laws have had to bear. As discussed in the preceding chapter, the concept frequently yields ambiguous or indeterminate results, because prevailing is not a statistical parameter or directly related to one. In the case of Davis-Bacon, the secretary did adopt a methodology as early as 1935 which, although it has caused great problems through

---

[52] There has been a slow erosion in the proportion of public construction over the longer time frame. In 1970, public construction was about 27 percent of the total. [THIEBLOT, *supra* note 4, at 97.]

[53] GENERAL ACCOUNTING OFFICE, *supra* note 3, at 3–4.

[54] Act of Aug. 30, 1935, Ch. 825, §1, 49 Stat. 1011 (1935).

The Davis-Bacon Act

the years, nevertheless did establish a structure for selecting a rate from those collected by survey of the existing workforce. This method was the secretary's own creation, and is not a statutory method under Davis-Bacon or any other law. The methodology remained informal until codified in 1952,[55] but governed determinations from 1935 until it was at last modified in 1985 (about which more later). It took the following form:

> The term "prevailing wage rate" for each classification of laborers and mechanics which the Administrator shall regard as prevailing in an area shall mean:
>
> (1) The rate of wages paid in the area in which the work is to be performed, to the *majority* of those employed in that classification in construction in the area similar to the proposed undertaking;
>
> (2) In the event that there is not a majority paid at the same rate, then the rate paid to the greatest number: Provided, such greater number constitutes *30 percent* of those employed; or
>
> (3) In the event that less than 30 percent of those so employed receive the same rate, then the *average* rate.[56]

This is the so-called "majority, 30-percent, or average" formula that dominated Davis-Bacon determinations for fifty years. Although always presented by the Department of Labor as a three-step formula, it should be obvious that in fact it has only two steps, since in all cases where a majority—that is, a 50-percent plurality—are paid the same rate, a 30-percent plurality is necessarily paid it as well, so the first step is superfluous. It should therefore be called the "30-percent or average" formula, and in fact is usually referred to outside the DOL as "the 30-percent rule."

Under rules introduced by the DOL in 1982 and finally approved by the courts in 1985, the formulation has changed to a two-step process of "majority or average," so the 30-percent rule has become a 50-percent rule.[57] Discussion of the development of this change and its implementation will be saved for a later section in the chapter, as will evaluation of the reasonableness or appropriateness

---

[55] Rules on administration and enforcement of the Davis-Bacon Act are contained in 29 C.F.R. parts 1, 3, 5, and 7 (1985). Part 1 outlines procedures for predetermination of wage rates. Part 3 concerns record keeping and payroll data submission requirements as interpreted from the Copeland Anti-Kickback Act. Part 5 deals with enforcement procedures and specifies the fringe benefit requirements of the act. Part 7 concerns the Wage Appeals Board, which was established within the Department of Labor in 1963 to adjudicate wage rate disputes following other internal review. Since these are non-statutory regulations, they can be modified after due notice of intended rulemaking and publication of revisions in the Federal Register, but after an attempt by Secretary Donovan to do so in 1981, the courts held that the right of the department to change its rules is limited.

[56] 29 C.F.R. Part 1, (1952) (Emphasis added.)

[57] Procedures for Predetermination of Wage Rates, 29 C.F.R. §§1.1–1.9 (1985).

of the procedure in any of its modes. Three factors are worthy of note about the formula, regardless of whether it is a 30-percent rule or a 50-percent rule:

1) It should be clear that the work of defining prevailing has not been finished by stating the above procedure; it is filled with words of art which must be defined in turn. Upon what basis, for example, should the administrator consider a *classification* of laborers and mechanics to be prevailing? How is the *area in which the work is to be performed* to be selected? By what taxonomy is *similar* work identified?

2) The formula presented is simply a selection device; it necessarily presupposes that some survey or other data-gathering method will be employed to collect wage rate information from the relevant locality. As any statistician can attest, data gathering is a much more difficult part of the statistical process than data reduction, and the place where mistakes can most easily be made.

3) The data-gathering and reduction process, extending as it does to every hourly-wage individual in an industry that is responsible for 7 to 15 percent of the gross national product, is a major administrative undertaking.

President Hoover showed remarkable prescience in his 1932 veto message about the administration of the Davis-Bacon Act. Over the years, the act has required the development of an extensive organization to: 1) define terms and give substance to the act; 2) search out, calculate, determine, and promulgate the prevailing wage rates; 3) handle inquiries and protests; 4) enforce compliance with the act's provisions; and 5) involve itself in other ways.

But the problem of Davis-Bacon administration is far more than just the size of its bureaucracy. Its regulatory and rate setting patterns evolved in a completely different way from those of its contemporary prevailing wage law, the Walsh-Healey Act, and are what have given Davis-Bacon its unique and obtrusive character. The law itself is vague and it apparently was deliberately designed to interfere as little as possible with the private negotiations between employees and employer. But from the first, the Department of Labor was lured into rulemaking and administrative procedures which took it further and further from the basic congressional intent and made it increasingly unlikely that the act could be fairly administered.

Some of the strongest arguments against Davis-Bacon are those raised to show that it is poorly administered to the point of unfairness, and is perhaps incapable of being administered well. Many

The Davis-Bacon Act

of these arguments key on the methods used by the secretary to search for and calculate the prevailing wage (the survey process). Before approaching this subject, however, we should look into the manner in which some of the administrative problems developed.

Comparison with Walsh-Healey Administration

Davis-Bacon's administrative procedures, particularly those developed to handle the prevailing rates, are a fascinating study. Davis-Bacon and Walsh-Healey, for example, were enacted at about the same time (mid-1930s) using an equally vague concept couched in similarly vague wording to accomplish very similar tasks. They used the same basic tools and gave about the same powers and duties to the same secretary of labor. In fact, there are only three differences between the acts that are not directly related to the fact that they cover different industries: 1) Walsh-Healey required payment of prevailing *minimum* wages, whereas Davis-Bacon required payment of straight *prevailing* wages; 2) Walsh-Healey required the rates to be set separately for employees performing "similar work *or* [performing work] in the particular or similar industries," whereas Davis-Bacon (which covered only a single industry) omitted the second part; and 3) the Walsh-Healey statute specified that prevailing rates would be required on contracts only if the secretary had made a wage determination for that industry, while the Davis-Bacon statute does not provide this exclusion.

The enormous differences that these few words made were not immediately apparent. In fact, until World War II, it was generally considered that Walsh-Healey was the more restrictive of the two laws because of the broader application of its required rates. An analysis performed in 1941 noted:

> [T]he Davis-Bacon Act is less rigid and more sensitive to changes in wage rates than the Walsh-Healey Act. This is especially true in times of changing wage scales. Under the Walsh-Healey Act, once a minimum rate has been determined for an industry all the contracts let to firms in that industry will automatically include the predetermined rate for that industry.[58]

Thus, it was assumed that a large number of supply contractors might have to adjust their wage rates actually paid, whereas construction contractors could generally follow their existing scales.

---

[58] Dadian, *supra* note 36, at 131.

Post-War Complications

After the war, as the amount of public construction work increased and as more and more federal-aid projects were brought under the Davis-Bacon Act, the relative impact of the two laws reversed.[59] Many of the economic changes brought on by the postwar expansion and construction boom made it increasingly difficult for the secretary to administer Davis-Bacon under the assumptions and procedures that had been sufficient during the 1930s. The differences came in many forms, some of which will be presented later in the chapter, but we will discuss three here by way of illustration.

Larger Rate Differentials. The rise of nonunion firms, with their developing capabilities outside of the residential market and increasing work in the building, commercial, and heavy segments of the industry, brought with it the complication of increasing numbers of job categories in which large wage rate differences existed for construction workmen doing the same job (or at least holding the same job titles). This made it both more difficult to identify the prevailing rate and more consequential if the rate were incorrectly determined. Nevertheless, in an increasing number of cases, the DOL lacked the manpower to do surveys and often relied instead on presumptions that the union rate prevailed. This continued despite the fact that union membership in the construction industry fell from an estimated 67 percent of the industry's employees in 1936, to 45 percent by 1967, and to no more than 30 percent in 1984.[60] Such presumptions were supported by the secretary's definition of the prevailing rate as the rate paid to a 30-percent plurality of the surveyed wages.

More Rate Categories Required. A second problem arose because of the increasing complexity of construction work and the greater use of new technologies (drywall instead of plaster, for example) and specialized equipment (such as push-cats, or flexometers, or wagon drills) creating new categories of workmen and operators who did not fit neatly into the traditional craft boundaries of the union building trades. This meant that whereas the typical rate determination of the 1930s might contain rates for a dozen categories of construction work, by the 1960s the typical determination might have 30 or 40 for commercial construction and over 150 for

---

[59] Fuller discussion of the development of Walsh-Healey and its administration is found in Ch. V, *infra.*

[60] Northrup, *supra* note 34, at 27 and 287.

heavy construction.[61] (Many recent wage determinations even contain separate rates for four or more categories of laborers, who are traditionally thought to be the undifferentiated common denominator of the construction industry.) When fringe benefits were added to the wage determination process in 1964, the task was again magnified because for each basic rate, up to four categories of fringe benefit payments also had to be determined.

More Determinations Required. But above all, the demand for wage determinations grew dramatically. The number of projects for which determinations were required was 4,453 in 1946. This skyrocketed to a peak of 46,397 in 1963, well beyond the capabilities of a few dozen wage specialists associated with the Employment Standards Administration.[62]

Consequences. During this era, the secretary found it increasingly necessary to make decisions for the sake of expediency, even if it involved the danger that the results might be inaccurate, unrepresentative, or not in keeping with the original congressional intent of Davis-Bacon. For example, in the early 1960s, when the number of contracts covered by extension of Davis-Bacon to federal-aid laws was growing and the burden of project wage determination surveys was increasing, the DOL began to issue general (or "area") determinations that were intended to remain in effect until superceded (compared with 120 days for project determinations) and apply to all contracts within the broad geography covered.

Although such area coverage seems to violate the rationale of the act to protect local wage rates, as well as the specific verbiage concerning "city, town, village, or other civil subdivision of the state," the secretary argued that it was necessary for effective administration. These area determinations are used for localities that have a rather steady flow of construction in a particular category and where there is some assurance that the rates are likely to remain fairly stable. Usually, this has meant areas which the secretary felt were prevailingly union rate, and which therefore required no surveys other than contacting local union business agents for information on the latest agreement terms. In some cases, the

---

[61] This does not take into account the fact that many of the rising nonunion firms employ workmen in such categories as "trainees," "construction mechanics," "forms carpenters," "electrician's helper," and other variations not found in the craft unions. The reason that they are not taken into account is that despite protestations to the contrary, the DOL until recently was almost never willing to countenance job titles other than the traditional ones used by the construction craft unions as titles for which rates might be determined, even if it could be shown that the use of such titles was a "prevailing" condition in a given locality.

[62] Fulton, *supra* note 37, at 16.

area is indistinguishable from nationwide, since some of the wage determinations cover up to 96 percent of the counties in the country.

A second example is the use of rates on file to make new determinations. Any interested party has always had the right to submit wage information on rates actually paid. File information comes from various sources, including contractors, employers' associations, labor organizations, and other interested parties. These may submit at any time:

1. Statements showing wage rates actually paid on projects.
2. Signed collective bargaining agreements.
3. Wage rates determined for public construction by state and local prevailing wage laws.
4. Information furnished by federal and state agencies.
5. Anything else that is pertinent.

There is little incentive for most individual contractors to submit such information, and there is none at all for contractors who are not oriented towards or interested in government work, which means the majority since government contractors tend to be larger firms. According to 1972 estimates, of the 921,000 construction contractors in the United States, 82 percent had fewer than four employees.[63]

Thus, whatever rates are on file come principally from the unions, who have a vested interest in ensuring that their most recent contract information is on file, and from employer trade associations. Trade associations are split, however, and many are all or partially composed of unionized firms that, even if they were opposed to Davis-Bacon, which many of them are,[64] would have to display incredible altruism to submit information that might tend to produce lower prevailing rate determinations. The net effect is that whatever wage information is on file tends to be high-rate information, except in a few lines of construction in a few areas of the country where the open shop firms felt they constituted more than a 70

---

[63] GENERAL ACCOUNTING OFFICE, *supra* note 3, at 4.

[64] The Associated General Contractors of America, for example, has strongly supported repeal of Davis-Bacon. "The Associated General Contractors of America subscribes to the [repeal of Davis-Bacon], although general contractors, theoretically at least, benefit from the Davis-Bacon Act by the elimination of wage costs as competitive factors in bidding on public construction. While the association might be expected, for this reason, to lean towards the protection of such laws, our actual experience with the Davis-Bacon Act, on an almost daily basis since its beginning 48 years ago, has convinced us that Davis-Bacon is not in the interest of the construction industry or the taxpayers and should be repealed." Testimony of the Associated General Contractors of America presented to the House Subcommittee on Labor Standards 14 (June 14, 1979).

percent plurality of the workforce, and therefore could force the average wage to be chosen as prevailing.

Mechanics of Administration

Under the original terms of the Davis-Bacon Act, the various contracting agencies of the federal government were individually responsible for determining if contractors were paying the prevailing wage. The 1935 amendments affixed the responsibility for predetermining the prevailing wage on the secretary of labor, but until 1950 the major responsibility for enforcement rested with the individual government agencies for whom the work was being performed.

In 1950, the federal establishment was reorganized. Reorganization Plan No. 14 affected the activities of the DOL, and authorized the secretary to prescribe appropriate standards and procedures to enforce the Davis-Bacon law.[65] By 1971, after a series of administrative and name changes, responsibility for rate determinations was vested in the Branch of Construction Wage Determinations of the Wage and Hour Division of the Employment Standards Administration.[66] In February of that year, President Nixon suspended the Davis-Bacon Act in an effort to curb inflation generally and construction wage escalation in particular. The DOL, acting as though the suspension were to be permanent, disbanded the branch responsible for prevailing wage determinations, and transferred most of the approximately sixty employees to other civil service positions.

The suspension, however, proved to be short-lived. After only thirty-five days, President Nixon bowed to construction union pressures, established an advisory board, the Construction Industry Stabilization Commission, with minor authorities to influence rates in construction in order to hold down wage-push inflation, and reinstated the act. At that time, to facilitate a return to rate determination service, regional offices of the Employment Standards Administration were given some field responsibility for wage surveys in their areas in addition to their existing duties, which was subsequently increased. The Wage and Hour Division retained final decision over the regional offices' determinations and continued to make all of the area (as opposed to project) determinations at the

---

[65] Reorg. Plan No. 14 of 1950 3 C.F.R. 107 (1985), *reprinted in* 5 U.S.C. app. at 1050 *and in* 64 Stat. 1267 (1952).

[66] For greater detail on the administrative structure of Davis-Bacon and its development, see THIEBLOT, *supra* note 4, at 28–43; and HINTZE, *supra* note 29, at 19–88.

Washington headquarters. After January 1978 all administration of wage determinations was transferred back to Washington, with the exception of performing wage surveys. These are still done by the field staff under the direction of headquarters.

In 1972, as a result of studies by the General Accounting Office showing misapplication of higher building construction rates to residential project determinations, the Department of Housing and Urban Development became dissatisfied with the accuracy of wages set by the DOL and began making its own surveys, the results of which it submits to the DOL along with any requests for determinations. Although there is no guarantee that the information it submits will be followed in making determinations (the DOL makes duplicate surveys and uses other "independent" wage data in an unknown number of cases), Housing and Urban Development has apparently found the exercise and the trouble worth the cost.

Number of Personnel. As of September 1973, the DOL had a total of thirty employees, twenty-one of them professionals and the rest clerks and typists, responsible for making wage determinations in Washington. These were supported by an approximately like number of specialists in the regional offices. By March 1978, the number had increased slightly, but there were still only twenty-four wage determination specialists or wage analysts at headquarters and twenty-six others located in regional offices.[67]

Extent of Task. The task faced by these approximately fifty persons is of monumental proportions. As noted earlier, there are about 600,000 public construction contracts in any given year. Approximately 10 percent of these might be for federal projects that require a prevailing rate determination, and each determination might consist of rates (and several fringe benefit amounts) for anywhere from 12 to more than 300 job categories.

As a result of the introduction of the area determination process, the number of separate determinations required began to decrease, since each area determination could replace a number of project ones.[68] By 1977, the total number of project determinations issued stood at 15,674 and the number of area determinations at 2,257.[69]

---

[67] GENERAL ACCOUNTING OFFICE, *supra* note 3, at 4.

[68] By 1985, the number of "safe union" areas of the country was diminishing rapidly. Simultaneously, the methodology for calculating the prevailing rate changed from one of "30-percent plurality or average" to one of "50-percent plurality or average." The significance of this is that the number of area determinations may have to decrease and the department revert to greater reliance on project rates. At the time of writing, it is too soon to tell if the methodological change will have major impact on the DOL in terms of the number of determinations issued.

[69] J.P. GOULD & G. BITTLINGMAYER, THE ECONOMICS OF THE DAVIS-BACON ACT: AN ANALYSIS OF PREVAILING-WAGE LAWS (1980) at 15.

In 1982, with volume down as a result of the construction recession, the DOL released 12,788 project and 1,238 area determinations.[70]

Even at this reduced figure, about fifty individuals are responsible for producing approximately 14,000 determinations per year, or 280 each—an average of more than one each working day.[71] The magnitude of this task is great enough to cause questions about the level of accuracy that is possible as a result of it.

Securing the Rate. The mechanics of securing a rate determination begin with a contracting officer requesting a project decision from the Employment Standards Administration. If the office has what it thinks is enough information on file to make the determination, it will. If not, it will ask one of the regional offices to conduct a survey, the results of which are forwarded to headquarters where the determination is made. In either case, once a rate schedule has been prepared and attached to the requests for bids (or forwarded to the bidding contractors if the requests went out before the rate decision was made), the cycle has been completed unless: 1) a subsequent modification is issued; 2) an interested party makes a protest; or 3) a clerical error is found in the determined rates.

Protesting a Rate. Although any of these might be of importance to a contractor, the only one that need concern us here is the second.[72] One of the problems with Davis-Bacon has been the lack of an easy mechanism to ensure that rates are accurately determined. Although rate protest is possible, it is not easy. Any inter-

---

[70] CONGRESSIONAL BUDGET OFFICE, MODIFYING THE DAVIS-BACON ACT: IMPLICATIONS FOR THE LABOR MARKET AND THE FEDERAL BUDGET (1983) at 19.

[71] If we were to assume, for the sake of argument, that all wage determinations were made on the basis of surveys, that a typical rate determination set wages and four different categories of fringe benefits for thirty categories of laborers and mechanics, and that for validity at least a dozen survey rates would be necessary to establish each one, then something over 200 payment numbers must be accumulated from a variety of sources (typically by telephone), verified for accuracy, analyzed to identify the prevailing rates (typically by hand), compiled into a determination, and issued by each wage determination specialist in every hour of a 2,000-hour work year. This amounts to 3.33 numbers per minute per man, or approximately one every 18 seconds, assuming no coffee breaks, or any other duties. Of course, surveys are not made for all wage determinations, many of the determinations issued are simply reissues of old rates, and many of the others—although called surveys—consist of little more than looking in the file for whatever negotiated rates might be found there. The above comments are included to illustrate the absurdly large task that would be required to administer Davis-Bacon as it is thought to be administered.

[72] Those interested in the operational details of Davis-Bacon administration should refer to at least one of the several compendia available from various trade associations. The DAVIS-BACON HANDBOOK (1976) of the Associated General Contractors of America is a particularly complete one (278 pages) and not yet too far out of date. Another is THE DAVIS-BACON GUIDE (1976) of the Building and Construction Trades Department, AFL-CIO (116 pages).

ested party can protest a rate, but in the period between the time that a wage rate is published and bids are opened, there is no contractor. The contracting agency might take an interest, but this would be rare. So at this point, only unions and contractors' associations are reasonable sources of interested parties. After bids are opened there is a contractor, but it is too late to protest, and only changes resulting from clerical error might be allowed.

Taking an appeal is basically a fact-finding operation. Although the Department of Labor is not required to justify the validity and accuracy of its rates, protestors must be prepared to prove their case. This involves the collection of prevailing wage information with an explanation of what it consists of, and a request to the appropriate Davis-Bacon representatives in Washington for redetermination based on that information. Depending on the timing, a request may also have to be made for extension of the bid-opening deadline.[73]

At the very least, challenge of a determination will require a trip to the regional office, and perhaps to Washington, to review the file of the wage information used to make the determination. If a review at this time by the DOL results in a changed rate, the appeal process is finished, a new determination is issued, and again depending on the time involved, invitations may have to be issued starting the bid process over again. If the judgment of the DOL is to reject the change, further appeal can be taken.

Even this first step of the protest process is difficult. An excellent summary of what is involved, and a good reason why it is not done more frequently by contractors, is provided in the testimony of Philip Abrams, a general contractor from Massachusetts, presented to a Senate subcommittee investigating Davis-Bacon administration in 1979:

> The reason that more contractors don't protest wages is that it's not easy to overturn wage determinations, no matter how outrageous they are.
>
> First of all, they must be done on bid projects before the bid documents are issued if you're going to protest, and that means that a contractor would have to be altruistic enough to conduct a study before he's even allowed to bid on the project.

---

[73] A request for postponement can be difficult. Neither the Wage Appeals Board nor the Davis-Bacon staff have jurisdiction over bid-opening dates. Only the contracting agency can delay a bid opening, and may not find it in its interests to do so, despite the fact that most rate protests have come from those seeking lower rather than higher rates which, if successful, might save the contracting agency some money.

The Davis-Bacon Act

> If it's a negotiated project, the contractor would have to be aware of the fact that he was going to be the contractor substantially before the time in which that contract was negotiated and signed. There's no time for the contractors or their associations to conduct the surveys that are necessary to police Davis-Bacon.
>
> It took the contractor on this particular project in Pennsylvania [that was successfully protested] over 8 months to conduct the survey, submit it to the Department of Labor to issue a favorable reduction in wages that had previously been submitted, and the only reason that that survey was able to be prosecuted was because it was delayed for other reasons.
>
> And the developer was willing to let the contractor go through the steps that were necessary in order to come up with wages that more accurately reflected those prevailing in that part of Pennsylvania.
>
> It's an onerous procedure to overturn a Davis-Bacon determination. It is not simple. The Department of Labor does not simply react to a statement by a contractor or his association that a wage is not accurate or is not prevailing. You must substantiate it. It takes a lot of time and effort to do that.[74]

In essence, in addition to the time constraints, the costs to contractors to protest a rate determination, and the fact that construction firms in an area might balk even more at sharing the details of wage information with a competitor than with a government agency, protests of determinations are inhibited by the fact that although the DOL does not have to verify the accuracy of its determinations, the protestor does. And even if a protest is successful and wage rates are modified accordingly, the protestor who paid for it all has no greater likelihood of winning the contract that the rates were determined for.

Assuming that the protest were refused, the next step would be a request for an in-depth field investigation and/or a conference with the Davis-Bacon staff in Washington to discuss the problem and review the wage data that the staff claims support their position. If still refused, a final appeal can be made to the Wage Appeals Board, an agency set up within the DOL in 1963 principally for this purpose.[75] (It also hears compliance cases.)

---

[74] *Davis-Bacon Legislation: Hearing Before the Subcommittee on Housing and Urban Affairs of the Committee on Banking, Housing, and Urban Affairs*, 96th Cong., 1st Sess. (May 2, 1979) (Statement of Philip Abrams, President, Abreem Corp., Needham Heights, Mass.) [hereinafter cited as *Hearings*].

[75] Established by Secretary's Order No. 32–63. In 1962, an effort had been mounted before the Special Subcommittee on Labor on Administration of the Davis-Bacon Act, of the House Committee on Education and Labor, to bring the secretary's Davis-Bacon determinations under judicial review in a fashion similar to that made part of the Walsh-Healey Act by the Fulbright Amendments. (See Ch. V, *infra*, note 41.) The Subcommittee rejected this approach, but suggested administrative review by a board selected from procurement experts and the construction industry. This was

There can be no appeal of a Wage Appeals Board decision. Courts do not entertain challenges to Davis-Bacon wage determinations, on the ground that "[t]he correctness of the Secretary's determination is not open to attack on judicial review."[76] Furthermore, no one has a litigable interest. A wage determination appeal can only be lodged before the bid opening, a time when there was no contract and therefore no interested party, from the courts' standpoint; after bids are opened, only clerical errors can be corrected, so no protest can be made.

CHALLENGES TO DAVIS-BACON ADMINISTRATION

There are three major challenges to the Davis-Bacon Act that have formed the basis of the calls for its repeal. The first centers on administration, and contends, in essence, that the complex structure necessary for implementation of a law that extends to so many contracts, involves so many judgmental decisions at the regulatory level about rates and surveys and applications, and has so few avenues for external review of accuracy, is not only unlikely to be fair, but also is unlikely ever to be made fair. The second centers on economic impact, and estimates the costs of the act, either on their own or as opposed to benefits provided, in terms of escalating wage rates, how much the government pays for construction projects relative to what it would pay in the open market, or costs to the economy through wage-push inflation. The third concerns the philosophy of the act, maintaining either that the act was the wrong way to achieve the original stated purposes, that those purposes are no longer socially necessary or desirable, or both. Although most of the challenges to Davis-Bacon through the years have encompassed some aspects of all three of these areas, some are more oriented one way than another. Those of the GAO, particularly under Comptroller General Elmer Staats, a Johnson appointee, have been among the most pointed in challenging the act's administration.

---

not a statutory suggestion, so the secretary declined the opportunity to subject his determinations to outside scrutiny, and set up the captive Wage Appeals Board instead. During its first years of operation, the Wage Appeals Board heard very few cases, but by the late 1970s was handling twenty to thirty a year. An excellent summary of the decisions made by the Board between 1964 and 1976 is presented in HINTZE, *supra* note 29, at 89–147.

[76] United States v. Binghamton Construction Co., 347 U.S. 171 (1954) (footnote omitted).

Comptroller General's Authority

The comptroller general has various enforcement responsibilities under Davis-Bacon dealing with reimbursements and debarments.[77] Additionally, he has responsibilities to the Congress to undertake studies of the effectiveness and the costs and benefits of government programs in any areas administered by the executive branch and to advise Congress of changes that should be made to improve such programs.[78] Finally, the comptroller general has specific responsibility to review the administrative results of the government procurement process.[79] Thus, the comptroller's agency, the GAO, has had the general and specific responsibility to review the activities of the DOL in administering the Davis-Bacon Act. It is not a complete authority. The comptroller cannot block the use of unauthorized wage determinations, for example, or remand them. He has no authorization to require the DOL to change its interpretations or to do, or not do, any particular thing. His statutory authority under Davis-Bacon is limited to controlling the disbursement of withheld wages to laborers and mechanics on federal construction.

Nevertheless, the position of the comptroller general is highly important. Because he is a watchdog of the Congress, on guard against waste of public funds, he has taken a continuing interest in Davis-Bacon wage determinations. He can make and has made investigations to document the misuse of funds and reports those findings to Congress which, although it has failed to act on them to date, is becoming increasingly hard-pressed to explain why not. Furthermore, the GAO is the only agency other than Congress itself with the ability to keep the DOL from being like the student who grades his own homework. The only other oversight of any kind is that provided by the Wage Appeals Board which, as we have seen, was created within and by the DOL and is at best quasi-autonomous.

---

[77] These are provided under 29 C.F.R., Part 5. Despite the complexity of the administrative machinery and the weight of the Copeland Anti-Kickback Act, there have been no great number of debarments. There were two in 1975, five in 1976, and seven in 1977 reported by the Congressional Research Service. [FULTON, *supra* note 37, at 21.] Secretary Marshall, however, noted that the Department of Labor debarred forty-one contractors because of Davis-Bacon violations in 1978. [*Hearings, supra* note 74, at 205 (Supplemental Testimony of Ray Marshall, Secretary of Labor.)] The apparent discrepancy is not explained.

[78] *Hearings, supra* note 74, at 12 (testimony of Elmer Staats, Comptroller General of the United States).

[79] Among other acts, the comptroller general has responsibilities under the Budget and Accounting Act, 31 U.S.C. 53 (1921) and the Accounting and Auditing Act of 1950, 31 U.S.C. 67.

Comptroller General's Activities

Despite limited authority, comptroller generals have taken their position as overseers of Davis-Bacon very seriously. The first comptroller general's decision, made in January 1938, interpreted the statutory language of the act precisely, and disallowed the contention by the secretary of labor that Davis-Bacon rates should apply to repair of a steamship on the ground that the location where the repairs were to have been made was not known beforehand, so local wage rates could not be protected.[80] Through the years, the comptroller generals' decisions have concerned such topics as correcting wage determination errors, preventing misclassification of laborers and mechanics, forestalling coverage of off-site facilities in connection with covered projects, expanding limits on uses of apprentices and other training classifications, selecting from among two or more wage schedules in effect for the same job, and limiting problems arising from expiration of wage determinations.

In these decisions, the comptroller has not always been on the side of the contractor, but he seems always to have been on the side of strict interpretation of the statutory language when the secretary of labor was attempting to extend it. Thus the comptroller challenged, among others, the secretaries' decisions to include negotiated wage increases without evidence that they actually were paid, to apply Davis-Bacon rates to off-site work, to refuse to determine rates for "beginner operators" on a highway project where their use was a prevalent practice, and to redefine the painter's job description in order to prohibit the use of paint sprayers.

Comptroller General's Challenge

The comptroller has also conducted a series of investigations of Davis-Bacon administration as part of his general oversight duties, and has made nine reports to Congress in the last twenty-five years. In a series of reviews starting in 1960, the GAO discovered distressing patterns of maladminstration of the act. Although these early reports are outdated with respect to such things as wage rates paid, later iterations of similar studies in the series, the most recent in

---

[80] Comptroller General's Decision *Vessel Tulip,* A-90983 (January 13, 1938). For a synopsis of fifty-six comptroller generals' decisions between 1938 and 1976, see HINTZE, *supra* note 29, at 150–56.

1979 and 1980, revealed that the problems identified were seldom corrected.[81]

By 1979, after the ninth study of Davis-Bacon administration, the comptroller general felt that the administrative burdens of the act had become too great and that the DOL, despite ample opportunity to do so, had demonstrated an unwillingness or an inability to rectify the problems identified earlier. He therefore recommended repeal of the act as the only realistic solution, citing incurable administrative problems as one and perhaps the most important of the three reasons. In the comptroller's view, despite fifty years of effort, the DOL had not developed an effective program to issue and maintain accurate wage determinations, and was unlikely to be able to do so in the future.[82]

The following extensive quote from the comptroller general's testimony to a Senate oversight hearing on Davis-Bacon administration in 1979 is presented here not only because it summarizes the GAO's position, but also because it introduces most of the administrative problems that have plagued Davis-Bacon from its inception:

> After nearly 50 years of administering the act, [the Department of] Labor has not developed an effective system to plan, control, or manage the data collection, compilation, and wage determination issuance functions under the Davis-Bacon Act. In fact, the policies, practices, and procedures developed by Labor for establishing wage rates under the Act have only rarely implemented the legislative intent. Rates issued have nearly always affected local wage standards—in many instances amounting to wage fixing and limiting or establishing worker classifications for Government construction with no consideration given to classifications and corresponding wages paid on similar private construction in the locality.
>
> Our evaluation of Labor's wage determination files and our inquiries regarding 73 wage determinations at five Department of Labor regional offices and headquarters showed that in many instances the wage rates were not accurately determined. About one-half of the area and project determinations reviewed were not based on surveys or wages paid to workers on private projects in the locality. Instead, union-negotiated collectively bargained rates were used.
>
> When wage surveys were made there were problems in identifying similar projects and collecting data from contracts on a voluntary basis. In addition, much of the wage and worker classification data

---

[81] Other researchers who have identified problems with Davis-Bacon administration include Professor Damodar Gujarathi, Professor Robert Goldfarb and John Morrall, and the author. Where their findings are similar to those of the GAO, they are not presented separately. See D. Gujarathi, "The Economics of the Davis-Bacon Act," (unpublished Ph.D. dissertation, U. of Chic., 1966), Goldfarb and Morrall, III, *The Davis-Bacon Act: An Appraisal of Recent Studies*, 34 IND. & LAB. RELATIONS REV. 191 (January 1981); and THIEBLOT, *supra* note 4.

[82] GENERAL ACCOUNTING OFFICE, *supra* note 3, cover summary.

collected was not used or was adjusted, upward or downward, by the regional and headquarters wage analysts. Further, Labor deleted, added, and changed the wage data received without adequate reason or rationale. As a result, many of the worker classifications and rates issued did not represent the prevailing wages paid in the locality.

We also found that Labor still followed some of the questionable practices and procedures we identified in prior reports. Labor: (1) Continued to use wages paid on Federal projects where Labor had previously stipulated rates to be paid; (2) applied data from surveys of projects that were not of a character similar to the proposed construction; (3) extended wage rates to adjacent and nonadjacent counties; (4) included wages paid to the same contractor's employees for several projects; and (5) applied its 30-percent rule, which has resulted in inflated wage rates.

We tried to quantify the errors and inconsistencies in Labor's wage determinations, especially where rates were supported by surveys, but often the files were so sloppily documented or incomplete, or could not be located, that this was impossible.

In our opinion, the Department of Labor's procedures for developing and issuing wage rate determinations provide no assurance that the rates stipulated actually prevail for corresponding classes of workers on similar private construction projects in the locality.[83]

It is important to note with respect to the GAO studies referred to above, the older ones as well as that performed in 1979, that with the exception of the 30-percent rule, they do not challenge the secretary's regulations or methods, but only the DOL's interpretations and applications of them. The GAO reports, therefore, mostly measure how well the DOL administers Davis-Bacon as compared with how the secretary has said it ought to be administered.

In 1979, the GAO made a followup review of administrative practices it had previously identified in its earlier studies:

> We observed that all of the ineffective practices identified ... still exist—inaccurate wage rates are still being issued. We found current examples of problems similar to those in our previous review:
>
> Rates were based on surveys made up to 8 years ago, or no survey was ever made in the locality.
>
> Voluntary participation by contractors in furnishing wage rates resulted in limited data acquisition, rates issued based on as few as one rate obtained in surveys.
>
> Data was not verified; inaccurate or false data was furnished to and used by [the Department of] Labor in determining rates.
>
> Data obtained in surveys was not used or was deleted and/or changed.
>
> Data on Federal projects in surveys distorted the prevailing wage determined in the locality.

---

[83] *Hearings, supra* note 74, at 7–8 (testimony of Elmer Staats, Comptroller General of the United States).

> Survey projects were not always of a character similar to each other or to the Federal project to which they were applied.
>
> Rates were extended from urban to rural localities on the basis of jurisdictional coverage in union collective bargaining agreements, or because that was all that was available.
>
> Duplicate counting of workers on more than one project in a survey distorted the prevailing determined rate.
>
> Rates were issued for a different type of construction than that requested by the agency.
>
> Rates obtained in surveys were not issued.
>
> Use of the 30-percent rule resulted in issuance of unrealistic rates, or it was not applied to avoid issuing too low a rate.
>
> Helper classifications were not issued even though surveys indicated a substantial use of the classification in the locality.
>
> Piece-rate wage data was not used in determining prevailing rates, although it was the prevailing form of payment in the locality.
>
> We also made surveys in each region. In two localities we found that wage rates issued by Labor were substantially greater than those that prevailed in private projects in the locality. For example, in Coweta County, Georgia, we found ... Labor issued union-negotiated rates on 11 of the 14 classifications we compared.... Of the 14 rates compared, our survey indicated that 13 were nonunion and lower than the rates Labor issued. Labor's rates averaged 47.8-percent higher than the rates we found prevailing, ranging from 7.1 percent to 141.2 percent.[84]

This is a rather thorough catalog of problems, and although they are not universal, it is unlikely that they are as isolated as the secretary of labor maintained in his counter-testimony, since they were obviously widespread enough to be picked up by a random selection of a few dozen determinations out of about 15,000 performed each year. Some of the specific areas identified as troublesome are discussed below.

Operating Patterns

The Davis-Bacon Act and its implementing regulations both require the determination of prevailing wages to be based on the wages paid the same classifications of laborers and mechanics found to be prevailing in the locality. One of the findings in several of the GAO studies conducted during the 1960s, however, was that the DOL applied the wage rates of one classification to another without investigating the rates paid to each classification or the work practices in the area for which the determination was being made.[85]

---

[84] GENERAL ACCOUNTING OFFICE, *supra* note 3, at 65–67.
[85] U.S. General Accounting Office, Comptroller General, *Report to Congress: Need for Improved Administration of Davis-Bacon Act Noted Over a Decade of General Accounting Office Reviews*, B-146842 (1971).

One might suppose this problem would arise only in a limited number of cases, such as on very small jobs by firms of limited resources or on unusual jobs requiring nonstandard skills. Actually, because of the difference in operating patterns and employee training methods between union and open-shop firms, the problem acquires significance both in terms of flexibility in work assignments and in the use of helpers and trainees. The National Association of Home Builders presented testimony to a congressional hearing in 1972 that:

> The job classifications prescribed by the Department of Labor frequently do not coincide with the job responsibilities of workmen in the residential construction industry. As is true with wages, these classifications are usually derived from job assignments in commercial and industrial construction.[86]

Thus, if a laborer picks up a hammer to nail up a temporary barricade, for example, he automatically becomes a carpenter and must be paid as such. Flexibility in work assignments is one of the most important contributions made by nonunion builders, and perhaps the principal factor that allows them a competitive advantage over their unionized counterparts.

> In broadest terms, this flexibility has three components: 1) the contractor's use of unskilled and semiskilled workers to perform work of which they are capable, rather than assigning such work to higher paid craftsmen; 2) the use of a skilled worker for a variety of tasks, some of which may be part of the job description of a different skilled occupation; and 3) dispensing with unnecessary and/or unproductive labor.
>
> Occupational distinctions in the open shop sector are often blurred. For example, cement may be poured and finished by mixed crews consisting of laborers, carpenters, ironworkers, and cement masons. Similarly, the helper (although he may be called by another name), a worker who labors alongside a craftsman and may perform the more routine aspects of the trade, is an integral part of the open shop work force.[87]

For example, Brown & Root, one of the country's largest construction companies, is a nonunion firm. The company president noted that construction workers in his company are classified under approximately 190 separate job classification titles which include skill or responsibility gradations in each discipline, such as three grades of helpers in each of a number of crafts, two grades of laborers, etc. The importance of the helper category is illustrated

---

[86] Banking, Housing, and Urban Affairs, *supra* note 15, at 169. (statement of Stanley Waranch, President, National Association of Home Builders).

[87] NORTHRUP, *supra* note 34, at 33.

The Davis-Bacon Act

by the fact that on a particular day in 1981, Brown & Root employed a total of 33,425 construction laborers and mechanics, of whom 20,586 were craftsmen, an estimated 10,000 were helpers or trainees, and an estimated 2,830 were laborers or equivalent.[88]

The helper category has rarely been recognized by the unions (and then in only a few of the craft classifications), and has been even more rarely recognized by Davis-Bacon.[89] The union "helper" classification had become almost extinct until somewhat revived by the givebacks of the early 1980s, and so was seldom a prevailing category for rate determinations, even when sanctioned by craft union rules.

The net effect is that nonunion contractors doing Davis-Bacon work, whether or not that work is covered by wage determinations at the union rate, must pay their helpers (and similar categories of semi-skilled workmen) the journeyman rate in accordance with the union craft rules. For example, a helper who nails up insulation would be paid the journeyman carpenter's rate, or one who unloads plumbing fixtures would have to be paid the journeyman plumber's rate (not even the specified laborer's rate). It also raises the absurd possibility that a nonunion contractor whose rates were the sole basis for a wage determination might have to change his scale of wages and reorganize his work assignments when using his same work crew on a Davis-Bacon job awarded under that determination.

Another element of human resource utilization is manning requirements: the stipulation of crew sizes; the required use of nonworking foremen; and limitations on the jobs a worker may perform or the number of times he may be shifted from one job to another in the course of the day. The open shop contractor is free of these restrictions even when working on a Davis-Bacon job, but shifting a worker from one job to another requires extremely careful record keeping, since each worker must be paid at the specified rate for each craft task for the time he is performing it. The result is that the contractor's flexibility in work assignment is severely limited.

---

[88] Affidavit of Thomas J. Feehan, President, Brown & Root, Inc., presented in Building and Construction Trades Department, AFL-CIO v. Donovan, Cir. A.N. 82-1631 (D. D.C. 1982).

[89] The Department of Labor denies that helper categories are deliberately excluded from rate determinations, but the General Accounting Office discovered that at least one regional wage specialist maintained it to be the stated regional policy for no helper rates to be determined. This apparent policy was confirmed in a project determination in the region (76-CA-33) which omitted to set helper rates for electrician helpers, tilesetter helpers, carpet-layer helpers, or plumber helpers, although all were represented in the survey in numbers as substantial as those for several crafts included in the determination for which rates were set. [GENERAL ACCOUNTING OFFICE, *supra* note 3, at 149-53.]

Much of the effect of Davis-Bacon administration on work practices is not part of the act or its regulations, but part of the unwritten rules of wage determinations, which generally adopt the "area practices" of the union crafts along with their wage rates. This is illustrated by the remarks of Philip Abrams, a general contractor, to a Senate hearing in 1979:

> [The problem with restrictive work practices is] difficult to quantify, but in general . . . if union wages have been determined and published, then therefore any restrictive work practices that are part of union agreements are then made a requirement in the name of area practice and are the responsibility of the contractor.
>
> The requirement, basically, on housing is that skilled people do unskilled work, that arbitrary rules like the tools of the trade determine the hourly wages that a working person receives. For instance, in one particular project, the fact that laborers were using hammers brought the Department of Labor and HUD to conclude that therefore they should be paid as carpenters, even though they were in fact doing laborers' work, even in accordance with union collective bargaining agreements.
>
> The sum and substance is that you lower productivity on construction sites by enforcing these restrictive work practices by not allowing helper categories, and by refusing to let unskilled people nail up insulation or carry pieces of steel or pull wire or unload plumbing fixtures.
>
> And the worst and most pernicious part of these regulations is that they are unwritten, there is no place where you can find these area practices written anyplace in any Government manual for anybody to reference. You're simply expected to comply with these [union] area practices, and they are enforced by the contracting officer and the Department of Labor arbitrarily and without any previous notice to the contractor. He's expected to comply with them.[90]

The lack of recognition of actual construction practices and job assignments, although it has no impact on unionized contractors, hurts nonunion firms on both ends of the determination process. In establishing rates, nontraditional job titles, such as "forms carpenter," or "pipelayer," or "construction mechanic," are seldom included in determinations, even in localities where such titles might be common or even prevailing and even if the open shop wage rate is determined to apply to a given project. In applying these rates, union "area practices" are applied even though they do not have the force of law or regulation behind them, to the effect that the higher-skilled and higher-paid workmen retain their job rights in unskilled work that could be performed with no impact

---

[90] Hearings, *supra* note 74, at 323-4 (statement of Philip Abrams).

on output quality of construction by lower skilled individuals at much lower cost.[91]

Classification of Workers

The above discussion serves as a preamble to the general problems of employee classification for both survey and wage administration purposes. The latter have been evaluated retrospectively in a number of the comptroller general's cases where enforcement actions were involved, and the former have been an issue in several of his reports to Congress.

Wage Administration. As we have already seen, with the increasing complexity of construction, the traditional divisions of the work force among a dozen-or-so crafts differing on the basis of the tools used no longer served. There are no precise definitions of the many categories of laborers and mechanics that are universally applied in the industry. The definitions depend on contractors' practices, which differ from one area to another and within given areas. Wages can differ substantially among individuals in the same locality holding the same job classification.

In the mid-1930s, Davis-Bacon administrators decided that contractors under the act would be required to follow the prevailing practice on work assignments as well as on wages.[92] The comptroller general disagreed with the prevailing practice theory. In *T.L. James Construction Company* in 1963, for example, he said that the classification rate required by the act is the one paid to a *substantial number* of men performing the work assignment on similar work in the area, and not necessarily to a *prevailing* number of men.[93]

The work in this case involved the installation of underground duct to carry electrical wiring. The International Brotherhood of Electrical Workers brought a Davis-Bacon enforcement action to compel the contractor to pay workers the electricians' rate instead of the lower pipelayers' rate. The comptroller general rejected the DOL's ruling that would have required the electricians' rate to be paid and said that the record showed "a substantial, although not preponderant, practice of installing similar duct with the use of laborers and pipelayers in the locality." Since the classifications

---

[91] A discussion of the impact of this issue on the structure of the industry and its ability to modernize effectively, and its impact on helpers and trainees, particularly minority group members, is presented in the section on policy questions, below.

[92] This section draws heavily on the summary of Comptroller Generals' decisions provided in HINTZE, *supra* note 29, at 160.

[93] Comptroller General's Decision in T.L. James Construction Company, B-147602, January 23, 1963.

existed and were used in the area on private work and since rates existed for the classifications in the determination, the comptroller general determined that contractors who chose to use them should not be questioned for wage adjustment purposes.

This decision was reaffirmed in a later opinion in a Brown & Root, Inc. case in 1966.[94] Here, charges of misclassification were made against the firm because it had paid the unskilled laborers' rate for the operation of small air tools. It was charged (and sustained by the DOL) that the contractor should have paid the rate specified for "air tool operators (jackhammer, vibrator)." The comptroller general rejected this contention and reversed the DOL on grounds that the term "air tool operators (jackhammer, vibrator) impliedly excluded small air tool operators and that there was a substantial area practice to classify small air tool operators as laborers."

In these and a number of related cases, the comptroller general seemed to be trying to free nonunion firms as much as possible from the importation of union work practices, but he could only do it retrospectively in enforcement cases, and his decision established no precedents that Davis-Bacon administrators were required to follow. The cases also further illustrate the propensity of the DOL to support the union line.

Surveys

The 1979 GAO study of Davis-Bacon administration found a number of examples where job classifications on wage rate data included in surveys had been arbitrarily changed by Davis-Bacon administrators. For example, the GAO was puzzled when it found that the wage rates for 113 carpenters making between $2.50 and $4.50 an hour in Stanislaus County, California, in 1976 had been dropped from the survey before the prevailing rate was calculated.[95] When questioned about it, the DOL responded that the rates were deleted because they showed an unusually broad range, which was taken to be an indication that the lower paid workers were generally trainees, not journeymen. On this logic, the DOL did not drop the rates, it simply reclassified them to a category for which rates were not determined, although the effect was the same. Had these rates

---

[94] Comptroller General's Decision in Brown & Root, Inc., B-152117, March 4, 1966.
[95] Project Determination 76-CA-33, reported in GENERAL ACCOUNTING OFFICE, *supra* note 3, at 149.

been included in the survey, the prevailing rate determined would have been $4.85 instead of $6.54, a decrease of about 25 percent.[96]

Because of the manner in which wage data are surveyed—often by telephone with responses based on the best remembrances of the contractor being interviewed—wage data are apparently often interpreted for validity by the wage specialists. If reported rates seem too low, the specialist might decide they should apply to helper or trainee categories. On the other hand, if laborer rates seem too high, they might be interpreted as being disguised journeymen's rates. Instances which seem to illustrate both of these possibilities were noted by the GAO.

Similar Construction

One question that administrators of Davis-Bacon must answer properly and consistently in making surveys for rate purposes is: what is similar construction? Is building a two-story frame house similar to building a seventeen-story hospital? Is building a levee more similar to building a superhighway than to building the seventeen-story hospital? Is building an atomic power plant sufficiently different from building a fossil power plant to require rates of its own? Here again is an area where the DOL is allowed considerable latitude in interpretation and one where a great many problems and apparent inequities have arisen.

The DOL classifies construction into four general categories: residential building, commercial building, heavy construction, and highway construction. This is both too few and too many categories. It is too few because there are perhaps clearer distinctions between high-rise and low-rise residential construction than there are between high-rise residential construction and office building (commercial) construction. It is also too few because the heavy category is a catch-all of fifty-or-so project types ranging from sewers to hydroelectric dams for which there is little commonality in skills required, job titles, or wage rates, so each such project type might require a completely separate set of rate determinations based on different comparability factors. It is too many because when multiplied by the number of job titles that might exist and localities

---

[96] In this instance, the GAO made further investigations which indicate that the reason for dropping the rates supplied by the DOL was inconsistently applied even for other rates within the same determination, and was probably developed after the fact. The real reason for dropping the rates was probably that the wage specialist simply felt they were too low because they were close to or below the laborer rate. That the wage specialist might feel free to do this raises a number of related questions that will be discussed later in this chapter.

for which rates might be needed, the rate-determining task becomes almost impossible to do fairly and accurately.

The heavy construction category has another problem as well. Typically, these projects have little in common beyond their large scale. One thing which they definitely do not share is a need for or reliance on the standard classifications of carpenters, glaziers, plumbers, electricians, roofers, tile setters, etc., of which the AFL-CIO building trades are composed—although, to be sure, some of these trades would be necessary to most of the projects falling within this category. A large proportion of the heavy jobs do require, however, extensive earthmoving, much of which is done by machinery similar to that employed in large scale roadbuilding. This creates a practical problem for Davis-Bacon rate determinations because such projects, if they are to be done as "heavy" construction, will likely be done at union rates, and if they are to be done as "highway" construction will likely be done at open shop rates.

Almost half of the Wage Appeals Board cases heard between 1964 and 1976 involved questions of whether building or residential construction rates would apply to high-rise residential projects, or whether heavy construction rates (often the same as building construction rates) or highway rates would apply to earthmoving projects.

Although the board's decisions in these cases are not inconsistent among themselves, their nature has made generalizations difficult. One common aspect to all of them, however, is that the burden of documentation is on the petitioner. The decisions of the DOL about similarity of work will stand unless challenged. If such a decision is challenged, it will become a matter of evidence in the individual case to determine what work is similar to that proposed and should be included in predetermination surveys. Another commonality is that in a majority of the cases, the DOL's initial decisions had been for the higher rate classifications and the protestors were seeking lower ones. While it is certainly possible to read too much into this, it is but one indication of many that the DOL may have a systematic bias towards establishing rates at the highest possible level.

Site of the Work

About a quarter of the Wage Appeals Board cases between 1964 and 1976 concerned questions involving the site of the work. Some of these involved the application of Davis-Bacon rates to repairmen or other nonconstruction workers who came on to the job site to, for example, repair factory-built kitchen modules being built into a residential project. Others involved extending Davis-Bacon rates to truck drivers, equipment operators, and other employees of borrow pit operators, or to stone, tar, or cement suppliers where the workmen did not work on the site of the job.

In these cases, the DOL had generally decided to extend coverage and the appeals were made to remove it. For the first type of cases, the Wage Appeals Board generally reversed the DOL. For the others, it built an elaborate system to determine whether the employees should be covered—depending on closeness to the project, sales to the general public, and other factors—and typically decided that they should. The comptroller general has consistently disagreed with the latter decisions.

The first opinion by a controller general on off-site facilities is dated July 26, 1963.[97] It involved a gravel pit three miles away from a construction site opened specifically for that project. The DOL held that the operator was a subcontractor rather than a materials supplier, and required prevailing rates to be paid his employees. An appeal was taken to the comptroller general who overruled the DOL and said that there was no Davis-Bacon coverage of the off-site pit. He noted that the term "directly on the site" in the Davis-Bacon Act was clear and not open to interpretation. He added that, "In our considered opinion, the Davis-Bacon Act does not undertake to provide minimum wage coverage for work off-the-site, whether by contractors, subcontractors, or materialmen, even though performed in the immediate community."

One might think that such an opinion (restated and reinforced in other cases in 1964 and 1976) would put an end to the DOL's attempts to extend coverage to off-site work; but as has been noted earlier, the authority of the comptroller general is limited except as to cases that come before him in his capacity as disburser of withheld funds under the act or as auditor of federal construction contract accounts. Thus, the DOL has continued to hold that gravel suppliers and borrow pit operators are subcontractors rather than materialmen, and as subcontractors are covered by the act even though their work is performed off site. In the most recent of such cases to be appealed to the Wage Appeals Board, the DOL had once again opted for coverage, and the board once again sustained the DOL, requiring back pay to employees at prevailing rates.[98]

---

[97] Comptroller General's Opinion in Hyde Construction Company (no number recorded) (July 26, 1963).

[98] D.A. Collins Construction Co., Wage Appeals Board Case No. 81-4 (September 20, 1984).

Importation of Wage Rates

Twenty years ago, Professor Damodar Gujarathi collected data on 372 wage determinations under Davis-Bacon for nine crafts in 300 counties selected in inverse proportion to the extent of unionization in them.[99] One of his most significant findings was the extent to which union wage rates were imported into a locality from noncontiguous areas. According to the data he collected, from 25 to 38 percent of the wage determinations for building construction, and from 46 to 73 percent of the determinations for heavy and highway construction were based on rates from noncontiguous counties or statewide union wage rates. In some cases, he found that the DOL had gone beyond state boundaries to noncontiguous states for prevailing wage data. He noted:

> The practice of "leap frogging" in search of prevailing wage rates does not conform to the act. . . . All the noncontiguous counties that were reached to obtain prevailing wage rates, were either metropolitan areas or areas of 50,000 and more population.[100]

For nine construction crafts studied, the average distance between the place of construction and the area from which the rates were taken ranged from a low of seventy-two miles to a high of eighty-four miles. The highest average distance for any craft, that for power equipment operators was 84.1 miles.[101]

In 1962, at about the same time that Gujarathi was making this study, the GAO was studying a wage determination for a Marine Corps School housing project in the vicinity of Quantico, Virginia. It concluded that the wage rates used on the job had been imported from Washington, D.C., an entirely different polity not even contiguous across a state line but separated by an intervening county by a distance of thirty-five miles. The wage determination so imported necessitated additional labor costs of more than $1 million, required deletions of some planned facilities, such as sidewalks, and considerable substitution of inferior materials, such as plywood siding for brick, to meet the limited funds appropriated. As a result, the project was of considerably lower overall quality than originally contemplated.[102]

In the 1972 Senate hearings, Senator John Tower noted that the problem of wage scales determined in large municipal areas but

---

[99] Gujarathi, *supra* note 81.
[100] *Id.* at 48–51.
[101] *Id.* at 62.
[102] General Accounting Office, U.S. Comptroller General, *Report to Congress of the United States: Review of Wage Rate Determinations for Construction of Capehart Housing at the Marine Corps Schools, Quantico, Virginia*, B-145200 (1962).

applied to rural counties was one of the three most often heard complaints from builders and sponsors.[103] This procedure, referred to as "importation of wages," is intimately connected with other problems involved in setting the boundaries on areas for the purpose of administering the Davis-Bacon Act.

Noncontiguous Areas. As noted previously, the act and its implementing regulations provide that the area to be considered for rate determinations is the "city, town, village, county or other civil subdivision of the State in which the work is to be performed."[104] This is perhaps the most specific language that can be found in the act and the closest the act comes to providing an operational definition of any term or specification. The DOL has chosen to honor it largely by ignoring it, however, and uses instead informal guidelines not sanctioned or contemplated by the law.

As early as 1935, the secretary of labor in informal discussions at the same time that the 30-percent rule was developed, decided that "county" was the standard civil subdivision which would be followed for rate determinations, and county has remained the standard ever since, except in the case of the even broader geography—often statewide and sometimes even nationwide—used in some area determinations since 1964. But there is ample evidence that even this demarcation has not been consistently followed.

In our 1975 study of the Davis-Bacon Act, we evaluated a statewide decision in effect for Maryland and found that metropolitan Baltimore residential construction rates were applied to the (noncontiguous) rural Cecil and Harford counties as well as in the suburban Howard County. We also discovered that the dredging rate in effect for Worcester County, the southernmost Maryland county on the Delmarva peninsula, was the same as the rate for Baltimore County, from which it was separated by seventy-five miles and five intervening counties by the most direct land route, but was different from the dredging rate for Somerset and Wicomico counties, the two counties contiguous to Worcester which pin it against the Atlantic Ocean and separate it from the general direction of Baltimore.

Findings of wage rates imported from outside of the local area are not confined to the older studies. The 1979 GAO report noted that of the fifty-six DOL determinations examined that were complete enough to reveal the source of the rates issued, nearly one-third used rates from counties other than the one in which the project was located. In Tennessee, for example, wage determinations for projects in two rural counties (population 26,000 and 73,000)

---

[103] *Hearings*, supra note 74, at 4 (statement of Senator John Tower).
[104] Procedures for Predetermination of Wage Rates, 29 C.F.R. § 1.2(b) (1985).

were based on the rates in a noncontiguous county of much higher population (447,000). In the case of one of these smaller counties, a survey had been undertaken before the determination was made, but the headquarters staff instructed the regional staff to ignore it and use instead the rates for the more populous county.

Union Jurisdictional Lines. To our knowledge, no one has been able to analyze Davis-Bacon wage determinations with sufficient precision to evaluate the degree to which imported wage rates follow union jurisdictional lines rather than geographic boundaries. It has been strongly suggested by individual contractors, however, that this is frequently the case. For example, a general contractor in Hagerstown, Maryland observed that the ironworkers' rate for wage determinations in his western Maryland city had typically been imported from those set by a powerful local in Harrisburg, Pennsylvania, even though no members of that local were normally active in Hagerstown. The reason for this was attributed to the fact that there were relatively few indigenous local ironworkers, and the Pennsylvania local was the nearest source of a large number of reported wage rates on file.

Emphasis on Union Rates

All of the empirical studies of Davis-Bacon have found corroboration of an emphasis on negotiated rates. This was true especially outside of the residential construction segment, but there is evidence it may occur even there. The best estimate available for the percentage of the residential construction industry represented by unions was 8.1 percent in 1977 and falling.[105] Yet in March 1979, the Davis-Bacon rates in effect in residential wage determinations in 23 percent of the 3,106 counties of the United States carried the union rate for some or all of its crafts.[106] Similarly, the best statistical estimates of the union proportion of commercial construction, also in 1977, were on the order of 35–40 percent, whereas building wage determinations in effect for 63 percent of all counties were all or partially at the union rate.[107]

---

[105] Based on an extensive survey conducted by the National Association of Home Builders. NORTHRUP, *supra* note 34, at 80.

[106] *Hearings, supra* note 74, at 217 (supplementary information provided by Department of Labor).

[107] Based on a finding by the Bureau of Labor Statistics surveying firms of over eight employees in all types of construction, in which it is estimated that residential construction firms are not heavily represented because of the size limitation, the union proportion in 1977 was 35 percent. For industrial construction in 1979, although no employment data are available, it was noted that 51 of the 400 largest industrial construction firms operated open shop, compared with only 13 ten years

Three reasons have been identified as contributing to the emphasis on union rates: First, rate determinations are based on counting rates identical to the penny. In a free market environment such as is found in open shop construction, the likelihood that different firms would settle on the same wages to the penny for any particular craft or class is remote. In any given locality, only three levels of wage rates are likely to appear in substantial numbers: the federal minimum wage; a previously issued Davis-Bacon rate; or a negotiated (that is, union) rate. Of these, the first is not much of a possibility in the high-wage construction industry, even for nonunion laborers, the lowest-paid traditional category of workmen; the second should not be a factor in wage determinations, given the clear legislative intent of prevailing wage laws to preserve local wage standards,[108] but was admittedly a part of the DOL's standard methodology until changed in the 1985 modifications, and so undoubtedly did have an effect on determinations;[109] the third, however, is by far the most significant, since it is the most common.

Second, the 30-percent rule, while it was active, encouraged use of the union rate by selecting a rate as prevailing even if it was the rate paid to fewer than one-third of the workers included in a survey. All of the empirical studies of Davis-Bacon administration have found instances of the union rate being determined as prevailing because of the 30-percent rule. The main charge against it, however, is that the proportion is low enough that the union rate could be presumed to prevail in various types of construction for

---

earlier. For highway and heavy construction it was also noted that in 1983 a survey by the Associated General Contractors of America found 64.2 percent of its members in heavy construction operating union, and 63.1 percent of its highway members operating union. [NORTHRUP, *supra* note 34, at 81, 100–106, and 199.] There is no easy way to reconcile these figures for industrial, heavy, and highway contractors into employment proportions, so the comparisons with Davis-Bacon determinations are not made for them, although it might be noted that for both heavy and highway determinations, half or slightly more than half of the counties showed union rate determinations. [*Hearings, supra* note 74, at 217.]

[108] The discussion in GENERAL ACCOUNTING OFFICE, *supra* note 3, at 154–7, cites the language of original supporters of the Davis-Bacon bills in 1930 and 1931 to the effect that prevailing wages were intended to be found by comparison with those in "*private* industries in the immediate vicinity" of the proposed job site [emphasis added].

[109] One contractors' association noted that in the event of a Davis-Bacon determination at the union scale, if a nonunion contractor won the bid and did the work at the Davis-Bacon rate, on the next round of surveys in the same locality the number of union-scale rates in the survey would have increased, and it would be even harder for a non-negotiated rate to be found to be prevailing. To remedy this situation, the group (the AGC) recommended that its members in such circumstances pay a few pennies more than the Davis-Bacon rate to avoid the reinforcement factor. It is doubtful, however, if any ever did so. [Hintze, *Unscrambling Davis-Bacon Administration*, CONSTRUCTOR (August, 1975).]

sections of the country where the union participation rates were estimated to be even moderately high, thus eliminating the need for surveys to support area determinations. One of the side effects of the 1982 regulatory changes eliminating the 30-percent rule should be that a large number of actual surveys will have to be conducted to verify the rates said to be prevailing for area determinations, but there is no evidence on this yet.

Third, union rates are the most likely to be on file for rate determinations purposes, and are the easiest to find if they are not on file. Thus, if rate samples are not chosen following statistical rules, or if sample size is not controlled, the sampling process will favor union rates. This problem of sample size is actually the most important aspect of the undue influence of union rates on Davis-Bacon determinations. It is an aspect of the wage determination process that is immensely complex, and seldom discussed in the empirical studies, because its arguments have usually been subsumed by analysis of the 30-percent rule. We will discuss it below.

It is important to point out that selection of the union rate, as such, in rate determinations is only a small portion of the overall problem of the influence of union rates on prevailing rate determinations. Assume for a moment a typical mixed market composed of some low, nonunion wages and some high, union wages. If rates are found in accordance with a 50-percent or 30-percent rule, they would most likely be the union rates, because union rates are more likely to be equal to the penny. But if there is no majority (or 30 percent) at the union rate, the alternative is *not* the open shop rate, as is commonly supposed.[110] The alternative is a rate made up of

---

[110] Such misconceptions are often reinforced by the posturing of people who know better, as in the following exchange between Senator Donald Riegel of Michigan, a supporter of the Davis-Bacon Act, and Donald Elisburg, then Assistant Secretary for Employment Standards (in charge of Davis-Bacon administration) in the Senate Hearings in 1979 [*Hearings, supra* note 74, at 111]:

> Mr. ELISBURG. That's correct. I would like to point out that on the average slightly less than half of our wage determinations are union rates and about a little more than half are open shop rates. There are some mixed rates.
> Senator RIEGEL. Would you say that—again, I want to make sure I'm clear on what you're saying.
> Mr. ELISBURG. Roughly a little less than half of our rates—that we issue are union rates—that is, collectively bargained rates.
> Senator RIEGEL. In other words, that would be established as the prevailing rate under your formula in that area?
> Mr. ELISBURG. Right. And a little more than half are open shop rates.
> Senator RIEGEL. Open shop rates would be nonunion rates but they would prevail as the prevailing rate in that area?
> Mr. ELISBURG. Right. And then there are some percentage of what you would call mixed rates—that is where it's a combination of collectively

The Davis-Bacon Act

the average of the high, union rates and the low, open shop rates, which by any arithmetical process is necessarily higher than the average of open shop rates. Under assumptions of a typical labor market and a current and accurate wage determination, there is substantially no possibility of the average open shop contractor not having to modify the wage scales of at least some of his employees on a Davis-Bacon job.

Furthermore, under such assumptions, the impact of prevailing rates fall *exclusively* on nonunion firms. It is another carefully nurtured misconception of Davis-Bacon that a rate established by it at less than the union rate will "drive wages down" in the industry. This is not true. Davis-Bacon rates are *minimum* requirements, and regardless of the level of rates determined they will not be higher than the union rate in a normal market, so the union contractors' agreements with their employees take precedence. Union contractors do not have to (and in fact cannot) adjust their wage scales downward because of Davis-Bacon. Open shop contractors, on the other hand, frequently must adjust their wage scales upward or change their job assignments.

Sample Size and Other Survey Problems

The principal reason cited by the DOL for importing wage rates from outside the locality in which a determination is being made is the lack of enough local data to form a sufficient sample size for determination purposes. Thus, in its response to the 1979 GAO study, the DOL maintained:

> Project data from other counties may be considered when there is a dearth of construction data in the county involved and we have already made a survey of an adjoining or close county with similar economic characteristics.[111]

---

bargained and open shop rates.
Senator RIEGEL. I would just say to my friend from Utah [Senator Jake Garn, an opponent of Davis-Bacon] that that doesn't sound like a stacked deck to me. The fact that the data would reflect more than half of the areas of the country where they are establishing rates does not substantiate the charge that there is a bias in favor of the organized labor side of things when in more than half the cases the rate that's established is below the organized labor rate in that area.

[111] GENERAL ACCOUNTING OFFICE, *supra* note 3, at 219. This particular quote continues with some assertions by the department that we would hope are simply in error rather than deliberately untrue. The DOL asserts, for example, that "Generally a metropolitan county is not used to obtain data for a rural county, and vice versa," which can be true only in the technical sense that the use of urban rates in rural counties is not the *prevailing* method of establishing rates in rural areas, but there is ample evidence that it does in fact occur in many project rates, and is even characteristic of area determinations. The DOL also asserts that in importing wage

Inherent in this answer is an implied concept of sample size sufficiency. Presumably, when looking for rates in an area upon which to apply a calculating formula such as the 30-percent rule or a weighted average calculation, some number of rates in the survey is enough, and some smaller number is too few, thus requiring importation of rates from somewhere else (or the use of rates from an earlier time period). Unlike the Walsh-Healey Act, the Davis-Bacon Act requires that some rate be said to prevail for every job category for every type of construction anticipated for a federal contract, even if there are *no* corresponding rates in the community on which to base a determination.[112] Once a determination is issued, contractors may use only the rates listed for paying wages. If no rate is issued for pipelayers, for example, the contractor must pay individuals at the electrician's rate, even though doing pipelayer's work.

The situation of having only one or two survey wages—or perhaps none—available upon which to base a rate is not as unlikely as it might seem. If the nation's 3,000,000 construction workers were evenly distributed among the country's 3,000 counties, there would be an average of 1,000 construction workers per county. Given that the typical wage determination for residential or commercial construction might have separate rates for 40 classes of workmen (for heavy or highway work this figure might reach 150), if we assume that the construction workforce in the county is equally divided by type of construction and neglect special variations among different types of heavy projects that would normally carry different rate schedules, we could expect to find an average of about 8 workers in each class and category per county. But of course these divisions are not equal: Los Angeles County, California, can reasonably be expected to have a greater number of construction workers than Wicomico County, Maryland, and one can confidently expect to find a greater number of carpenters on commercial construction projects

---

rates from another county, "State boundaries are not crossed." Examples of areas where this has occurred, however, were presented earlier in this chapter. As will be seen later, one of the hard-fought rule changes finally implemented in 1985 concerned this application of metropolitan rates to rural areas. That it is likely to have minimal impact on Davis-Bacon administration is illustrated above.

[112] The DOL does not have an out, in the sense that it can decide not to issue a rate for a particular trade because of insufficient data upon which to base a determination. In such a case, however, it must follow a conformance procedure that consists of negotiating between the contracting officer and the contractors establishing a mutually acceptable rate for that trade and communicating the result to the DOL which then includes it in the determination. This, however, is a cumbersome process, and the GAO found that some wage specialists would issue a determination based on a single rate in a survey rather than go through it. [See GENERAL ACCOUNTING OFFICE, *supra* note 3, at 145.]

than iron workers in residential construction. If the usual 80–20 rule of thumb applies, we could expect that 80 percent of the counties would have in aggregate only 20 percent of the construction workers, meaning that in some 2,400 counties, fewer than 2 individuals might make up the survey base for a particular prevailing rate.

The DOL may attempt to survey all of the contractors in a locality, using perhaps the Dodge Construction Reports of activity (in which case it will miss most small, residential contractors), but it has no exact knowledge of how many rates comprise the universe of construction employment in the area (again because of the lack of data of smaller employers and also because both contractors and construction workers are mobile and may not be from the immediate locality, even for private work). Furthermore, it has no authority to require participation in its survey, and many contractors may simply decline to become involved.[113]

The DOL is under no compulsion to identify *all* of the contractors or *all* of the construction workers who received wages in the locality.

Problems and Opportunities for Error

This leaves the DOL with the problem that the universe from which survey rates are to be drawn contains an unknown number of rates paid, and that the surveys collect a partial response of unknown proportions, perhaps resulting in as few as one or two rates. Since it must determine a rate, the DOL may take the opportunity to decide that its results, however scanty, are sufficient to establish the rate, or it may decide to bring in rates from another county, from a nearby union local, from the nearest previous Davis-Bacon job, or from an earlier time period. In the overwhelming majority of cases, whatever it decides will go uncontested because there is no external review of its decisions.

The wage specialist also can apply his own discretion in accepting wage rates reported in a survey as actually paid, without external

---

[113] In reference to the voluntary collection of survey information, the GAO noted complaints from a number of DOL field staff representatives concerning problems with and/or shallowness of survey returns. For example, one compliance officer complained of encountering increasing resistance to wage surveys from subcontractors: "A number of these contractors flatly refused or were reluctant to furnish the data until a combination of cajolery, flattery, logic, and endless explanation of the purposes of the survey was brought into play.... [It] is an absolute impossibility to do a competent job within the time frame expected." Another mentioned that "In many trades, the majority of employees are paid on a salary or piece rate basis or are owner-operator type businesses. The excluding of these employees sometimes results in just one or two hourly employees being recorded in a particular trade." [Both cited in GENERAL ACCOUNTING OFFICE, *supra* note 3, at 132.]

verification of their accuracy, and can also eliminate from the surveys rates he feels might be too high or too low, again without external check. He can stop searching for additional rates whenever he feels he has enough. By these methods, the wage specialist could control the range of rates that are included in the survey and to which the prevailing rate formula is applied, and thereby, in large measure, control the final rate. At the very least, the unrestrained survey process creates the opportunity for error and the possibility of an unrepresentative, unfair, or simply wrong rate being determined.

Hypothetical Examples. The critical aspect of this is that by deciding one way or another what constitutes a sufficient base for determinations and what rates will be allowed to be a part of it, the result of the determinations can be varied tremendously. Consider the following hypothetical examples:

1) If the DOL were to decide for whatever reasons that the cement mason's rate in a particular determination should be at the negotiated union rate rather than at one of the open shop rates that might have been paid in the locality to, say, sixteen of twenty-two workmen found in a survey, it could opt to disregard the survey results as insufficient and add to them an appropriate number of rates from another locality where the negotiated rate might be known to exist. Then it could apply its calculating formula with total accuracy and determine the negotiated rate to be the prevailing one in the locality.

2) In another case, the DOL could choose to set the prevailing rate for all of the pipelayers to work on a new federal building project based on the rate actually paid to only three individuals found in a survey of existing jobs in the county, while it could simultaneously decline to set a rate for drywall hangers on the same project because only three rates could be found in a survey of existing jobs in the county.

3) The DOL might decide to eliminate 113 carpenter rates found in a survey for a residential construction project because they simply appeared to be too low.

4) It could decide to adopt as prevailing the statewide union rate for boilermakers even though it found no boilermakers at all in its survey.

5) The wage specialist could selectively drop rates from a survey for truck drivers because they were lower than laborers' rates, or reduce the amount of the rate paid to thirty of ninety-eight ironworkers in a survey because they exceeded the union rate.

Do such things actually happen in wage determinations? Most empirical evaluations of Davis-Bacon administration have been unable to analyze how the DOL and its field staff conduct this aspect of prevailing rate determinations for the simple reason that they do not have access to the details or to the personnel involved. Only an independent oversight organization such as the GAO is in a position to do so, and has done it sporadically over the years. Although it has had occasional success in persuading the DOL to adopt different practices, such as issuing separate rate determinations for low-rise and high-rise residential projects, in many more cases it has been unsuccessful, because it has no direct or statutory authority over the DOL's administrative practices. All of the hypothetical examples presented above closely resemble actual practices found by the GAO to have taken place among the seventy-three determinations it investigated and reported on in its 1979 report.[114]

Arbitrary Wage Scales. Before turning to the DOL's response to the comptroller general's administrative challenge, we might note that although no other agency has, to our knowledge, audited prevailing rate determinations in the way that the comptroller general has, several researchers have attempted to measure the difference between average wage rates in a locality and those set for the locality by Davis-Bacon determinations. One such study was performed for the Council on Wage and Price Stability in 1976.[115] The study attempted to determine whether there would be significant cost savings to the government from switching to a prevailing wage determinations procedure based on an average rate calculation to warrant the change. (The economic, as opposed to administrative, findings of the study will be discussed later in the chapter.) To conduct the analysis, the council used data covering union, nonunion, and average rates drawn from a Bureau of Labor Statistics special construction wage survey. These data were compared with actual Davis-Bacon determinations in effect for the same time period (1972). The study base consisted of bricklayers, electricians, and laborers working in commercial construction, and carpenters and laborers working in residential construction in nineteen cities.

In the comparisons between Davis-Bacon and average rates, the study found that in the residential construction area thirteen of

---

[114] *Id.* at 141–53

[115] "An Analysis of Certain Aspects of the Administration of the Davis-Bacon Act," (mimeo) Council on Wage and Price Stability (May 1976), published as Morrall & Goldfarb, *An Analysis . . .* CONSTRUCTION LAB. REP. No. 1079 (June 30, 1976). Also, slightly different earlier version using same data: R.S. Goldfarb & J.F. Morrall III, "Cost Implications of Changing Davis-Bacon Administration," ms. (May 1975). Summarized, with slightly revised conclusions, in Goldfarb & Morrall, *supra* note 81.

the rates set by determinations were below average construction wages, which the council attributed to the possibility of lags in updating the files used to make the determinations, but which could also have resulted from incomplete data collection or some of the other problem areas already discussed. On the other hand, almost as many rates, twelve of the thirty-eight, were set at arbitrarily high levels, including four cases in which the Davis-Bacon rate was set *higher* than the union scale. In one case, the Davis-Bacon rate for carpenters in residential construction was set $2.49 an hour above the average wage in a city in which the Bureau of Labor Statistics was unable to identify *any* union carpenters in residential work.

In the comparisons for commercial construction, thirty Davis-Bacon rates, or 33 percent of the total, seem arbitrarily low, and another twelve (20 percent) seem arbitrarily high, including six which are above the union scale. Also, in twenty-eight cases, the Bureau of Labor Statistics could find no nonunion commercial bricklayers, electricians, or laborers. In such cases, the rate set by Davis-Bacon rules should have reflected the union rate. But this was true in only six of the twenty-eight cases. In twenty others, the Davis-Bacon rate was set below the union rate, and in the remaining two, above it.

Thus, the data used in the study show some cases in which Davis-Bacon rates were set below average construction wages and others in which they were set above union rates. The most reasonable conclusion is that the rates were set arbitrarily.

Another aspect of the arbitrariness of prevailing rates is also illustrated by the data used in this study. In the nineteen cities studied, in September 1972 when the data were collected, Davis-Bacon rates established for bricklayers varied from $5.12 to $8.79; for electricians, from $6.50 to $9.20; and for laborers, from $3.85 to $7.025. On residential work, the ranges were: carpenters, $2.50 to $8.57; laborers, $1.60 to $7.025. It is impossible to reconcile the wide ranges of rates established with differences in cost of living among the cities, and it would be foolish to assume that they reflected skill differences. To suppose that rates in these ranges were necessary to protect local wage levels from itinerant outsiders strains credulity. In fact, the only thing these disparate determinations are likely to reflect accurately is the DOL's perceptions of the differences in union strength in the different cities, which is probably not what the originators of Davis-Bacon had in mind. This, however, is what the act seems to have accomplished.

DEFENSE OF DAVIS-BACON ADMINISTRATION

The DOL has always shown a protective interest in Davis-Bacon quite unlike that apparently felt for Walsh-Healey. Although the act had been often challenged in the past, the challengers were generally hampered by an inability to apply the considerable resources necessary to evaluate the administration of Davis-Bacon in detail. Furthermore, they have lacked the authority to compel attention to the results by either the DOL or the general public. The comptroller general at least had the former, and his report to the Congress in 1979 was a devastating attack on the quality of Davis-Bacon administration.

GAO Report Restated

With respect to administration (again we shall leave economic discussions for later), the GAO's 1979 report was an examination of seventy-three Davis-Bacon wage determinations, chosen by a structured random sample. In summary, the report found that most of the undesirable practices cited in earlier GAO reviews of Davis-Bacon administration persisted; it found that nearly half of the determinations reviewed were not supported by surveys of wages paid on similar construction projects in the locality; and it found that the DOL had invariably relied on wage rates and corresponding worker classifications and work practices established in union-negotiated collective bargaining agreements without verifying either that the union rate actually prevailed or that the negotiated rates had actually been paid.

The GAO selected thirty locations from its random sample and audited the accuracy of the prevailing rates determined by the DOL by conducting actual on-site surveys, which are rarely done by the DOL. The audit found that 100 percent of the DOL's determinations were inaccurate. In comparison to rates properly calculated by Davis-Bacon rules, 40 percent of the DOL's determinations were too high, and the remainder were too low. Not every rate in every determination was wrong, however. Of the 277 worker classifications, the prevailing rates prescribed by the DOL were found to be correct in 35 cases (13 percent) and incorrect in 242 cases (87 percent). Errors ranged from $5.44 high to $5.30 low. Still, an 87 percent error rate is not an enviable result.

Specific administrative problems cited by the GAO, each illustrated by at least one example drawn from the audit, included use of inaccurate and unverified data in surveys, arbitrary revision of data to drop or change survey information, inappropriate extension of wage determinations across counties, the use of wage data from dissimilar projects, and the use of previous determinations in establishing new ones (which may or may not be an error, depending on interpretation of the rules, but which congressional intent clearly did not contemplate). The report concluded that Davis-Bacon was not being properly administered, and that the complexities of the situation quite possibly precluded proper administration.

Response of the Department of Labor

The GAO study was a massive undertaking—294 staff days were required just to conduct the surveys in the Dallas region, one of five reviewed—and was performed by an agency charged specifically with an auditing function, and one which is noted for its objectivity. Nevertheless, the report to some extent met with the same fate at the hands of the DOL as had the previous private studies. In essence, the secretary of labor stonewalled the challenge.

As is its custom, having made its surveys and produced a draft of the results, the GAO invited the DOL's comments so that any misconceptions could be cleared up before final publication. The formal response of the secretary was one of fustian, bluster, and thinly disguised disdain: with respect to administration, the secretary refused to acknowledge that a single one of the problems uncovered was germane or accurate, and that the problems did not exist except in the eyes of the beholders.[116] The formal response was contained in a letter from Secretary Marshall to Comptroller General Staats:

> On the basis of an examination of 73 of about 10,000 Department wage determinations which were made in the first six months of 1976, or applicable during that period, the GAO review team found "inadequacies" and "problems" in the Department's program and concluded that it is ineffective. [*n.b.* Actually, the GAO review team found 13 different classes of problems which, in its estimation, caused 87 percent of the individual rate classification determinations ex-

---

[116] The informal reply was considerably more emotional. As reported in the testimony in the Senate hearings in 1979 [*Hearings, supra* note 74, at 29] by Senator Tower (interviewing the comptroller general): "Mr. Staats, Secretary Marshall called your report a sloppy piece of work and said, 'If it had been done by one of my people, I would have flunked him.' Do you have any comment on that?" Mr. Staats replied, "Well, I think he's entitled to his opinion. I'm sure that he's attempting to carry out his responsibilities in the most effective way he knows how and I'm sure he may be fully reflecting the administration position on this matter. I don't see that that excuses him for some of the inflammatory and emotional comments that he's made about this report of ours. I think it should be dealt with on its merits. I might suggest to him that when he decides to become a college professor again that he might take a different position than he has."

The Davis-Bacon Act

amined to be inaccurate.] About 30 examples of the team's judgments were included in the draft's Appendices. In almost all 30 examples the Department found the alleged inadequacy or error to be that of the review team, rather than the Department. The reasons in most cases were a failure to conduct an in-depth analysis of the presumed errors and a lack of understanding of the industry terms and practices. The Department's wage determination procedures, as the enclosed detailed response points out, have been adopted as a result of a long experience in dealing with the particular characteristics of the various segments of the construction industry.[117]

The letter goes on to support the secretary's contention that Davis-Bacon is being "competently and effectively administered" by pointing out that "contracting agencies, contractors, and employees, or their representatives, have a right to seek a review of any wage determination in which they are interested parties," and that appeals are "available to an impartial Wage Appeals Board."[118]

In the accompanying attachment, a seventy-four-page critique of the GAO report, the secretary attempts a point-by-point refutation of the administrative problems cited by the GAO, and presents the small number of appeals taken to the Wage Appeals Board on disputes over the level of wage rates (eight in 1976, seven in 1977 and fourteen in 1978) as "evidence of the high degree of accuracy which our wage decisions achieve."[119] There is considerable other information relating to the economic impact of Davis-Bacon or its continuing necessity in the current economic situation, but the secretary's defense of his department's practices is based essentially on three points: 1) that of a great many determinations issued each year, the comptroller general audited only a very few; 2) that the problems found did not exist; and 3) that rates must be accurate as determined because so few are protested to the Wage Appeals Board.

Nonsubstantive Response. Only the second of these points is substantive. The first, that the comptroller examined only a few determinations, has no bearing unless the secretary could show that the projects chosen (by using a random number generator to select from subsets within half of the ten DOL regions of the country stratified by type of construction and type of project), were a biased sample or were not representative of other determinations. There is no such claim. The third point, that the rates must be accurate because of the small number of appeals to the Wage Appeals Board,

---

[117] Letter of Ray Marshall, Secretary of Labor, to Elmer Staats, Comptroller General, January 15, 1979. In the files of the Senate Subcommittee on Housing and Urban Affairs.

[118] *Id.*

[119] "Department of Labor's Comments Upon GAO Draft Report on Davis-Bacon and Related Acts" (mimeo) (1979) at 11.

is disingenuous in the light of the costs, lack of standing, and other problems associated with appeal which were discussed above. Furthermore, the secretary's total rejection of the challenges to the accuracy of wage determinations brought by a federal auditing agency armed with hundreds of man-days of field surveys and the authority to poke into hidden recesses of the survey process is a rather clear indication that protests from individual contractors or their associations are not likely to get very far.

Substantive Response. Thus, the secretary's principal defense of his assertion that the Davis-Bacon Act is being fairly and accurately administered rests on his assertion that the errors which resulted in 87 percent of the individual wage classifications being inaccurately determined did not exist. The secretary's assertions, however, are not well supported in the interchange that took place between the DOL and the GAO. An example is provided by a project determination in Texas, determination 76-TX-89, which was one of those reviewed by the GAO in its original draft report. With respect to this determination, the GAO found that the DOL's regional staff had made numerous changes and additions to survey data, and it specifically challenged the rates set by the DOL in four situations involving five different worker classifications. For each of these four situations, the original GAO draft report findings, the DOL's response to them, and the GAO's followup rejoinder are reproduced below:

1. *Asbestos Workers.* The survey had found the hourly rate for asbestos workers to be $8.00 plus fringes. The GAO charged that this rate was arbitrarily increased by the DOL field staff to $8.45 plus fringes by applying the union-negotiated rate of the prior year and updating it to the current rate issued, and that the amount was then further increased by DOL headquarters staff to $9.50 plus fringes.

DOL Response:

> A union rate was updated and issued for the asbestos workers, rather than using survey data because the Department independently found that the union rate still prevailed for asbestos workers.[120]

GAO Rejoinder:

> [The Department of] Labor stated that, since the union-negotiated rate was found to prevail, it was updated and issued. However, in the same survey a negotiated rate was paid to 42 percent (97 of 231) of the carpenters, but at more than one rate because of the extended period covered by the survey. These were not similarly updated to

---

[120] *Hearings, supra* note 74, at 268.

the current union rate and, since no one single rate was paid to more than 30 percent of the carpenters in the survey, rates were averaged and a nonunion rate was issued. Under the 30-percent rule, and to be consistent with Labor's comments above, the negotiated rate should have been updated and issued, but it was not.[121]

2. *Boilermakers.* Although a survey was performed, no rates for boilermakers were discovered. The $9.28 rate that was issued for boilermakers was based on a statewide union-negotiated rate.

DOL Response:

With respect to the boilermakers used in the example, a rate for them was included in the final wage determination because the prevailing rate for this occupation was a union rate which was independently found to be prevailing in the county.[122]

GAO Rejoinder:

No rates were obtained on this classification in the survey. This is an example of using the jurisdictional coverage of a union collective bargaining agreement to search for a rate even though the rate may never have been paid to workers in the locality, and may never be paid except on Federal or federally assisted projects. The conformance procedures... should have been applied in this case. We asked [Department of] Labor officials how it was independently determined that the rate prevailed, and we were furnished a manual citation which said that collective bargaining agreements may be used.[123]

3. *Ironworkers, Structural and Ornamental.* In the survey performed, the hourly rate found for ironworkers was $8.00. Before being issued, this rate was lowered by the field staff to $7.03 plus fringes. The union rate for ironworkers in the area was $7.03 plus fringes.

DOL Response:

The rate which the Department issued for the iron worker was lower than that which GAO asserts the survey disclosed because GAO improperly included fringe benefits in the hourly rate for iron workers. The Department's action on this determination is consistent with page 26 of the Manual which provides that where wage data contains hourly rates, which includes fringe benefits in the basic hourly rate, because the employer paid them as a lump sum payment, the fringe benefits must be broken out prior to compiling the data.[124]

---

[121] GENERAL ACCOUNTING OFFICE, *supra* note 3, at 147.
[122] *Hearings, supra* note 74, at 268–69.
[123] GENERAL ACCOUNTING OFFICE, *supra* note 3, at 148.
[124] *Hearings, supra* note 74, at 269.

GAO Rejoinder:

We did not improperly include fringe benefits in the hourly rate for ironworkers. The contractor, whose rates at $8 an hour prevailed in the survey, told us that this was his basic hourly rate on both the federally funded and the private projects included in the survey. He had simply advised the wage analyst in the telephone survey that his basic hourly rate was more than the union-negotiated rate, including fringe benefits, required of a nonunion contractor on Davis-Bacon Act projects in the survey.

Only 5 of the 98 rates in the survey were paid at the union-negotiated rate of $7.03 plus fringe benefits (the rate issued), while 30 were paid at $8 (more than 30 percent). In our opinion, the wage specialist's reason to reduce the rate (i.e., it was higher than the union-negotiated rate) was controlling in this instance and resulted in the issuance of an inaccurate rate.[125]

4. *Tilesetter Helpers and Air Conditioning Mechanics.* The survey hourly rate for tilesetter helpers was $2.50 and that for air conditioning mechanics was $5.00. No rate was issued for these classifications.

DOL Response:

The rates issued for the tile setter helper and the air conditioner mechanic were deleted because the survey data provided too little data for an accurate finding, and were sufficiently inconsistent with other information in the survey to raise substantial questions about their validity.[126]

GAO Rejoinder:

[The Department of] Labor explained that these crafts were deleted because too little data was obtained in the survey to issue an accurate rate, or that the data might not be valid. Rates were obtained on 28 tilesetter helpers and 25 air conditioning mechanics—the majority in each classification were paid at the rate shown. In the same survey, rates were issued for other classifications on the basis of far less than 25 rates. For example:

	Number of rates
Boilermaker	0
Bulldozer operator	1
Backhoe operator	2
Foundation drill operator	5
Painters, spray	4
Painters, tape and bed	8

[DOL's] survey files did not indicate any followup to question the validity of the rates deleted. If they were substantially questionable, they should have been verified. In our opinion, they were deleted on the basis of the regional wage specialist's comments [that the rate

---

[125] GENERAL ACCOUNTING OFFICE, *supra* note 3, at 148.
[126] *Hearings, supra* note 74, at 268.

found for tilesetter helpers was below the rate for laborers and that the rate for air conditioning mechanics was below the rate found for plumbers], but were representative of those prevailing in the locality and should have been issued.[127]

It is possible to draw various conclusions from these exchanges and from the similar ones found with respect to each specific example of administrative problem originally noted by the GAO, but it would take an extremely staunch supporter of the DOL to claim that the department sustained its defense in all or even very many of the exchanges. Perhaps the most charitable approach is to say that the environment of wage determinations is so variable and the situation so changeable that experts will disagree about the proper method of handling a particular survey or establishing a particular rate. Even under this interpretation, one must conclude that Davis-Bacon determinations made in an environment that contains many opportunities for error are often based on arbitrary and questionable decisions which may offer expediency, but no assurances of accuracy.

Other Defenses of Davis-Bacon Administration

Other defenses of the administrative adequacy of Davis-Bacon are rare. The AFL-CIO, in its most complete defense of Davis-Bacon, makes this comment about administration:

> The vulnerability of the Davis-Bacon program stems in large part from the fact that the program's administrators must constantly exercise discretionary judgment in order to arrive at a wage determination. The language of the statute is, after all, not very precise in that it calls for determinations to be based on the wages paid to "corresponding classes of laborers and mechanics employed on projects of a character similar in the city, town, village, or other civil subdivision of the State in which the work is to be performed." The Department must, therefore, make judgments as to occupational classifications and project classifications, and it must, for example, sometimes come up with a determination for a locality in which "projects of a similar character" are nonexistent.
>
> The Department of Labor issues thousands of prevailing wage determinations each year, and they apply to workers in many different crafts and occupations at tens of thousands of covered projects. Occasional errors must be expected. It is the errors, however, which get highlighted by the program's critics.[128]

---

[127] GENERAL ACCOUNTING OFFICE, *supra* note 3, at 147–48.
[128] "A Report on the Davis-Bacon Program," Testimony of Robert A. Georgine, President, Building and Construction Trades Department, AFL-CIO, before the House Subcommittee on Labor Standards (Mimeo) (June 14, 1979) at 32–33.

Many of the program's critics feel that it is their function to highlight errors in Davis-Bacon administration, and although they might sympathize with the magnitude of the task faced by the DOL, they also suggest that the construction industry (and the general public) have a right to program administration that does, in fact, produce only "occasional" errors. As was stated earlier, the observed error rate in determinations studied by GAO was 87 percent.

The only other common defense of Davis-Bacon administration was offered by Secretary of Labor Ray Marshall:

> I think many of the criticisms of the administration of the act are valid and one of the first things we did when we came in was to try to change that. You will note, however that their [GAO's] data refers to 1976 and therefore it refers to the administration of the act in previous years and not to the administration as it is now. These particular matters are difficult, but we have been doing everything we could. I outlined a long list of those in my formal paper to improve the timeliness and validity of the data and to get data from as many sources as we can. We believe, unless we do accurately determine prevailing wages, that our administration is subject to criticism and it should be.[129]

Mr. Marshall's position would be more believable if he had not flatly denied the GAO criticisms of activities that took place under his predecessor's leadership. Obviously, if he was unwilling to admit there was a problem, he had no reason to change anything. Thus, he put himself in the position of ascribing to his predecessor's patterns by refusing to change them or acknowledge their inadequacies.

ADMINISTRATIVE CHANGES

During his first presidential campaign, Ronald Reagan promised that he would not actively seek repeal of the Davis-Bacon Act. But when his administration took office in 1981, he did encourage the new secretary of labor, Raymond Donovan, to undertake a review of the aspects of the act that had provoked the most criticism in recent years and that were administrative procedures within the purview of the secretary to modify. On the basis of the review, a number of specific changes were contemplated.

1982 Proposals

It is likely that the impetus for these changes included consideration of the fact that public clamor for total repeal was growing, and that unless something were done by the DOL to ameliorate the

---

[129] *Hearings, supra* note 74, at 109 (testimony of Ray Marshall, Secretary of Labor).

impact of the act administratively, the President might be pressured to go back on his promise. This is not to suggest, however, that the proposed changes were window dressing. Indeed, among them were modifications dealing with fundamental aspects of the act's administration that were well beyond what might have been necessary simply to assuage critics and divert attention from repeal. There were five substantive changes among those published in the Federal Register for comment August 14, 1981. These were proposals to alter the regulatory scheme then current by:

1) eliminating the 30-percent rule and creating as the new "federal formula" a two-step process of selecting the prevailing rate as the rate found in a survey to be that paid to a majority, and if no majority received the same rate, then the weighted average of all the rates in the survey;

2) combining data from adjacent rural counties but excluding any nearby urban counties when wage data in a given rural county was insufficient to determine a locally prevailing wage, thus eliminating the importation of metropolitan wage rates to rural areas;

3) excluding wages paid under previous Davis-Bacon determinations from new surveys for prevailing wage calculation for most building projects (but not heavy or highway work, where almost all the work is public and done under Davis-Bacon rates), thus breaking the self-repeating cycle of perpetuation of erroneous rates;

4) expanding the permitted use of semiskilled helpers in a number of ways, including permitting such a classification (in a ratio of no more than two helpers for every three journeymen) in areas where the use of helpers is only an "identifiable" practice rather than a "prevailing" one, and eliminating the requirement that helpers do only tasks distinct from those undertaken by other classes of workers; and

5) allowing contractors to submit a weekly statement certifying compliance with Davis-Bacon wage requirements, thus eliminating the burdensome, unnecessary, and unused requirement of submitting copies of actual weekly payrolls.[130]

Although there were projections of cost savings associated with these provisions—variously reported at between $500 and $700 million, but estimated by the Congressional Budget Office to be towards the high end of the scale,[131] principally from the expanded

---

[130] *See* 46 Fed. Reg. 41444–41450, 41456–41470 (1981) (codified at 29 C.F.R. parts 1, 5).
[131] CONGRESSIONAL BUDGET OFFICE, *supra* note 52, at 37.

use of helpers ($360 million)[132] but also from cutting down the reporting requirement ($100 million)[133] and eliminating the 30-percent rule ($145 million)[134]—the changes were basically put forward as solutions to some of the administrative problems that had been aired by various critics of the act. As such, they were applauded by many long-time opponents of Davis-Bacon who may have felt that persuading the DOL to adopt a more responsive administrative stance meant that the hard part of the Davis-Bacon reform had been accomplished. They had reckoned without Judge Harold Greene.

Judge Greene. Shortly after the revised rules were promulgated on May 28, 1982, the unions brought suit seeking declaratory injunctive relief from their implementation. After a hearing on a motion for interim relief and cross-motions for summary judgment, D.C. District Court Judge Harold Greene, on July 22, 1982, five days before the new regulations were to take effect, granted a preliminary injunction barring implementation of all five provisions.[135] On December 23, 1982, after further hearings, Judge Greene granted summary judgment for the plaintiffs (the unions) on four of the five provisions at issue, permanently enjoining implementation of all the changes except the elimination of the 30-percent rule.[136]

Although seeming to acknowledge that Congress left the entire administration of Davis-Bacon up to the secretary of labor, Judge Greene argued that since fifteen previous secretaries of labor since the 1930s had not seen fit to make these changes, the current one should not be allowed to do so, and that furthermore, the proposed changes (except for elimination of the 30-percent rule) were "wholly

---

[132] *Id.* at 28. This is the figure for the two-helpers-to-three-journeymen case. Unlimited use of helpers would have resulted in estimated savings of $480 million. The figures were taken from U.S. Department of Labor, *Final Regulatory Impact and Regulatory Flexibility Analysis on Davis-Bacon Related Regulations (1982)*. With respect to them it was noted that "These estimates have been criticized as too high. . . . [However] the DoL described a number of factors that might cause its estimates to be too low [also]. To adjust for these opposing factors, the DoL produced a range of estimates (reflecting varying assumptions) and then chose the mid-point as its final estimate."

[133] *Id.* at 29. Number suggested by the Department of Labor. The Congressional Budget Office felt it was too high, and reduced the estimate to $50 million, as will be discussed below.

[134] *Id.* Derived from $155 million figure presented in Table 3, page 36, corrected to the year 1982.

[135] Building & Construction Trades Dept., AFL-CIO v. Donovan, 543 F. Supp. 1282 (D.D.C. 1982).

[136] Building & Construction Trades Dept., AFL-CIO v. Donovan, 553 F. Supp. 352 (D.D.C. 1982).

inconsistent" with his reading of congressional intent and the legislative history of Davis-Bacon.[137]

This curious (and inconsistently applied) logic was challenged by the secretary of labor in unusual association with various contractors' groups, who pointed out that because of the secretary's broad authority, his regulations could be set aside only if they were "arbitrary, capricious, an abuse of discretion, or otherwise not in accordance to law."[138] Specifically, the secretary and his allies felt that Judge Greene had misread not only the secretary's authority to modify his own regulations but also the congressional intent embodied in the act.

They argued, for example, that importing urban wage rates to rural areas defeats the idea that prevailing rates should reflect local conditions, and that previous Davis-Bacon rules already discouraged the practice. They also argued that insofar as the clear legislative intent of Davis-Bacon was to leave private wage scales undisturbed, only private wage scales should be surveyed for determinations; that the increasing presence in the industry of nonunion contractors using helpers virtually required the secretary to recognize a helper classification; and that replacing the filing of weekly payroll reports by contractors with a single "statement of compliance" would meet the technical requirements of the Copeland Act and eliminate a lot of useless paperwork.[139]

Based on this logic, they filed a appeal from Judge Greene's permanent injunction. The Building and Construction Trades Council, of course, did not agree, but it filed an appeal also, arguing that Judge Greene had been inconsistent in failing to enjoin elimination of the 30-percent rule along with the other changes.

Higher Courts. Effective June 28, 1983, the DOL reissued its proposed regulations, stripped of all the changes except for the elimination of the 30-percent rule and some minor provisions for enforcement. This was done between the time that the D.C. Court of Appeals heard the combined appeals (May 5, 1983) and handed down its decision (July 5, 1983),[140] but the DOL maintained that there was no significance to the timing.[141]

---

[137] *Battle Lines Drawn in Davis-Bacon Appeal,* ENGINEERING NEWS-RECORD 60 (March 17, 1983).
[138] *Id.*
[139] *Id.*
[140] Building & Construction Trades Dept., AFL-CIO v. Donovan, 712 F.2d 611 (D.C. Cir. 1983), *cert. denied,* 52 U.S.L.W. 3527 (Jan. 17, 1984).
[141] *Labor Department Issues Davis-Bacon Rules Minus Provisions Voided by District Court,* 85 DAILY LAB. REP. A-9 (May 2, 1983).

In the appeals court decision, the earlier logic of the district court was partially sustained and partially overturned. As a result, 1) the 30-percent rule was eliminated; 2) injunctions against the new rules for surveying wages, that is, for not including previous Davis-Bacon rates and not importing metropolitan rates, were lifted; 3) the injunction against dropping the weekly submission of payroll records was sustained; and 4) changes for helper classifications were allowed insofar as they related to expanding the definition of helpers, but not to determining rates unless their use was a prevailing, not just an identifiable, practice in an area. The unions appealed to the Supreme Court in the October term, 1983, but *certiorari* was denied January 17, 1984, allowing the Circuit Court's interpretations, listed above, to stand.[142]

Judge Greene, Again. Since further appeals were impossible, there the matter should have stood. The DOL should have been able to institute the rules it had originally published in May 1982 minus the change affecting reporting requirements, and substituting the words "prevailing practice" for "identifiable practice" when referring to setting rates for helpers. Again, however, this did not give due consideration to Judge Greene. Despite the fact that his decision to permanently enjoin application of the original rule change (always excepting the 30-percent rule exclusion) had been overturned by the Circuit Court in July 1983, he declined to lift it. Even after the Supreme Court decided not to review the case in January 1984, he declined to lift it. Not until December 21, 1984 would Judge Greene comply with the Circuit Court's ruling of the previous year and issue an order releasing his injunction, thus allowing the DOL to get on with implementing the new regulations.[143]

Greene declined, however, to let the DOL take the easy approach to modifying the helper ruling. Instead, he refused to rescind his injunction with respect to the entire helper issue (apparently substituting his own judgment for that of the higher courts), and suggested (somewhat disingenuously, given the history) that "This does not mean, however, that the secretary is precluded from issuing a new regulation concerning classification and wage rates for classes of laborers and mechanics."[144] Thus, if the DOL wanted to ease the rules for helpers, even if they form a prevailing category of work-

---

[142] 52 U.S.L.W. 3527.

[143] *Court Lifts Davis-Bacon Injunction,* ENGINEERING NEWS-RECORD 10 (January 10, 1985).

[144] *Id.*

men, it will have to start over again with a notice of intended rulemaking.[145]

Implications of the Changes

In January 1985 the DOL began implementing the changes concerning the use of previous federal rates in new surveys and the use of metropolitan rates in rural determinations.[146] These, along with the previously implemented 30-percent rule elimination, were obviously as far as the original proposals were going to go. From an economic standpoint, the residual changes were not nearly as significant as the original ones, for most of the savings anticipated would have come from changes in rules for using helpers and from eliminating the senseless weekly submission of payroll copies. The prospective administrative impact of each of the three follows.

Urban Rates in Rural Determinations. Eliminating the application of urban rates to rural determinations probably will not be very significant, despite the fact the average urban construction wage is about 25 percent higher than the rural one.[147] Earlier Davis-Bacon rules had already discouraged the practice, and in final analysis, the decision of the wage specialist to take rates from where he can find them for surveys will probably continue. There are many examples in the GAO report and discussed earlier in the chapter of similar regulations being honored in the breach.

Previous Davis-Bacon Rates. Similarly, eliminating previously determined rates on public building projects from being included in new surveys may not have a major effect, although it is a change for the better and should be applauded.[148] It does not apply to heavy and highway rates, of course, because such projects are almost never bought by private individuals, and there will undoubtedly be complications arising in the surveying process for joint rates, such as "building and heavy" rates, which are about 5 percent of the area determinations, as to what rate base should be included in surveys for them. Still, the elimination of previously determined rates is a

---

[145] This is an example of an unusual occurrence—that of a district court being able to thwart a decision handed down by an appeals court and allowed to stand by the Supreme Court.

[146] *Labor Department Issues Final Rules for Setting Davis-Bacon Wage Rates,* 22 DAILY LAB. REP. A-3 (Feb. 1, 1985).

[147] *See* Bureau of Labor Statistics *Current Population Survey* (May 1979).

[148] The 1979 GAO study found that the DOL had relied on previous Davis-Bacon wages in 20 of the 277 craft rate determinations it reviewed. [GENERAL ACCOUNTING OFFICE, *supra* note 3, Appendix VII.] If this had not been done, wages on 14 of the 20 would have been 4 to 50 percent lower, and wages on 6 of the 20 would have been 3 to 23 percent higher than those actually set by the DOL.

worthwhile change, and will undoubtedly have greater effect in the longer term, because it will slow the spread (and sometimes the institutionalization) of erroneous Davis-Bacon rates.

The 30-Percent Rule. The most important change is undoubtedly the elimination of the 30-percent rule—but for reasons that are perhaps not readily apparent. The 30-percent rule was unique to Davis-Bacon for almost fifty years. Because of its obvious arbitrariness, it became a focal point for Davis-Bacon opponents, who often used it to dramatize the law's complex problems as tersely as possible. This may have given the 30-percent rule an appearance of undue importance. Actually, the elimination of the 30-percent rule (more accurately, the shift from a 30-percent rule to a 50-percent rule) will not prompt any cataclysmic change in the way Davis-Bacon is administered. Since the 30-percent rule simply provides a calculating methodology for fixing on one of the rates found in a survey, it has not been the only, or even the major administrative failing of the act. Changing to a 50-percent rule, for example, decreases but does not eliminate the influence of negotiated rates, which are still the only ones in a survey likely to be the same to the penny.

Nevertheless, the change has the potential to be immensely important because of its indirect effects. Under the current system, about half of all wage determinations are made without survey of existing rates because the DOL "knows" that the area or locality for which the determination is being made is negotiated-rate territory. Instances were also reported above in which survey results were neglected in favor of union rates because the DOL "knew from independent sources" that the union rate prevailed in the locality. Under the new 50-percent rule, *a priori* judgments of this kind will have to be conditioned by the higher percentage requirement. This should cause the DOL to question the actual dominance of union rates in many areas previously considered safe union territory and result in more actual surveys being performed.

Because implementation of this aspect of the change remains largely within the control of the Employment Standards Administration staff, it may be that its effect will not be fully realized. Although it is too soon to tell what final direction the DOL will take, however, there is already some evidence of the type of impact that is possible. A recently revised rate schedule was released in May 1985 covering building construction in a three-county area of Atlanta, Georgia's metropolitan area. The new schedule set different (and much lower) rates for Clayton County, the most rural of the three counties, and higher rates for Fulton County, the most urban. In the previous (1983) determination, the three counties had been undifferentiated, and each had rates higher than for any of the counties in the current wage schedules.[149]

SUMMARY OF ADMINISTRATIVE IMPACT

The recent administrative changes have not cured the problems of the prevailing wage concept. All three of the new rules are improvements, but the only one likely to have any major effect is the change from the 30-percent rule to a 50-percent rule. This change has the potential to reduce the number of cases in which union rates are accepted as the default position by making it harder for the DOL to assume that there is enough union representation in a given type of construction in a given locality to accept the unions' negotiated rates as prevailing without actually conducting a survey.

To be effective, however, the changes must be properly applied. The effect will be minor if the DOL assumes, for example, that union rates continue to dominate in all of the places where area determinations were in effect before the changes were made. Unfortunately, there is no system established within the Davis-Bacon administration to ensure that judgments about union domination of an area are accurate. We have only the word of the DOL in many cases that it knows "from independent sources" that a union rate prevails. In this as in every other aspect of rate setting under Davis-Bacon, there is no external check on the DOL's decisions: its determinations do not have to be made on the record; courts will not normally question their accuracy;[150] and they are not subject to general or even sampling review by any auditing agency that has the authority to compel a reasonable standard of accuracy and consistency. Therefore, whether a 30-percent rule or a 50-percent rule applies, we will probably have to continue to accept the DOL's judgment that the necessary pluralities exist for determinations that are made without survey.

Furthermore, problems will exist even if more surveys are made. All other factors aside, a prevailing wage law makes no sense if the rates it establishes are not actually prevailing. The finding of the comptroller general that 87 percent of the wage rate classifications

---

[149] *Prevailing Rates for Atlanta Area Sharply Lower in New DOL Survey*, 31 CONSTRUCTION LAB. REP. 279–80 (May 8, 1985).

[150] A suit brought by the Southeastern Legal Foundation challenging a Davis-Bacon determination affecting a construction contract in the state of Virginia resulted in 1979 in the Fourth Circuit U.S. Court of Appeals ruling that Davis-Bacon determinations would be reviewable by the courts, but it is uncertain how this might apply. Reported in GOULD & BITTLINGMAYER, *supra* note 69, at 63.

he reviewed were inaccurately determined stands as indictment of the adequacy of Davis-Bacon's administration. The errors found by the comptroller general were for rates measured with respect to what they should have been under Davis-Bacon's old rules, but their frequency would have been only marginally smaller under the new rules. Therefore, there is little reason to anticipate that the results of future surveys will be any more accurate than in the past.

The controversy between the comptroller general and the secretary of labor over the accuracy of rates illustrates another point. Both the wage specialists of the DOL and the auditors of the GAO applied essentially the same rules to the same situations and came up with different prevailing rates in 87 percent of the determinations studied. In only two classes of instances (accounting for fewer than 10 percent of the cases) did the differences result from differences in interpretation of Davis-Bacon rules rather than misapplication of the rules.[151] Although the GAO's rates appear to be better supported by the facts, the case against Davis-Bacon administration is equally strong whether errors were made by the GAO or by the DOL. In either event, the result is a *prima facie* case that Davis-Bacon determinations are so complicated that even experts are unable to agree on what the proper rate should be.

The possibilities for administrative error in Davis-Bacon are many. Partly they result from the size and complexity of the environment within which determinations take place, and partly they are endemic to any rulemaking system founded on subjective differentiations (such as "corresponding classes of laborers" and "projects of a character similar"). In the text above, we have not reviewed all of the problem areas, or even all of the thirteen cataloged by the comptroller general as having distorted the wage determinations he reviewed in 1979. Nevertheless, it should be clear from those that have been reviewed why Davis-Bacon administration is responsible for so much dissatisfaction, and why the comptroller general felt that the act was probably incapable of being well administered.

In the introduction to the chapter, we posed the question of why the case against Davis-Bacon has not been more compelling. With respect to the act's administration, that is a very difficult question to answer. A great step forward was taken in 1981, when the sec-

---

[151] In two classes of instances, those involving the use of previously determined federal rates in new surveys and those involving multiple counting of rates for the same individual, the secretary argued that his rates were set correctly with respect to previous practice, whereas the comptroller argued that the previous practice was a misinterpretation of legislative intent. In these cases the differences found may be more properly attributable to philosophical differences rather than to error.

retary acknowledged that serious problems existed, but it is clear from the courts' reactions that even obvious improvements that are well within the authority of the secretary to make, are not easily brought about. Furthermore, the changes implemented thus far apply to only a few of the many problem areas identified by the comptroller general and other critics, and fail to get to the heart of the matter—that the wages set by prevailing wage laws are arbitrary and fundamentally unfair, and will most likely remain so.

ECONOMIC IMPACT OF DAVIS-BACON

A second broad avenue of appraisal of Davis-Bacon concerns not how well it carries out its function, but how much it costs. Most recent studies of the act have been devoted to estimating one or another aspect of how the prevailing wage process raises wage rates above what they would be without it, how the increased wages translate into unnecessary government spending for construction above what would be needed to buy the same output on the open market, how the artificial wage rates induce other unnecessary expenditures on the part of contractors in the form of job assignment restrictions which would not exist except for the act, or how wages inflated by Davis-Bacon cause direct or induced wage-push inflation. Some also have made estimates of such things as the cost of maintaining the prevailing wage machinery, or the cost to contractors of complying with paperwork requirements. These studies are all different from one another in subtle or obvious ways. They ask different questions, make different assumptions, and use different methodologies. They also arrive at different results, and depending on the conservatism of the authors, or the unavailability of needed parameters, may express their results as being somewhere within a wide range.

Realistically, regardless of the approach taken by the studies, no level of precision greater than order of magnitude is likely, given the great many simplifying assumptions that must be made. On the other hand, no greater level should be required, since the purpose of making the estimates is to condition policy judgments. For this requirement, it matters very little if the true economic cost of Davis-Bacon is one-half or twice as large as the typical estimate. The urgency of action might be somewhat affected, but the fundamental policy prescription would not be altered.

Nevertheless, there is a certain attractiveness to having a particular number as a benchmark. Davis-Bacon economic impact estimates have been presented during the past ten years ranging from less than $50 million to more than $2 billion. These apparently disparate estimates have caused unnecessary confusion over the economic impact of the act. In fact, most of the estimates are more compatible with one another than they seem, and differ principally because they measure different things. In terms of the amount of money that the government could save by buying the same type and volume of public works construction free from Davis-Bacon requirements, the preponderance of the credible estimates supports a conclusion that the cost of Davis-Bacon is approximately $1 billion per year.

Costs Based on Wage Differential Estimates

As discussed earlier, although there is no direct way to measure Davis-Bacon impact, there are a number of surrogates. One method is to estimate the degree to which prevailing rates inflate the wage costs on some sample of government projects, translate this wage cost difference into project costs or savings, and then expand the result to the universe of such work, namely all federal or federally aided construction. The obvious mechanical problems with this methodology include concerns over adequacy of sample size and precision of estimates, and estimation of the wage proportion of contracts and the universe size of federal projects.

Reasons have been offered as to why studies performed by this method, which might be called the wage differential approach, are either generically or individually biased towards underestimation or overestimation of the actual economic impact. The AFL-CIO has suggested, for example, that the higher wage rates required by Davis-Bacon determinations may not translate proportionately to higher project costs because they may be partially offset by productivity increases, by better management encouraged by the higher rates, or by reduction of first-line supervision.[152] Others have suggested that factor substitution (the replacement of the more expensive on-site labor by increased use of prefabricated parts assembled elsewhere, perhaps, but in general the shift from production labor to nonproduction labor and/or increased use of capital) will occur to offset any cost increases.[153] Conversely, the point has been raised

---

[152] Georgine, *supra* note 128, at 35–37.

[153] Allen, *Much Ado About Davis-Bacon: A Critical Review and New Evidence*, 26 J. L. & Econ. 707–36 (October 1983). (Allen notes [at 707]: "The first draft was written while I was receiving research support from the Building and Construction Trades Department of the AFL-CIO.")

that most of the existing studies fail to measure the wage difference properly or to consider the impact of union work rules.

Despite these problems, the wage differential approach is one of the few that allow generalization about total costs. Three basic studies have adopted it, those of the Congressional Budget Office, the General Accounting Office, and the Council on Wage and Price Stability. As will be the case with all of the quantitative analyses, we shall provide a brief overview of the methodology and results, and then see the degree to which the results support the $1 billion total cost estimate.

Congressional Budget Office (1983). The Congressional Budget Office study is the most recent, and is the only study of this type that relies on basic input data developed by the DOL. Therefore, it is not subject to challenge on the basis of anti-DOL bias. It is also the only study of the type that attempts to find the full cost of Davis-Bacon, rather than just the wage impact.

The study was undertaken at the request of the Subcommittee on Labor of the Senate Committee on Labor and Human Resources and described the act and its effect on wages, federal construction costs, inflation, and employment in accordance with a mandate to provide objective and impartial analysis. The study contains no recommendations. Basic input data were drawn from materials used by the DOL when justifying its proposed administrative rule changes in 1981.

The Congressional Budget Office conceived of the total impact of Davis-Bacon costs—and therefore the amount that could be saved by repealing it—as the sum of the impacts derived from each of three sources: first, a wage impact resulting from wages required under Davis-Bacon exceeding average construction wages in the community; second, a workforce utilization impact resulting from restrictions on the use of helpers; and third, an administrative impact resulting from the paperwork associated with contract administration. No consideration was given to savings that might result from elimination of the Davis-Bacon bureaucracy at the DOL and other federal agencies, and social benefits or costs were not estimated. Separate estimates were made in many cases for the impact on "budget authority" and "outlays," the former being a representation of the steady-state effect after full digestion of the repeal, while the latter recognizes that full savings would not be realized at once, since contracts in progress would continue to use the old rate schedules under which they were let, and firms require some time to adjust to new possibilities for workforce utilization.

In its 1982 justification for rule changes, the DOL had estimated from analysis of a sample of both project and area determinations in effect in April 1981 that Davis-Bacon rate determinations were, on average, higher than the average wage in the locality. From this sample, the DOL had estimated that "the difference between average wages on Davis-Bacon projects and on private projects was 5.3 percent in building construction and 5.4 percent in residential construction."[154]

To derive the impact on the universe of federal construction, these wage differences were first reformed as percentage savings of construction costs. Since labor accounts for about 35 percent of construction costs, the wage difference of about 5.4 percent was expected to produce cost savings of approximately 1.9 percent of federal construction costs. Then this percentage cost savings was expanded to the universe of federal construction, estimated to be $30 billion. On this basis, the Congressional Budget Office estimated the total wage-related direct impact of Davis-Bacon rate increases to be $568 million.

Even if the Congressional Budget Office had gone no further, it would have performed a valuable service by bringing to light the DOL estimates of Davis-Bacon impact. At least these cannot be accused of having insufficient sample size or anti-DOL bias. Nevertheless, the results would have been open to criticism for having measured the wrong labor cost difference. The difference between Davis-Bacon rates and average rates is not the relevant difference for estimating the impact of repeal. If Davis-Bacon were repealed, government contracts theoretically would have to be awarded to the contractors with the lowest wage rates, rather than to an average of all contractors. Therefore, rates set by Davis-Bacon determinations and the lowest rates generally available in the community should be compared for a proper comparison of Davis-Bacon costs.

In actuality, if Davis-Bacon rate determinations were eliminated, each sector of the industry would eventually find some equilibrium position where the level of bids would depend on: first, the strength of unionization in the sector and the ability of open shop firms to compete effectively against union firms on technological grounds; second, the average open-shop labor rate as applied in accordance with open shop work practices; third, the ability of union firms to offset their higher wage rates with greater worker productivity or

---

[154] CONGRESSIONAL BUDGET OFFICE, *supra* note 52, at 26, citing U.S. DEPARTMENT OF LABOR, *Final Regulatory Impact and Regulatory Flexibility Analysis on Davis-Bacon Related Regulations* (1982).

better management; and fourth, cost-of-living and other conditions in the local labor market. This equilibrium position would be different in each sector, but would probably rest at a higher level than open shop rates only in the heavy construction sector, where there are very few open shop firms. In this sector, the relevant comparison would be that between Davis-Bacon rates and average of all sector rates; in all others, it would be between Davis-Bacon rates and the average of only the open shop rates.

The Congressional Budget Office did not make this estimate, but it did provide an estimate to correct for cost savings attributable to freeing the nonunion sector from the constraints placed upon its workforce utilization practices by the Davis-Bacon rules. The DOL had estimated in 1982 that allowing unlimited use of helpers on Davis-Bacon work would result in the saving of 1.6 percent of total project costs.[155] As the Congressional Budget Office put it:

> Although the effect of Davis-Bacon on wages receives the most attention, the act's largest potential cost impact may derive from its effect on the use of labor. [n.b. Actually it is not quite as large as the wage impact.] For one thing, DoL wage determinations require that, if an employee does the work of a particular craft, the wage paid should be for that craft even if the employee does not carry that job title. For example, carpentry work must be paid for at carpenters' wages, even if performed by a general laborer, helper, or member of another craft. In addition, ... the DoL generally has not issued wage determinations for helper and apprenticeship classifications....
>
> A DoL regulatory impact analysis concluded that the current policies regarding semi-skilled workers—helpers, in particular—do not adequately reflect local practice and therefore raise project costs. The DoL estimated that allowing unlimited use of helpers on federal construction projects would have reduced costs by approximately $480 million in fiscal year 1982.[156]

The Congressional Budget Office estimated a slightly larger amount, 1.6 percent of federal construction costs, or $500 million, as the total effect of not only allowing more widespread use of helpers, but also allowing more flexible use of labor generally.

The third portion of the estimate was that associated with paperwork costs. Again, the DOL had made estimates for the 1982 rule changes. It had relied on the only known estimate of this expense, a survey in 1972 by the Associated General Contractors of America of its members performed at the request of the Commission on Government Procurement.[157] That survey had estimated paperwork

---

[155] *Id.* at 29.
[156] *Id.* at 27, 28.
[157] Described in THIEBLOT, *supra* note 4, at 79–82.

costs to be one-half of one percent of total contract costs, or a total of $190 million at the $38 billion level of federal spending. The DOL felt that this estimate was too high, and arbitrarily cut it back to $100 million. The Congressional Budget Office felt that the DOL had not cut it back enough, and arbitrarily reduced it to $50 million.

Adding these three factors—$568 million for wage-related cost increases, $500 million for eliminating work practice restrictions, and $50 million for eliminating contractor paperwork—led to a total savings estimate from repealing the act of slightly over $1.1 billion per year. This number, which obviously is consistent with the $1 billion benchmark, was then projected to account for increasing levels of government spending in fiscal years 1984-88, to produce savings estimates increasing from $1.4 billion in 1984 to $1.6 billion by 1988.[158]

General Accounting Office (1979).[159] In its 1979 review of Davis-Bacon administration, the GAO made field audits of thirty projects on which it discovered differences between the wage rate determined by the DOL and that which actually prevailed in the locality in 87 percent of the individual wage classifications it identified. In 40 percent of these cases, the DOL's determinations were higher (by an average of $2.04), and in 60 percent of them, they were lower (by an average of $.99). Noting that where the determined rate was lower than that actually prevailing in the community there was no effect on the wages actually paid, the GAO estimated that the 36.8 percent raw wage cost increase found resulted in increases in construction costs in these projects of from 1 percent to nearly 9 percent, with the average at 3.4 percent. It concluded that,

> While GAO's selection of the 30 projects was made on a random sample basis, the sample size was insufficient for projecting the results to all Federal or federally assisted construction costs during the year with statistical validity. However, even in the absence of statistical certainty, the random nature of GAO's sample leads it to believe that, if these projects are representative (and GAO has no reason to believe they are not), the act results in unnecessary construction costs of several hundred million dollars annually.[160]

---

[158] CONGRESSIONAL BUDGET OFFICE, *supra* note 52, at 36.

[159] GENERAL ACCOUNTING OFFICE, *supra* note 3.

[160] *Id.* at iv. The comptroller estimated that a sample of 1,200 projects would have been required to achieve a statistically valid result at the 95 percent confidence level but maintained that the results found in the small random sample were representative and indicative of the conclusion presented. During the Senate hearings at which the comptroller presented this study, Senator Williams (as part of what can only be described as a deliberate effort to blur the impact of its conclusions) imagined that he could not interpret so nonprecise a number as that presented by the comptroller:

Mr. STAATS. We know the costs are very high, but the question is the precise

In the body of its report, the GAO did go through the exercise of expanding the 3.4 percent differential found in the sample to the universe of federal construction that it felt would be similarly affected to estimate a cost of the errors made by the DOL in misapplying Davis-Bacon rules. It used two methods: one assumed that costs on 40 percent of federal construction (the same proportion as found in its sample) were raised by 3.4 percent; the second expressed the costs of the twelve projects in which it had found increases as a percentage of the costs on the total of thirty projects in the sample, and then assumed that this calculated percentage (17.8) of all federal construction experienced increases of the same amount (3.4 percent).

This second calculation, which results in the smaller number, gives recognition to the fact that the DOL's error rate was higher on smaller projects, which is logical given the approximate proportionality that exists between project size and degree of unionization; but given the nature of the sample and the fact that the average difference in construction cost was already weighted by project size, this method of calculation does not necessarily produce a superior estimate—simply a different one.

Depending on which expansion assumption was made, the results were as follows:

> Setting prevailing wages for federally financed construction, as required by the Davis-Bacon Act, has increased the direct cost of Federal construction. We estimate that, as a result of wages being established at higher rates than those actually prevailing in the area of the projects, construction costs for federally financed projects could be increased by an estimated $228 million to $513 million annually.[161]

Two notes should be added at this point. First, the comparison being made by the GAO is between prevailing rates as calculated and prevailing rates as they *should have been* calculated by the Davis-Bacon rules. It is therefore an estimate of DOL error rather than an estimate of Davis-Bacon cost. Projecting this figure to the total market does not take into account either of the two principal advantages that would obtain from repeal of the act—eliminating the distortion to open market rates caused by government-mandated super-minimum wages, or freeing the market from the workforce utilization constraints that the act imposes.

---

figure. It's a question of what would be the precise nationwide figure. That's all we're qualifying.
Senator WILLIAMS. You know the costs are very high? I don't know what you mean there. All costs for everything are very high today. We all know that.
[*Hearings, supra* note 74, at 31.]
[161] *Id.* at 76.

Second, the figure as calculated may be conservative. One later review of the GAO report done at Oregon State University noted that the GAO had found labor cost increases averaging 36.8 percent but project cost differences of only 3.4 percent, and suggested that the figure may have been in error.[162] Labor costs—as opposed to capital and material costs and profits—are typically estimated to be no less than 30 to 35 percent of construction costs, so these results would seem to be grossly distorted. On the other hand, on some projects the increases in rates were not uniform or universal, and in some cases they occurred in lesser-used trades. The result is the difference between the straight average of rate differences (about 37 percent) and the weighted average including the rates of all those on a project whose rates did not change (11 percent). In one specific example, the review noted that "[l]abor costs for the Barron, Wisconsin vocational school amount to only 7 percent of total costs, which is unusually low for a building of this type. Excluding this observation yields an increase in wage costs of 28.2% and an increase in total costs of 4.5%."[163]

If one were to expand these figures following the same two procedures as used by the GAO, estimates for the total error cost would be from approximately $153 to $646 million. The fact that the "more conservative" GAO expansion results in a decreased total cost—$153 million compared with $228 million—even though the wage cost difference increased from 3.4 percent to 4.5 percent, leads one to question whether the method might not be *too* conservative. The small sample size is obviously a factor here.

The GAO's findings in the economic impact area have also been attacked as not being conservative enough. Professor Steven G. Allen, of North Carolina State University, reanalyzed the GAO's wage difference statistics and determined that the comptroller had erred in this interpretation, leading to an "implied cost (using GAO's methodology) of Davis-Bacon [of] $75.6 million, not several hundred million as claimed by the GAO."[164]

The analysis is somewhat difficult to summarize, but Professor Allen's basic contention seems to be that if the error in determining an excessive rate cannot be clearly determined, it should be concluded that the GAO erred in finding it too high. Thus, in reviewing

---

[162] M. N. FRAUNDORF, J. P. FARRELL, & R. MASON, EFFECT OF THE DAVIS-BACON ACT ON CONSTRUCTION COSTS IN NON-METROPOLITAN AREAS OF THE UNITED STATES, 4 (1982).

[163] *Id.* We were unable to verify this observation of unusually low labor costs in the GAO report.

[164] Allen, *supra* note 153, at 716. Allen incorrectly identified what the GAO study was measuring—which is actually DOL error rather than Davis-Bacon cost.

the twelve determinations in which the GAO found rates too high, he attributes the difference in "sampling error" to the GAO (although not even the DOL, itself, in its vigorous rebuttal of the report makes this claim) and discounts them. He claims that in only four instances did it seem likely that the DOL had arbitrarily applied union rates from nonadjacent counties to the projects in "small, rural counties in southern states with low unionization."[165] Thus, he used these four instances, along with parts of two others, to project the differences by the more conservative projection method, and arrived at his conclusions, which he feels debunks the GAO's report.[166] Since he offers no support other than the mere assertion of his judgments in these findings, they are not very compelling.

Since the range of estimates provided by the GAO itself is between about $225 million and $500 million, it would seem that the comptroller's estimate is not supportive of the $1 billion benchmark. This, however, is not the case. As emphasized repeatedly above, the GAO estimate is an error-rate calculation. In some sense it might be thought of as a correction that would have to be added to an estimate based on wage rate differentials, like that of the Congressional Budget Office. Furthermore, it does not include effects for workforce utilization or contractors' administrative expenses. If these are added at the same levels as found by the Congressional Budget Office, the GAO estimate would be from $778 million to just over $1 billion. Both of the comptroller's estimates derive from different expansion methods applied to the same estimate. One of them, which applies the 3.6 percent increase in construction costs to 40 percent of the projects reviewed, translates into a 1.4 percent cost impact on federal construction generally. Given the fact that the GAO was measuring a slightly different thing, this result is fully compatible with the $1 billion estimate.

---

[165] *Id.* at 715.

[166] It is interesting to note that in evaluating the GAO's determinations of prevailing rates in one area, Allen finds examples of rates determined for electricians to be below those of cement masons, carpenters, bricklayers, and roofers, and rates for laborers to be above those of painters. For these, he feels, GAO should have obtained more data, or dropped the rates from the sample. [*Id.* at 716 n. 31.] Since the GAO did not calculate these rates from a sample, as he implies, but from a full field survey to which the Davis-Bacon determination rules were applied, they are quite likely to be accurate (and were not challenged for their accuracy by the DOL in its rebuttal). Thus, what Professor Allen has discovered is not a flaw in the GAO survey, but a flaw in the prevailing wage concept, which, even when properly applied, often results in arbitrary and inconsistent wage determinations. He has also stumbled on a factor that may motivate the wage specialists to disregard, add to, or modify the rates found in regular Davis-Bacon surveys, or to import wages from other counties, etc. In other words, he has done a fair job of summarizing the GAO's contention that the rate-setting process is arbitrary and unfair.

Goldfarb & Morrall (1976, 1981).[167] Robert Goldfarb and John Morrall performed a study on behalf of the Council of Wage and Price Stability in 1976 to evaluate whether significant cost savings to the government could be obtained by switching to a prevailing wage determination procedure based on an average calculation instead of the 30-percent rule. They used data from a Bureau of Labor Statistics special construction wage survey, which they compared with actual Davis-Bacon determinations in nineteen cities for three construction trades in commercial construction and two in residential construction.

In residential construction, the original study showed that the Davis-Bacon rates were higher than the average wage rates by 3.1 percent, but that in commercial construction, they were lower than the average rate by 2.7 percent. This caused the authors to draw the conclusion, often repeated by Davis-Bacon supporters, that "if average rates were used instead of Labor's procedures, some savings would be obtained in certain cities and occupations but that the widespread savings expected by some observers were unlikely."[168] The AFL-CIO went one step further, not totally inaccurately, in saying that "A study prepared by the Council on Wage and Price Stability ... found that Davis-Bacon prevailing wage rates are not 'typically higher' than average rates paid to craft workers in a local labor market."[169]

This unexpected result can be explained by the fact that, despite having derived an extensive data base on comparisons between average rates and rates set by Davis-Bacon determinations in the cities studied, Goldfarb and Morrall inexplicably shifted to a new calculation base in the original study when they attempted to expand their conclusions to estimate the direct impact of the act. Instead of using the Davis-Bacon-to-average comparisons, they used union-to-average comparisons. Their 1972 sample showed that union rates exceeded average rates by 2.1 percent for commercial construction and 5.4 percent for residential construction. This difference, along with an estimate that labor was 35 percent of total construction costs, was applied to the estimated total public construction market of $30.2 billion to produce a "rough estimate" of the cost savings of changing from what they described as union-based Davis-Bacon rule to an average-wage rule of between $222 million and $571 million.

---

[167] Goldfarb & Morrall, *supra* note 115.

[168] Letter from William Lilley III, Acting Director, Council on Wage and Price Stability, to William J. Usery, Secretary of Labor, June 23, 1976.

[169] Georgine, *supra* note 128, at 56.

This was a misleading number, since it answered a question no one was asking, but was apparently the best Goldfarb and Morrall could do faced with the unexpected negative result in the difference between Davis-Bacon and average rates found in the commercial sector. (The authors presumably knew that no Davis-Bacon determination could *decrease* construction costs, since even if it set rates at zero, contractors would have to continue to pay market rates. But had they expanded the negative difference, it would have resulted in just such a decrease.)

In 1981, logic developed by the GAO provided a means through which Goldfarb and Morrall could not only improve their analysis of rate comparisons, but also expand their results to the universe of federal construction answering (this time) the proper question of how much might be saved by shifting from the existing Davis-Bacon methodology to one based on average wages, although they do not explain this in their study. Using the same 1972 estimates of total federal construction and proportion of labor costs, Goldfarb and Morrall reviewed their original data and modified their conclusions considerably:

> It is important to recognize [that] "below average" Davis-Bacon rates in city A do not really "cancel out" or "average out" high Davis-Bacon rates in city B. Instead, city B has a high "minimum wage," while city A has an ineffective (or less effective) minimum wage. City A's "low" Davis-Bacon determination does not necessarily result in below-average wages in federal projects in that city; instead, it merely "abandons the field" to the market wage.
>
> This line of reasoning suggests another calculation not in our earlier paper. Since Davis-Bacon rates are less likely to affect actual wages when determinations are below actual average wages, we recalculate the average-rate Davis-Bacon comparison . . . by assuming that Davis-Bacon determinations above the actual average wage raise costs by the difference between the Davis-Bacon determination and the average, while those below the average have no effect. This recalculation shows Davis-Bacon rates exceeding the average wage by 4.0 percent in commercial and 9.1 percent in residential construction.[170]

Using this new approach, Goldfarb and Morrall now estimated the economic impact of repealing Davis-Bacon at between $423 million and $962 million.[171]

Although these figures are in the approximate range of compatibility with the $1 billion benchmark, they are a bit high. They measure only the wage-related impact of average-to-Davis-Bacon rates, neglecting savings that would obtain from eliminating work-

---

[170] Goldfarb & Morrall, *supra* note 81, at 196–97.
[171] *Id.* at 199.

rule restrictions and paperwork requirements. It might be noted, however, that they were expanded to the federal construction universe by a rather crude methodology that did not account for sample proportionality as did the GAO study (that is, this study did not calculate the weighted average error) or acknowledge that there are about six times as many commercial projects as residential ones (so the 9 percent residential difference is not nearly as significant as the 4 percent building difference). Finally, no data were gathered or estimates made for highway or heavy construction, which together account for about 38 percent of the federal total.

On the other hand, the estimates, although revised in 1981, are in 1972 dollars. Corrected for best estimates of current volumes of federal construction spending, they would be about 25 percent higher. Thus, although the results are compatible with the $1 billion figure, the authors' original warnings in 1976 that these were "rough estimates" should be respected.

Direct Analysis of Project Costs

A pure analysis of how much Davis-Bacon requirements increase the costs of public construction is impossible. To be able to make such a thing, it would be necessary to rerun history, once with the prevailing law in effect, and once without it—with no time difference in between, or any other changes. There is only one empirical example which, although flawed, comes close: it is based on the suspension of the Davis-Bacon Act during the spring of 1971.

Davis-Bacon Suspension.[172] One section of the Davis-Bacon Act specifies that its provisions may be suspended during time of emergency by the President. On February 23, 1971, following a year in which wage increases in construction union contracts had averaged 15 to 18 percent, President Nixon exercised his prerogatives, declared an emergency, and suspended the operation of the act. The suspension lasted for thirty-five days and ended when organized labor agreed to a program of voluntary wage constraints that limited increases in negotiated construction wages to an annual rate of about 6 percent.

During the suspension, 288 projects of over $10,000 on which bids had been received but no contracts awarded were reopened without Davis-Bacon prevailing wage requirements. Analysis was made of the bids submitted under both circumstances by 914 contractors, and also of the 288 lowest bids and rebids. Exclusive of the infla-

---

[172] Details of a study by the author on this subject are in THIEBLOT, *supra* note 4, at 89–94.

tionary factor of 1–2 percent which might have applied during the forty-five-day average period between bids and rebids, the first set of comparisons (between all competing bids and their matching rebids) showed the rebids to be 2.93 percent lower than the initial bids. The second set of comparisons (between initial low bids and subsequent low rebids) showed the rebids to average 0.63 percent lower than the initial bids.

A disclaimer to this estimate, is necessary, however, because the bid-rebid process was not pure. In addition to the time difference problem, all of the original bids were disclosed before rebids were made, which points to the high probability that some gamesmanship was at work in the process, independent of the prevailing rate elimination. Yet, although gamesmanship certainly influenced the general level of competing bids (towards the initial low bid, perhaps), its impact and even its direction were much less distinct in the case of the low bid comparisons. Using the bid-rebid difference as a base and applying it to all federal construction, an estimate was made of the savings allowable from the repeal of Davis-Bacon, which was put at $240 million per year.

A reexamination of the data from which that estimate was derived in 1975 demonstrates, however, that the savings estimate was probably too conservative, as it did not account for the amount of inflation affecting the construction market in that time period. For approximately half of the total construction volume represented by the 288 bids, the type of project was known, and for the other half, the percent difference (0.78 percent) was close enough to the average (0.63 percent) that we can assume it was distributed in about the same way among the categories. By category of construction, the percent differences between the lowest rebids and the lowest bids were as follows: residential, −4.02 percent; highway, −2.91 percent; building, −1.16 percent; and heavy, +4.33 percent.

Two factors become apparent from ranking the differences this way. First, the percentage savings are inversely proportional to the estimated degree of unionization by segment (residential, the least unionized segment, shows the highest savings, etc.). Second, the most unionized segment showed an increase rather than a decrease in its rebids. The implications of this are not only that bids tended to go down most in those areas where elimination of the Davis-Bacon requirement allowed freer competition actually to take place, but also that in those heavily unionized areas where such competition could not take place because union rates rather than prevailing rates controlled, some factors other than prevailing rates (such as actual or anticipated inflation in the cost of labor or materials) caused the bids to increase. To the degree that those factors were common to all segments of the market (and there is no reason to suppose they were not), the real savings that the elimination of Davis-Bacon would make possible are much higher than previously estimated.

Taking as the actual savings for each category the difference between the 4.33 percent increase of heavy construction and the figures noted above, weighting them by the construction volume in each category, and calculating a weighted average yields an overall savings figure of 4.74 percent. Expanded to cover the entire federal construction universe (assumed to contain the same proportional mix of project types as the sample—12 percent building, 38 percent heavy, 9 percent highway, and 41 percent residential), this yields a total savings estimate of $1.1 billion annually.

Although there are problems with this figure, it is obviously compatible with the $1 billion benchmark. It might be an overstatement because of the unknown amount of gamesmanship involved in the bid-rebid process, but even if such gamesmanship existed, it is difficult to tell in what direction it may have influenced the bidding, much less by what amount. A second problem is that the contracts involved in the rebidding during this period do not seem to be representative of all federal contracts, since they show a considerable under-representation of building projects, and over-representation of both heavy and residential projects. If the weighted average savings figure of 4.74 percent were to be applied to a synthetic distribution of contract types composed of 53 percent building projects, 19 percent heavy, 19 percent highway, and 9 percent residential, an estimated savings of $1.4 billion would result.

Another researcher, Professor John Gould of the University of Chicago, arrived independently at a similar conclusion using the same data and the same type of analysis:

> The importance of breaking down the figures from the suspension is underscored by figures assembled by Thieblot.... For a variety of projects on which new bids were submitted during the act's suspension, the new low bids were substantially higher, in particular for heavy construction projects. Even defenders of the Davis-Bacon Act do not contend that the act lowers construction costs or that the suspension of the act should result in higher costs. The higher bids are most reasonably interpreted as arising from other factors, such as changes in the expectations held by contractors about future prices and the bias that results from rebidding. If we assume that the categories that had higher average rebids give an indication of the strength of these influences, and that the remaining groups combine those influences *and* the effects of the Davis-Bacon Act, we can arrive at a measure of its net effect. Taking the lower figures, we find that

the combined influence of factors exclusive of the Davis-Bacon Act increased the lowest bids by 3 to 4 percent. Decreases in bids, again taking the lower figures, were on the order of 1 to 3 percent, these figures representing the combined influence of Davis-Bacon suspension and all other factors. The effect of Davis-Bacon alone on the basis of Thieblot's evidence should probably be placed in the neighborhood of 4 to 7 percent for a large fraction of projects. If a third of the projects are affected to this degree, then we can place the costs at between $500 million and $1 billion per year.[173]

Survey of Contractors

There has been only one extensive survey of contractors' opinions about the effects of Davis-Bacon. That was performed by the Industrial Research Unit of the University of Pennsylvania during the late spring and summer of 1974.[174] A detailed questionnaire was mailed to every other member (alphabetically by location) of the Associated General Contractors, the Associated Builders and Contractors, the American Road Builders Association, the National Electrical Contractors Association, the Associated Independent Electrical Contractors, and the Mechanical Contractors Association. Approximately 10,000 questionnaires were mailed. These associations were chosen to provide a good cross section of the construction industry. Some are oriented towards union firms, some towards open shop, some towards larger firms, some towards smaller. The National Association of Home Builders (mostly open shop) was not included because its vast number of members (about 28,000 at the time) would have skewed the results towards that sector of the industry. As a result, the residential construction sector is probably somewhat underrepresented in the study.

Just over 1,400 usable responses were received, which was considered to be a slightly better than average response rate for a survey of this kind. Each contractor was asked thirty-two questions (some with subparts) about his firm, his firm's experience with Davis-Bacon, and his opinions of several aspects of the law, of which only the middle set are of interest here. Most of the respondents (more than 80 percent) reported some direct experience with the act during the preceding two years, either as a bidder for government work or as a contractor or subcontractor on it. They had submitted an average of 25.2 bids each, and won an average of 10.1. Davis-Bacon work averaged 40.6 percent of all the work done by the group as a whole, but a few (7.6 percent) did all Davis-Bacon work, and a few (8.2 percent) did none.

---

[173] GOULD & BITTLINGMAYER, *supra* note 69, at 58–59.
[174] THIEBLOT, *supra* note 4, at 153–66.

Asked if the Davis-Bacon rates were "greatly different in either rate or benefits from your own on private work," 10.8 percent of the union firms and 78.0 percent of the nonunion firms responded affirmatively. Where Davis-Bacon had an effect, contractors reported that it raised their wage rates for selected trades by an average of 36 percent, broken down as follows: carpenters, 32.4 percent; cement masons, 31.1 percent; laborers, 40.6 percent; plumbers/pipefitters, 32.6 percent; other, 43.2 percent.

The simple average (36 percent) of these rates was taken as representative of all trades and was applied, for the approximately one-half of all the firms responding, to the 31.1 percent labor cost proportion of Davis-Bacon jobs to produce an estimate of a 5.6 percent cost increase for federal construction. Since total federal construction was taken to be $38 billion annually, the total cost impact reported was $2.1 billion. Because of the usual data problems, this number was presented in the study as an indication of order of magnitude only, and it was noted that limitations precluded analysis of size of firm or type of construction engaged in, which would have skewed the results upwards if the firms reporting increases due to Davis-Bacon requirements were the smaller firms, as was considered likely.

In terms of compatibility with the $1 billion benchmark, we might point to the fact that this study produced a 36 percent simple average wage increase, which is the same as that found by the GAO in its 1979 review. It is therefore possible that if data composition were known, and if it was similar to that used by the GAO, the weighted average wage savings might be much lower. In addition, the universe of public construction used, $38 billion, included spending by state and local polities which should probably not have been included. (More refined estimates developed since the report was written would have put the federal total at no greater than $30 billion.) In summary, although this $2.1 billion figure is higher than acceptable for compatibility with the $1 billion benchmark, it is undoubtedly an overstatement, and under some assumptions could be decreased considerably.

Econometric Analyses

Some analyses have been performed on the impact of Davis-Bacon by economists using econometric models. Econometric analyses tend to be incomprehensible to anyone other than other econometricians, and are highly dependent on the quality of the behavioral assumptions and parameters upon which all such models depend. Nevertheless, two analyses that present direct cost estimates of Davis-Bacon appear below.[175]

John P. Gould (1971).[176] Professor Gould developed a model to estimate changes in demand and wage levels in the union and nonunion sectors of the construction market that might be caused by a shift in government demand from one sector to the other, depending on the level of wages set by the prevailing wage requirement. Full use of the model required values for four elasticities, which were not available, but a very simplified application prepared by Congressman John Anderson found that Davis-Bacon determinations resulted in excessive demand for union-rate construction workers. If Davis-Bacon were eliminated, part of the excess demand would shift to the open shop sector. The difference in the equilibrium wage was 6.5 percent, which, when applied to the 6.6 billion man-hours estimated in the industry in 1970, resulted in a cost of the act to the economy of about $2.1 billion. The share of the cost to the government, which purchased or financed about 27 percent of all construction that year, was thus about $567 million.[177]

This application, besides being highly simplified, assumed that Davis-Bacon rates were all determined at the union wage; that government could take advantage of all lower rates and that wages in the unionized sector were elastic, meaning that they could respond to demand; and that government purchasing of construction is perfectly inelastic with respect to union wage rates, meaning that the government would buy the same amount of construction, regardless of project costs. Therefore, the results can only be viewed as a ballpark estimate.

As presented, the model does not contemplate any shift in workforce utilization practices by nonunion firms. If this factor and the paperwork burden factor were added, in the same way as done by the Congressional Budget Office, the result would be almost identical to that study's $1.1 billion final result.

Steven G. Allen (1983).[178] A much more sophisticated-looking demand model was created by Professor Allen in 1983. It hypothesizes a demand function for labor in which substitution of capital

---

[175] The presentations are relatively brief. We rely on the fact that for every econometrician there is an equal and opposite econometrician who will provide comprehensive analysis for the benefit of anyone who can read it.

[176] J. P. GOULD, DAVIS-BACON ACT: THE ECONOMICS OF PREVAILING WAGE LAWS (1971).

[177] THIEBLOT, *supra* note 4, at 95–97, derived from the Statement of Representative John B. Anderson (Ill.) in Subcommittee on Housing and Urban Affairs, *supra* note 15, at 391.

[178] Allen, *supra* note 153.

and nonproduction labor occurs if the price of labor is increased arbitrarily by Davis-Bacon determinations. Therefore, if Davis-Bacon were eliminated and production labor costs allowed to fall back to previous levels, savings arising from the resubstitution of production labor for capital and nonproduction labor would result, in addition to the wage savings. This savings is the measure of actual Davis-Bacon costs. It is not a sector model, like the one above, and does not contemplate the competitive effects of a shift in government demand from one sector to the other, but presumes that government purchases after elimination of Davis-Bacon would be made in the same proportion from union and open shop firms.

According to Allen, previous studies that failed to take the resubstitution factor into account underestimated the cost of Davis-Bacon:

> Previous estimates of the increased cost of public construction projects resulting from the Davis-Bacon Act have been based on the assumption of a fixed-coefficients production function. The average difference between wages in the Davis-Bacon determination and a survey estimate of the average wage in a sample of markets is multiplied by aggregate annual manhours in public construction to produce the estimate. *This procedure underestimates the cost of Davis-Bacon* because it fails to take into account the substitution of other factors for labor which takes place when wages on public projects are constrained to be above market levels.[179]

Based on the results of his model, Allen claims that "the most reasonable estimates of the increase in public construction costs resulting from inaccurate determinations are between $41 million and $224 million per year."[180] Although the highest number given here is compatible with the lowest estimated by the GAO—which also was a measure of error rate—and therefore is compatible with the $1 billion benchmark, Allen makes it clear in the text that the higher figure was calculated by the inferior, three-factor version of his demand model. The range of impact estimated by the superior, four-factor model is from $41 million to $107 million per year, which would clearly be outside the range of support for the benchmark (as well as considerably less than any other available estimates).

Part of the reason that the model produces such low results has to do with the fact that it uses as input the results of another econometric model Professor Allen designed to measure the error rate in Davis-Bacon determinations. This model attempted to measure the level of unionization in seventy-three Standard Metropol-

---

[179] *Id.* at 725 (emphasis added).
[180] *Id.* at 734.

itan Statistical Areas (SMSAs) for which rate determinations and union wage rates were known, against the level of union-rate determinations made by the Department of Labor. An arbitrary basis, varying by type of construction, was established to test whether the union rate was properly applied or if a bias towards the union rate existed in Davis-Bacon determinations.

To determine if a union-rate bias existed, Allen assumed that any segment in which unionization was over 50 percent should have had rate determinations at the union rate. (This is approximately the same logic the DOL uses in making area determinations.) This criterion was modified, however, to account for the differences in propensity of various construction sectors to unionize. Thus, if the union percentage in construction work in an SMSA were, say, 50 percent, the union percentage in heavy construction, which is heavily unionized, might be over 50 percent and that in residential construction, which is not heavily unionized, might be under 50 percent.

Allen establishes his determination of Davis-Bacon error on the assumption that various population proportions of construction worker unionization will yield a union majority at different population proportions for different types of construction. In the process, he seems to give the DOL broad leeway. For example, by his calculations the union percentage among the construction population in an SMSA could be as low as 20 percent (or 27 percent by a tighter analysis), and the DOL will have made no error if its determinations reflect the union rate as prevailing in the SMSA for heavy and highway construction projects. Similarly, for some different SMSA, no error would be attributed to the DOL if it found the union rate as prevailing for residential construction in an area where union percentage was only 44 percent (or 50 percent by the tighter rules).

This seems to contradict the logic above, which implies that a proportion greater than 50 percent would be necessary for the lightly unionized residential sector to show an effective union majority; but Allen further rationalizes that within the residential proportion of the industry, the single-family subsector is totally union free—an erroneous assumption[181]—so the multiple-family residential subsector, the only one of interest to Davis-Bacon according to him—another error[182]—would have a union majority

---

[181] NORTHRUP, *supra* note 34, at 65, estimates that the single-family residential sector of the construction market is "probably more than 90 percent" nonunion, but does not estimate it to be at or near 100 percent.

[182] Although it may be true that very few single-family projects are built under Davis-Bacon determinations, what is under discussion is not projects built, but wage

even if only 44 percent of all construction workers in the locality were unionized. Thus, in all sectors of the construction industry, by either standard of strictness, a union population proportion of 50 percent or less will yield an effective union majority, according to Allen.

By these relaxed standards, it is surprising that Allen found any error at all in the determination process. He did find a few, however:

> [T]he results indicate that the selection of union versus nonunion rates in Davis-Bacon area determinations is sensitive to percent union [i.e., unbiased]. This is especially true in the residential and heavy and highway sectors. A bias toward union rates remains in the building sector, however, and the decision rule for the other sectors seems to vary across regions. The latter phenomenon suggests that the real problem with the Wage and Hour Division's administration of Davis-Bacon is inconsistent application of existing regulations rather than, as is usually claimed, a bias toward adopting union rates regardless of percent union.[183]

Besides the loose standard being applied, the methodology contains a few other questionable features. For example, rather than being a measure of error in applying Davis-Bacon rules correctly, it is actually a measure of error in finding the union rate, applied backwards. That is, it measures the times when the union rate was determined when it was not justified, rather than the times when the determined rate was higher than the average rate or higher than the rate properly calculated by the rules (as was done by the GAO). Second, it evaluated determinations only in SMSAs, where the necessary supporting data was available. Since these are generally the most unionized areas, and since there is no error if the DOL finds the union rate in a union area, the error rate drawn from such a nonrandom sample should be expected to be low. Furthermore, the methodology applied cannot recognize the local differences that would presumably be identified by a survey of wage rates, does not realize that many construction workers working in the open shop and being paid open shop wages have union cards, and fails to consider local aberrations that might exist, such as the presence of a strong local union leader. The best that can be said of the analytical method is that it measures some aspect of the

---

rates that should be included in a survey. Because the DOL divides the residential construction sector into high- and low-rise subsectors but not into single- and multiple-family subsectors, wage information for single-family residential construction workers is included in surveys for low-rise residential determinations regardless of whether the determinations are for single- or multiple-family projects.

[183] Allen, *supra* note 153, at 724.

The Davis-Bacon Act

difference between the DOL's and Allen's perceptions of when an area is "safe union territory."

If Professor Allen used only the output from his rate-bias model as input to the demand model discussed above in order to calculate the costs of Davis-Bacon error, it might have been safe to assume that the reason his demand model's cost estimates were so low was due to the construction and assumptions applicable to the error rate determination. But Allen used the demand model to calculate estimates based on GAO rate bias figures as well,[184] which yielded equally low results. This indicates that both his error rate and his demand models may be flawed.

According to Allen, the principal function of his demand model was to capture the additional Davis-Bacon costs presumably associated with factor substitution. But in applying the model to common data, the result, rather than capturing any additional costs, seems to have lost track of some costs. Allen's impact estimate, by the superior, four-factor version of the model, was $213 million, as compared with the GAO's estimate of $228 million.[185] On this basis alone, the validity of the demand model seems suspect.

Summary of Cost Estimates

Estimates of the impact of the Davis-Bacon Act are not nearly as divergent as they might at first appear. Every estimate that has been produced in recent years is consistent with a total cost of $1 billion per year except two: one not-very-scientific survey of contractors resulted in estimates that were considerably higher, and one apparently flawed econometric model resulted in estimates that were considerably lower. Nevertheless, caution should be exercised in viewing the conclusion, for all of the studies admit to data problems in varying degrees. Even so, the $1 billion per year benchmark figure should provide a suitable order-of-magnitude estimate.

PRODUCTIVITY AND RELATED MATTERS

It has been suggested by Professors Bourdon and Levitt, of Harvard and MIT, respectively, that the real cost differences between union and nonunion labor are less than suggested by the wage rate

---

[184] The GAO used two alternative methods of expanding the error rate found in its sample of Davis-Bacon determinations. (See note 161, *supra*, and accompanying text.) Without explaining why the alternative might be unsuitable, Allen used only the GAO's more conservative method in his demand model.

[185] Allen also presents estimates of costs between $54 million and $118 million based on what he calls his "Revised GAO Estimates," which, as discussed above [note 166 *supra* and accompanying text] are methodologically suspect.

difference between them, and that the economic impact of Davis-Bacon may be overstated to the degree that it does not consider these offsets.[186] There are two principal lines to this argument: 1) higher Davis-Bacon rates may cause contractors to hire better or more productive workmen, thus cutting down on the number of manhours needed to complete the job or the level of supervision needed, and furthermore, employees have more incentive to perform well if they are being well paid; and 2) if employees are more costly as a result of Davis-Bacon, management will have greater incentive to control their time well, or to improve output by buying labor-saving devices.

Management Incentive Argument

The second of these two points can be dismissed out of hand. If it were true that artificially elevated wages produced a sort of "shock effect" on management, forcing it to be more efficient, then a wise government would impose such burdens (superminimum wage rates, special taxes or tariffs, additional paperwork requirements) on any sector of the economy it wished to foster—which of course is nonsense.[187] Furthermore, in a competitive environment such as building construction, any management will naturally make use of all its wiles, however minimal or extensive they might be, to control employee time and to augment the output of labor by whatever labor-saving devices it can afford to buy. Management's motivation is the simple one, that unless these things are done, the company will fall prey to its competition. Holding a fire to management's feet in the form of mandatory wage rates that are set higher than market rates for labor does not cause management to be smarter or more efficient, or provide it with any additional means to these ends; rather, it restricts management's options by eliminating the possibility of trading off wages for productivity, and absorbs funds that might otherwise have been available for buying labor-saving devices.

Productivity Argument

The question of whether productivity is increased by the higher wages of Davis-Bacon determinations is closely related to the larger one of whether union labor and practices are enough more produc-

---

[186] C. BOURDON & R. LEVITT, A COMPARISON OF WAGES AND LABOR MANAGEMENT PRACTICES IN UNION AND NONUNION CONSTRUCTION, Research Report No. R78-10 (Boston: MIT Department of Civil Engineering, 1978).

[187] For further discussion, see Reynolds, *supra* note 7, at 303.

tive than nonunion labor to overcome the latter's admitted cost advantage. This broader question is discussed by both sides in the Davis-Bacon debate, but need not concern us here.[188] Our interest is restricted to evaluating whether the increased wage rates associated with Davis-Bacon determinations generate offsetting productivity gains.

Exogenous Increases. No formal analysis should be required to see that with respect to labor productivity as to other things, the truism "you get what you pay for," is a syllogism and is intransitive in logic. Highly productive labor costs more: if you want to buy highly productive labor, you will have to pay more for it. But paying more for labor does not make it more productive. Summarized in colloquial terms, you get what you pay for, but you should only have to pay for what you get.

In economic terms, to the degree that the elevation of wage rates by Davis-Bacon requirements is exogenous (external) to the wage offer terms of contractors, it has no productivity effect, because exogenous change provides no motivation. If the level of wages is fixed without regard to individual productivity, that productivity will tend to be low, regardless of the level of wages.[189]

Furthermore, for reasons that have already been fully discussed, the wage impact of rate determinations is limited exclusively to increases in wages that may be required for employees of nonunion firms. The contractors who head such firms have two choices if they win a Davis-Bacon job: either they can use their current employees, paying them the exogenously determined higher rates, in which case they can expect no offsetting productivity gains; or they can replace them with other employees who, being more expensive, may be more productive. In this case, the higher wage rates are no longer independent of productivity, but can be used as motivators. Thus, the entire productivity argument hinges on the fact that higher wage rates required by Davis-Bacon may encourage nonunion contractors to replace their existing employees with "better" ones.

---

[188] See NORTHRUP, *supra* note 34, at 51–56 for a summary of the arguments on both sides. That study found that the amount of construction work going to open shop firms in almost all construction trade sectors has been increasing, indicating that the open shop sector's claims of greater effectiveness are being accepted by the private construction marketplace.

[189] An illustrative, though contrived, example is provided by the U.S. mails: Assume that it costs 23 cents to mail a letter first class from Baltimore to New York and takes three days to be delivered. If one wanted greater speed (productivity), a special delivery stamp could be bought for, say, $2.50, and one would make the decision to buy based on the value of the speed compared with its cost. But if one was required by any outside force arbitrarily to put 35-cent stamps on one's letters (or $1, for that matter), it would not cause one's letters to be delivered any faster.

Involved here are normative, structural, and operational questions. The normative questions ask why a prevailing wage law should be a vehicle for forcing contractors to alter the productivity-cost mix of his workforce from one that he was satified with to one that reflects his competitors' practices. The structural questions address the impact on the expectations and potentials for youths, minorities, women, and other workforce learners when subject to an obviously elitist requirement that trades off lower-paid but less productive employees for more highly paid, more productive ones. Even deferring both of these questions (on the grounds that they are not appropriate to the purely economic matter of whether such trade-offs actually take place) the questions of operational impact remain. First, do nonunion contractors actually replace their low-wage employees with others? Second, if so, does the replacement result in higher productivity and therefore lower wage and contract costs?

Measures of Productivity Effect

Direct evidence on worker replacement is both scanty and anecdotal. Bourdon and Levitt report that some contractors may use the higher rates of Davis-Bacon work as a reward, by assigning their better employees to government work instead of private work if the company is doing both kinds simultaneously.[190] On the other hand, our earlier study of Davis-Bacon reported conversations with contractors who declined to bid on Davis-Bacon work because "if they got themselves in a position where they had to pay the higher wages and then had to go back to privately financed construction, it would disrupt their relations with their own workers."[191] This evidence is both too scanty and too mixed to allow conclusions to be drawn one way or the other. But for the sake of argument, let us assume that some such replacement does occur. If it does, and there is a resultant impact on productivity and contract costs, then that impact should be measurable. Specifically, if other variables are controlled or eliminated by multiple regression analysis, for this thesis to be true, regardless of the mix of union and nonunion contractors,[192] buildings

---

[190] LEVITT & BOURDON, "Cost Impacts of Prevailing Wage Laws in Construction," 105 J. CONSTRUCTION DIVISION, 298, Proceedings of the American Society of Civil Engineers, (December 1979).

[191] THIEBLOT, *supra* note 4, at 86.

[192] The analysis is independent of the union status of contractors because regardless of the level of rates set, Davis-Bacon determinations have no effect on union wage rates or productivity. If, as the unions contend, higher union wage costs are already offset by increased productivity, the entire argument must center on the impact or lack of it on the nonunion sector. To the degree that union firms construct a larger

The Davis-Bacon Act

constructed under Davis-Bacon rules should cost less than comparable ones constructed privately.

We shall examine two situations in which the cost of Davis-Bacon work is compared with that done free from the prevailing wage requirement. The first, taken from a report of school construction in Florida between 1974 and 1977, is a direct but not scientific comparison of schools built before and after school construction was dropped from that state's prevailing wage law. The second, based on an extensive and carefully controlled study done at Oregon State University in 1982, compares the costs of private rural building projects with those built under Davis-Bacon rules.

Florida Schools Report. In 1974, the Florida Legislature exempted construction by school boards and community colleges from the requirement of the state's prevailing wage law. These are projects which are totally state funded, and therefore do not carry Davis-Bacon provisions in the absence of state law requirements. In 1978, a bill was filed in the state senate providing that school board construction again be included under prevailing wage. In an effort to defeat this measure, many school boards calculated their total construction during the three years since repeal and developed an estimate of the savings due to the exemption.

The figures provided by twenty-two counties were compiled by the State School Board Association in 1978. Although unverified and unaudited, they were thought by the association to be representative. Total school construction during the period was $242.7 million, which county school boards estimated would have cost $37.0 million more, had the prevailing wage law still been applicable. In individual counties, the cost differences ranged from 2 percent to 25 percent, and the average for all counties was 15 percent.

Although prior to its repeal in 1979 the Florida statute calculated prevailing rates on the same basis as Davis-Bacon (using the 30-percent rule), the savings figure estimated here may not be indicative of what would happen nationally, because only a single type of construction was included. Additionally, there is room to question the accuracy of the estimates. Nevertheless, the figures give very little support to the contention that prevailing wage requirements might not raise project costs because the higher wages bring about offsetting gains in work productivity. It might also be noted that repeal of the Florida law in 1979 was greatly influenced by the possibility of similar savings on other state projects. In the six years

---

portion of Davis-Bacon work than of private work, therefore, the total impact of cost saving might be diminished, but it would not be eliminated unless union firms did all of the Davis-Bacon work.

since that repeal, although there have been several bills to reinstate the act, the state has apparently been satisfied that savings have occurred, since none of the reinstatement efforts have been successful.[193]

Oregon State University Study.[194] In 1982, three professors from Oregon State University collaborated on one of the most extensive researches done to date on Davis-Bacon. Their study uses a multiple regression model to estimate the total project cost differences (as a measure of savings that could result from eliminating Davis-Bacon) for nonresidential buildings in nonmetropolitan areas of the United States.[195] By going directly to the cost of construction, the study sought to bypass the problems associated with assumptions regarding cost composition, factor substitution, productivity effects and the like.

To develop a data base, face-to-face interviews with contractors were required. First, a representative number of counties which fit the definition of rural (meaning, in general, that they were not part of an SMSA) was selected from all regions of the country in proportion to the rural population in each region. Next, as complete a list as possible was prepared of all of the Davis-Bacon construction projects completed in those counties in 1977 or 1978, which were stratified as to type and size. Only building projects were included, excluding residential projects of any size, and heavy and highway projects. Another list was prepared of all of the private projects completed in the counties, stratified in the same way. If a match existed for one pair of projects of each type, that pair was included in the sample. If more than a single pair was found, a match was randomly selected. If no match was found, the search was extended to other parts of the same region. In this way, 537 projects were selected, half Davis-Bacon and half private, with respect to which 215 interviews were conducted, about evenly divided between Davis-Bacon and private work.

A multiple regression model was constructed to estimate the effect of the Davis-Bacon Act on construction costs after correcting for project scale, technical characteristics (seventy-three individual alternatives for twelve major components such as the number of stories, type of foundation, or bearing wall construction) building type (office commercial, industrial, storage, medical, amusement,

---

[193] See discussion of Florida state prevailing wage law in Ch. IV, *infra*.

[194] FRAUNDORF, FARRELL, & MASON, *supra* note 162. Summarized in Fraundorf, Farrell, & Mason, *The Effect of the Davis-Bacon Act on Construction Costs in Rural Areas*, 66 REV. ECON. & STATISTICS 142–46 (February 1984).

[195] The reason for the nonmetropolitan (rural) orientation of the study is that it was funded by a grant from the American Farm Bureau Federation.

or other), and region (Northeast, North Central, South, or West) in which the project was located.

The results of the study showed the impact of Davis-Bacon to be much larger than expected. It found that Davis-Bacon Act requirements caused wage rates on 24.8 percent of the public projects to increase by 12.9 to 23.2 percent. The authors were also surprised to find that the increases in total construction costs were even greater than the wage rate differences, ranging from 26.1 to 37.7 percent. Variables such as firm profit margins, the cost of paperwork, and the sometimes excessive cost associated with hiring minority subcontractors, had already been factored into the model, leading the authors to conclude that the total project costs increased more than wage rates as a result of the limitations Davis-Bacon imposes on work assignment.

Overall, the study found that the cost per square foot for the public projects in the sample was $41.12, considerably higher than the $33.90 found for private projects. Although the authors were careful to point out that the magnitude of the differences discovered might have been influenced by the fact that their sample was drawn exclusively from rural areas and was composed entirely of building construction projects, both of which are likely to be more influenced by Davis-Bacon determinations than some other alternatives might be, and that some of the difference might be attributable to specific federal requirements for quality, safety, or affirmative action, which would always apply whenever Davis-Bacon applied, they are satisfied that the results are valid for the projects studied.

The conclusions of this study support (and are supported by) those drawn independently from totally different data sources by the Congressional Budget Office, which has also determined the cost of work assignment restrictions to be greater than the cost of wage differences. By the same token, the conclusions provide no support whatsoever for the unions' contention that productivity gains might offset wage rate differences.

Summary of Cost-Related Questions

All but two of the major studies of Davis-Bacon costs that have been undertaken during the past few years are consistent with a benchmark total cost of $1 billion per year. Of the two that are not consistent, one estimates the costs to be higher and one estimates them to be lower than the benchmark. The increased wages required by Davis-Bacon are not offset by increases in productivity. In fact, both of the two studies from which comparisons can be made of wage rates and total project costs show that total costs increase by larger percentage amounts than do wage rates, which leads to the opposite conclusion.

POLICY CONSIDERATIONS

Analysis of Davis-Bacon implementation and administration has indicated that the act is poorly administered, and is likely to remain so, despite recent efforts by the DOL to ease its burdens. Analysis of its economic impact has indicated that the act's requirements drive up costs on federal projects by amounts on the order of $1 billion per year. In the face of these damaging findings, it remains only to see if the act achieves its original purpose, or offers any social advantages which are not already provided by other legislation.

Original Purpose—Stated Rationale of the Act

The stated rationale for the Davis-Bacon Act, as developed in 1931, was one of protecting local contractors and local labor from the predations of itinerant, low-wage contractors. Although it is not known why this should be a socially desirable effect for the heavy, highway, or specialty construction segments of the industry, it has appeal in the residential and commercial sectors where there is at least the likelihood of having a local industry to protect. Since the very existence of itinerant, low-wage contractors is problematic in the current economy, Davis-Bacon easily achieves this purpose, but in the same trivial sense that a pussycat succeeds in keeping the house free from elephants.

Nevertheless, the more vociferous supporters of Davis-Bacon see the act as a means of preventing reversion to "the chaotic conditions of the early 1930s with itinerant contractors traveling from locality to locality, underbidding local contractors and causing local unemployment."[196] Until recently, the impact of Davis-Bacon on preserving federal contracts in an area for local contractors was unknown, and proponents and opponents of the act were compelled to trade conclusions derived from feelings, opinions, and inferences. Since 1979, however, two empirical studies have provided evidence on the question of whether the act improves the opportunities of local contractors to be the successful bidder on federal projects. In both cases, they have found that it does not.

---

[196] Statement of Frank Bonadio, President, Building and Construction Trades Department, AFL-CIO.

The Davis-Bacon Act

The Oregon State University study of paired federal and private building construction projects in rural areas found that a significantly higher percentage of the federal projects went to outsiders:

> There appears to be some validity to the charge that the way the Davis-Bacon Act is now administered puts local contractors at a disadvantage instead of ensuring local firms and residents their share of the jobs as the law apparently intended. Compared to contractors on private projects, contractors on public projects are less likely to be within the same county as the project. Only 27.8% of the public buildings were built by local contractors, compared to 46.6% of the private ones, a statistically significant difference. ... If we use private project experience as a guide to what would happen in the absence of Davis-Bacon, the Act does seem to have the effect of making it more difficult for local contractors to successfully bid on public projects.[197]

The other study, by the General Accounting Office, found similar evidence of Davis-Bacon working in reverse from its intended effect. In the GAO's comparisons of thirty Davis-Bacon determinations, it found twelve determinations to be above the actual prevailing rate in the locality, and eighteen to be below. For the twelve that were too high, the majority of the projects performed (and all of the projects performed in the smaller of the counties by population) were done by nonlocal contractors. For these, the GAO noted, "The higher rates may have had an adverse effect on competition by discouraging some local contractors from bidding on the projects."[198] On the other hand, in the eighteen counties for which the rates were below those actually prevailing in the community, local contractors were the successful bidders on fifteen of the eighteen projects. "Thus, the act's intent—to maintain the local prevailing wage structure—was carried out when Labor established rates that were lower than those prevailing in the communities."[199]

The GAO found no instances where outside contractors took advantage of the low rates by importing low-paid workers into the locality. This led to the final conclusions, expressed by the comptroller general: "Thus, we found that the act's intent—to maintain the local prevailing wage structure—is carried out only when the administration of the act has no effect."[200]

---

[197] FRAUNDORF, FARRELL, & MASON, *supra* note 162, at 17–18.
[198] GENERAL ACCOUNTING OFFICE, *supra* note 3, at 72.
[199] *Id.* at 75.
[200] *Hearings, supra* note 74, at 8 (statement of Elmer B. Staats).

Imputed Purpose of the Act

The above examples demonstrate clearly that the stated purpose of the Davis-Bacon Act is not being effectively carried out. Another purpose, however, has been imputed to Davis-Bacon by its adherents in more recent times. Former Secretary of Labor Ray Marshall formulated this position in an informal, but apparently complete, way in an interview granted in 1981 to a union magazine:

> The basic rationale for the Davis-Bacon law is really quite simple. It is based on the idea that the federal government should not use taxpayers' money to undercut local area employment conditions.[201]

Asked to explain how Davis-Bacon achieved this purpose, Secretary Marshall gave his opinion that without the protection to local wage standards offered by prevailing rate requirements, the competition for government business would "drive down wages,"[202] Thus:

> [U]nder the pressure of competition, in the search for business—when the employer has practically no control over these other major cost factors [such as land, materials, and interest rates]—he will seek to underbid his competitors and still make a profit by reducing his wage bill, by cutting wages. And since there tends always to be a pool of unemployed workers competing for available jobs, the employers who are inclined in this direction will be able to hire workers at substandard rates of pay.[203]

As hypothesized by Marshall, these "substandard rates of pay" would spread through the industry:

> In order to compete, other contractors would be forced to lower their bid prices, and they, too, would be compelled to pay substandard wages.[204]

The prevailing rate requirement eliminates this competition and "[s]o far as wages are concerned, . . . puts all bidders for the federal construction dollar on an equal footing."[205]

The impact envisioned by Marshall of the elimination of the Davis-Bacon Act would be considerable and far reaching:

> Can you imagine what the impact would be if the federal government permitted its construction dollars to be used [in this way to] undercut prevailing pay standards? We would be helping to drive down wages

---

[201] *Davis-Bacon Works and Works Well!: An Interview with Former U.S. Labor Secretary Ray Marshall*, 3 BUILDERS SPECIAL REP. np. (March 7, 1981).
[202] *Id.* Secretary Marshall also refers to this elsewhere as "wage busting."
[203] *Id.*
[204] *Id.*
[205] *Id.*

The Davis-Bacon Act

in any community in which such federal or federally-assisted construction was taking place, and it wouldn't take very long for this to be felt by the merchants in those communities—that is, by the people who own the shops, the stores, and the markets where construction workers spend their income.[206]

We believe that this is a fair statement of the secretary's (and the unions') principal defense of Davis-Bacon on policy grounds: irrespective of the quality, accuracy, or fairness of Davis-Bacon administration, and independent of any additional costs that might be incurred on government buildings as a result of it, the act is necessary because, without it, the pressures of competition for government work cause contractors to offer substandard wages as the only way to achieve low bids, since they cannot control their other factor costs.

There are two flaws in this line of argument, both of them fatal. The first is supplied by the secretary, himself. With respect to the costs of Davis-Bacon, Secretary Marshall argued that the productivity factor was being overlooked:

> The claim ... that lower wages produce lower costs assumes you get the same quality of labor, regardless of the pay scale. That just isn't so. The more skilled workers will shun the lower paying jobs and gravitate toward the jobs where the pay is higher. ... If lower wages mean less productive labor, the end result can be higher total labor costs for any construction project. This is because the contractor paying lower wages will have to employ more labor to handle any given project.[207]

If this point is true, then the secretary must concede that only a stupid contractor would attempt to produce a low competitive bid by deliberately seeking low-wage employees, much less offer substandard wages.[208] Unless he is willing to claim that the relationship between wage rates and productivity is known only to union contractors, he cannot simultaneously maintain that it exists but would not affect the bidding process. Therefore, there is a clear alternative to contractors lowering wage rates in order to get bids, and his contention that this is the contractor's only recourse is not supportable.

As one critic of the act has noted, if the relationship between productivity and price exists as the secretary claims it does, the act is unnecessary:

---

[206] *Id.*
[207] *Id.*
[208] Although in this same interview, Secretary Marshall characterizes nonunion contractors as "incompetent," he apparently means this to apply to the hypothesized quality of their output (requiring higher maintenance and repair costs after the project is completed) rather than to their ability to calculate low-cost bids.

> [The relationship] implicitly assumes that those closest to the situation, *i.e.,* contractors, lack the elementary business acumen to make productivity decisions on their own. Certainly, a contractor would realize that if a worker demands a 40% higher wage, but was 60% more productive, it would be in the contractor's interest to hire the higher paid worker since the costs per unit of output would be lower. The statute in this case would be superfluous.[209]

It might be argued that we hoist ourselves on the same petard as the secretary, since we found earlier that the secretary was incorrect also in his hypothesis that productivity differences offset wage differences in Davis-Bacon cost analysis. But this is not the case. Our earlier analysis found only that arbitrarily high wage rates do not cause or induce offsetting increases in productivity. We not only acknowledge a general relationship between productivity and wage rates (quality and price), we insist on it. Furthermore, we suggest that improper understanding of the relationship is the second fatal flaw in the secretary's argument.

As anyone familiar with the construction industry can attest, a substantial portion of many skilled jobs involves unskilled or at most semi-skilled work. For example, sweeping the debris off of a roof before the roofers begin their task is a job that can be done by a helper in an open shop firm, but only by a journeyman in the union environment. There is, therefore, ample room for less skilled personnel without affecting in any way the quality of construction output. Skill, training, and experience are not necessary for sweeping debris, nor is the quality of a swept area improved for having been swept by a journeyman at $15 an hour instead of a helper at $6.

In hypothesizing a situation in which contractors hold down bids by offering low wage rates, Secretary Marshall overlooks entirely the possibility that lower wages might be offered for lower skills. He assumes that the only way a contractor can be competitive is to undercut wage rates, "driving down wages" in the industry; in doing so, he overlooks the principal economic advantage enjoyed by open shop firms, that of flexibility in work assignments.

Other Policy Issues

As the basic arguments over Davis-Bacon have developed, both proponents and opponents have discovered additional policy considerations involving such matters as skill development in the construction trades, minority employment, the quality of construction,

---

[209] Schulman, *supra* note 8, at 32.

construction wages, and contractors' profits. Most of the considerations raised in these arguments are basic issues of union versus nonunion building practices, and fuller discussion of them all is available in this broader context from a variety of sources.[210] Although they deal with important topics, they are peripheral to the main analysis of Davis-Bacon, whose impact on them is limited to the degree to which the act serves as a union-protective measure rather than a wage-setting measure. For these reasons, our coverage is limited to a brief overview.

Construction Quality. Former Secretary of Labor Ray Marshall, among others, has suggested that the Davis-Bacon Act is needed because without it "government construction work could go to incompetent contractors who would be competitive only by virtue of the lower wages,"[211] whose putatively shoddy buildings would require higher maintenance and repair costs. This is a familiar claim of the unions, and has arisen frequently in state prevailing wage hearings as well as federal ones, but has never to our knowledge been supported by other than anecdotal evidence. Such evidence is necessarily suspect, because it is not difficult to find specific examples of both well and poorly constructed buildings built by either union or nonunion workmen.

Empirical analysis is also difficult because of the number of variables involved in product quality, including the precision of product specifications, differing abilities among architects and engineers, imposed time and budgetary constraints, and lack of an objective standard of acceptable quality. There is in the literature, however, one econometric analysis of the impact of Davis-Bacon on product quality. Based on hypothesizing a penalty associated with not meeting the desired quality standard, that study concludes that "the 'construction quality' argument for the Davis-Bacon Act is seriously flawed, since quality may in fact fall because of Davis-Bacon coverage."[212]

One reason for this, although not cited in that study, was included in the above discussion on wage-productivity relationships. That is, that a large proportion of many construction jobs is unskilled work such as sweeping, unloading, carrying, and the like, which have no relationship to product quality, whether they are done well or poorly, by high-priced or low-priced workmen.

---

[210] See for example, NORTHRUP, *supra* note 34, *passim.*
[211] *Davis-Bacon Works, supra* note 200.
[212] Metzger & Goldfarb, *Do Davis-Bacon Minimum Wages Raise Product Quality?* 4 J. LAB. RESEARCH 265 (Summer 1983).

The broader marketplace of private construction provides additional evidence. Buyers in the private market must continually make decisions as to whether to buy union or open shop, and these decisions are typically predicated on the reputation and past performance of the contractors under consideration. It would be fair to assume that acceptable quality output is a part of this. Since open shop firms are doing an increasing proportion of private construction work, especially in the residential and building sectors, but also in highway and heavy, one must conclude that if there is a difference in quality of output, it is more than compensated for by the decreased cost.

If government would rather not make this trade-off in a similar fashion, but insists on quality regardless of the cost, even in this case the Davis-Bacon Act is a poor quality control device. A better alternative than Davis-Bacon is direct control of output quality through the procurement system. The specifications on which contractors bid can, and in fact already do, contain mandatory output quality standards covering such matters as safety and environmental features as well as selection of materials, required strengths, mandatory ratings, and the like.

Construction Wages. The unions have suggested that Davis-Bacon is needed in order to maintain wage levels in an unstable industry, and that without it there would be a tendency for wages to fall. This contention again neglects the evidence of the 75 percent of the industry that is not covered by prevailing wage requirements. Furthermore, construction workers are among the best paid in the nation. Weekly earnings in construction were $398 in 1981, compared with $318 in manufacturing. Although construction workers typically do not work a full year, in a given year one-half of all construction workers will have earnings outside the industry, and one-half of those who work outside the industry will earn more money there than in construction. This led one author to conclude that the net effect of Davis-Bacon in "[p]roviding a 'superminimum' wage to a group with above average earnings is tantamount to a perverse subsidy—the 'poorer' subsidizing the 'richer.' "[213]

Contractors' Profits. Davis-Bacon or the lack of it seems to have no impact on the rate of contractors' profits. The Oregon State University study of comparative Davis-Bacon and private construction projects found that the profit on public projects was 8.7 percent of project cost, and on private projects was 8.5 percent.[214] This small percentage difference is not statistically significant, from which it

---

[213] Schulman, *supra* note 8, at 39.
[214] FRAUNDORF, FARRELL, & MASON, *supra* note 162, at 24.

may be concluded that the rate of profit is about the same on public or private projects. But the study also found Davis-Bacon jobs to be 26.1 to 37.7 percent costlier than equivalent private ones,[215] indicating that the dollar amount of profits on Davis-Bacon work is considerably more than it would be on the same job done privately.

Thus, in arguing for repeal of Davis-Bacon instead of for some middle alternative such as rate determinations based on survey averages, which would achieve the same competitive advantage over union firms while retaining artificially high wages and costs (and therefore profits), open shop contractors demonstrate that they are motivated by something other than the desire for maximum profits that is sometimes attributed to them.

Minority Employment. Davis-Bacon opponents have maintained that to the degree that the act imposes arbitrarily high wage rates and inflates the cost of government projects, minority groups and those without jobs are the most negatively affected, both through decreased job opportunities and, in the case of all disadvantaged groups, the diminished amount of subsidized housing being built.[216] It has also been noted that prevailing wage requirements are sometimes onerously imposed on neighborhood self-help homesteading projects and on construction projects on Indian reservations.[217]

Davis-Bacon affects job opportunities in two ways. First, the route to journeyman status is more readily available in open shop than in union firms. Second, the work rule restrictions of Davis-Bacon eliminate helpers and trainees and promote their unemployment where they were previously employed. In the words of one contractor:

> We simply cannot pay ... over $13.00 an hour to an individual to carry electrical conduit or unload lighting fixtures. If we have to pay that kind of rate, we will simply have to put our journeymen electricians on those chores since they can do other work at other times.[218]

The unions counter with the argument that repeal of the act would produce instability within the construction industry, adversely affecting apprenticeship programs in the union sector, thus hurting minority trainees, and furthermore, that a "low-wage, migratory firm employing the cheapest available labor on an ad hoc

---

[215] *Id.* at 27.

[216] Schulman, *supra* note 8, at 36.

[217] Keyes, *The Minimum Wage and the Davis-Bacon Act: Employment Effects on Minorities and Youth*, 3 J. LAB. RESEARCH 404 (Fall 1982).

[218] "Impact of the Davis-Bacon Threshold on Small Business Construction Contracts," Hearings Before the Subcommittee on Government Procurement, February 2, 1982 at 96, cited in Schulman, *supra* note 8, at 37.

basis may have little interest in human capital development."[219] They also maintain that their apprenticeship programs indenture higher proportions of minorities than those of open shop contractors.[220]

In rebuttal, three observations are offered. First, one would much more likely find minorities among the helpers and trainees of non-union firms than in the registered apprenticeship programs. Second, the only prominent black economist known to have taken an opinion on Davis-Bacon favors its repeal because, "to the extent that the Davis-Bacon Act discriminates against the non-union sector of the construction work force, blacks bear the heaviest burden of the discrimination."[221] Third, based on Bureau of Labor Statistics figures, minorities are underrepresented in construction craft labor unions. As of 1980, minorities constituted 9 percent of the construction workers and 9.4 percent of that industry's union-represented workers; among carpenters, however, minorities were 7.4 percent of the labor force, but only 5.2 percent of union-represented workers; and for construction craft workers except carpenters, minorities were 10.8 percent of the labor force, but only 8.5 percent of those union represented. These statistics indicate that open shop firms employed a higher proportion of minority workers as craftsmen.[222]

Test of the Impact of Repeal

Short of actually repealing the Davis-Bacon Act and observing the result, there is no convenient way to determine absolutely the impact such a repeal would have. There are three factors, however, which give strong support to the contention of opponents that the effect would be minimal.

First, the Davis-Bacon Act does not apply to all construction work, but only to that portion of it performed for the federal government, which is no more than 25 percent of the total. The other 75 percent is done without the protection of prevailing rates. The majority of private construction work is contracted in about the same way that federal work is contracted, in that plans and specifications are

---

[219] Whittaker & Bolle, *The Davis-Bacon Act: Consideration During the 97th Congress,* Issue Brief IB 81038, Congressional Research Service, Library of Congress (March 10, 1981) at 5.
[220] Georgine, *supra* note 128, at 29.
[221] *Davis-Bacon Hurts Minority Groups, Economist Declares,* Washington Post, May 18, 1981. The economist is Dr. Walter E. Williams, Professor of Economics at Temple and George Mason universities.
[222] NORTHRUP, *supra* note 34, at 539.

drawn up and then put out to bid, with the contract typically going to the lowest bidder.[223]

In the private sector of the construction industry, there seems to be ample room for both unionized and open shop firms, despite wage rate differences of as much as 40 percent between the two. There is no evidence of low-wage itinerants swooping into local areas and taking away all the private work from local contractors, and in fact local contractors perform a higher percentage of private contracts than they do of Davis-Bacon jobs. Union contractors dominate the heavy construction field, and are a very strong presence in highway and in building construction. Hourly union construction craft wages are among the highest of any blue-collar occupation. In short, the private sector of the construction industry, both union and open shop, seems to be holding its own even though it is free from Davis-Bacon protection.

Furthermore, the Davis-Bacon Act does not apply to all public construction, but only to that portion of it that is federally involved. State prevailing wage laws apply to the construction of schools, prisons, roads, and other projects that have no federal involvement. Beginning with Florida in 1979, seven states have repealed their state prevailing wage laws, without observable consequence to the contractors or construction workers of those states.

Finally, not all prevailing wage laws affecting federal procurement are effective. Wage determinations have not been issued under the Walsh-Healey Act since 1964. Nevertheless, chaos does not reign in the material and supply industries which used to have prevailing wage protection.

SUMMARY AND RECOMMENDATIONS

The Davis-Bacon Act is badly administered, and probably is too complex to be administered well, regardless of the administrative effort made. It is an expensive piece of legislation, adding perhaps $1 billion a year to the cost of federal building projects. It does not fulfill either its original stated purpose or other purposes that have

---

[223] There are, to be sure, times when a private party can decide to use a contractor other than the lowest-bidder—an option that is not directly available to the government. But as anyone familiar with government contracting can attest, the bidding system is far from a pure price competition to which all are invited. See, for example, Thieblot, *Government Interference with the Development of Small Business,* Center for the Study of American Business, Washington University (mimeo) (1975), which outlines several cases where low-price bidders on government contracts were denied them on various technicalities. These were all contracts for supply items rather than construction, but the principle is the same.

been imputed to it. Eliminating it will not disrupt the economy or the construction industry, although it might be more difficult for building trade unions to maintain practices that are not cost effective. For these reasons, it seems clear that Davis-Bacon is an idea whose time is past, and that it ought to be repealed.

If Davis-Bacon is repealed, some other federal laws must be repealed as well. The Copeland (Anti-Kickback) Act should be repealed as no longer germane, or at the very least that section of it requiring weekly wage reporting should be rescinded. Additionally, the appropriate sections of the federal-aid programs which specify Davis-Bacon rates on their construction projects should also be rescinded. The repeal bill should exert federal preemption over state prevailing wage laws, as was done during the Davis-Bacon suspension in 1971, so that joint federal-state projects would be free from prevailing wage requirements regardless of the status of the states' laws.

To vitalize the construction industry thoroughly, we would also recommend rescinding the sections of the Contract Work Hours and Safety Standards Act requiring overtime pay for work in excess of eight hours in any one day, and modifying the Miller Act (requiring performance bonds for contractors on contracts of over $25,000) to eliminate the double standard that currently exists for federal-aid projects, so that state or agency standards will apply on all federal-aid projects regardless of amount, rather than only on those costing less than $100,000, as is now the case. At the present time, on jobs costing over $100,000, both bonding laws must be complied with.

Alternatives Short of Repeal

Although the results of this study indicated the desirability of outright repeal of the Davis-Bacon Act, there are those who feel that its administration can be improved enough to make it palatable, or who feel that too much risk is involved in eliminating it entirely. Below are twelve alternatives short of repeal that might be considered either individually or in various combinations as fallback positions. Although we have tried to sort out their major impacts and explain their merits, additional analysis would generally be necessary to refine them sufficiently for actual legislative consideration.

Increase Contract Threshold. Increasing the cost threshold for activating applicability of Davis-Bacon to some substantial amount, such as $1 million, would greatly reduce the number of Davis-Bacon projects to administer but would nevertheless preserve the act's applicability to the majority of federal spending. It is estimated that only 4 percent of the contracts under Davis-Bacon are for $1 million or more, but these account for 60 percent of all construction dollars spent.[224]

Increasing the threshold would also improve the potential for accurate wage determinations, since conceivably all wage rates could be based on actual surveys. On the other hand, such a raise would not be in keeping with the original rationale of the act's threshold, which was to exclude only contracts considered too small to disrupt a community's wage structure or living standards.

Define Prevailing as Average. The Congressional Budget Office estimates that modifying Davis-Bacon to include a definition of the prevailing rate as meaning the average of all rates for workmen doing similar work on similar projects in the locality would achieve about 8 percent of the savings attributable to full repeal of the act.[225] Savings of even this amount would be worthwhile, but such an approach would leave untouched all of the administrative and cost problems associated with the act except those associated with rate determinations not based on surveys. It would further increase the administrative burden on the DOL by requiring a greater number of surveys of a larger number of rates, and would tend to leave problems in place for nonunion contractors, add problems for union contractors, and save the government relatively little. Furthermore, there is no more essential logic to using the average rate as the minimum for all determinations than there is now to using it on some determinations.

Change to Pre-Existing Wage. If the intent of the Davis-Bacon Act is to prevent contractors from debasing their wage rates in their effort to achieve the lowest bid, that purpose can be achieved by changing the law from a prevailing wage concept to a pre-existing wage concept. Under this concept, every contractor might be required to submit a certified copy of a payroll record along with his bid, and agree to a stipulation that no wage of any employee on the federal project would be less than the corresponding wage included on the record. Any craft or class of employee not covered on the payroll record would be paid a rate at least equal to the nearest equivalent class of employee included on the record. A table of equivalences could be constructed similar to those now used by the DOL in grouping equipment operator rates in heavy construction determinations.

Admittedly, this alternative does not speak to the question of low-wage itinerant contractors, but the evidence indicates that these

---

[224] CONGRESSIONAL BUDGET OFFICE, *supra* note 52, at 35.
[225] *Id.* at 36.

are somewhere between rare and mythical, and are certainly not a major factor in the industry. Otherwise, the alternative achieves most of the economic effect of repeal without eliminating protection from competitively lowered wages.

Change to "Prevailing Minimum" Law. Amending the Davis-Bacon Act by adding the word "minimum," so that it would require payment of wages "determined by the secretary of labor to be the prevailing *minimum* wages for the corresponding classes of laborers and mechanics," would be easy to do and would bring the language into line with that of the Walsh-Healey Act. For this revised standard to be effective, however, some other modifications would be necessary, because the definition of prevailing as currently applied has the curious characteristic of being unable to distinguish between minimum and maximum: by either its old or its current rules, it would identify the prevailing minimum wage, the prevailing wage, and the prevailing maximum wage as being the same number.

If construction wage rates followed a statistically normal distribution, it would be easy enough to define the prevailing minimum as, perhaps, the rate which occurred closest to the point two standard deviations below the mean; but construction wage rate distributions tend to be bi-polar, with one pole at the union rate and another at the mean of the normally distributed nonunion rates. Therefore, the prevailing minimum would have to be defined as something like the average of the nonunion rates.

Set Rates for Laborers Only. Another amendment that could be readily made is replacing the words "corresponding classes of laborers and mechanics employed on projects of a character similar" with the word "laborers." With this change, the act would require payment of prevailing wages to various classes of laborers and mechanics at rates determined by the secretary of labor to be no less than those prevailing for laborers employed in the city, town, etc.

This amendment would allow the wisdom of the market to establish rates for all other job categories, depending on their traditional relationship to the laborer's rate. Naturally, one would hope to find all journeymen's rates higher than laborers' rates, and most helpers', apprentices', or trainees' rates lower. (Since helpers, apprentices, or trainees are not "classes of laborers or mechanics," their rates would float freely, and could be less than the rate set for laborers.) But if this did not happen on some particular contract because a contractor decided to classify all of his journeymen as helpers and pay them all less than laborers, it is likely that his journeymen would be able to settle the score without help from the government.

Although this proposal might sound a bit odd, it is essentially the mechanism by which Walsh-Healey set rates—for the lowest-paid workmen only. It is a totally reasonable and realistic alternative, and one that would eliminate many of the arbitrary decisions now forced on wage specialists in categorizing employees and project types; it would cut down on the administrative burden of wage surveys by dramatically reducing the number of different rates under consideration from as many as several hundred to one; and it would come closer than any other modification short of repeal to providing a floor under wages while disrupting local practices as little as possible.

Use Whole Dollars. If in wage surveys reported rates were rounded down to the nearest dollar, the rate-to-the-penny problem would be assuaged. The current practice, which sometimes goes to fractions of a cent, gives a false aura of accuracy to determinations that seldom actually have this characteristic.

Provide Rates for All Jobs. Work assignment restrictions that accompany Davis-Bacon determinations are responsible for much of the cost of the act and much of the dissatisfaction with it voiced by nonunion contractors. These could be eased by adding the word "all" at the appropriate place, so the secretary of labor would be required to determine the prevailing rate for "all corresponding classes" of workmen and defining the classes to include helpers, construction mechanics, pipelayers, or whatever other titles actually exist and are found in surveys. Not every contractor would make use of all of the titles, but this is often true under current practice, especially in area determinations. An easier way to accomplish the same end is provided by the next alternative.

Eliminate Nonprevailing Rates. Under the Walsh-Healey Act, if a prevailing rate has not been determined by the secretary of labor, the contractor was free to pay the market rate. The same effect could be achieved under Davis-Bacon by recognizing that in many instances, a prevailing rate simply does not exist in a locality, and when that is the case there are no local wage standards to uphold, so no arbitrary wage rate should be applied. This alternative is a bit broader than the preceding one, in that it would allow floating rates for helpers and other categories not now determined but would also permit floating rates for unusual trades, the rates for which are now often set based on only one or two surveyed wages. Accompanying this change might be formal guidelines to the secretary as to the sample size needed to ensure adequacy in determining a particular rate, as in the next alternative.

Require Surveys. Require all rates to be set by survey, and establish a minimum number of sample rates to be found before determining a rate. A reasonable number might be at least a dozen rates from at least three different sources. This alternative cannot stand alone, since there will be times when in a given county fewer than that number of rates will be available. It is probably best used in conjunction with the preceding alternative.

Require Verified Rates. It is a common practice for some union locals to negotiate a wage rate and then offer contractors what amounts to a discount from the negotiated rate to enable them to bid jobs away from open shop firms. This practice should be forestalled lest it establish a two-tiered union rate schedule with the higher applicable to government jobs only. This could be done by requiring that wage rates used in samples be verified as having actually been paid. Since the DOL maintains that it currently verifies wage rates (although the evidence is to the contrary), this alternative would have to be accompanied by one or another of the oversight alternatives that follow.

Determinations on the Record. An amendment made to the Walsh-Healey Act in 1952 required that wage determinations under that act be made "on the record," meaning that some formal method is established to ensure that the rates are fairly and accurately determined. If Davis-Bacon were similarly modified, it would have the effect of increasing the accuracy of determinations and eliminating many of the arbitrary shortcuts now taken by wage specialists.

Under present administrative rules for Davis-Bacon, however, such a requirement might be impossible for the DOL to fulfill because of the vast number of determinations needed. This would probably lead to a situation similar to Walsh-Healey's where no rates are determined. Therefore, it would have to be coupled with some provision to cut down on the number of determinations required. It might be used, for example, in conjunction with an increase in the contract threshold to $1 million, or with a provision that allowed work to be done at market rates unless prevailing rates had been determined.

Audit Determinations. As an alternative to the foregoing, an annual review by some auditing agency (such as the GAO or a reconstituted Wage Appeals Board) of a sample of the determinations made in the previous period would probably yield superior accuracy and fairness, particularly if the results of the audit (along with responses documenting corrective action to be taken with respect to any problems found) were made public. If this were done, the reappearance of similar problems in later determinations could provide a litigable basis for adjudication.

Summary

Many other possibilities exist for modifications to the Davis-Bacon Act that fall short of total repeal. All of them have some merit in terms of relieving problems that the act has been observed to cause, or of saving some portion of the excess costs it imposes on government construction. The very fact that there are so many plausible modifications lends additional support to the conclusion that the only effective cure for the ills produced by the Davis-Bacon Act is its elimination.

CHAPTER IV

State Prevailing Wage Laws[1]

The Tenth Amendment to the Constitution limits the ability of the federal government to dictate contract terms selectively for the states. Therefore, public works contracts in which the federal government does not have a direct interest, that are entered into by states or by local polities such as cities or school districts, cannot be made subject to provisions of the Davis-Bacon Act or other federal prevailing wage legislation. States desiring to have wage requirements similar to those of the federal laws for public contracting in their own jurisdictions must establish such requirements through state legislation.

Not all states have chosen to establish prevailing wage laws, and not all of those that have enacted such legislation have followed the example set by the federal statutes. Where they do exist, state prevailing wage laws tend to be almost exclusively for public works construction, and are, in effect, little Davis-Bacon acts. The Walsh-Healey and Service Contract Acts have no counterparts at the state level, although a few state prevailing wage laws do cover employees other than construction workers.

State prevailing wage laws are highly dissimilar. They are alike only in that all of them set some level of super-minimum wage rates for construction workers on public works. Even those state prevailing wage laws patterned on the federal Davis-Bacon Act usually contain concepts, definitions, procedures, or rules so changed from the original that no standard form can be said to exist. The thirty-five little Davis-Bacon acts (those of thirty-four states plus that of the District of Columbia) are all effectively different, tied together by little more than a common name.

This chapter analyzes all of the state prevailing wage laws. The first section examines their history and characteristics collectively.

---

[1] Materials in this chapter are derived from Armand J. Thieblot, Jr., *Prevailing Wage Laws of the States*, 4 GOV'T UNION REV., 1–65 (Fall, 1983). Coverage in that article is somewhat more complete for the period prior to its publication. Philip W. Northrup handled the 1982 field interviews with state departments of labor. The articles from local newspapers that are cited throughout this chapter were obtained from the Public Service Research Council Clipbook, a weekly news clipping service.

This is followed by a review of each individual law and recent legislative activities surrounding it. A final section provides a brief summary and conclusion.

HISTORY AND OVERVIEW OF STATE PREVAILING WAGE LAWS

Although the prevailing wage laws are different in each state, their development and intentions have followed a number of common patterns. This is shown by their history and current operations. The earliest state prevailing wage laws actually predate the Davis-Bacon Act by many years. They began to appear on the record around the turn of the century, first in Kansas in 1891. Typically, however, these earliest laws (there were seven in effect before the Davis Bacon Act was passed in 1931) were essentially eight-hour laws; that is, they standardized an eight-hour work day instead of ten, and provided that overtime—when it was authorized at all—was to be paid on the basis of an eight-hour day. Many were subsequently modified to accommodate the prevailing wage concept.

Even modified, the early laws tended to be extraordinarily vague. The relevant portion of the country's first, that of Kansas, said in substance that:

> not less than the current rate of per diem wages in the locality where the work is performed shall be paid to laborers, workmen, mechanics, and other persons so employed by or on behalf of the State of Kansas, or any county, city, township, or other municipality of said State.[2]

The Kansas act did not provide for predetermination of wage rates, for definition of prevailing, for administration by the state's department of labor or other body, or for enforcement other than through the courts.[3] Other states that passed prevailing wage laws before the Davis-Bacon Act include New York (1897), Idaho (1911), Arizona (1912), New Jersey (1913), Massachusetts (1914), and Nebraska (1923). Among these, the laws in New York, New Jersey, and Massachusetts, as might be expected in these areas of high labor union concentration, have been modified and strengthened through the years, and have become among the most restrictive in

---

[2] KAN. STAT., ch. 114 (1891). Now, KAN. STAT. ANN., §§ 44-201 to 205.

[3] Until 1978, the Kansas statute was considered to be administratively unenforceable, but a state supreme court decision at that time [Anderson Construction Co. v. Weltmer, 23 Wage & Hour Cas. (BNA) 904 (Kan. Sup. Ct., 1978)] and a newly activist stance by the state's department of labor have revitalized it, making Kansas one of only a handful of states in which the prevailing wage law has become stronger rather than less restrictive in recent years. [See detailed discussion below.]

the nation. Nebraska's law is unique in that it has retained much of its original character, making it the least typical and least restrictive of all the state acts. Prior to its repeal in 1985, Idaho's law had been modified to become more like state laws passed subsequent to the Davis-Bacon Act. Arizona's law had become staunchly prounion before its method of rate selection was found to be unconstitutional in 1979; thereupon the law became ineffective, and was finally repealed by voter referendum in the general election of 1984.[4]

Most legislative activity concerning prevailing wages at the state level occurred in the few years following the passage of the federal Davis-Bacon Act in 1931. Six of the state laws were put on the books in 1931; then, between 1931 and World War II, fourteen additional states added prevailing wage statutes. (See Table IV-1.) Additionally, the District of Columbia, in which all public works funds are federal, did not require a statute, but was covered automatically by the federal law. (Alaska and Hawaii, still territories at the time, were covered when they became states. Alaska, which now dates its statute to 1931, is included among the first six mentioned above, but Hawaii, which chose its statehood date of 1955 as the date for its statute, is not.) The total number of statutes by 1945, therefore, stood at twenty-eight.

Fourteen other states added prevailing wage statutes or replaced older laws with new ones in the years since World War II, so that forty-two states (of fifty-one, counting the District of Columbia on both sides) had such statutes by 1973.[5] The count held at forty-two until 1979. Since 1979, there have been at least fifty-one bills introduced to twenty-three state legislatures to repeal or substantially curtail existing prevailing wage laws; and these repeal efforts have met with some success. Florida repealed its statute in 1979, and both Alabama and Utah repealed theirs in 1981. The citizens of Arizona, in a ballot referendum, repealed that state's already moribund act in 1984. Idaho, Colorado, and New Hampshire all repealed their prevailing wage laws in early 1985, leaving the number of states with effective prevailing wage laws for state (and sometimes local) public works at thirty-five.

---

[4] The law was found unconstitutional in Industrial Commission v. C & D Pipeline, Inc. 34 Wage & Hour Cas. (BNA) 313, (Ariz. Ct. App., 1979); 607 P.2d 383 (1980). The results of the voter referendum on repeal are reported, among other places, in *Arizona State Prevailing Wage Statute Repealed by Voters in Ballot Initiative*, DAILY LAB. REP. No. 218, P. A-8 (November 9, 1984).

[5] Unless specifically exempted by the context, the District of Columbia will be counted as a "state" for the purpose of numerical presentations. Thus, since 1955, there have been fifty-one "states" in the Union.

TABLE IV-1
Existence of Prevailing Wage Laws, by State

States Having Prevailing Wage Laws	Date of Law	States Without Prevailing Wage Laws		
Alaska	1931	Georgia		
Arkansas	1955	Iowa		
California	1931	Mississippi		
Connecticut	1935	North Carolina		
Delaware	1962	North Dakota		
District of Columbia	1931	South Carolina		
Hawaii	1955	South Dakota		
Illinois	1931	Vermont		
Indiana	1935	Virginia		
Kansas	1891			
Kentucky	1982			
Louisiana	1968			
Maine	1933			
Maryland	1945	States With Repealed Laws	Date of Law	Date of Repeal
Massachusetts	1914			
Michigan	1965			
Minnesota	1973			
Missouri	1957			
Montana	1931	Alabama	1969	1981
Nebraska	1923	Arizona	1912	1984
Nevada	1937	Colorado	1933	1985
New Jersey	1913	Florida	1933	1979
New Mexico	1937	Idaho	1911	1985
New York	1897	New Hampshire	1941	1985
Ohio	1931	Utah	1933	1981
Oklahoma	1965			
Oregon	1959			
Pennsylvania	1961			
Rhode Island	1935			
Tennessee	1953			
Texas	1933			
Washington	1945			
West Virginia	1933			
Wisconsin	1931			
Wyoming	1967			

Source: Individual state laws and Wharton Industrial Research Unit survey, state departments of labor, 1982.

Characteristics of the State Prevailing Wage Laws[6]

The state laws differ significantly in both their applicability and their provisions. Definitions of public works vary, as do the types and sizes of contracts covered, applicability to municipal contracts

---

[6] Information on the state prevailing wage laws was derived from several sources: 1) individual contractors or contractors' organizations were surveyed in a majority

or to contracts also funded by the federal government, the types of employees for whom prevailing wage rates will be calculated or to whom they will be applied, and the methods used for identifying, categorizing, selecting, calculating, and issuing the wage rates and fringe benefits the laws require.[7]

Very few state prevailing wage laws match the degree of coverage or the definitions of the federal Davis-Bacon Act, but most of them use it as a starting place. Therefore, it is helpful to review how the Davis-Bacon Act defines public works, and how far it extends coverage.[8]

The Davis-Bacon Act covers construction of public works for the federal government or in which the federal government has a financial interest, provided that the contract is for an amount larger than a threshold of $2,000. All types of building construction, maintenance, and repair are covered, including construction of residential, commercial, and industrial structures, highways, and heavy projects such as bridges, dams, airports, or waterways.

Workmen employed in all of the standard building crafts, including those working in demolition (if it is incidental to a construction project), in painting and decorating, and in carpet laying are included, provided that their job title is a "prevailing" job title. In some circumstances, rates may be issued for apprentices or helpers, but rates for job titles that might be used exclusively by non-union contractors (e.g., construction mechanic or [multi-trade] helper) are not found.

---

of states by the author in the spring of 1980 for their interpretations of how the acts were implemented in their areas; 2) officials of each state's department of labor were either interviewed in person or by telephone, or were surveyed by a mailed questionnaire during the summer of 1982 by Philip W. Northrup for the Industrial Research Unit, The Wharton School, University of Pennsylvania; 3) newspaper reports of legislative activity concerning state prevailing wage laws during the period 1979–1985 were secured from the Public Service Research Council clipping service and from the files of the *Construction Labor Report*, and the *Engineering News Record;* 4) the statutes and, where available, the administrative regulations supporting them, were reviewed; and 5) judicial decisions and summaries of relevant opinions by states' attorneys general were also reviewed where available.

[7] The state laws also differ widely in matters of administration, enforcement, compliance, and the handling of grievances. Enforcement provisions, for example, run the gamut from no enforcement to substantial fines and the possibility of black listing or even felony criminal convictions; in some states, the public agencies awarding contracts, as well as contractors themselves, can be held liable. Compliance provisions are sometimes spelled out in the statutes, but often are found only in the states' regulatory manuals or labor department operating procedures. Furthermore, there is often only a mild degree of relationship between compliance provisions on the books and enforcement actually applied. For these reasons, these matters are not summarized or covered in this chapter.

[8] For a full presentation of the Davis-Bacon Act and its requirements, see Ch. III, *supra*.

Contracts by public agencies related to the federal government are not covered unless the enabling legislation of the agencies include it by reference. Contracts by included polities (such as states, counties, or municipalities) are not covered unless federal funding is involved.

Some states adhere to the pattern of the Davis-Bacon Act rather closely, but others do not. In the overviews and summaries that follow, the provisions for the District of Columbia, which are the same as those of the Davis-Bacon Act, can be used as a benchmark. The overviews will cover the contract threshold amounts, applicability to local and public agency contracts, applicability in the event of overlap with the federal act, and the methods used to establish prevailing rates.

Contract Threshold

The purpose of a contract threshold is to eliminate the bother and expense of administering a prevailing wage law for a contract the cost of which will be likely to have little impact on local competition or the local labor market. Table IV-2 shows the contract thresholds in effect for the District of Columbia and the thirty-seven states that have prevailing wage acts. Only the District of Columbia and four states use the same $2,000 threshold amount as the federal government. Two states have lower thresholds, at $1,000, and twelve others do not specify a threshold at all, usually covering instead "all public works." Sixteen states have higher thresholds, with Maryland the highest at $500,000.

Most of the threshold amounts are straightforward, and are at such minimal levels as to have little or no impact on applicability. But every aspect of prevailing wage laws is capable of complication, and four states have found ways of providing it in this case: Connecticut varies the threshold amount depending on whether the work is new construction (for which the threshold is $200,000) or remodeling (for which it is $50,000); Kentucky has established a threshold at $250,000, but has tied it to changes in the consumer price index, so that the amount will increase with inflation; Minnesota applies different amounts depending on whether only a single construction trade ($2,500) or multiple trades ($25,000) will be used on a project; in Wisconsin, either state or local contracts for building or heavy construction, and state contracts for highway work, are covered if they exceed $2,500 for a single trade or $25,000 for multiple trades, but local contracts for highway work have a threshold of $7,500 for a single trade and $75,000 for multiple trades.

TABLE IV-2
Contract Threshold Amounts in State Prevailing Wage Laws

State	Threshold amount
Alaska	$2,000
Arkansas	$75,000
California	$1,000
Connecticut	$200,000 for new construction, $50,000 for remodeling
Delaware	$2,000
District of Columbia	$2,000
Hawaii	$2,000
Illinois	0
Indiana	0
Kansas	0
Kentucky	$250,000
Louisiana	$25,000
Maine	$10,000
Maryland	$500,000
Massachusetts	0
Michigan	0
Minnesota	$2,500 for single trade, $25,000 for multiple trades
Missouri	0
Montana	0
Nebraska	0
Nevada	$20,000
New Jersey	$2,000
New Mexico	$20,000
New York	0
Ohio	$4,000
Oklahoma	$600,000 for school districts, counties, cities, and public trusts
Oregon	$10,000
Pennsylvania	$25,000
Rhode Island	$1,000
Tennessee	$5,000
Texas	0
Washington	$17,500
West Virginia	0
Wisconsin (except local highway contracts)	$2,500 for single trade, $25,000 for multiple trades
Wisconsin (local highway contracts)	$7,500 for single trade, $75,000 for multiple trades
Wyoming	$25,000

Source: Individual state laws.

Indiana adds a double complication. Although its legislation specifies no threshold amount, the state department of labor has provided one administratively. The amount is $5,000 for all state contracts except those for work done for state universities, for which it is $50,000. Finally, in Pennsylvania, where subcontractors sometimes bid separately on a job, the prevailing rate requirements will apply if the total job price—not just the price of the subcontract—exceeds the threshold of $25,000.

Local and Public Agency Contracts

None of the states have constitutional prohibitions that would keep them from applying their prevailing wage laws to contracts entered into by county or city governments, but the applicability of some of the state acts is circumscribed by the statutes. The acts of Maine, Michigan, and Wyoming specify that prevailing wages will not be required on local government contracts. Those of Tennessee and Louisiana allow local governments the option of being covered or not, at their discretion. The Maryland and Kentucky statutes will apply to a local government project only if 50 percent or more state funds are used to pay for it. States follow varying procedures for applying their acts to projects funded by off-budget revenue sources, such as bond sales for industrial development, economic recovery, or schools. Two states, California and Ohio, go beyond all the others in defining a public work, so that if a private developer in those two states builds an office or other structure whose space is intended to be leased to the state, even though no public monies of any sort are used in the construction, the project will be subject to the statute and require prevailing rates.

Some states make distinctions in coverage based on the type of construction work involved. Nebraska and Oklahoma exclude highway work, and three others—Connecticut, Indiana, and Texas—cover highway work under separate laws or by separate sections of their statutes, usually specifying a long-outdated minimum wage payment (e.g., $.30 per hour is mandated in Texas). Wisconsin has differing provisions for four separate situations: state contracts for building construction, state contracts for highway construction, local contracts for building construction, and local contracts for highway construction. Arkansas' act excludes not only highway work, but also heavy construction and school construction. Maryland, besides the highway exclusion mentioned above, also excludes school construction unless 75 percent or more of state funds are used. Missouri excludes work on drainage and levee projects, and New York excludes some work for school districts. Pennsylvania and Texas, on a slightly different tack, exclude maintenance work (as differentiated from repair).

Among the odd inclusions for coverage by the acts are a number of prevailing wage and other requirements which are, at best, peripherally related to construction work. California covers janitors.

Massachusetts has provisions for movers, janitors, draftsmen, teamsters, public employees, truck rentals, printing for the state, and of all things, meatcutters. Truck rentals are also covered in Minnesota, Rhode Island, and Wisconsin; and printing contracts are covered in Pennsylvania. New York covers serving labor, able bodied seamen, public employees, and others. These items are outlined in Table IV-3.

Federal-State Overlap

Many public works projects involve funding from both federal and state sources, raising the possibility of conflict between the prevailing wage laws of each. One might suppose that the general doctrine of federal preemption would control in these cases. But because the Davis-Bacon Act does not of itself set rates, but merely requires payment of whatever wages are currently prevailing in the community where the work will be performed, the federal law will allow precedence to state statutes requiring prevailing rates, even though such might differ from those set by the U.S. Department of Labor.[9]

Thus, discretion as to which law will apply is left to the state statutes, the administrators of the state laws, or decisions of the states' attorneys general. In those cases where precedence is not given to one act or the other, it is presumed that both apply simultaneously, meaning that the higher rate mandated by the laws in each category will apply, and that the contractor must satisfy the administrative and reporting requirements of both. The summary of applicability in the event of overlapping jurisdiction is in Table IV-4.

Establishment of Prevailing Rates

In the methods used to established the level of their prevailing rates, the states can basically be divided into five categories: (1) those which set rates that approximate the free market; (2) those which survey local rates and use some measure of central tendency—arithmetic mean, geometric mean, or median—to select the prevailing rate; (3) those which adopt the Davis-Bacon rates as their own; (4) those which set rates by a formula similar to that used to

---

[9] This was not always the case. Applicability used to be set by 50 U.S.C. 885, which gave precedence to the federal act. That was repealed about 1956, and applicability is now governed by 10 U.S.C. 2237. In October 1985, the Federal Highway Administration proposed a regulation which would require the states that pay higher prevailing rates than those set pursuant to the federal Davis-Bacon Act on federally funded or assisted highway projects to pay the entire difference out of state funds.

TABLE IV-3

Major Items Included in or Excluded from Coverage by State Prevailing Wage Laws

State	Exclusions	Inclusions
Alaska	—	surveyors
Arkansas	highways, schools, heavy	—
California	irrigation, pub. utilities	janitors, leases
Connecticut	highways (sep act)	—
Delaware	—	—
D.C.	—	—
Hawaii	—	—
Illinois	—	—
Indiana	highways (sep act)	—
Kansas	—	—
Kentucky	schools, local (unless 50% state funds)	—
Louisiana	local (unless ordinance)	—
Maine	local	—
Maryland	local (unless 50% state funds), schools (unless 75%)	—
Massachusetts	—	truck rental, moving, meat cutting, janitors, public employees, etc.
Michigan	local	school boards, printing
Minnesota	local (unless ordinance)	truck rentals
Missouri	drainage, levees	—
Montana	—	—
Nebraska	highways	—
Nevada	—	truck rents, pub. utils.
New Jersey	—	—
New Mexico	schools	—
New York	—	serving labor, seamen, public employees, etc.
Ohio	—	serving labor, leases, off-site fabrication
Oklahoma	highways	—
Oregon	—	—
Pennsylvania	maintenance	printing
Rhode Island	—	teamsters, truck rents
Tennessee	—	—
Texas	highways, maintenance	—
Washington	—	—
West Virginia	—	—
Wisconsin	—	teamsters, truck rents
Wyoming	—	—

Source: Individual state laws.

administer the Davis-Bacon Act; and (5) those which specify union rates.

One of the astonishing aspects of all of the prevailing wage laws, including the federal ones, is that so many different methods are used to establish or calculate the rates that are said to prevail for

TABLE IV-4

Methods Used by the States to Handle Overlapping Coverage by Davis-Bacon Act and State Prevailing Wage Laws

State	Rates That Apply
Alaska	Higher rates.
Arkansas	Davis-Bacon.
California	State act, if state does contracting.
Connecticut	State law, "if there is any state money in the job."
Delaware	State law, if state involvement exceeds $5,000.
D.C.	Davis-Bacon.
Hawaii	Law of whoever administers contract.
Illinois	State act, if state does the contracting.
Indiana	Davis-Bacon.
Kansas	Higher rates.
Kentucky	Higher rates.
Louisiana	Davis-Bacon.
Maine	Davis-Bacon.
Maryland	Higher rates.
Massachusetts	Higher rates.
Michigan	Davis-Bacon.
Minnesota	Higher rates.
Missouri	Spokesman for the state's labor department was unable to say, but rates are about the same.
Montana	Davis-Bacon.
Nebraska	Davis-Bacon.
Nevada	State law.
New Jersey	Higher rates.
New Mexico	Davis-Bacon.
New York	Higher rates.
Ohio	Davis-Bacon.
Oklahoma	Unknown.
Oregon	Davis-Bacon.
Pennsylvania	Davis-Bacon.
Rhode Island	State "works with" federal department of labor differently, depending on proportion of funding from each source.
Tennessee	State law, if over $50,000 of state funding.
Texas	Unknown; applicability is unspecified by statute, and the state's department of labor is prohibited from administering the state law.
Washington	Higher rates.
West Virginia	Unknown.
Wisconsin	Higher rates.
Wyoming	Higher rates.

Source: Individual state laws.

given job categories in the community. This is perhaps a reflection of the fact that no logically defensible definition of the term prevailing has ever been advanced.

The Old Federal Formula. The Davis-Bacon Act does not attempt a definition of prevailing, but leaves that task, along with other administrative details, to the secretary of labor. In 1935, Secretary

Frances Perkins, the first to administer the act, adopted the survey as the means of identifying rates, and this method has been continued by her successors. The geographic extent of surveys has usually reflected county boundaries. Within counties, data are compiled or sampled of wage rates paid to workmen in various classes of labor working on various types of construction work. The formulation originally established by Secretary Perkins to select the prevailing rate from the sample data remained in effect for about fifty years until modified, as explained below. By the original formula, if any specific rate (to the penny) was paid to a majority of workmen in the survey sample, that rate was taken as prevailing; but if there were no such rate, then a specific rate paid to at least 30 percent of workmen was selected; otherwise, the average of all of the rates in the survey was adopted, even if no individual workman actually received that rate.

This process has sometimes been called the "federal formula," or the "majority, 30 percent, or average" formula, or sometimes just the "30-percent rule." Although it is said to involve a three-step process, in fact, there are only two steps, because in every case where the same rate is paid a majority, it is necessarily also paid to at least a 30 percent plurality. Therefore, the formula is really a "30 percent or average" formula. In the text which follows, it will be called the "old federal formula."

The New Federal Formula. Since 1983, a new administrative definition of prevailing, without the 30-percent provision, has been in existence, and was cleared for implementation in 1985.[10] This necessitated a new federal formula for selecting the prevailing rate, which is one of "majority or average," and might be called the "50-percent rule." When applied, the new federal formula will select as the prevailing rate the rate (to the penny) paid to a majority of workmen in a survey, if there is such a rate, or else the average of all sample rates. At the time this study was prepared, none of the state acts that had followed the old federal formula had yet changed to the new one, except the District of Columbia, for whom the change was automatic. Additionally, Alaska had previously followed a regulatory method of "majority or average," and both Oregon and Washington use the same formula with the minor variations. Finally, Arkansas and Connecticut skip formulas and calculations entirely, and adopt the most recent federal Davis-Bacon rates as their own. Thus, without additional changes by state legislatures,

---

[10] See discussion in Ch. III, *supra.*

six states will set their prevailing rates based on the new federal formula or a minor variation of it.

Individual State Methods. Of the thirty-five state-level prevailing wage laws, seventeen fail to specify how the prevailing rate should be calculated. Although several mention that surveys should be performed, or that the act's administrator should "ascertain and consider" collectively bargained rates, Davis-Bacon rates, and such rates as are generally paid (or some similar combination), these statutes do not specify a selection procedure or other means of establishing the prevailing rate. In some states, administrative regulations are more informative, but not in all. In Texas, for example, there are no state-wide administrative regulations and the entire decisionmaking process is left to the awarding agency; in Indiana, the rate-making process is performed by special three-person committees without state guidelines; and in Illinois, Louisiana, Missouri, Montana, Nevada, Pennsylvania, and Rhode Island methods for calculating the rates are specified by neither law nor regulation. Where administrative regulations do contain selection methods, they frequently use the old federal formula (New Mexico, Oklahoma, Wyoming); other variations include adopting Davis-Bacon rates (Arkansas, Connecticut), using the new federal formula (Alaska, District of Columbia), or taking the simple mode (California).

The statutes of the other eighteen states do provide guidance for selecting the prevailing rates, but their methods differ sharply: Kansas, Nebraska, and West Virginia specify that the majority rate should be chosen, but fail to identify a method for proceeding if there does not happen to be a majority paid the same rate. (Furthermore, rate predetermination is not required by either the Nebraska or the Kansas statutes.) Delaware requires selection of "the average of a majority" of wage rates in a survey, which is statistically indeterminate. (Delaware solves the problem by rank ordering the wage rates in the survey by size of workforce and taking the average of the highest 50 percent.) Nine states specify the mean, the median, or the mode in some combination or variation.

The mean and the median are central-tendency rates, but the mode (used alone) is not, because wage rates in construction do not follow a statistically normal distribution. Tennessee uses the arithmetic (unweighted) mean of statewide rates, plus or minus 6 percent. Maine uses the median of survey rates. Hawaii, Kentucky, Maryland, Oregon, and Washington use the mode, at a specified level, then the average of all rates if the specified level is not met. Minnesota and Wisconsin (by three of its four procedures, as explained below) use the modal rate alone. This is simply the rate that appears most frequently in the survey. Using the mode to select construction wage rates is often tantamount to selecting the union rate, because only the minimum wage or the union scale is likely to be represented in any number of individual cases. Free market rates will naturally vary from one another by at least a few pennies, and most of the construction industry is well above the minimum wage.

Finally, four states (Massachusetts, Michigan, New Jersey, and Ohio) adopt collectively bargained rates as prevailing, and New York also adopts collectively bargained rates in practice. The rules in New York specify that the collectively bargained rate will be taken as prevailing if at least 30 percent of the workforce is unionized. The state department of labor assumes this to be the case, and performs no surveys to verify it. States that have regulations that cause rates to be set higher than those established pursuant to the federal Davis-Bacon Act may reconsider their policies if new federal policies, such as that described in note 9, *supra,* require the states to bear the full costs.

In Table IV-5, the statutory, regulatory, and effective methods of establishing the prevailing rates are presented in somewhat abbreviated form. Much of the minutiae associated with particular acts has been eliminated. Some states calculating an average, for example, use the simple (arithmetic) mean of individual survey rates; others use the mean of the wages weighted by the number of hours worked (the geometric mean).

INDIVIDUAL STATE LAWS:
SUMMARY, ANALYSIS, AND PRESENT LEGISLATIVE AND JUDICIAL ACTIVITY

Although the state prevailing wage laws fit into general categories, each has its own idiosyncrasies. In this section, the specific state acts are analyzed separately, along with recent legislative and court action associated with them. They are arranged in alphabetical order.

Alabama

The Alabama prevailing wage statute was repealed in 1980.[11] The law was originally enacted in 1941, and had most of the usual provisions applying to public works contracts for the state or, by local ordinance, its subdivisions.[12] The law was unusual in that it

---

[11] *Alabama Votes to Repeal Prevailing Wage,* ENGINEERING NEWS-RECORD 41 (May 24, 1979).

[12] ALA. CODE tit. 25.

required a wage ceiling rather than a floor. Prevailing rates set by it were to be no higher than the lowest of collectively bargained rates, rates set under the Davis-Bacon act, or "wages actually paid for similar work" in similar areas.

A bill to repeal this statute was narrowly defeated in 1978. The following year, a similar measure passed both houses of the legislature, but in a compromise to avoid a filibuster, its effective date was postponed until the end of the 1980 legislative term, so that it might be reconsidered or reinstated during the 1980 session. Efforts by prevailing wage proponents in the 1980 session to retain the law or pass a substitute were unsuccessful, and in May 1980, Alabama became, after Florida, the second state in modern times to repeal its prevailing wage statute. With the repeal, the entire South from Virginia to Mississippi, with the exception of Tennessee, became free from state prevailing wage laws.

Bills to reintroduce a prevailing wage law similar to the old one were brought to the legislature in 1983 and again in 1984. The 1983 bill passed the state senate when the lieutenant governor broke a tie and voted with the proponents, but failed by a wide margin in the house of delegates.[13] The 1984 bill also failed in the house.[14]

Although there is no prevailing wage law for the state, local prevailing wage laws are not prohibited in Alabama, and there is at least one of those, for the city of Mobile. Mobile's prevailing wage policy is said to accept union wage scales as prevailing for city-sponsored construction.[15] Since the repeal of the state act, this local law has acquired new significance both for the unions, which would like to protect it as the basis for new statewide measures, and for nonunion construction firms, which would like to eliminate the last vestige of applicability.

Alaska

Alaska's statute is relatively old, dating back originally to the federal act of 1931, when Alaska was still a territory. Its present law dates from 1960.[16] Although the new law remains similar in many respects to the federal statute, it has been modified to reflect local concerns seemingly centered on the surveying process. Besides laborers and mechanics, field surveyors are the only workers ex-

---

[13] *Wage Bill Strikes Out in House,* Advertiser (Montgomery, Alabama) July 13, 1983.
[14] *The 1984 Prevailing Wage Roundup,* GOV'T UNION CRITIQUE 5 (June 1, 1984).
[15] *City's Wage Policy Waste of Tax Money,* (editorial) Mobile Register, June 10, 1983.
[16] ALASKA STAT. tit. 36, ch. 05.

TABLE IV-5

Methods Used to Calculate or Select Prevailing Rates by State Prevailing Wage Laws*

State	Statutory Method	Regulatory Method	Effective Rate Chosen
Alaska	Discretion of admin.	Majority or average	Approximately D-B
Arkansas	Ascertain and consider	Adopts D-B rates	D-B
California	Discretion of admin.	Simple mode (most frequent rate)	Weighted strongly towards C/B
Connecticut	Unspecified	Adopts D-B rates	C/B, because "safe union territory"
Delaware	Average paid a majority	Average of top 50%	Weighted towards, but below, C/B
D.C.	Unspecified	Majority or average	C/B, because "safe union territory"
Hawaii	Old FF (cannot be less than D-B)	Same	C/B, because "safe union territory"
Illinois	Unspecified; awarding agency sets rates	Consider surveys, public hearings, C/B	"Usually" C/B, by newspaper opinion
Indiana	Unspecified; awarding agency establishes 3-man committees	Unspecified	C/B "99% of time," by DOL opinion
Kansas	Rate paid to greatest number (interpreted as majority)	Unspecified	No predetermination
Kentucky	Majority or simple average	Same	Approximately D-B
Louisiana	Ascertain and consider	Same	C/B, according to university study
Maine	Median rate in annual survey	Same	Probably below D-B, over free market
Maryland	Majority, 40 percent, or average	Same	Approximately D-B
Massachusetts	Depends on job level, usually C/B	Same	C/B
Michigan	C/B	Same	C/B
Minnesota	Simple plurality (mode)	Same	Heavily weighted towards C/B
Missouri	Ascertain and consider	Unspecified	Unknown
Montana	Ascertain and consider	Same	C/B
Nebraska	Scale paid by 50% of contractors	No predetermination	Free market
Nevada	Discretion of admin.	Survey, per court ruling	Approximately D-B
New Jersey	C/B	Same	C/B

Table IV-5 (Continued)

State	Statutory Method	Regulatory Method	Effective Rate Chosen
New Mexico	Unspecified	Old FF	Approximately D-B
New York	C/B, if 30% union	Union assumed, unless challenged	C/B
Ohio	C/B	Same	C/B
Oklahoma	Unspecified	Old FF	D-B
Oregon	Majority or average in largest city in vicinity	Same	Above D-B outside of cities
Pennsylvania	Ascertain and consider; C/B fringe benefits automatic	Same	"Almost invariably" C/B, in opinion of DOL
Rhode Island	Survey	Same	C/B, because "safe union territory"
Tennessee	Annual survey, arithmetic mean plus or minus 6%; no fringes	Same	Mean
Texas	Set by awarding agency	None	Varies
Washington	Majority or average in largest city in locality	Same	Above D-B outside cities
West Virginia	Majority, then unspecified	Unknown	Unknown
Wisconsin	Majority or plurality, except local highway, set by locals	Same; prospective rate increases included	Heavily weighted towards C/B
Wyoming	Awarding agency ascertains and considers	Old FF	Varies, but approximately D-B

*Note: The following abbreviations and conventions are used in this table:

C/B = Collectively Bargained rates
D-B = Davis-Bacon rates or Davis-Bacon Act, depending on context
Admin. = Administrator, Department Head or other designee, regardless of actual title
DOL = State's Department of Labor, by whatever actual title
Old FF = Old "federal formula," of "majority, 30 percent, or average"

plicitly covered. Although not mentioned in the statute, a representative of the state's wages and hours division thought it important to note that construction camp cooks are not covered by the prevailing wage law.[17]

The Alaska act covers public works contracts in excess of $2,000, including highway construction and work done for local and municipal subdivisions within the state. The method of determining and selecting the prevailing rate is left to the commissioner of labor. His office reports that the prevailing rate is determined by surveying "all licensed contractors, unions, contractors' associations, state and federal agencies, and minority groups" through a sequential process of mailed questionnaires, telephone contacts, and personal interviews.[18]

The rate paid the majority, or if there is no majority, the average of all rates paid, is selected as the prevailing rate. The Alaska formula thus anticipated the "new federal formula." No appeals are possible because the discretion of the department of labor is held to be absolute.

One anomaly of the act which sets it apart from all others (except those of New York and Ohio) is that the prevailing rates mandated for a construction project can change during the life of the contract. This provision has the potential to increase contractors' risks considerably, because costs may increase for reasons that are beyond the contractors' control, whereas revenues are fixed by the contract.

An amendment introduced in 1981 would have increased the prevailing wage threshold amount from $2,000 to $25,000, but it did not pass the legislature. A bill to repeal the prevailing wage law failed to pass the legislature in 1983. Some controversy having to do with applicability of the act to construction contracts let by state-supported nonprofit organizations arose in 1983. In the opinion of the deputy attorney general, projects such as day care centers, not traditionally built by municipalities, might be exempt when built for state-funded nonprofit organizations.[19]

Arizona

Arizona's statute dated from 1912. It began as an eight-hour-day law, but became a prevailing wage law during the 1930s.[20] As it evolved, the statute became increasingly prounion, so that by 1973

---

[17] Response to Wharton Industrial Research Unit survey, July 15, 1982.

[18] *Id.* How "minority groups" might thus be surveyed is not explained.

[19] *Davis-Bacon Flap with Non-Profits not Quite Settled,* Drums (Bethel, Alaska) April 7, 1983.

[20] ARIZ. REV. STAT. tit. 34.

it surveyed rates only for classes of workmen who were members of statewide or national labor organizations, and specified that these rates be accepted by the Industrial Commission as prevailing, and therefore required, on public works. In the event there were no suitable labor organizations in the locality where a prospective job was to be performed, the Industrial Commission was instructed to extend its search to the nearest similar locality having one.

During the 1970s, the constitutionality of the law was challenged as an unlawful delegtion of legislative power to private persons (organized labor) over whom the legislature had no control, and a violation of due process.[21] A lower court ruled that the section of the statute instructing the Industrial Commission to extend its search to the nearest locality with national unions if none were present where the work was to be performed was unconstitutional.[22] As a result of the ruling, the Industrial Commission temporarily ceased issuing wage rates, because it had no mechanism in the statute to specify rates for localities where no national unions were represented.

In late 1979, the Arizona Court of Appeals upheld the lower court on the extension issue, and went further, striking down the entire procedure and thereby the entire law.[23] As a result of the court's

---

[21] The constitutionality of such action was established by, among others, Carter v. Carter Coal Co., 298 U.S. 238 (1935) and affirmed by Arizona courts in Patrack v. City of Phoenix, 86 Ariz. 88, 91; 340 P.2d 997, (1959).

[22] C&D Pipeline, Inc., v. The Industrial Commission of Arizona, Maricopa Cty. Super., C-320557 and C-32685 (1979) (consolidated).

[23] Industrial Commission v. C&D Pipeline, Inc., Ariz. Ct. App., 24 Wage & Hour Cas. (BNA) 313 (1979); 607 P.2d 383 (1980). Similar findings of unconstitutional delegation were found in Illinois in Bradley v. Casey, 415 Ill. 576; 114 N.E. 2d 681 (1953), and in Wisconsin in Wagner v. Milwaukee, 177 Wis. 410; 188 N.W. 487 (1922). In other states where the prevailing wage requirement was similar to that in Arizona in adopting collectively bargained rates as prevailing, courts have upheld the constitutionality of the practice. Such cases were decided in Kentucky in Baugn v. Gorrell & Riley, 311 Ky. 537, 541; 224 S.W.2d 436, 438 (1949), in New Jersey in Male v. Ernest Renda Contracting Co. Inc., 122 N.J. Super 526; 301 A.2d 153. aff'd; 64 N.J. 99; and in Michigan in West Ottawa Public Schools, v. C. Patrick Babcock, 107 Mich. App. 237; 309 N.W.2d 220 (1979). Related cases were decided in New Hampshire in Union School District of Keene v. Commissioner of Labor, 103 N.H. 512; 176 A.2d 332 (1961), and in California in Kugler v. Yocum, 69 Cal. 2d 371, 445 P.2d 303; 71 Cal. Rptr. 687 (1968) and in Metropolitan Water Dept. v. Whitsett, 215 Cal. 400; 10 P.2d 751 (1932). More recently, in Illinois the constitutionality of the statute (revised since 1953 decision in Bradley v. Casey, above) was upheld even if union rates were determined to be prevailing. [Herbert Hayden v. The County of Ogle, Ill. Sup. Ct. No. 58833, Agenda 31, April 19, 1984.] In contrast, in David L. Hunter v. City of Bozeman, Mont. Sup. Ct., Case No. 84-381, May 30, 1985, the constitutionality of Montana's statute was upheld, but only because it did allow the state's secretary of labor discretion in ascertaining and considering rates other than union rates in making wage determinations. The court noted that had the statute not allowed such discretion, the constitutionality of the statute would not have been upheld.

ruling, Arizona's Industrial Commission no longer issued prevailing rates and the statewide wage law became nonoperational.

For seven consecutive years, beginning in 1972, bills had been introduced in the lower chamber of the legislature to repeal the prevailing wage law, but none had made it to the senate floor before 1979. In that year, a bill to repeal the (moribund) prevailing wage bill passed both houses of the legislature, but was vetoed by the governor.

In 1982, an attempt was made by Republican legislators to place repeal of the law before the voters as a referendum question in the 1984 election. If successful, it was argued, the voter referendum would be proof against the governor's veto; furthermore, the referendum would prohibit any charter city or other political subdivision from enacting an ordinance requiring payment of prevailing wage scales. (During 1980, the cities of Tucson and Globe had enacted prevailing wage laws of their own.)[24] The measure died in the house in 1983.[25]

Early in the 1984 session, both houses passed the same repeal and local prohibition measure, which was promptly vetoed by the governor.[26] In response, the legislature considered the question again, this time successfully sending it to referendum by the voters in the 1984 general election. The voters approved it, repealing the act and prohibiting local communities from implementing their own versions.[27]

Arkansas

First enacted in 1955 and reenacted in 1969, Arkansas's statute is one of the more recent ones.[28] It covers only state and local building contracts (no highways or bridges) in excess of $75,000. It specifically exempts public school construction (except community colleges), and is inapplicable to force account employees (workmen who are employees of any public body).

Like many other state prevailing wage laws, Arkansas' leaves the method of selecting rates unspecified, but calls for collectively bargained rates, Davis-Bacon rates, and "such rates as are generally paid" to be ascertained and considered. The state's department of

---

[24] *Davis-Bacon: Get Rid of It,* (editorial) Tucson Daily Citizen, February 19, 1982.
[25] *Budget, Health Care Dominated Legislature,* Arizona Daily Star (Tucson), May 1, 1983.
[26] UPI (wire service), 04-02-84, 03:41 pps.
[27] *Arizona Voters Repeal Little Davis-Bacon Act,* GOV'T UNION CRITIQUE 6 (November 16, 1984).
[28] ARK. STAT. ANN. tit. 81.

labor, however, acknowledges that it has no mechanism available for surveying wage rates, but "adopts the wage rates established by the U.S. Department of Labor . . . updated as new determinations are issued."[29] This would seem to be a dangerous procedure for Arkansas: the 1955 predecessor to the present act was declared unconstitutional because, among other things, it delegated legislative authority to the federal government and discriminated between areas with and without federal wage determinations.[30]

During 1979, a bill to exempt county and city projects from the state act failed narrowly in the legislature. In 1980, the Supreme Court of Arkansas ruled that construction projects financed by industrial development bonds ("Act 9 bonds") would be exempt from the statute. In 1981, a bill to repeal passed the senate, but was tabled for study in the house.[31] Following the unsuccessful repeal effort, a prevailing wage task force was set up which in 1984 resulted in the first actual wage rate survey in the state since 1969.[32] This survey brought about wage floor reductions of up to 39 percent in one county, and an average reduction of 25 percent for all the wages surveyed.[33]

California

California's statute is another of the many passed during the Depression,[34] but it differs in many details from its contemporary, the Davis-Bacon Act. In almost all particulars, it is more restrictive and more highly labor oriented than the federal law. Its minimum contract amount is only $1,000 (raised from $500 in 1981), and it covers such items as demolition work, construction of streets and sewers, hauling refuse from job sites and from the University of California and the state colleges, and laying carpeting, as well as surveying and ordinary building maintenance (janitorial work). Although work done for irrigation and other special districts and for public utilities is excluded, more than 6,000 public agencies or bodies in the state can award contracts requiring prevailing rates.

---

[29] Response to Wharton Industrial Research Unit survey, July 8, 1982.

[30] Crowly v. Thornbrough, 31 Lab. Cas. 70, 236; 226 Ark. 708; 294 S.W.2d 62 (1956).

[31] *Arkansas Labor Rally Helps Defeat Bill,* IBEW J. 4 (June 1981). The article notes: "on the morning of March 4, the day scheduled for public hearings by the House Labor Committee, over 3,000 hard hats answered the call and set the stage for one of the largest rallies in labor history in the state of Arkansas. . . . The [hearing] room was packed with hard hats and labor supporters."

[32] *Arkansas Wage Survey Trims Prevailing Wages,* ENGINEERING NEWS-RECORD 59 (September 13, 1984).

[33] *Id.*

[34] CAL. LAB. CODE part 7, ch. 1.

One unusual provision specifies that the employees of private contractors working on private buildings are covered by the law if the buildings are to be leased at least 50 percent to the state or a political subdivision for its use after completion. Finally, a California Court of Appeals ruled that the prevailing wage law applies to all force account (public) employees engaged in construction, which is also unusual among the state laws.[35] All told, the California statute is one of the most all-encompassing of the state laws.

The means of setting rates is not identified in the legislation but is left to the discretion of the director, whose determinations are final. Prior to 1976, the director required that many awarding agencies (such as school boards) be responsible for determining their own wage rates and issuing them along with their requests for bids, but since that time, all determinations have been made by the state department of labor.[36]

Administrative rules issued by the department of labor specify that collectively bargained rates and "such rates as are generally paid" shall be ascertained and considered, with further data to be collected only if these two are not actually prevailing. In practice, although the state department of labor says wage surveys are occasionally made, such surveys would seem to be largely wasted effort, since the regulations specify that the prevailing rate shall be the rate paid the majority, or if there is no majority, then the rate paid the greatest number. In effect, therefore, the law specifies a purely modal rate. (Only Minnesota also uses the modal method.) Such a choice will typically have the effect of selecting a negotiated rate as prevailing if there is any union representation in an area, since it is unlikely that the free market wage will be identical for many workmen within any given category of work.

In 1979, a bill to add state printing contracts (as in Pennsylvania) was introduced in the legislature, but it failed to pass. An interesting measure to require an independent survey by a private firm for wage rates applicable to substantial jobs (over $500,000) was also introduced that year, but it was withdrawn for amendments and never returned.

The 1981 legislature considered bills to increase the threshold amount from $500 to $3 million (which would have effectively eviscerated the law), to exempt certain school construction or repair work, and to exempt counties with a population of less than 500,000 from the act. None of these bills survived both houses of the leg-

---

[35] Bishop v. City of San Jose, Cal. Ct. App. 19 Wage & Hour Cas. 13.
[36] Wharton Industrial Research Unit interview, California Department of Labor, San Francisco, July 22, 1982.

islature, but a bill to increase the contract threshold by an insignificant amount (from $500 to $1,000) was successful. A 1983 bill to modify the act by localizing the wage survey procedure failed.[37]

It is interesting to note that the actions of local polities have the opposite effect in California from those in Alabama and Arizona. In the latter states, local polities have enacted prevailing wage laws in the absence of state laws. In California, the cities of San Diego and Porterville (in Northern California) have passed ordinances approved by the courts freeing themselves from having to pay prevailing wage rates on local construction projects.[38]

In the event of overlapping coverage of public works jobs by both the California prevailing wage statute and the Davis-Bacon Act, California's act takes precedence, provided that the state does the contracting.

Colorado

Colorado's prevailing wage law was repealed in 1985. The 1933 law had been among the shortest of the state laws,[39] being only one paragraph in length as it pertained to building construction. Other portions of the statute established an eight-hour day and provided preference on public works employment to Colorado residents. The law did not apply to highway work (which is covered by its own minimum wage provisions, well below the federal standard)[40] but did apply to local contracts, according to a spokesman for the state department of labor.[41]

The Colorado statute had been unusual in that the method for establishing the prevailing rate was not mentioned in the statute, and no one was even empowered to determine or post the rate unless a dispute arose, in which case the dispute was referred to the director of the division of labor for resolution. Nevertheless, the head of a local contractors' association in 1980 felt the state prevailing rate was set exclusively by reference to union contracts in effect at the time, and went on to point out that an effort in 1979 to provide funding and a specific method for making wage determinations by

---

[37] *A Needless Penalty on Taxpayers,* (editorial) Los Angeles Times, December 13, 1983.

[38] *Prevailing Wages No Longer Demanded,* Recorder (Porterville, California) April 20, 1983.

[39] COLO. REV. STAT. § 80-17-1 *et.seq.* (1953).

[40] *Id.,* Sec. 80-14-1. This section sets minimum rates of between $0.50 and $1.25 per hour depending on location and skill level required.

[41] Wharton Industrial Research Unit interview, Colorado Department of Labor, August 9, 1982.

survey was vetoed by the governor.[42] On the other hand, a spokesman for the state's department of labor maintained in 1982 that prevailing wages were determined by surveys of urban and rural rates, both union and nonunion.[43]

Regardless of which rate method actually existed, there was considerable dissatisfaction with the law on the part of local contractors, at whose behest several bills to repeal the prevailing wage statute were introduced in the legislature during the late 1970s. Although none of these were successful, in 1981 a repeal measure passed both houses of the legislature before being vetoed by Governor Richard Lamm.

In 1984, with the same governor in office and the likelihood of veto high, the legislature compromised short of repeal by passing a measure to raise the threshold amount from $5,000 to $150,000,[44] and requiring the state department of labor to conduct actual surveys for wage rates.[45] The following year, with a new legislature seated having close to a two-thirds majority opposed to the prevailing wage law, another repeal bill was introduced and passed. Despite indications that he might not do so, Governor Lamm vetoed the repeal measure.[46] This time, however, the votes were there to override the veto (24-9 in the senate and 48-15 in the house), and the prevailing wage law was repealed, effective June 13, 1985.[47]

There is at least one municipal ordinance, for the town of Pueblo, Colorado, which establishes its own prevailing rates for local work bids.[48] Its continuing fate or application following the state law's repeal is unknown.

Connecticut

Connecticut's prevailing wage statute is another Depression-era law (1935).[49] It follows most of the Davis-Bacon provisions, except that the minimum contract amount, raised to $50,000 for new construction and $10,000 for remodeling and repair in 1979, was further increased to $200,000 for new construction and $50,000 for remod-

---

[42] Response to author's survey, April 1980.
[43] Wharton Industrial Research Unit interview, Colorado Department of Labor, August 9, 1982.
[44] *The 1984 Prevailing Wage Roundup*, GOV'T UNION CRITIQUE 4 (June 1, 1984).
[45] UPI (wire service), 03-09-84, 04:01 pcs.
[46] *Colorado Governor Vetoes Repeal of State Prevailing Wage Statute*, 31 CONSTRUCTION LAB. REP. 406 (June 5, 1985).
[47] *Lawmakers Override Lamm Wage Bill Veto*, Denver Post, June 14, 1985, p. A4.
[48] *City Needn't Follow Davis-Bacon on Local Bids*, Pueblo Chieftan (Colorado), September 9, 1983. See also, *The City Should Scrap Outdated Wage Ordinance*, (editorial) Pueblo Chieftan (Colorado), December 1, 1983.
[49] CONN. GEN. STAT. §§ 31-53.

eling in 1985.[50] It also differs in that locality is specified in the statute as "town," and that state highway work is covered separately.[51]

Although the method of selecting rates is unspecified, a spokesman for the Connecticut department of labor reports that for the past several years the state has simply reissued the federal Davis-Bacon rate. Because the U.S. Department of Labor considered Connecticut to be "union-rate territory" for which prevailing rate surveys were not conducted, union rates have almost invariably been prescribed in Connecticut. The definition of locality as "town" by the state act and, effectively, "state" by the U.S. Department of Labor, does not seem to be reconciled.

Two Connecticut cities, New Haven and Shelton, have separate rate requirements based on Davis-Bacon determinations,[52] but these cities are not otherwise excluded from the state act. Therefore, the status of their statutes, in the (unlikely) event that the state-determined rate differs from the Davis-Bacon one, is unclear for joint state-local projects. The state, itself, defers to the federal act when funds are used from both sources.

Connecticut has an unusual approach when it comes to handling contractors' appeals on prevailing wage rates: it takes the position that because its rates are reissues of the federal rates, dissatisfied parties should take the matter up with the federal government. It therefore has no appeals procedure.[53] Efforts to repeal the state statute were mounted during the 1980 and 1985 legislative terms, but without success.

Delaware

Delaware's 1962 law provides for a somewhat adventurous method of selecting the prevailing wage—namely, the "average of actual wages paid a majority" in the county where the work is to be performed.[54] This definition, although similar to that last used by the federal Walsh-Healey Act, is statistically difficult. The Delaware Department of Labor has chosen to interpret it by rank ordering the responses within each of Delaware's three counties to

---

[50] *Legislative Update*, GOV'T UNION CRITIQUE, June 28, 1985, p. 5.
[51] CON. GEN. STAT. §§ 31–54. This section contemplates hearings to establish prevailing rates only for state highways and bridges. The only apparent difference from the main statute is in the broader definition of locality used in the highway portion.
[52] New Haven: Special Act No. 297, Acts 1945. Shelton: Special Act No. 516, Act 1959.
[53] Wharton Industrial Research Unit interview, Connecticut Department of Labor, New Haven, July 6, 1982.
[54] DEL. CODE § 6913, tit. 29.

a statewide survey by number of employees in each of fifty-seven categories of employment. From all valid responses for the top 50 percent (*i.e.*, the largest firms) the state compiles the average wage rate as weighted by the number of hours worked. The procedure is repeated for calculating fringe benefits. The survey is extensive, and is performed annually. Almost 900 firms responded to a recent one.[55]

The statute is silent about its applicability to highway work, but the survey covers building, industrial, heavy, and highway construction. The threshold amount is $2,000. In the event of joint projects with the federal government, Delaware takes the position that if the level of state funding exceeds $5,000, the state prevailing wage law will apply, leaving relatively few contracts indeterminate. Contracts for political subdivisions of the state are covered by the law.

No recent or current legislative activity is reported concerning the statute, which was last amended in 1972, but a special commission was assigned by the governor to evaluate and refine the survey technique for 1983. Its efforts, in conjunction with a concerted effort by nonunion contractors to respond to the questionnaire, resulted in dramatically lower rates specified as prevailing in 1984.[56]

District of Columbia

The Davis-Bacon Act serves without modification as the District's own prevailing wage law.[57] It dates from 1931, and covers contracts for buildings or highways in excess of $2,000.[58] There are no local polities within the District of Columbia, and therefore no complications involving overlapping state and local coverage.

As is also true of many state statutes, the Davis-Bacon Act leaves determination of almost all operational details to the act's administrator, in this case, the U.S. secretary of labor. For example, it does not specify how prevailing rates are to be selected or determined. In 1935, the secretary of labor issued administrative regulations which remained largely unchanged as the basis for rate setting until 1983. Those regulations called for finding existing wage rates by survey and selecting the prevailing rate by a formula of "majority, 30 percent, or average" applied to the survey results. In

---

[55] Wharton Industrial Research Unit interview, Delaware Department of Labor, Wilmington, June 18, 1982.

[56] *New Prevailing Wage May Cost Some 50% in Pay,* Morning Journal (Wilmington), March 8, 1984.

[57] Davis-Bacon Act, tit. 40, § 27a, U.S. CODE.

[58] See Ch. III, *supra,* for details of Davis-Bacon Act coverage.

recent years, however, actual surveys have been considered unnecessary in the District, because earlier ones had consistently found that union rates prevailed. Therefore, except in unusual circumstances, rate determinations were made by simply taking the rates from the most recent collective bargaining agreements in effect.

Since 1971, there have been at least twenty-nine bills introduced in Congress to repeal, restrict, or amend the Davis-Bacon Act, but none has passed both houses. There have also been several administrative changes, instituted in 1983, that survived legal challenges through the court of appeals, but remained under a lower court injunction until early 1985.[59] These changes modify some of the rules for conducting prevailing rate surveys and also change the formula for selecting or calculating the rates. One of the changes, prohibiting the use of previously determined rates in new surveys, may well have substantial impact in the District, because so much of the construction work there is government sponsored. The change in the formula for selecting the prevailing rate (dropping the 30-percent provision and creating the new federal formula of "majority or average") may also be significant for some trades in the District.

Florida

The Florida statute was repealed over the Governor's pocket veto, effective April 25, 1979—the first such legislative repeal in many years. An act to prohibit political subdivisions and agencies from adopting any prevailing rates was passed by the legislature but vetoed by the governor in 1979. Prior to repealing the entire act, the Florida legislature had experimented with the effect of eliminating coverage by dropping it for school construction. In 1978, when a legislative attempt was made to reinstate the school coverage, the Florida State School Board Association surveyed its districts and found that in the period 1974–1978, the taxpayers of the state had saved $37 million, or approximately 15 percent of the total construction cost of $243 million.[60] (In individual counties, the savings estimates ranged from 2 percent to 25 percent.) This information was persuasive to the legislature, which declined to reinstate

---

[59] Building & Construction Trades Department, AFL-CIO v. Donovan, 712 F.2d 611, D.C. Cir., July 5, 1983. For a full discussion of this case and these changes, see Ch. III, *supra*.

[60] "An Informational Report: The Impact of the State Prevailing Wage Law on State and Local Construction Costs," (mimeographed) Florida Advisory Council on Intergovernmental Relations, January 1979. Table 4, "Survey of School Boards by the State School Board Association: Spring 1978."

coverage for school construction and in fact began to contemplate eliminating the entire act, which it did the following year.[61]

Bills were introduced to both houses of the legislature in 1980 and again in 1981 to reinstate the prevailing wage law, but without success. In 1983, Broward County imposed a local prevailing wage law, under a procedure allowed by the state legislature, which required prevailing wages at the federal Davis-Bacon level on county projects of more than $250,000. Several cities within Broward County passed similar requirements, raising a call for the state legislature to move to prohibit such local options.[62] Although there is no reported action at the state level, the Dade County Commission in 1984 rejected adopting a local option when it learned that the change would have increased the county's construction costs by $60 million over the next six years.[63]

Georgia

Georgia has no prevailing wage legislation on its books.

Hawaii

The Hawaii law was enacted in 1955 and last amended in 1969.[64] It applies to local as well as state contracts for over $2,000, and contains several unusual provisions: it applies to the transportation of goods to and from job sites and to the manufacture and supply of materials if persons performing those services are employed offsite by the contractor; in general it applies to "every person paid by a contractor for his labor" (although, presumably, not to supervisors or management); wages must be paid at least every five working days; and a copy of wage rate schedules must be given to every workman not a member of a collective bargaining group.

The method for establishing the prevailing rate in Hawaii is set by the law itself, and follows the old federal formula. Although set by surveys conducted four times a year, a spokesman for the state's department of labor indicated that the prescribed rates are usually the union scale, because of the large proportion of union representation in the islands.[65] The statute is unusual in specifying that the

---

[61] *Florida First State to Repeal State Prevailing Wage Statute,* 1233 CONSTRUCTION LAB. REP. A-14 (April 25, 1979).

[62] *Prevailing on Wages,* (editorial) Miami Herald, December 30, 1983.

[63] *State Wage Laws Attacked,* ENGINEERING NEWS-RECORD 139-40 (April 19, 1984).

[64] HAWAII REV. STAT. ch. 104.

[65] Wharton Industrial Research Unit interview, Hawaii Department of Labor and Industrial Relations, Honolulu, July 7, 1982.

State Prevailing Wage Laws

wage rates set cannot be less than those established by the Davis-Bacon Act for the state.

In the case of joint federal-state projects, Hawaii takes the position that the prevailing wage law of whichever agency administers the contract will apply. A 1979 proposal to extend coverage to work contracted for by certain public utilities died in committee.

Idaho

Idaho's was a very early law, first enacted in 1911 as an eight-hour-day law,[66] although it was extensively amended as recently as 1965. It covered "persons doing any form of manual labor on public works," and took as prevailing the Davis-Bacon rate for the county seat of the county where the work was to be performed, where such a rate existed; otherwise it specified that a survey of actual wages and fringe benefits paid at or near the job site was to be taken. In practice, wage rates were set for geographic regions that did not follow county boundaries, so somewhat modified Davis-Bacon rates were used.[67] There was no threshold contract amount.

The law applied to all subdivisions within the state. It did not mention highways, but the state prevailing rate schedules were published for highway-related jobs.[68] The Idaho department of labor's compliance officer was unsure of how the law applied to projects jointly funded by the federal and the state government, but since the state act relied on reissue of federal Davis-Bacon rates, this was not a problem.

A bill to repeal the statute failed to pass the legislature in 1979. Another attempt in 1981 passed the house, but was not acted upon by the senate before adjournment. In 1982, both houses passed a repeal measure, but it was vetoed by Governor John Evans, allegedly on technical grounds.[69] The vote to override the veto passed the house but failed by one vote in the senate. A new bill was thereupon introduced which corrected the technical defects. It was passed by

---

[66] IDAHO CODE tit. 44.

[67] Wharton Industrial Research Unit interview, Idaho Department of Labor and Industrial Services, Boise, August 11, 1982.

[68] See, e.g., "Prevailing Wage Rates for Use on All Public Works Projects in Conformity with the Provisions of Section 44-1006, *Idaho Code,*" Schedule 2. This twelve-page schedule lists 192 separate rates determined for various times in 1982 for approximately 500 job titles in building, highway, and heavy construction in North Idaho, one of four sections of the state for which determinations were made.

[69] *Evans Veto Results in Introduction of New Prevailing Wage Bill,* News (Kellogg, Idaho), March 11, 1982.

both houses and sent on to the governor, but he vetoed it again, this time on political grounds.[70]

In 1983, proponents of reform offered a new approach, to replace the prevailing wage requirement with one based on a super-minimum wage, identified as such. It would have established a mandatory minimum crew average wage of three times the federal minimum wage. This was attacked by union leaders, who said it would "open the door to abuses by employers who could pay workers 'starvation wages' in a buyers' market for wages."[71] This bill, offered as a compromise from full repeal, passed but was also vetoed by the governor, whose veto, again, was narrowly sustained.[72]

In the face of strong and at times vitriolic opposition from organized labor, the legislature tried again to reform the prevailing wage act in 1984, this time passing a bill which would have curtailed application of prevailing wages to public school and college projects. Following tradition, the governor vetoed, and his veto was narrowly sustained.[73] The house prepared yet another compromise measure, calling for state rather than federal determination of wage rates, but a house committee, anticipating the veto, did not report it out.[74]

In 1985, with the same governor but a new "veto proof" legislature sitting,[75] yet another repeal bill was introduced, the seventh in as many years. It passed by a vote of 68–16 in the Idaho House and 36–5 in the Senate. Faced now with the certain prospect of an override of his veto, Governor Evans took no action on the bill when it reached his desk on February 6, 1985. Because it had been passed as emergency legislation, the repeal bill took effect five days later without the governor's signature.[76]

Also repealed were the sections of the state's public works law requiring payment of overtime for work over eight hours in one day. The only operative section remaining in the statute is one which requires preference in employment of Idaho residents. No more than 10 percent nonresidents may be employed on projects

---

[70] *Evans Tells Unions They've Got It Right,* Press (Coeur d'Alene, Idaho), June 9, 1982.

[71] *Smooth Sailing for 'Davis-Bacon' Change,* North Idaho Press (Wallace, Idaho) February 17, 1983.

[72] *Idaho Governor Vetoes Changes in Davis-Bacon Law,* Intermountain Contractor (Salt Lake City, Utah) April 18, 1983.

[73] UPI (wire service), 02-23-84, 04:14 aps.

[74] *The 1984 Prevailing Wage Roundup, supra* note 44, at 6.

[75] *Conservative Idaho Legislature Pushes Right to Work, Repeal of Prevailing Wages,* 10 DAILY LAB. REP. A-1 (July 15, 1985).

[76] *Idaho's Prevailing Wage Statute Repealed, Effective Immediately,* 30 CONSTRUCTION LAB. REP. 1374 (February 13, 1985).

using fewer than fifty persons, or more than 5 percent nonresidents on those employing more than fifty persons.

Illinois

The prevailing wage law of Illinois was passed at about the same time as the Davis-Bacon Act, in 1931.[77] It covers highway work and applies to local as well as to state contracts, and contracts by most, if not all, special districts. The act does exclude maintenance (janitorial) contracts, and work by materials producers and suppliers, tree trimmers, and convicts.

The method for establishing the prevailing rate is not specified by law. The Illinois Department of Labor says that rates are established by three methods—personal surveys of job sites, public hearings, and collection of collective bargaining agreements.[78] In 1953, before amendments now incorporated were added, the use of collectively bargained rates as prevailing was found to be unconstitutional.[79] Nevertheless, observers on the scene in Illinois suggest that collectively bargained rates are again the rule.[80]

One unusual aspect of this act is that the public body doing the contracting is supposed to find and set the prevailing rate, with the department of labor doing it only if the public body desires. If neither is able to set the rates, the Court of Appeals is empowered to set them. In 1982, Ogle County attempted to exercise its option to design a prevailing wage scale of its own, using data compiled in a survey of union and nonunion contractors in the county.[81] The local circuit court overturned the wage rates so calculated, and the county took its case to the Illinois Supreme Court, where, in 1984, the constitutionality of the act was upheld and the Ogle County rates were rejected.[82]

In the event of joint coverage by the state act and the federal Davis-Bacon Act, the state act will apply if the state does the contracting. In 1963, the Illinois Supreme Court found that the extension of prevailing rates to force account labor (public employees doing construction on public works), was unconstitutional.[83] Chi-

---

[77] ILL. REV. STAT ch. 48, § 393.
[78] Wharton Industrial Research Unit interview, Illinois Department of Labor, Springfield, August 3, 1982.
[79] Bradley v. Casey, 415 Ill. 576; 114 N.E.2d 681 (1953).
[80] Author's survey, spring 1980.
[81] *Ogle Wage Case May Have Big Effect,* Journal Standard (Freeport, Illinois) March 10, 1982.
[82] *Illinois Wage Law Upheld,* ENGINEERING NEWS-RECORD (May 17, 1984).
[83] City of Monmout v. Lorenz, Ill. Sup. Ct., 16 Wage & Hour Cas. 177 (1963).

cago, however, has a local ordinance providing such coverage, which the mayor of Chicago pledged in July 1983 to overturn.[84]

In 1979, bills to establish a threshold at $250,000 (there is none in the present law) died in assembly, as did one to require all service contracts over $2,000 to be performed by employees receiving prevailing wage rates.[85] In the same year, a bill to repeal the act failed in committee. Several bills were introduced in 1980 and 1981 to exempt certain types of projects or certain public bodies from coverage, and one bill would have required an average rather than a general prevailing wage. None of these passed.

Indiana

Indiana's is a depression-era statute, passed in 1935.[86] It covers all state and local contracts, and has several unusual provisions. For example, wage rates are set by special three-man committees set up by the awarding agency. The law specifies that if these committees cannot agree on rates, the awarding agency will make its own determination, but in practice if two of the three persons on the committee agree on a rate, that rate is final, so the awarding agency would seem to have little need to get involved.[87] Rates set by the committees for the eighteen geographic regions into which the state is divided for the purpose are final and are subject to neither review nor appeal. Judicial review would have been required by a 1981 bill, but it failed to pass the legislature. Another unusual aspect of the law is that although no threshold is specified, the statute is applied only to state contracts of over $5,000, except for state universities, for which the amount is $50,000.[88] A representative of the Indiana division of labor stated that "rates are determined by the local collective bargaining agreements 99 percent of the time."[89]

Although highway work is covered by a separate provision calling for wage rates at least equal to those paid by the state to workers employed as common laborers on its highways, an opinion of Indiana's Attorney General in 1960 provided that the scale of wages and classifications of labor approved by the Bureau of Public Roads of the U.S. Department of Agriculture on highway projects must

---

[84] *Mayor Prevails upon Union,* (editorial), Chicago Times, July 12, 1983.

[85] If this measure had passed, Illinois would have been the only state with a "little Service Contract Act."

[86] IND. STAT. §5-16-7-1.

[87] Wharton Industrial Research Unit interview, Indiana Division of Labor, Indianapolis, July 28, 1982.

[88] *Id.*

[89] *Id.*

be used if any part of the project is paid for by state funds.[90] There is no record of this unusual opinion's ever having been tested. For regular building construction, if the Davis-Bacon Act applies, the Indiana law does not. There are no local prevailing wage laws.

In 1979, several bills calling for detail changes to the statute were introduced, but failed to pass. A bill to repeal also failed. In 1982, the school board of one Indiana county voted to challenge the constitutionality of the law on the ground that rate-setting procedure does not provide sufficient guidelines for committees to establish wage rates, thus forcing them to rely on collective bargaining rates instead of rates actually paid in the community. The case was pending hearing at the time of this writing.[91] Two additional bills to repeal failed in 1985 to clear the Indiana House Committee on Labor.[92]

Iowa

Iowa has never had a prevailing wage law. In 1984, an effort was mounted to establish one. It passed the state house, but failed in the state senate.[93] In 1985, subsequent to a study by local economists which reportedly estimated increases in state highway costs of only 1 to 3.5 percent and pointed to a "positive effect to the state's general fund revenues because of the additional taxes that would be generated on increased income of the [highway] workers,"[94] a new bill to establish a prevailing wage law for all state projects of over $2,000 in counties with a population of greater than 20,000 passed the Iowa Senate by a vote of 26–19, and the house by 54–44.[95] Although vetoed by Governor Terry Branstad,[96] the votes were such that it seems likely that efforts to pass a prevailing wage law in Iowa will continue.

Kansas

Kansas passed the nation's first prevailing wage statute in 1891 as an eight-hour-day law.[97] Although it has been updated, the major changes were made in 1919, 1923, and 1931, before the present

---

[90] Op. Att'y Gen. No. 5 (1960).
[91] *Shelbyville School Board to Challenge State Wage Law*, Indianapolis Star, March 4, 1982.
[92] *Legislative Update*, Gov't Union Critique 5 (March 22, 1985).
[93] *The 1984 Prevailing Wage Roundup*, supra note 44, at 6.
[94] *Prevailing Wage Bill Helps Iowans*, (guest editorial by Phil Kraft, President, Iowa Council of Building and Construction Trades) Globe Gazette (Mason City, Iowa) April 29, 1985.
[95] *Legislative Update*, Gov't Union Critique, May 3, 1985, p. 5.
[96] *1985 Prevailing Wage Roundup*, Gov't Union Critique, May 20, 1985, p. 6.
[97] Kan. Stat. Ann. tit. 44, §§ 201–205.

federal law was passed. Therefore, this prevailing wage law is a greater anachronism than most. It devotes most of its attention to prohibiting overtime except in emergencies, and specifying that in such emergencies workmen will be "paid on the basis of eight hours constituting a day's work."

The prevailing wage rate is taken as the rate paid to "the greater number of workmen" (interpreted by Kansas to be the majority rate, although the same language is interpreted by California to be the modal rate), or the average, if there is no "greater number," in the county or in cities of the "first or second class" (population greater than 2,000) where the work is to be performed.

Very little in this act is defined or specified. Furthermore, unlike the situation in many other states, little is delegated to the state department of labor or other administrative authorities. There is no threshold amount, no method established for identifying the prevailing rate, and, surprisingly, no method of enforcement except through the courts. Highway work is not specifically mentioned, but it is covered, as are local contracts. Some local polities have their own prevailing wage statutes as well.[98]

Because no one is authorized to do it, prevailing wage rates are not pre-determined in Kansas, and bid specifications sent out to contractors may only mention that prevailing wages are required, or only require compliance with all relevant Kansas statutes. Prior to 1978, an opinion of the state's attorney general governed application. It maintained that contracts that did not specifically identify a schedule of prevailing rates were not enforceable as to them, and therefore, in effect, the statute was inoperative since it did not provide for predetermined rates. That opinion, however, was reversed by the Kansas Supreme Court in 1978.[99]

Since that decision, activists in the state department of labor (and, seemingly, the courts) have been seeking various means of mandating specific wage rates. The state supreme court's opinion was that any public agency can adopt whatever rules, regulations, and wage rates it wishes, so long as they are in the project specifications. In conjunction with this opinion, the department of labor has been seeking enforcement through a different Kansas statute, the Kansas Wage Payment Law,[100] that requires the regular pay-

---

[98] Topeka and Shawnee counties are mentioned as having such laws in *County to Focus on Prevailing Wage Issue,* Union (Junction City, Kansas) January 16, 1983.

[99] Andersen Construction Co. v. Weltner, 23 Wage & Hour Cas. 904, Kan. Sup. Ct. (1978)

[100] KAN. STAT. ANN. ch. 44, §§ 313 *et seq.*

ment of "all wages due," thus entirely circumventing the legislative process.[101]

A bill to repeal the statute failed to pass the 1981 legislature. Another bill, which would have authorized the secretary of the department of human resources to determine the prevailing wage rate and to make rules and regulations necessary to carry out the provisions of the prevailing wage act (subject to review by a wage review panel) also failed in the 1981 legislature.

In 1983, the Supreme Court of Kansas ruled that the state department of transportation could require bidders on state-funded highway projects to pay federally established Davis-Bacon rates, and that where overlapping jurisdictions applied, the higher of the prevailing rates under each would apply.[102]

Late in 1983, the Governor proposed making surveys to establish prevailing wage standards for twenty-one Kansas communities where state construction work was expected.[103] In reaction, the legislature prepared a repeal bill,[104] but in the face of a certain veto, it instead reported out a bill to survey wages by counties, rather than separately for the individual cities, and to hold up any implementation of survey rates found until after the 1985 legislative session.[105]

Kentucky

The Kentucky law, first passed in 1940,[106] was extensively modified during the 1970s, and again in 1982 subsequent to an economic impact analysis of the law ordered by the state senate in 1980.[107] The new law attempted to rectify several of the problem areas that the study found to be creating excessive costs in Kentucky and other states.

The 1982 legislature did not repeal the prevailing wage law, but it did restrict its coverage considerably. As revised, the statute applies to contracts of over $250,000 (increasing each year after 1982 in accordance with the consumer price index) for public works, which are defined to include highways, but to exclude school con-

---

[101] Wharton Industrial Research Unit interview, Kansas Employment Standards Section, Topeka, August 6, 1982.
[102] Ritchie Paving, Inc. v. Kansas Department of Transportation, 645 P.2d 440 (Sup. Ct. Kan., 1982).
[103] UPI (wire service), 10-20-83, 08:03 ped.
[104] *Wage Law May Be Nullified,* Capital Journal (Topeka) January 28, 1984.
[105] *Legislative Update,* GOV'T UNION CRITIQUE, March 9, 1984.
[106] KY. REV. STAT. ch. 337, §§ 505-550.
[107] *Economic Impact: Kentucky Prevailing Wage Law,* Legislative Research Commission, Research Report No. 185 (October 1981).

struction and construction by local polities unless the construction is at least 50 percent state-funded. The prevailing rate is taken as the majority or simple average (not weighted by hours worked). The commissioner of labor is to determine the prevailing rate by survey. If the Davis-Bacon Act overlaps the state law, the higher rate required for each classification will apply.

In 1983, the Legislative Research Commission was asked by the legislature to compare the costs of projects before and after the reform went into effect in July 1982. On projects that had become exempt from the law (local government and school projects) the commission estimated savings to be 11 percent. Total savings estimated on all state projects during the year (some of which still carried prevailing rates) amounted to more than $38.5 million.[108]

During the 1984 legislative session, a bill to undo some of the reforms and broaden coverage of the act passed a house committee but was withdrawn by its sponsors before going to the floor, reportedly to avoid the possibility that amendments for outright repeal of the prevailing wage law might be added and approved by the full house.[109]

Louisiana

The Louisiana statute was enacted in 1968 to cover state construction contracts over $25,000.[110] It is silent on applicability to highway work but highway and heavy construction are covered by administrative regulation. It "ascertains and considers" collectively bargained rates, Davis-Bacon rates, wages actually paid, and "other" rates, but does not say how the prevailing rate is to be chosen. According to a 1971 report by the Public Affairs Research Council of Louisiana, "nearly all the actual wage rates the department has in its file reflect collectively bargained pay rates."[111]

If federal and state laws overlap, the Louisana administrator of labor says that the federal law will apply unless the federal administrators decline coverage, in which case the state law will apply.[112] The act does not set rates for local contracts if there is a local ordinance requiring them and if local funds provide at least

---

[108] *Prevailing Wage Reforms Saved Taxpayer Dollars,* Gleaner (Henderson, Kentucky) December 9, 1983. (From the Paducah *Sun.*)

[109] *The 1984 Prevailing Wage Roundup, supra* note 44, at 7.

[110] LA. REV. STAT. tit. 38.

[111] W. D. WAGONER & T. RYAN, ECONOMIC IMPACT OF THE LOUISIANA PREVAILING WAGE LAW ON CONSTRUCTION COST IN STATE-FUNDED CONTRACTS, 20 (Research Study No. 25, Division of Business and Economic Research, University of New Orleans, 1978).

[112] Response to Wharton Industrial Research Unit survey, July 8, 1982.

90 percent of those required for the job. But the state act does not apply unless 90 percent of the funds are state or federal, so local contracts which are funded by more than 10 percent but less than 90 percent local funds do not seem to be covered.

Bills to repeal the prevailing wage law and to increase its threshold from $25,000 to $5 million failed to pass the 1981 legislature. Earlier unsuccessful bills to repeal the measure had also been introduced each year since 1968, when the law was first enacted. In 1985, both house and seante overcame procedural roadblocks and passed repeal bills that were consolidated and then vetoed by Governor Edwin Edwards.[113] Although the senate voted to sustain the veto, members of the house attempted to circumvent the veto by substituting a resolution calling for a fourteen-month suspension instead of outright repeal. Such a resolution would have required the concurrence of the senate, but could not have been vetoed by the governor, since it did not require his signature. The resolution, however, did not carry.[114]

Maine

Maine's law was enacted in 1933, reenacted in 1967, and amended at various times since.[115] It covers only state contracts (no local) for construction and highway work in excess of $10,000, except for temporary or emergency repairs, and gives hiring preference to state residents. The hiring preference applies even when the state act is superseded by the Davis-Bacon Act for jointly funded projects.

The prevailing rate (called "fair minimum wage" in the statute) is established by an unusual method. All construction contractors in building, highway, or heavy construction having five or more employees during the second and third weeks of September are surveyed. Statewide median (middle) rates are then set for each of 133 categories of trades or crafts having more than ten employees in the state. It then applies the median as the fair minimum rate for each "labor market area" as defined by census commuting-pattern data.[116] This is the only state statute that uses the median rate as prevailing. Occupations and job categories that fail to meet the above numerical test do not have prevailing rates assigned, and may use free-market rates. Fringe benefits are not included. No recent litigation involving this act is reported.

---

[113] *Legislative Update,* GOV'T UNION CRITIQUE 7 (July 12, 1985).
[114] UPI (wire service) 07-02-85 06:39 acd.
[115] ME. REV. STAT. tit. 26, §§ 1304 *et seq.*
[116] Response to Wharton Industrial Research Unit survey, July 14, 1982.

Maryland

Maryland's 1945 law was reenacted in 1969 and amended most recently in 1983.[117] It applies to highway and water works as well as to building construction for state contracts in excess of $500,000. Projects that are at least 50 percent state-funded (down from 100 percent by 1983 amendment) are covered, except for school projects, which must be 75 percent state-funded. Local contracts are covered only if there are local ordinances. (There is a separate statute for Prince Georges County, and one for Baltimore City included in the state statute.)[118] Helpers or trainees are specially excluded.

Rates are set semi-annually. The act had been silent about the method of prevailing rate selection, but regulations used to mandate the old Davis-Bacon formula of "majority, 30 percent, or average." This was changed to an unusual variation and legislated in the 1983 amendments to be "majority, 40 percent, or average."[119] The only similar formulation had been used by the New York state prevailing wage law, but New York changed to a different formulation the same year that Maryland adopted it.

Legislative efforts to change Maryland's law have gone in both directions. A bill to reform the act by adopting average rates and making other administrative changes failed in committee during the 1980 legislative session. On the other hand, a bill to extend coverage to all state printing contracts of $1,000 or more failed the following year. Nevertheless, the 1983 amendments made it clear that Maryland's statute, although less restrictive than most, is becoming broader in application. A suit filed by a union group in August 1984 charges the state with lack of vigilance in investigating complaints and enforcing the act, citing alleged problems with use of nonregistered apprentices and with job assignments. As of the time of this writing, the matter remained open.[120]

During the 1985 legislative session, five bills were enrolled for repeal, suspension, or phase-out of the prevailing wage law, or for reforms such as requiring that rates be set for helpers and trainees. Only the helper bill made it to the house floor, but it was defeated there.[121]

---

[117] MD. ANN. CODE art. 21, §§ 8-501 et seq.

[118] City of Baltimore: art. 4, § 6, Subsection 4(B), MD. CODE, and BALTIMORE CITY CHARTER. Prince George's County: MD. CODE OF PUB. LOCAL L., Art. 17.

[119] *Analysis of Prevailing Wage Legislation,* Maryland Department of Fiscal Services (November 1983).

[120] Washington Building and Construction Trades Council v. Dominic N. Fornaro, Montgomery Cty. Cir. Ct. (August 27, 1984).

[121] Letter from Robert H. Kittleman, member, Maryland House of Delegates, February 22, 1985. In the author's files.

Massachusetts

The prevailing wage statute of Massachusetts is complex, involuted, and the most restrictive of all the state statutes. It was first enacted in 1914, was reenacted in 1963, and has been amended since.[122] It covers highway work and applies to local as well as state contracts. There is no minimum contract threshold amount.

In addition to construction work, the statute applies to the rental of trucks by state and local agencies, and to moving office furniture and fixtures by state or local agencies. It also applies to firms supplying meats and meat products to the commonwealth. It mandates that housing authorities must bargain collectively, and requires that architects, engineers, draftsmen, and other technical employees of housing authorities be paid at 80 percent of the prevailing rate. The law also covers public employees employed in construction or repair work for which at least a $1,000 special appropriation has been provided. It requires that employees engaged on public works lodge, board, and trade where and with whom they elect.

For construction work, the statute mandates prevailing rates for the installation of resilient flooring, and for those doing soil tests and borings; also for teamsters, chauffeurs, and gravel transporters; and for janitors and maintenance workers, at 80 percent of the prevailing rate. The method of determining and selecting the prevailing rate is convoluted, but arrives at the collectively bargained rate. Laborers' wages are to be not less than those paid laborers in municipal service in the town (or the highest of the towns, if applicable) in which the prospective work is to be performed, unless there are collective bargaining agreements in effect, in which case collectively bargained rates apply. Craftsmen's wages are taken as the collectively bargained rates in the town, if they exist, or otherwise as the wages paid (to an unspecified plurality or majority) by private employers. The Massachusetts department of labor says that regardless of the circumstances, the union rate is used, because "by law, the rate cannot be less than the collective bargaining rate."[123] Fringe benefits, also, are taken as the equivalent of those required by collective bargaining agreements.

Locality is defined as the jurisdictional districts of local unions. In the event of joint coverage with the federal Davis-Bacon Act, the higher rate is used, which is usually the state rate. (In Massachu-

---

[122] Mass. Gen. Laws ch. 149, §§ 26 et seq; ch. 149, §§ 26 and 26Z; ch. 7, § 22; ch. 30, § 39L.

[123] Wharton Industrial Research Unit interview, Massachusetts Department of Labor, Boston, July 7, 1983.

setts, even spokesmen for the department of labor agree that if there is a difference, the state rate is almost invariably higher than the federal rate.)[124]

In 1979, four bills were introduced to the legislature calling for various modifications, but none was passed. Two bills were introduced during the 1980 session: one, calling for a study of the economic impact of the act on local government, received a favorable report from committee; the other, for raising the contract threshold to $150,000, received an unfavorable committee report. Both died. In 1981 there were four more bills, one again calling for a study of the impact of the law on local government, and the others seeking various extensions of the act, including coverage of contracts awarded by the Massachusetts industrial finance agency, requiring contractors to furnish proof of paying for certain fringe benefits, and providing for changing the rates during the life of contracts.

In 1983, a major effort was undertaken by a coalition of legislators, contractors' organizations, taxpayers' groups, and local officials to allow cities and towns the option of dropping the prevailing wage requirement for their own local contracts.[125] This was seen as an "odious and insidious attempt to destroy organized labor" and a "threat to the labor movement from the 'new right' which wants to destroy unions" by spokesmen for the 600 union members who "jammed a State House auditorium and hooted, howled, jeered, and applauded through a seven-hour hearing" by a state senate committee which then reported unfavorably on the measure.[126]

Proponents of repeal or modification of the law promised continuation of the effort in 1984.[127] This took the form of a proposal to establish a $250,000 threshold, and to set wage rates at 80 percent of prevailing (that is, 80 percent of the union rate) for other public works. it would also have established a helper category, in which wages at no less than twice the federal minimum wage would be allowed, and would have increased the ratio of apprentices allowed.[128] It was not reported out of committee, but during the 1985 legislative session the hearings on similar measures attracted a crowd of "about 1,000 union laborers"[129] to oppose them. Although the measures were defeated, their sponsors were reportedly heart-

---

[124] *Id.*

[125] *Coalition Fights Prevailing Wage Law,* Daily News (Springfield, Massachusetts) February 16, 1983.

[126] *Prevailing Wage Law Seems Sure to Survive,* Sun (Lowell, Massachusetts) April 15, 1983.

[127] *The* Other *Prevailing Wage Laws,* NATION'S BUSINESS 68 (June, 1983).

[128] *State Wage Laws Attacked,* ENGINEERING NEWS-RECORD 139 (April 19, 1984).

[129] *Taking on the Labor Lobby,* Sun (Lowell, Massachusetts), April 24, 1985, p. 7.

ened by their relatively stronger support, and set out to broaden the coalition seeking repeal or reform by including the Rural Caucus and other groups affected by high construction costs. Additional legislative studies were also sought.[130]

Michigan

Michigan's 1965 act covers highway work, competitively bid school board contracts, and public housing contracts, but not local or municipal contracts.[131] There is no minimum contract threshold. The act takes as prevailing the collectively bargained rates in the locality where the work is to be performed, or the nearest locality where they exist. The provisions of the act do not apply if they overlap Davis-Bacon rates on jointly-funded projects. Also included within the prevailing wage act is a provision requiring that printing done for the state must be done in-state, and (with minor exception) carry the union label.

By judicial opinion in 1975, the Michigan act did not apply to school construction for public school districts;[132] but a 1979 amendment extended the statute to school construction work again, provided that it was "sponsored or financed in whole or in part by the State."[133] Two western Michigan school districts that planned to undertake new construction in 1979 financed by local bond sales without using prevailing rates were required by the state's department of labor to apply prevailing rates to the work, since in such bond sales the state acts as surety on the bonds. The school districts challenged this presumption, and in the ensuing trial, the district court granted an injunction against applying the prevailing rate pending resolution of the question of whether the state's statute involved an unconstitutional delegation of authority to unions because of the method of rate selection.[134] The injunction was appealed by the Michigan department of labor, and was subsequently vacated by the appeals court which upheld the constitutionality of the Michigan statute, and in effect, sided with precedent from New Jersey rather than from Arizona.[135]

In 1983, a new economic development program, called the Michigan Strategic Fund, was created for the state; and the governor

---

[130] *Legislative Update,* GOV'T UNION CRITIQUE 6 (July 26, 1985).
[131] MICH. STAT. ANN. §§ 408.551 *et seq.,* (Act No. 106, 1965 Mich. Pub. Acts).
[132] Bowie v. Coloma School Board, 58 Mich. App. 223 (1975).
[133] Statutory language, 1965 Mich. Pub. Acts § 2, Act No. 166.
[134] West Ottawa Public Schools v. C. Partick Babcock, Cir. Ct. the County of Ottawa, 79 4801 CZ.
[135] West Ottawa Public Schools v. C. Partick Babcock, 107 Mich. App. 237, 309 N.W.2d 200 (1979). *See generally,* note 24, *supra.*

decreed that the prevailing wage bill would apply to construction projects financed by it, although prevailing rates had not applied to either of the predecessor economic development authorities which had been combined to create it. During the year, bills were introduced to the legislature to block the wage law's application to projects where local economic development corporations were involved in the financing, to abolish the law, and to eliminate the prevailing wage requirement.[136] In the legislative maneuvering, although the senate favored the bills, the house blocked their adoption. Similar measures were introduced in 1984, some of which advanced as far as a joint house-senate conference committee, but were again rejected.[137]

Minnesota

Minnesota's current law goes back only to 1973.[138] It covers multi-trade contracts over $25,000 and single-trade contracts over $2,500 for state projects only. Bills introduced in 1980 and 1981 would have mandated that municipalities establish prevailing wage rates also, but they did not pass the legislature. The present act allows the city councils of cities of the second class—over 20,000 and less than 50,000 population—to establish residency requirements and adopt wage scales for construction workmen; another section of the act separately allows municipalities to adopt rules establishing prevailing wage rates.

There is a separate provision for highway work which establishes prevailing hours of work as well as prevailing rates.[139] For the prevailing hours of work, any work over the prevailing hours, even though less than eight hours per day or forty hours per week, must receive overtime at time-and-one-half. Another section specifies that highways constructed in the state with federal funds, if administered by the state, must provide for wage rates at least as high as the state rates. There are exceptions to this last provision which exempt contracts with railroads or public utilities for the alteration or relocation of their facilities where the work is to be performed by the regular employees of the railroad or utility.

Like the Massachusetts act, this one seems to have been influenced by teamster concerns, in that it covers not only truck drivers but also the rental rates for truck hire. In the event of overlapping coverage with the federal Davis-Bacon Act, "whichever is most strin-

---

[136] UPI (wire service), 11-03-83, 07:16 pcs.
[137] *The 1984 Prevailing Wage Roundup, supra* note 44, at 7–8.
[138] MINN. STAT. §§ 177.44 *et seq.*
[139] MINN. STAT. §§ 177.42, 177.43

gent upon the employer and/or most beneficial to the employee" prevails.[140]

To establish the prevailing rate, a mail survey is conducted and the simple plurality rate (the rate paid to the largest number) is taken. This method of establishing the rate, the same as used in California, would normally guarantee that AFL-CIO collective bargaining rates would be found to be prevailing, but in many rural areas of Minnesota, the issue is complicated by the presence of the Christian Labor Association, a non-AFL-CIO union whose wage rates are generally lower than those of the traditional craft unions.[141] Critics of the Minnesota act maintain, however, that the Christian Labor Association rates are as neglected as open shop rates, leaving the AFL-CIO union rates as the ones most generally specified.[142]

Bills for repeal were proposed in both 1979 and 1980 following allegations of improprieties in the wage survey process, including failure to conduct actual surveys, accepting dubious statements from union officials, using forms which contain inaccurate wage rates and instances of forgery, and for not accepting the wages found by field investigators.[143] Neither of the bills passed.

Mississippi

The public works prevailing wage law of Mississippi establishes a two-year residency requirement for employment on public works contracts, but does not set, establish, or require prevailing rates.

Missouri

The Missouri law dates from 1957.[144] It covers highway contracts and work performed for public utilities whether state or local, but does not cover work for special drainage or levee districts. To set the prevailing rate, collectively bargained rates and rates that are generally paid are ascertained and considered, but the selection process is not defined. Wages must be paid in cash. In an interview in August 1982, the administrative assistant for the Division of Labor Standards, Missouri Department of Labor, did not know

---

[140] Response to Wharton Industrial Research Unit survey, August 17, 1982.

[141] *Uncle Sam Pays Too Well, Says Construction Contractor,* Free Press (Minnesota) July 20, 1983.

[142] *Minn. ABC Calls for Grand Jury Investigation of State's Prevailing Wage Law Administration,* A-15 CONSTRUCTION LAB. REP. 1264, February 13, 1980.

[143] *Fraud Uncovered: Probe Reveals Improprieties in Minnesota Davis-Bacon Pay,* ENGINEERING NEWS-RECORD 51 (August 2, 1979).

[144] Mo. ANN. STAT. §§ 29-210–290.340. (Vernon).

which wage rates apply when federal and state acts overlap, and was unable to say if any local prevailing wage laws existed in the state.[145]

Specification of the union rate as prevailing is apparently certain enough that one union is reported to have taken advantage of the system. In 1983, an electricians' union negotiated a labor agreement that called for a wage rate of $2.89 per hour more for its members when working on public contracts than when working on private ones. The state department of labor obliged by adopting this contrived rate as prevailing, even though it had never been paid to anyone.[146]

A 1979 bill which would have limited application to projects more than 50 percent state-funded died, as did a bill to shift authority from the state department of labor to individual contracting agencies. The constitutionality of the Missouri statute's rate determination methodology was tested but affirmed by the state supreme court in 1981.[147]

Montana

Montana enacted its prevailing wage law in 1931 and last amended it in 1981.[148] Like many other state acts, this one has no minimum contract threshold, and so covers all public works. An attempt to introduce a $50,000 threshold failed to pass the legislature in 1981. The prevailing wage law covers school work, highway work, and contracts for political subdivisions; it requires hiring preference for state residents except where contracts are federally aided. If the federal law applies, the state statute does not. The housing authority is given permission—rather unnecessarily—to comply with requirements for prevailing rates on federally funded housing projects. Another seemingly unnecessary provision in the statute specifies that prevailing rates cannot be set higher than those determined by collective bargaining contracts.

The Montana Commissioner of Labor is directed to determine the prevailing rate, and has some discretion in choosing it, in that he is to ascertain and consider collective bargaining agreements and other information on wages in effect in the county or locality for

---

[145] Wharton Industrial Research Unit interview, Missouri Department of Labor and Industrial Relations, Jefferson City, August 2, 1982.

[146] *Prevailing Wage System Is a Rip-off,* (editorial) News-Press/Gazette (St. Joseph, Missouri) December 3, 1983.

[147] From information contained in Richard R. Nelson, *State Labor Legislation Enacted in 1981,* 105 MONTHLY LAB. REV. 8 (January, 1982). No case citation given.

[148] MONT. CODE ANN. § 18-2-403 (1978).

each craft, classification, or type of worker needed to complete the contract.[149] The administrator of the state's labor standards division in 1982 maintained that rates were set after reviewing information from various sources, including, in addition to collective bargaining rates, Davis-Bacon rates and data provided by the state's job service.[150] Locality for prevailing rate purposes is set following collective bargaining boundaries.

A bill to drop state wage determinations in favor of federal rates was killed in the state senate in 1979, as was a bill to use the arithmetic average of survey rates. The Montana department of labor was granted somewhat stronger enforcement procedures in 1981. The new procedures specified that if public agencies did not notify contractors that they must pay the prevailing wage rates, the public agencies themselves could be forced to compensate employees who were paid less. In 1982, the Montana Association of Counties called for repeal of the law.[151]

Nebraska

Nebraska's law, dating from 1923, is among the most atypical of the state statutes.[152] Among other things, it does not intend to establish prevailing rates, but rather "fair labor standards." It expressly prohibits actions under the act that will increase cost to the state of public works contracts. Furthermore, it does not apply if public works contracts stipulate rates of pay and conditions of employment. Finally, it does not contemplate predetermination of wages, their issuance, or their posting.

What the act does require is a statement of compliance to be filed by contractors at the time of the bid submission to the effect that the contractors will pay a scale of wages paid by 50 percent of contractors in the same business. On a showing, satisfactory to a public contracting agency, that a contractor has not complied with fair labor standards, that contractor's low bid may be disqualified, and the next lowest bid accepted instead. The act, such as it is, does

---

[149] The constitutionality of the statute in its delegation of authority from the legislature to private hands was tested in David L. Hunter v. City of Bozeman, Mont. Sup. Ct., Case No. 84-381, May 30, 1985. This court found the statute constitutional, since it directed the secretary of labor to consider information other than collectively bargained rates. The judge in this case indicated, however, that a statute making the union scale absolutely determinative of union rates would be unconstitutional. [*Montana Supreme Court Upholds State's Prevailing Wage Law*, 31 CONSTRUCTION LAB. REP. 466 (June 26, 1985).]

[150] Response to Wharton Industrial Research Unit survey, July 27, 1982.

[151] *Repeal of State Wage Laws Sought*, Missoulian (Missoula, Montana) May 12, 1983.

[152] NEB. REV. STAT. tit. 73.

apply to highway work. In the event of conflict with the federal act, the federal provisions apply.

A representative for the state department of labor, interviewed by telephone in July 1982, felt that, realistically, Nebraska has no substantive prevailing wage law.[153] Nor does the Nebraska Department of Labor attempt to enforce the prevailing wage requirement. The Nebraska job service (the unemployment office) performs annual surveys of wage rates in the whole state, which contractors are expected to rely upon in complying with the law. Enforcement is by individual action through the courts, but there have been no such actions in fourteen years.

Although Nebraska's act is the least typical of all of the state acts, it probably does come closer than any other to achieving the stated intent of prevailing wage laws—to build protection into the contracting system to prevent competition for public works from driving down wages in the industry. It achieves this purpose, apparently, with little fuss or controversy.

Nevada

The Nevada statute, passed in 1937, covers both highway and construction contracts, and specially covers work for public utilities, and on water mains and sewers, public parks, and playgrounds.[154] The law does not mention contracts for political subdivisions, but the commissioner of labor has ruled that such contracts are covered also.[155] By a 1982 attorney general's opinion, all public works contracts, even those that are in part federally funded, are covered by the state act if a state or local agency is in any way involved in the administration or monitoring of that project.[156] Like Massachusetts and Minnesota, Nevada concerns itself with special provisions applying to the rental of trucks by contractors.

The level of prevailing rates is set at the discretion of the commissioner of labor, and no method of selecting the prevailing rate is mentioned, although the commissioner is instructed to hold hearings if in doubt as to what the rate should be for a given locality. For prevailing wage purposes, the commissioner has elected to divide the state into two districts, comprising a northern district (dominated by the city of Reno) and a southern district (dominated by the city of Las Vegas). According to a local newspaper report,

---

[153] Wharton Industrial Research Unit telephone interview, Nebraska Department of Labor, July 8, 1982.
[154] NEV. REV. STAT. tit. 338.
[155] Response to Wharton Industrial Research Unit survey, July 13, 1982.
[156] Op. Att'y Gen. No. 82-18.

Reno union wage scales are taken as the prevailing rates for the entire northern half of the state and Las Vegas union wage scales establish the prevailing rate in the south.[157]

A 1979 bill removed some limitations on work hours (based on an eight-hour day) from the act. In 1981, a bill that would have repealed the prevailing wage law failed to pass the legislature, as did another that would have adopted the federal Davis-Bacon Act procedures and rates. However, the legislature did pass a bill establishing a contract threshold amount of $4,000. (None had existed previously.)

In 1982, a coalition of rural municipalities and counties sought relief from the imposition of the city union rates by seeking (without success) to have additional wage districts established for the more rural regions, where local rates would be more adequately reflected in wage determinations.[158] In 1983, the effort continued, and was joined by several other public bodies and school boards. Other amendments sought would have exempted county projects from the prevailing wage requirement.[159] These amendments were unsuccessful, but a suit brought by two rural counties to force the state labor commissioner to hold hearings in each county before establishing prevailing rates for it did much better. An Elko district judge ruled in July 1983 that the commissioner could not enforce the prevailing wage in Elko County until he held a public hearing to learn the proper wage levels.[160] The state supreme court upheld the lower court's ruling in 1984.[161] In a separate case, the state supreme court also ruled that the commissioner's division of the state into two arbitrary districts for wage making was in excess of his statutory authority.[162]

Commissioners of labor in Nevada have traditionally been appointed from the ranks of metropolitan labor organizations, and over the years they seem consistently to have used their office to interpret the prevailing wage law restrictively and favorably towards union interests. These new rulings may limit their discretion in the future. Two bills were introduced to the 1985 legislature. One of them, calling for rates to be established by hearings at the

---

[157] *Public Works: Paying the Price,* Independent (Elko, Nevada) February 2, 1983.

[158] *County Seeks Relief from Davis-Bacon Act Wage Scale,* Mason Valley News (Yellington, Nevada), July 16, 1982.

[159] *Douglas Seeks Injunction Against State in Wage Flap,* Nevada Appeal (Carson City, Nevada) March 25, 1983.

[160] UPI (wire service), 05-07-84, 02:05 ppd.

[161] *Nevada Counties Win Prevailing Wage Ruling,* GOV'T UNION CRITIQUE 1 (September 21, 1984). (Case citation unreported.)

[162] *Id.*

town level, was held for further study, but the other, calling for repeal, was unanimously defeated in the assembly Labor and Management Committee after construction workers showed up in force at the hearings.[163]

New Hampshire

The New Hampshire statute, dating from 1941, tied with Maryland's for the highest contract threshold: $500,000.[164] It applied to both local and state contracts, in the same manner and to the same extent as the Davis-Bacon Act. Like the federal act, it left selecting the prevailing rate to its regulations which paralleled the "majority, 30 percent, or average" of the old federal formula.

In practice, New Hampshire's rates were weighted towards larger firms (and therefore, by inference, towards higher wage rates) by excluding small jobs, part-time employees, and helpers from surveys and by taking each contractor's peak payroll period wages.

A 1979 bill to repeal the statute passed the senate, but died in the house. In 1985, however, after indications that prevailing rates on one school project may have inflated costs by over 9 percent[165] and that their existence on another may have caused local contractors to withdraw and leave the field exclusively to "out-of-state contractors with high-wage crews,"[166] separate repeal bills were introduced in both houses of the legislature. Both passed, and the repeal became effective sixty days later, in August 1985, without the signature of Governor John Sununu.[167]

New Jersey

New Jersey's 1913 law was reenacted in 1963 to cover building and highway work on state or local contracts in excess of $2,000.[168] Collectively bargained rates are specified as prevailing. Although the New Jersey Department of Labor maintains that it relies mainly on county boundaries,[169] local contractors have said that reliance on union practices in different jurisdictional areas can and does cause problems with the classification of certain workmen, and

---

[163] UPI (wire service) 04-22-85 06:03 pps.

[164] N.H. STAT. ANN. tit. 280.

[165] *Bill Would End Public Wage Rates,* Coos Co. Democrat (Lancaster, New Hampshire), May 20, 1985, p. 1.

[166] "Prevailing Wage Issue Before House," UPI (wire service) 04-16-85 07:23 pes.

[167] *Taxpayers Rejoice* (editorial), Sentinal (Keene, New Hampshire) June 4, 1985.

[168] N.J. STAT. ANN. §§ 34:11-56.25–34:11-56.44.

[169] Wharton Industrial Research Unit interview, New Jersey Department of Labor, Trenton, June 18, 1982.

therefore with their wage rates.[170] Additionally, the rules for overtime depend on union craft practices, which differ by craft and area, requiring more than ten different provisions to be accommodated.

Although not mentioned by the statute, local and municipal contracts are covered. For joint federal-state projects, the higher rate prevails. Public employees employed in construction work are excluded.

In 1979, several modifications were proposed to provide for tougher enforcement procedures; other proposals would have excluded towns with less than 10,000 or less than 25,000 population. None of these proposals was successful. In 1980, the legislature extended payment of prevailing wages to construction projects receiving financial assistance from the Economic Development Authority. In 1981, it voted against extending coverage to work performed on private property that was or would be leased to the state.

New Jersey's is one of the most pervasively prounion prevailing wage statutes. This is at least partially attributable to the fact that the individual who has been the assistant commissioner of labor in charge of administering the New Jersey prevailing wage law for more than twenty years, is staunchly prounion: "No bones about it, I'm a union man."[171] Furthermore, this individual considers the statute to be his very own. In his words, "This is my law."[172] When interviewed in June of 1982, the assistant commissioner expressed the opinion that prevailing wage statutes are specifically for the purpose of protecting *union* employees, and if they do not adopt the union scale, they are of no value. (He also feels that surveys at any level, including those by the U.S. Department of Labor, are not and cannot be accurate.)[173]

The pro-labor orientation of the law's administrators seems to be shared by members of the judiciary, including the federal court judiciary, in New Jersey. In a recent district court opinion, the federal judge concurred that "the purpose of the Act is to prevent unfair competition by nonunion employers with unionized employers providing similar goods or services, by payment of wages below those paid to union employees."[174] The judge went on to point out that the "Act represents a reasonable attempt by the state to deal

---

[170] Author's survey, spring 1980.
[171] Wharton Industrial Research Unit interview, New Jersey Department of Labor, Trenton, June 18, 1982.
[172] *Id.*
[173] *Id.*
[174] *Garden State Brickface Co. v. New Jersey,* N.J. Dist. Ct., No. 80-635, March 11, 1981. (Unreported).

with an undisputed economic evil"—presumably that of free market wages.[175]

New Mexico

New Mexico's law, dating from 1937, covers both construction and highway work in excess of $20,000 (raised from $2,000 by a 1979 amendment) for both state and local contracts.[176] Although not specified by the statute, New Mexico uses the old federal formula of "majority, 30 percent, or average" to determine rates.[177] Most of the provisions of the New Mexico law seem similar to those of the federal act.

Local as well as state contracts are covered. School work is excluded if school boards serve as prime contractors and hire laborers and mechanics on their own. State employees are not covered. In the event of overlap with the federal Davis-Bacon Act, the federal act takes precedence, but only if its rates are higher.[178]

The New Mexico legislature killed a bill in 1979 which would have restricted coverage to only those projects for which the total contract amount was under $1.00. In 1981, the legislature passed a bill to repeal the prevailing wage law, but it was vetoed by the governor.[179] Another repeal bill died in 1985.[180]

New York

New York had a prevailing wage statute as early as 1897; its current law dates from 1921.[181] Amendments through the years and contrary opinions by various attorneys general have made it one of the nation's most turgid and confusing. It applies, for example, to garbage men employed by private contractors, but not to county sanitation men (although public employees, except those in graded municipal service, are supposed to be included); it applies to employees of the Thousand Islands Bridge Authority, but not to employees of the New York Port Authority; it covers able bodied seamen scaling ships, but not stationary firemen in state hospitals. Serving labor is specifically included, whereas electricians, engi-

---

[175] *Id.*
[176] N.M. STAT. § 13-4.
[177] Author's survey, spring 1980.
[178] Op. Att'y Gen. No. 71-114.
[179] *New Mexico Joins Other States in Repealing State 'Davis-Bacon Act,'* DAILY LAB. REP. A-2 (April 3, 1981).
[180] *Public Works Wage Measure Dies in House,* Record (Roswell, New Mexico) March 7, 1985.
[181] N.Y. LAB. LAW ch. 31. (McKinney).

neers, and elevator men in the Bureau of Building Management of the Office of General Services during the annual session of the legislature are specifically excluded. Finally, an entirely separate prevailing wage law is on the books to cover work on eliminating railroad grade crossings.

As the law applies to construction work, it covers both highways and buildings. There is no threshold contract amount, although a 1915 attorney general's opinion mentions $500. Prior to 1983, wage rates under the statute were purportedly based on semi-annual universe surveys (100 percent sample size) with rates chosen by an unusual formulation of "40 percent plurality or average."[182] In 1983, surveys were dispensed with, and the prevailing rates are now taken as the union scale, if unions comprise 30 percent of the workforce, or the average if they do not.[183] Since no mechanism is provided to determine if unions do comprise at least 30 percent of the workforce in any given locality in the state, the state's department of labor takes the position that the union rate prevails unless challenged, and if challenged, leaves it up to the challenger to prove that it does not.[184] New York is thus effectively a union-rate state.

Wages are per diem, and must be paid in cash unless prior arrangement is made with the commissioner of labor. New York City has its own prevailing wage law for local contracts (which generally requires the union rate) as do a number of other cities in the state.[185] When there is joint application at the state-local or at the federal-state level, the higher rates apply.

Fringe benefits are handled in a unique way. Unlike the federal government or other states which mandate fringe benefits as part of the prevailing wage, New York City requires that they be paid in kind under the state law. That is, nonunion (or other) employers cannot "cash out" fringe benefits in the usual way or provide their employees with equivalent supplements. If such employers do not participate in the particular benefit programs that are determined to be prevailing, their only alternatives are to purchase the same benefits for their employees, which is often impossible, or to pay them the cash value of the supplements as they would be purchased

---

[182] Maryland is the only other state whose prevailing wage law specifies a "40 percent plurality or average" formula. Maryland adopted the formula in 1983, the same year it was dropped by New York.

[183] "The New York State Prevailing Wage Law: An Investigative Analysis," State of New York Commission of Investigation, December, 1983, pp. 10–18.

[184] *Id.*, p. 18.

[185] New York City's Public Works Law, Sec. 343-09.0, NYC Administrative Code, requires only a minimum wage rate (of $2.50 per hour), safe and sanitary working conditions, and minimum wages for male and female employment. The Board of Estimates, however, is empowered to "adopt necessary rules and regulations."

by an individual.[186] Insofar as these benefits are typically much more expensive when purchased for small groups or for individuals, the New York law has succeeded in making nonunion labor costs higher than union costs on public construction.

This interpretation of fringe benefit requirements was the subject of a New York Court of Appeals decision in 1985, which found nothing in the state law that "expressly prohibits an employer from providing the prevailing supplements either totally in payments in cash, partially in benefits and partially in cash, or totally in benefits by direct contribution to a benefits fund.[187] The court found the city's enforcement "arbitrary and irrational" because it did not allow contractors to pay cash to workers in lieu of fringe benefits,[188] but the court did not broach the question of benefit equivalence.

Another problem area involves apprentices and trainees. As in other parts of the country, duly registered apprentices, who tend overwhelmingly to be employed by union contractors, may be paid at starting rates of from 30 to 50 percent of prevailing, increasing with experience. Trainees are minority group members or other individuals who could not meet the age or educational requirements for apprenticeship established by the unions, but who are registered with the United States Department of Labor. It is a requirement of both New York City and New York State that trainees be employed in the ratio of one trainee for every four journeymen on public works projects in New York City.[189] Since June 1980, however, the city comptroller's office has refused to issue wage rates for trainees, requiring them to be paid at the full journeyman's rate.[190]

A state supreme court decision in 1979 affirmed a 1975 amendment which allowed the Industrial Commission to redetermine rates during a contract's life and to require the new rates on existing contracts.[191] As is the case also in Alaska and Ohio, this provision would seem to increase contractor's risks significantly in taking on public works jobs. It also applies to public employees, whose wages, although tied to collective bargaining rates, tend to lag behind them

---

[186] Op. Att'y Gen. No. 106,336 and No. 108,138 (May 7, 1975).

[187] *N.Y. High Court Clashes with City over Wage Law,* ENGINEERING NEWS-RECORD 60 (January 17, 1985).

[188] *Id.*

[189] New York City: Executive Order 20, July 1970 and Executive Order 50, April 1980; New York State: Executive Order 43, January 1971.

[190] "The New York State Prevailing Wage Law: An Investigative Analysis," *supra* note 183, at 33-54.

[191] N.Y. LAB. LAW ch. 31, subdiv. 3, as amended by ch. 336, L. 1978 (McKinney). Constitutionality upheld in Meaott Construction Corp v. Philip Ross, N.Y. Sup. Ct., Albany Calendar No. 7, June 22, 1979, affirmed N.Y. Sup. Ct., App. Div. No. 37151, May 29, 1980 (unreported).

in time of application. As of July 1982, the state had lost more than 140 suits on this ground.[192]

Recent legislative efforts, as might be expected of New York, have been numerous and unusual with respect to efforts in other states. During 1979, bills were introduced to the state assembly calling for tougher enforcement of existing regulations, for new penalties on contractors for underpaying employees, for extending coverage to employees engaged in fabricating steel and other architectural metals, for eliminating coverage for towns and villages, and for requiring payment of interest by contractors on late wages. The penalty and interest provisions became law in 1980; the others failed. Several of the same measures were introduced again in 1981, but failed again. Another 1981 bill would have extended prevailing wage coverage to the printing trades, but it was tabled in committee.

In 1982, a bill which would have required the union rate to be chosen as prevailing disappeared in the senate, but it was resurrected in slightly modified form and passed in 1983.[193] This amendment, in addition to requiring collective bargaining rates (if at least 30 percent of the workers in a trade in the locality are covered by collective bargaining agreements) also changed the definition of locality, defining it as that area of the state described and defined in the current collective bargaining agreements between employers and bona fide labor organizations.

In late 1983, the State of New York Commission of Investigation issued a lengthy analysis of the state prevailing wage law, concluding that the law "is cumbersome to administer and can often result in inaccurate and inflationary wage and benefit determinations."[194] It made seven specific recommendations to the legislature, including changing the plurality cutoff point from 30 percent to 50 percent to reflect the new federal rules, but the legislature took no action on them during 1984.

North Carolina

North Carolina has no prevailing wage statute.

---

[192] Wharton Industrial Research Unit interview, New York Department of Labor, Albany, July 8, 1982.

[193] Co-sponsored: S.1904-A and A.2043-A. Passed by the legislature on June 24, 1983 and signed into law by the Governor on July 15, 1983, effective immediately.

[194] "The New York State Prevailing Wage Law: An Investigative Analysis," *supra* note 183, at 65. *See also, New York Wage Law Blasted,* ENGINEERING NEWS-RECORD, 66–7 (January 19, 1984); *Report Says City and State Pay Too Much for Buildings,* New York Times, January 11, 1984; and *New York State Prevailing Wage Law Criticized for Role in Cost Increases,* 7 DAILY LAB. REP. A-4–A-6, (January 12, 1984).

North Dakota

North Dakota has a public works law which gives contracting preference to in-state contractors who employ at least 90 percent state residents, but it has no prevailing wage statute.

Ohio

Although many of the state laws passed at about the same time as the Davis-Bacon Act reflect the federal legislation, Ohio's does not.[195] Its threshold amount for building or highway work is $4,000 instead of $2,000, but in most other respects, Ohio's law varies on the side of expanded coverage. It applies, for example, to serving labor, and to off-site laborers, workmen and mechanics working on any materials to be used in connection with public work, who are to be paid prevailing rates applicable in the same trade in the locality where the materials are to be used—a provision which must be close to impossible to administer. It extends, as does California's, to cover privately owned buildings being constructed for public lease, and to such diverse activities as tree trimming and removal along city streets. It requires, as does Hawaii's, that each nonunion workman on a job be given separate notification of the schedule of wages to be paid. It applies to local and municipal contracts. It even extends to private contracts if funded through industrial development financing.

As is the case in New York and Alaska, its rates may change during the life of the contract if collectively bargained rates change. It applies to regular salaried employees of municipalities engaged in constructing public improvements (force account labor), unless the municipality has adopted charter under the state constitution and has its own civil service regulations.[196] Perhaps the only area of flexibility of this statute is that it does not apply where joint coverage exists with the federal Davis-Bacon act.

The prevailing rate established by Ohio's law is that found in the collective bargaining agreements in the county where the work is to be performed, and if it should happen that no such agreements exist, the Department of Industrial Relations is required to take the rates of the nearest and most similar area which has such agreements. Wages must be paid in case, and are set on a per-diem basis.

In 1979, an unsuccessful proposal was made to raise the threshold for construction on school jobs to $100,000. In 1980, bills to exempt

---

[195] OHIO REV. CODE ANN. § 4115.03.
[196] Op. Att'y Gen. No. 1181 (1960).

construction of public schools and hospitals, facilities and projects constructed by private entities with state financial assistance, and construction of nonprofit health care facilities were suggested, but all were killed in committee. In late 1982, after an effort to eliminate prevailing rates from a state-sponsored housing loan program failed, another try was made to substitute the federal Davis-Bacon rate. It failed also.

All told, Ohio's is one of the most thoroughly prounion prevailing wage laws. An unsuccessful repeal effort on behalf of minority construction workers was mounted in late 1979. In October 1978, one Ohio city, Upper Arlington, passed an ordinance specifically excluding incorporation of prevailing rates in its contracts, but it is not known if the legality of that ordinance has been tested.[197] A recent head of the prevailing wage division in Ohio expressed the opinion that the prevailing wage law is unconstitutional and inflationary, and should be repealed. She, however, was an administrative rather than a policy setting executive.[198]

Oklahoma

The current Oklahoma statute dates back only to 1965.[199] It covers building construction (no highways) for the state or its political subdivisions, including some but not all special districts. There is no minimum contract threshold amount. For setting the prevailing rate, the statute is silent, but its regulations follow the old federal formula, with determinations based on an annual peak-period wage survey.

Prior to 1981, fringe benefits were not included in the statute, but were set by regulation as the same proportion that fringe benefit costs were to basic rates found in the most recent collective bargaining agreements on file in the state. This procedure usually resulted in fringe benefit amounts of about 10 percent of the base wage rate, and simplified the problem of calculating fringe benefits, which otherwise would have entailed a separate survey. The method was dropped because the resulting full rates (base plus fringes) were different from the rates set by the Davis-Bacon Act.

A bill to repeal the statute passed the senate in 1981, but failed narrowly in the house. The same fate met another bill aimed at improving administration of the act. Modifications were approved,

---

[197] Ordinance No. 75-78, City of Upper Arlington. In *Lawmaker Opposed to Prevailing Wage,* Dispatch (Columbus, Ohio) September 4, 1979.

[198] Wharton Industrial Research Unit interview, Ohio Department of Industrial Relations, Columbus, July 23, 1982.

[199] OKLA. STAT. § 196.

however, that mandated using federal Davis-Bacon rates where they were available, added fringe benefits to the definitions of hourly wages, established a wage appeals board, and adopted procedures for determining rates in the absence of federal rates based on four classes of public works: building, residential, heavy, and highway. In 1983, the Oklahoma senate, through an amendment to an unrelated bill, voted by a two-to-one majority to abolish the law, but the repealer was killed by the house.[200] A number of other unsuccessful attempts to abolish the act were made in 1983.[201]

During the 1984 session, little Davis-Bacon repeal became one of the major issues of the legislative term. A bill to repeal was introduced early in the session. After clearing the state assembly by a comfortable margin, intensive lobbying in the senate resulted in a procedural amendment which, by a single vote, sent the bill to a joint conference, where it was allowed to die.[202] In 1985, several bills calling for the phase out or repeal of the law failed to pass both houses of the state legislature.[203] Late in October 1985, however, the Oklahoma legislature passed a bill to partially repeal its little Davis-Bacon act. The bill exempts projects under $600,000 from prevailing wage requirements and prevents the labor commissioner from using urban wage scales in rural determinations, but it applies only to school districts, counties, cities, and public trusts, not state building projects.[204]

Oregon

Oregon's is a recent statute, having been enacted in 1959.[205] Local as well as state contracts over $10,000 are covered. In setting the prevailing rate, what has become the new federal formula of "majority or average" is used. Locality is defined as the largest city and its vicinity in the district (of which there are sixteen in the state) where the work is to be performed, and if data are not available for it, the Davis-Bacon rate is used instead. Where it is the practice among the construction trades in the state for wage rates to increase progressively based on the distance between the job site and a

---

[200] *Challenge to Prevailing Wage Sparks Both Sides into Action,* Tulsa Daily World, April 13, 1983.

[201] *State AFL-CIO Race Heats Up,* Tulsa Daily World, July 15, 1983.

[202] *Senate Buries Wage Bill,* News (Enid, Oklahoma) April 26, 1984.

[203] *Wage Proposal Needs Approval,* Eagle (Enid, Oklahoma) March 25, 1985; and *House Passes Prevailing-Wage Bill,* Journal Record (Oklahoma City) March 15, 1985, p. 1.

[204] *Partial Davis-Bacon Victory,* Daily Oklahoman (Oklahoma City) November 3, 1985.

[205] OR. REV. STAT. § 279.

specific landmark, these increases become part of the prevailing rate required.[206] Because of the reliance on metropolitan rates in the survey structure, the prevailing rate procedure is said to favor union rates.[207] Local contracts are covered. If Davis-Bacon rates apply, the state rates do not.

In 1979, a bill to repeal the statute was tabled, and another bill, which would have required certification of the name and address of each worker and the individual wages paid each, died in committee. A similar bill in 1981 also failed. A bill to replace the word "workmen" with "workers" passed, but was vetoed for undetermined reasons. Several administrative and enforcement procedures were proposed during the 1981 legislative session, including one which would have allowed the labor commissioner to seek an injunction against employers to prevent future failure to pay the prevailing wage. These measures passed the senate but failed in the house.

A bill to repeal the act was entered in 1983 but failed to clear the legislature.[208] A compromise bill which would have stopped application to local and school district contracts also died, even though it had the support of the Oregon Association of Counties, the League of Oregon Cities, and the Oregon School Boards Association. Despite these efforts to soften or eliminate the prevailing wage measure, the only bill actually to pass in 1983 expanded coverage to certain workers previously exempted, required posting of prevailing rates at the job site, and made other administrative changes. It did, however, also raise the minimum contract threshold from $2,000 to $10,000.[209]

Pennsylvania

As is true in several other industrial states, prevailing rates in Pennsylvania are established for trades outside the construction industry. In Pennsylvania, commonwealth printing contracts and some local printing (at local option) fall under the act.

The minimum contract amount for this much-modified 1961 law is $25,000.[210] Highways are not mentioned, but local contracts are covered. The secretary of labor is given broad discretion in defining

---

[206] Op. Att'y Gen. No. 7947 (1980).

[207] *Little Davis-Bacon Repeal,* Journal of Commerce (Seattle, Washington) March 7, 1983. (Dateline Salem, Oregon).

[208] *Prevailing Wage Law Under Fire,* Aloha Breeze (Hillsboro, Oregon) November 17, 1982.

[209] *State's Wage Rate Law Has Six Changes,* Mail Tribune (Medford, Oregon) October 18, 1983.

[210] PA. STAT. tit. 43, §§ 165-1–165-17.

the prevailing rate for the state and establishing the localities to which it applies. Although he is instructed to ascertain and consider a variety of wage scales in the commonwealth, it is generally agreed by members of the labor department, as well as by local contractors, that the rates chosen as prevailing are almost invariably the rates found in union agreements.[211] By statute, collectively bargained fringe benefits are automatically considered prevailing. If the state and federal acts overlap, the state act provisions do not apply. The law is unusual in that it is one of the few which do not cover maintenance work. This has produced a number of court cases, since the dividing line between reconstruction and maintenance is a fine one.[212]

A bill to repeal the statute was introduced in 1979, but was not successful. Its constitutionality was tried and sustained in 1980.[213] Another repeal attempt, in 1981, also failed, and an attempt in the same year to increase the minimum contract threshold from $25,000 to $50,000 was bottled up in committee. During 1982, there was talk by a member of the labor relations committee of the house of representatives of trying to modify the statute to the extent of eliminating coverage on any contracts sponsored by a public municipality regardless of how they were funded, but the measure was never formally introduced.[214]

Rhode Island

Rhode Island's 1935 law covers highways and local contracts over $1,000.[215] To a greater degree than most, it reflects teamster concerns: teamsters, chauffeurs, and those engaged in transportation of gravel or fill to or from the job site are covered; grading and clearing are mentioned; and the statute contains a provision that contractors must pay for trucking and for materials within ninety days of the invoice or the invoice amount may be withheld by the contracting authority.

---

[211] Wharton Industrial Research Unit interview, Pennsylvania Department of Labor and Industry, Harrisburg, June 22, 1982.

[212] A contract for replacing the cell block roof at a state correctional institution was held by the Pennsylvania Secretary of Labor and the Pennsylvania Wage Appeals Board to be "repair" work, but the Commonwealth Court of Pennsylvania reversed and determined such work to be "maintenance" work, because it "did not change or increase the size, type, or extent of the cell block." Kitson Bros. v. Com. Dept. of Labor, etc., Pa. Commw., 414 A.2d 179 (1980).

[213] Keystone Chapter, Associated Builders and Contractors, Inc. v. Commonwealth of Pennsylvania, Pa. Commw. No. 749, May 30, 1980.

[214] Wharton Industrial Research Unit interview, Pennsylvania House of Representatives, Harrisburg, July 22, 1982.

[215] R.I. Gen. Laws tit. 37, §§ 37-13-1 to 37-13-16.

No specifications are made for the calculation or setting of prevailing rates, but the director of labor is empowered by the statute to adopt Davis-Bacon rates, and by the administrative regulations to conduct surveys. Surveys, however, have reportedly not been conducted for the past six or seven years.[216] For unusual job categories, such as scuba divers needed for bridge construction, where Davis-Bacon rates are not available, union rates are taken as prevailing. In the particular case of scuba divers, the union rate for carpenters was chosen as prevailing, although no one seems to know why.[217]

A 1981 amendment modified the law by establishing an eighteen-month black list for persons or firms found in violation of the prevailing wage law.

South Carolina

South Carolina has no law providing specifically for prevailing rates. There is only a provision giving preference to South Carolina workmen and materials on public works.

South Dakota

Prevailing rates are not required in South Dakota, but there is a statute giving hiring preference to veterans and to state residents.

Tennessee

Tennessee had a prevailing wage law as early as 1953, but the current law was enacted in 1975.[218] It covers all highway contracts and state building contracts over $50,000. Local contracts are not covered, but a number of cities, such as Nashville, are reported to have local prevailing wage ordinances which adopt the state rates.[219]

Rates are set by a special five-man commission based on an annual survey for highway work and a biennial survey for building construction. The surveys attempt to be comprehensive of all workmen in the state. The commission is empowered to modify the rates found in its survey by plus-or-minus 6 percent from a base established by taking the arithmetic mean of the survey returns from the twelve areas into which the state is divided for the purpose. Only "straight"

---

[216] Wharton Industrial Research Unit interview, Rhode Island Department of Labor, Providence, July 7, 1982.
[217] *Id.*
[218] TENN. CODE ANN. tit. 12. (Prevailing Wage Act of 1975.)
[219] Wharton Industrial Research Unit interview, Tennessee Department of Labor, Nashville, July 27, 1982.

wages are mentioned; fringe benefits are neither surveyed nor determined.

Although the statute does not mention procedures to follow in the event of joint federal-state coverage of a project, for highway work Tennessee rates are followed, and for building construction the whole Tennessee law applies, provided that the state puts more than $50,000 into the project.[220]

Attempts to amend the statute in 1981 by adding two labor representatives to the commission and requiring annual determination of wage rates for building construction were unsuccessful.

Texas

The Texas law, enacted in 1933, extends to both state and local contracts but only for building construction.[221] Highways are covered under a separate act by minimum wage provisions mandating thirty cents per hour. As in Pennsylvania, maintenance work is excluded.

Rates set by the act are supposed to be per diem, and hiring preference is given to U.S. citizens. What sets the Texas law apart from most other state prevailing wage laws is the fact that determination and enforcement of prevailing wage rates in Texas is done by each public body or board commissioning work, rather than by some central department of labor, and their decisions are final and not subject to appeal. The Texas Department of Labor and Standards is prohibited from enforcing prevailing wage matters.[222] Each body is free to apply its own definition of what makes a wage prevail. Thus, certain state school boards, such as the Houston Independent School District, have adopted as prevailing the rates paid public employees in construction-related jobs, whereas other local agencies, such as the City of Houston, have adopted the local union rates as prevailing.[223]

Surveys of the Houston area show that neither of these rates is truly representative. In a 1978 law suit, the Houston Gulf Coast Building and Trades Council admitted its membership comprised only 24 percent of the construction market in Harris County,[224] so the free-market rate would seem to be the most reasonable candidate. This hypothesis was partially confirmed by a Texas A&M

---

[220] *Id.*
[221] TEX. STAT. ANN. tit. 83, art. 5159a (Vernon).
[222] Op. Att'y Gen. No. H-845 (1976).
[223] *Construction Wage Survey Has Unions, Foes Ready for Battle,* Houston Post, April 1, 1983.
[224] *Brown Seeks Wage Law Repeal,* Sun (Alvin, Texas) May 31, 1983.

State Prevailing Wage Laws

University wage survey in the county for carpenters, which found the prevailing rate to be the merit shop wage of $8.87 per hour, whereas the union scale, and therefore the prevailing scale used by the City of Houston, was $13.52 per hour.[225] As a result of the diversified wage-setting procedure, prevailing rates in Texas show much greater variation than is common in other states.

A bill to repeal the act was introduced in 1979, but was tabled in the house. Bills in both the house and senate in 1981 to repeal the law failed to pass, and in 1983, bills to repeal, to exclude cities of population less than 1.5 million, and to exempt school boards failed. Because of the nature of the administration of this act, much of the pressure for reform of rate determinations that occurs at the state level in other jurisdictions occurs here at the local level. Recent efforts to adopt more representative wage scales have occurred in San Antonio and Houston.[226] In 1985, a bill to eliminate application to school construction projects failed, as did a bill to repeal.[227]

Utah

The Utah prevailing wage statute was repealed in 1981. The state had a prevailing wage law since 1933 that covered both state and local contracts, but not highway work.[228] It was an unusual law in several respects, setting prevailing rates by hearings held in three districts into which the state was divided for the purpose, and establishing prevailing rates for piece work.

Similar to other wage law repeal efforts, the repeal process in Utah was lengthy, and required the legislature to override a governor's veto. A bill to repeal the statute was originally introduced and passed by the legislature in 1979. It was vetoed by the governor, and although the house voted to override the veto, the senate did not act before the legislative term expired for the year. In 1981, both houses again voted to repeal, and again the governor vetoed the bill. This time, however, the repeal was passed over his veto by a substantial majority. The statute expired in March 1981.[229]

---

[225] *City Should Pay Realistic Wages*, (editorial), Express (San Antonio) September 4, 1981.
[226] *Assault Begun on Construction Pay*, Houston Chronicle, April 1, 1983.
[227] *Prevailing Law Needs Striking*, Dispatch Record (Lampass, Texas) April 18, 1985.
[228] UTAH CODE ANN. § 34-30-2.
[229] *Utah Wage Law Repealed*, ENGINEERING NEWS-RECORD 81 (March 12, 1981).

Vermont

The Vermont public works statute gives hiring preference to local workmen but neither sets nor requires prevailing wages. The state's highway board is empowered to set minimum (not prevailing) wages for various classes of highway labor.[230] Although it has no prevailing wage law, Vermont became embroiled in a prevailing wage controversy in 1985 concerning construction of a bridge linking the state with New York. Federal Davis-Bacon rates applied to the project, but workers on the New York side would receive more than twice as much per hour as their counterparts on the Vermont side. Vermont's governor, Madelaine Kunin, bowed to political pressures and ordered a 50 percent increase in wages to be paid workers on the Vermont side of the bridge.[231]

Virginia

Virginia's prevailing wage law is limited to a passage which says that laborers and mechanics employed in construction, alteration, or repair undertaken by the Metropolitan Transit Authority (mainly the subway for Washington, D.C.) must be paid rates not less than those prevailing on similar construction in the locality as determined by the U.S. Secretary of Labor. Other projects by state or local agencies are not covered by a prevailing wage provision.[232]

There is a provision that specifies that contractors living outside the state who come into it to do work on public works contracts of value not less than $300 nor more than $60,000 (an odd range) must register with the Department of Labor and Industry, at Richmond, on a prescribed form which reports, among other things, the rates of pay and number of persons employed at each rate.

Washington

Washington's law was enacted in 1945 to cover state and local contracts.[233] Highways are not mentioned. Rates are set by the industrial statistician of the Department of Labor and Industries who uses a mail survey and calculates rates by a majority-or-average formula applied to the largest city or locality in the area.[234] Rates set are typically about the same as Davis-Bacon rates, or perhaps

---

[230] VT. STAT. tit. 19, § 4 and § 18.
[231] UPI (wire service) 04-16-85 11:24 pes.
[232] VA. CODE art. 14, § 64.
[233] WASH. REV. CODE tit. 39.
[234] Wharton Industrial Research Unit interview, Washington Department of Labor and Industries, Olympia, August 12, 1982.

State Prevailing Wage Laws

a bit higher, since they are often on more current data.[235] In cases involving overlapping applicability with the federal act, the higher of the rates prevail.

The threshold was raised to $17,500 in 1979. In that same year, a bill to restrict coverage to laborers, by eliminating rate setting for workers and mechanics, died in committee. Administrative provisions requiring the posting of wage rates and other information on the job site were approved in 1981.

West Virginia

The 1933 West Virginia prevailing wage law was reenacted in 1961 to cover both state and local contracts, and highway work.[236] It requires payment of "fair minimum" rates, set annually by the West Virginia Department of Labor. Spokesmen for the department report that in setting rates, surveys are made and collective bargaining agreements are ascertained and considered, but no further information is available.[237]

No recent legislative activity is reported.

Wisconsin

The Wisconsin prevailing wage law for state projects was enacted in 1931, and a separate section for municipal contracts was added in 1933.[238] Rather than a single law, this statute is a bewildering patchwork of laws covering applicability and enforcement for four separate conditions: state contracts for building construction; state contracts for highway work; local contracts for highway work; and local contracts for public works other than highways. Contracts are covered, for example, if they exceed $2,500 for a single trade, or $25,000 for multiple trades—except in the case of local contracts for highway work, for which the threshold is $7,500 for a single trade and $75,000 for multiple trades (up from $3,500 and $35,000, respectively, in 1982).

This is one of the teamster-oriented statutes, covering the delivery of mineral aggregates deposited in place directly or though spreaders, and truck rental rates. Prevailing rates are determined by a variety of methods depending on the specific law involved. Political subunits set their own prevailing rates for highway work. The City of Appleton, for example, had a local ordinance that required em-

---

[235] *Id.*
[236] W. VA. CODE § 21-5A.
[237] Response to Wharton Industrial Research Unit survey, July 12, 1982.
[238] WIS. STAT. §§ 66.293, 103.49, 103.50.

ployers to pay wages equal to those paid city employees doing the same kind of work, but the city rescinded it in 1982, and adopted instead the federal minimum wage as prevailing.[239]

Prevailing rates for both local and state building construction and state highway work are set by the state department of labor. The department takes as prevailing the majority or plurality (modal) rate found by survey, including in its calculations prospective rate increases as of their effective date of application. In those areas where the state department has determined that collectively bargained rates reflect the modal wage rate, surveys are not made and the collectively bargained rates are used.[240]

When rates are set by the state, prevailing hours are also established. Capped at eight per day, the prevailing hours establish the point at which time-and-one-half is required. The portion of the law applying to local contracts for construction work requires that plumbing, mechanical, and electrical work must be separately contracted, if possible. Finally, if a joint project is undertaken with both state and federal or municipal funds, the higher rate required for each trade must be paid.

Despite the law's complexity, or perhaps because of it, no legislative attempts at modification are currently reported.

Wyoming

Wyoming's law dates from 1967 and applies only to state contracts over $25,000 (increased from $5,000 in 1979).[241] Highway work is not mentioned. Although the method of selecting the prevailing rate is unspecified, each contracting agency is expected to set its own rates, based on a mail survey of collective bargaining rates and "such rates as are generally paid," and apply the old federal formula of "majority, 30 percent, or average." According to a spokesman for the state's department of labor, the union scale is specified 50 to 60 percent of the time.[242] On a joint project with the federal government, the higher rate must be paid. Inmates on work release programs are required to to be paid the prevailing rate.

A bill to repeal the act failed in 1979. Several contractors' groups were expected to sponsor new repeal efforts after 1983, but no activity has been reported.

---

[239] *Prevailing Wage Suit Dismissed,* Post-Crescent (Appleton, Wisconsin) June 25, 1982.

[240] Response to Wharton Industrial Research Unit survey, July 12, 1982.

[241] Wyo. Stat. Rev. § 27-4.

[242] Wharton Industrial Research Unit interview, Wyoming Department of Labor, Cheyenne, August 10, 1982.

SUMMARY AND EVALUATION OF THE PREVAILING WAGE LAWS

The purpose of this chapter is to analyze the state prevailing wage laws and catalog recent legislative activity with respect to them, rather than to argue their merits. Most of the arguments for and against these state laws have been raised also for or against the federal Davis-Bacon Act, covered in Chapter III, above. They will not be repeated here.

But is is interesting to note that arguments for repeal of the state laws, or for reform to make them less restrictive, have become increasingly persuasive to both the general public and legislatures across the country. Changes that have been proposed to, or enacted by, state legislatures in the past few years have overwhelmingly been directed towards eliminating or reducing the scope of prevailing wage laws.

Summary of Recent Legislative Activity

In 1978, the Florida legislature was asked to reinstate prevailing wage coverage for school construction, which had been dropped from the state law in 1974. But when a survey of the state's school districts revealed that the state had saved $37 million (about 15 percent) on school construction since coverage had been dropped, without any perceptible diminution in the quality of the work done, the legislature the next year decided instead to repeal the entire statute.

Since that repeal in 1979, state prevailing wage laws throughout the country have come under increasing scrutiny. Between then and 1985, well over one hundred bills concerning prevailing rates have been introduced to thirty-four state legislatures. Most of these bills have attempted to restrict applicability, ease rate requirements, increase thresholds, or eliminate the statutes. Fifty-one bills to repeal, in addition to several others that would have had the effect of repeal, were introduced.

During this period, legislatures passed fourteen repeal measures in nine states: Alabama (1979), Arizona (1979, 1984), Colorado (1981, 1985), Florida (1979), Idaho (1982, 1982, 1985), Louisiana (1985), New Hampshire (1985), New Mexico (1981), and Utah (1979, 1981). In every state except Alabama, where the governor signed the measure, these bills were vetoed by the state's governor or were allowed to become law over his pocket veto (that is, without his signature). Thus, the statutes were effectively repealed in Alabama, Colorado, Florida, Idaho, New Hampshire, and Utah, but were saved by vetoes in Arizona, Louisiana, and New Mexico. The Arizona statute was also repealed in 1984, but by voter referendum.

On the other hand, only a few states acted to reintroduce or strengthen prevailing wage laws. There were two bills to institute a new law in Iowa, one of which passed and was vetoed, and two bills for reinstatement in each of Alabama and Florida, all of which failed. Only three states passed bills strengthening their prevailing wage laws: a bill in Maryland increased coverage of local and school board contracts (1983); one in New Jersey extended coverage (1979); and two in New York strengthened enforcement and extended coverage (1979), and adopted the union rate as prevailing (1983). Other bills to strengthen coverage were few in number as well as unsuccessful. Overall, the trend is definitely in the direction of fewer and less obtrusive prevailing wage laws.

Ranking of the State Laws

State prevailing wage laws vary considerably in many ways, but for the purpose of ranking, we have chosen to evaluate them here on the basis of how well they approximate the free market. Thus, laws that intrude more into the free marketplace by covering greater varieties of construction work, larger numbers of different types of workmen, and larger numbers of contracting agencies are considered to be more restrictive than those which do not. Similarly, the laws that either require or encourage the use of collectively bargained rates are considered more restrictive than those that adopt the federal Davis-Bacon rate, which, in turn, are considered to be more restrictive than laws using a simple average of survey rates. All of these are more restrictive than laws using free market rates.

To rank order the state laws, a factor comparison was established giving equal weights to coverage factors and to prevailing rates selected in practice by the laws. These factors are presented in Table IV-6, and the results of performing the comparison are presented in Table IV-7, where the states are listed in groups from least restrictive to most restrictive.

Of the states which have substantive prevailing wage acts, Nebraska clearly has the least restrictive requirements. Predetermination and publishing of prevailing rates is not required by this statute, and each contractor within the state is individually responsible for meeting the bill's requirements, subject to court review on complaint. Tennessee's statute scores next lowest in the comparison for several reasons: it has a relatively high contract threshold ($25,000), it does not burden its rates with fringe benefits, it

TABLE IV-6
Factors and Ratings Used in Comparing
State Prevailing Wage Laws

	Factor and Rating
1. Coverage	
A. Contract threshold	0 over $10,000 1 $2,000 to $10,000 2 under $2,000
B. Breadth of local coverage	0 no local coverage 1 local option 2 local covered
C. Extent of work coverage	0 less than Davis-Bacon 1 same as Davis-Bacon 2 greater than Davis-Bacon
2. Prevailing Rates	
D. Prevailing rates established in practice	0 free market rates 1 simple average 2 more towards free market than Davis-Bacon 3 same as Davis-Bacon 4 more towards union rates than Davis-Bacon 5 simple plurality 6 union rates or approximately union rates

does not extend to local contracts, and it establishes its rates by taking the simple average of rates found in its surveys. Maryland's law (although it is one of the few that have recently been made more restrictive) and Kentucky's new statute, which come next, are aided in their scores by their high thresholds and by the fact that each law requires substantial proportions of state funding in county and municipal construction projects before the state prevailing wage law applies to local work.

At the other extreme is Massachusetts, which has the most restrictive act. The Massachusetts law requires collectively bargained rates in practice, but scored as more restrictive than several other states with the same requirements because of the breadth of its coverage. It has no threshold, applies to local contracts, and extends to many more employee types—including janitors, teamsters, draftsmen, public employees, movers, and meatcutters—than most of the other acts. New York's act is the next most restrictive, followed closely by those of Michigan, Ohio, California, and New Jersey.

It should not be inferred from Table IV-7 that the acts that scored lower in the listing are not intrusive or administratively burden-

TABLE IV-7

Rank Ordering of State Prevailing Wage Laws Based on Factor Comparisons of Coverage and Rates

1. Least restrictive acts. Factor comparison aggregate score, 3.

    Nebraska   Tennessee

2. Less restrictive acts. Factor comparison score, 4 or 5.

Arkansas	D.C.	Kansas
Kentucky	Louisiana	Maryland
New Mexico	Wyoming	

3. Restrictive acts. Factor comparison score, 6 to 9.

Alaska	Connecticut	Delaware
Hawaii	Illinois	Indiana
Maine	Minnesota	Missouri
Montana	Nevada	Oklahoma
Oregon	Pennsylvania	Rhode Island
Texas	Washington	West Virginia

4. More restrictive acts. Factor comparison score, 10 or 11.

California	Michigan	Montana
New Jersey	Ohio	

5. Most restrictive acts. Factor comparison score, 12.

    Massachusetts   New York

Note: States are ordered alphabetically within categories.

some, but rather that they are merely less so than those that scored higher. The District of Columbia's prevailing wage law, for example, is the Davis-Bacon Act itself. As noted in Chapter III, above, the Davis-Bacon Act has been under intense repeal pressure in Congress for several years because of its costs and its impositions on the construction industry. Yet the District of Columbia's act scores among the less restrictive statutes in the table.

Conclusion

All state prevailing wage laws subject contractors to risks and to the possibility of civil or criminal prosecution for carrying out their businesses in ways that are perfectly acceptable to all other purchasers of construction except governments and the government agencies. All of them tend to make buildings and projects more expensive and therefore give governments less value for their construction dollar than a private person would receive. All of them tend to use the contracting mechanism as a hidden conduit for income transfers from taxpayers to construction workers. Additionally, to the degree that they interfere with the market mechanism for construction labor rates, they ensure that wage inflation in the construction industry will outpace that in other fields. Finally, our survey of state departments of labor found that the acts collectively require the services of more than 500 administrators, whose talents might well be put to better use elsewhere.

All told, the state prevailing wage laws seem to be neither necessary for effective state procurement policies, nor beneficial to the economy of the states and their taxpayers or to the majority of the firms and workers in the construction industry. Now may be the time for the remaining states which have prevailing wage laws to examine the effect of the repeals in Alabama, Arizona, Colorado, Florida, Idaho, New Hampshire, and Utah to see if there is any valid reason for their own laws to be retained.

CHAPTER V

The Walsh-Healey Public Contracts Act

The Walsh-Healey Public Contracts Act was the second of the federal prevailing wage laws. Just as the Davis-Bacon Act applied the concept of prevailing wages to that portion of the construction industry interested in doing contracting business with the government, the Walsh-Healey Act extended it to goods-producing industries. It is surprising, therefore, how different the two acts are, in the construction of the legislation, the way each has been administered, and in the impact each has had on the economy and on industrial wage rates and working conditions. Davis-Bacon and the state prevailing wage laws (which apply mostly to the construction of buildings and public works) continue to have a great impact on this industry, and add costs of well over $1 billion each year to government purchases. But its contemporary, the Walsh-Healey Act, although applying to a far greater volume of purchasing and a much wider industrial base, has always been relatively insignificant.

Despite this, however, the Walsh-Healey Act is worth investigating. It raises some interesting questions about the concept of prevailing wages and further highlights the difficulties posed by such legislation in trying to apply a subjective criterion in an objective way. It is also interesting to compare and contrast Walsh-Healey with Davis-Bacon since they use the same tools to accomplish about the same purposes and were drafted at about the same time.

HISTORY AND DEVELOPMENT OF THE WALSH-HEALEY ACT

The Davis-Bacon Act and the Walsh-Healey Act share a common environmental heritage. Both use the quasi-voluntary participation of contractors with the federal procurement system as a means of influencing specific and general levels of industrial wages. Both set minimum wage rates based on the concept of matching those prevailing in similar circumstances. Both use prevailing wages rather than minimum wages because at the time they were passed Congress was still afraid to interfere with free competition by imposing a mandatory wage level on employers. Both owe their existence to the depressed economy of the early 1930s.

The Davis-Bacon Act was first passed in 1931. Two years later, the National Industrial Recovery Act (NIRA) sought to extend the principle of a legislated minimum wage, at least for the duration of the crisis brought on by the Great Depression, to all firms of entire industries involved in interstate commerce.[1] Under temporary suspension of the antitrust laws, business groups acting under governmental administrative supervision were to establish codes setting the parameters for "fair competition" by fixing minimum commodity prices *and minimum wages* for all the firms within their industries.

This effort to extend a system of controlling minimum industrial wages was extensive but short lived. In May of 1935, after at least the outlines of such codes were in place for some 500 industries, the Supreme Court held that Congress had gone beyond its powers and had improperly delegated the legislative function.[2] Less than a month later, the Wagner Act was passed.[3] It was basically a rewrite of one section of the NIRA dealing with and encouraging group action by workers. The other sections of the recovery act were not resurrected for general application,[4] because of continuing doubts that the Supreme Court would allow Congress to control wage rates as part of its regulation of interstate commerce.

The real or perceived limitations of the interstate commerce clause prevented Congress from attempting to set across-the-board minimum wage rates for industrial employees, but few doubted that the government could control the terms of its own purchase decisions to at least some degree, or use those controls as a means of spreading to the general economy via the industrial structure. Based on the precedent established by the Davis-Bacon Act, Congress could feel secure that extension of the prevailing wage concept to other industries that were government suppliers would be able to run the gamut of the Court, although a minimum wage law even in this restricted area would have been less likely to succeed.[5] Accordingly,

---

[1] National Industrial Recovery Act, 48 Stat. 195 (1933).
[2] Schechter Poultry Corp. v. United States, 295 U.S. 495 (1935).
[3] National Labor Relations Act (popularly the Wagner Act), 49 Stat. 449 (1935).
[4] There was an attempt made by Senator Joseph Guffey to establish a recovery act for the single industry of coal mining, the Bituminous Coal Conservation Act, 49 Stat. 991 (1935), but it need not concern us here.
[5] The original Walsh Bill (S. 3055, 1935) did not use the adjective "prevailing" in requiring payment of a minimum wage, nor did the Mead bill (H.R. 8701, 1935), the

at about the same time the Wagner Act was introduced, new legislation was also entered to extend some form of wage protection to the wider audience of federal contractors than were already covered by the Davis-Bacon Act.

Enactment and Goals of the Walsh-Healey Act[6]

In June of 1935, Senator Walsh and Representative Healey introduced their bills to extend prevailing wage requirements to employers whose firms sought to provide goods (but not personal or professional services which did not involve goods) under contracts with the federal government.[7] After wending through the congressional process, Senator Walsh's amended bill was signed into law by President Roosevelt one year later, on July 30, 1936, as the Walsh-Healey Public Contracts Act.[8]

The language of the original bills was provided in large measure by then Secretary of Labor Frances Perkins.[9] It should be no surprise that the principal stated rationale of the Davis-Bacon Act, protection of local contractors from the competition of low-wage itinerants, was not mentioned. Few other industries are like construction, where the work must move to wherever it is purchased.[10] The pur-

---

ideological predecessor of the Healey bill on the House side. During the Senate debates in 1935 and in the second ("clean") Healey bill introduced to the House in 1936 (H.R. 11554, 1936), various formulations were discussed for ways to require a minimum wage without running afoul of similarities with the unconstitutional NIRA codes or with language associated with the New York State minimum wage bill, which had been determined to be unconstitutional by that state's highest court shortly before the clean Healey bill was introduced. Thus, it was only late in the congressional process that the idea of prevailing rates was introduced into Walsh-Healey. One suggestion raised in a bill by Representative Monaghan, among other places, was that the contracts act require the payment of prevailing *union* wages (H.R. 11927, 1936). There is a section in this bill emphatically stating that "Federal judges are forbidden to declare [this bill] unconstitutional" and specifying that any judge who made such a determination would be automatically guilty of violating his constitutional requirement of good behavior and replaced, but this was more a reflection of congressional frustration than a realistic legislative attempt. The idea of requiring a prevailing union rate as the minimum was rejected because of its almost certain unconstitutionality. This left following the example of the Davis-Bacon Act, which had already proven to be successful in the sense that it had not been invalidated by the Court, as the only reasonable alternative.

[6] Much of this section derives from C. L. CHRISTENSON & R. A. MYREN, WAGE POLICY UNDER THE WALSH-HEALEY PUBLIC CONTRACTS ACT, Ch. 1, (1966) [hereinafter cited as CHRISTENSON & MYREN].

[7] S. 3055 and H.R. 8558, 74th Cong., 1st Sess. (1935).

[8] Walsh-Healey Public Contracts Act (popularly the Walsh-Healey Act), Pub. L. No. 846, 74th Cong., 2d Sess. (1936).

[9] CHRISTENSON & MYREN, *supra* note 6, at 11.

[10] As will be discussed below, Walsh-Healey could not shake itself totally from a local orientation. Problems with defining locality led to the first court challenge of the act, and were indirectly responsible for the fact that it no longer sets wage rates.

pose of Walsh-Healey was stated less obliquely than was Davis-Bacon's. It was to salvage at least a part of the influence sought or enjoyed by the NIRA in increasing the purchasing power of employees. Along with this, it also sought to decrease the hours of work in order to spread employment among the potential workers.

These two goals, increased purchasing power and restricted work hours, were undoubtedly more correlative in 1935 than they have come to be in the fifty years since. With unemployment at record levels, it was just as important to put a ceiling over work hours (to spread the opportunity for jobs by prohibiting or restricting overtime) as it was to put a floor under wages. In the post-depression economy, trends in work hours have undergone a reversal. Whereas in 1935 many workmen wanted to work longer hours, so long as they were paid for them, to improve the amount of their take-home pay, in modern times it is much more common for industrial workers to prefer no overtime, or even a shortened workweek, so as to increase their leisure time. Additionally, with the introduction of the Fair Labor Standards Act in 1938, overtime beyond forty hours in any one week was mandated to be paid at time and one-half; so this major goal of Walsh-Healey was at least partially co-opted. Nevertheless, it is the work hours provisions of Walsh-Healey rather than the wage setting ones that remained significant. In sharp contrast to the results of the Davis-Bacon Act, where the prevailing wage clause continues to have major impact on industry structure and costs, prevailing wages set by Walsh-Healey caused relatively minor perturbations in free market wage rates in the industries for which they were set.

In presenting the provisions of Walsh-Healey, below, comparisons and contrasts will be drawn with the similar ones contained in the revised Davis-Bacon Act. That revised act had been redrafted in August, 1935, about halfway through the congressional review of Walsh-Healey.

The Walsh-Healey Act in Its Original Form

The Walsh-Healey Act applies to contracts entered into by "any executive department, independent establishment, or other agency or instrumentality of the United States [or the District of Columbia] for the manufacture or furnishing of materials, supplies, articles, and equipment in any amount exceeding $10,000."[11] It requires that

---

[11] All quoted materials in this section, unless noted otherwise, are taken from the Walsh-Healey Public Contracts Act, Pub. L. No. 846, 2d Sess., 49 Stat. 2036 (1936). Where specific provisions are contrasted with those of the Davis-Bacon Act, the Davis-Bacon materials are synopsized from materials presented in Ch. III, *supra*.

stipulations be included in all such contracts concerning minimum wages, maximum hours, the use of child or convict labor, and safe and sanitary working conditions.

Davis-Bacon provisions apply only to contracts to which the United States or the District of Columbia is an actual party. Statutorily, Davis-Bacon is thus more narrowly applied than Walsh-Healey, although its actual application has been broadened to about the same extent by its inclusion in the public works procurement contracts of various agencies related to the federal establishment. Furthermore, Walsh-Healey has a higher contract threshold.

Contract Threshold. The contract threshold establishes the minimum contract size for which prevailing wage laws will prescribe rates. Davis-Bacon's threshold was set at $2,000 by its 1935 amendments, and Walsh-Healey's was established at $10,000 in the final version of that bill, passed in 1936. This is curious insofar as the amounts represent opposite movements in the two bills. In 1935, Davis-Bacon was amended downward from its 1931 threshold of $5,000. On the other hand, the original Walsh bill as passed by the Senate had no minimum threshold at all. The clean bill Representative Healey introduced to the House in 1936 had a threshold of $2,000 (matching the revised Davis-Bacon threshold), which was increased to $10,000 just before final passage of the act. The increase apparently resulted from objections lodged by the National Association of Manufacturers that a threshold of at least $10,000 was necessary to "avoid the terrible confusion that would arise in the case of thousands of small contracts"[12] without it.

Minimum Wage Stipulation. The Walsh-Healey wage stipulation requires that:

> All persons employed by the contractor in the manufacture or furnishing of the materials, supplies, articles, or equipment used in the performance of the contract will be paid, without subsequent deduction or rebate on any account, not less than the minimum wages as determined by the Secretary of Labor to be the *prevailing minimum* wages for persons employed *on similar work or in the particular or similar industries or groups of industries* currently operating *in the locality* in which the materials, supplies, articles, or equipment are to be *manufactured or furnished* under said contract. (Emphasis added.)

The minimum wage stipulations in this act differ from those in the Davis-Bacon Act in subtle but important ways. Both provide

---

[12] Statement of James W. Hook, President, Geometric Tool Company, on behalf of the National Association of Manufacturers, in *Hearings on H.R. 11554,* cited in CHRISTENSON & MYREN, *supra* note 6, at 23–24.

that the respective groups covered will be paid, without subsequent reduction or rebate, minimum wages as determined by the secretary of labor; but Walsh-Healey bases the wages on what the secretary determines to be the prevailing *minimum* wages, whereas Davis-Bacon bases them on prevailing wages (without the modifier).

The word *minimum* makes a world of difference. Had it been included in the Davis-Bacon Act, the impact of that act would undoubtedly have been measurably less as the economy improved and the spread began to occur between minimum, market, and union wages; and largely because it was included in the Walsh-Healey Act, the economic impact of that act has been relatively small. With it, Walsh-Healey essentially allows market forces to set all wage rates above those paid to the lowest-paid individual; without it, Davis-Bacon essentially suppresses market forces and frequently requires that a high wage rate (typically the union rate) or some central-tendency (average) rate be used as the minimum paid to all workers in each craft and class.

Wage Applicability. The differences between the two acts are increased by the fact that Walsh-Healey sets the minimum for all persons doing like work (of any sort) within an industry based on an industry-wide (albeit sometimes regional) minimum, whereas Davis-Bacon sets a different minimum for each craft in the construction industry based on the prevailing (not prevailing minimum) rates found in several different classes of construction projects. Specifically, Walsh-Healey looks for prevailing minimum wages "for persons employed on similar work or in the particular or similar industries or groups of industries," whereas Davis-Bacon seeks the prevailing rate for *corresponding classes* of laborers and mechanics employed on projects of a *character similar* to the contract work. Thus, one Walsh-Healey wage determination might apply without variation to *all* employees of the pumps and compressor industry, regardless of whether the covered employees were janitors, machinists, molders, die sinkers, assemblers, roughnecks, draftsmen, or what have you; but Davis-Bacon would set a different rate for even slightly different jobs—for the operator of a hydraulic backhoe rather than for a cable-operated backhoe, for example—and would set rates for all of these differently if they were to be established for a highway construction project, for construction of an airport runway, for laying a parking lot for a military housing apartment unit, or for constructing an automobile access ramp for a federal office building.

Locality. The final difference of interest is that of the locality over which the secretary of labor is instructed to search for existing rates in determining the levels of prevailing wages for each act. In the case of Walsh-Healey, he is to determine the prevailing minimum wages for persons employed "in the locality in which the materials, supplies, articles, or equipment are to be manufactured or furnished"; and in the case of Davis-Bacon, he is to determine the prevailing wage for persons employed on projects of a character similar to the contract work in the *city, town, village, or other civil subdivision of the state* in which the work is to be performed. Since whole industries, such as the miscellaneous chemical products and preparations industry (one of those for which Walsh-Healey set prevailing rates), can be quite widely scattered in terms of the loci of their manufacturing facilities and distribution points, it is clear that Walsh-Healey has very little local orientation despite the lip service paid the word *locality* in the act.[13] The Davis-Bacon Act, on the other hand, is so localized, in addition to being fractionated with respect to the crafts of workmen and types of construction which can serve as input to the rate determination process, that it frequently cannot be administered as written, because an insufficient pool exists from which to draw a valid conclusion about what rates prevail.[14]

Work Hours Stipulation. The original Walsh-Healey work hours stipulation required that no persons employed by contractors covered by the act "shall be permitted to work *in excess of eight hours in any one day* or in excess of forty hours in any one week." Although the secretary of labor was empowered to "make any rules and regulations allowing reasonable variations, tolerances, and exemptions to and from any or all provisions" of the act regarding maximum hours, it was specified that whenever they involved overtime the secretary was restricted to setting a rate at not less than one-and-one-half times the "basic hourly rate received by any employee affected."[15] Furthermore, sufferance of any overtime work at all was at the secretary's discretion. Only in 1942, by amendment, did it become possible for Walsh-Healey contractors to employ persons for longer hours (and pay them time and one-half in compliance

---

[13] In application, most prevailing rate determinations under Walsh-Healey were industrywide or nationwide. One exception, discussed later in this chapter, occurred in the steel industry, where the country was divided into four parts. Another was in the coal industry, where the division followed regional boundaries that had been established under the NIRA. In both of these, the geography covered was considerably greater than would be considered "local" by most definitions.

[14] This also results in Davis-Bacon rates being highly variable—if not arbitrary—because they are based on small sample sizes which are in many cases much influenced by extremes. *See* Ch. III, *supra*, for further discussion.

[15] This provision became difficult to interpret in regard to piece rate workers.

with the Fair Labor Standards Act of 1938) without a dispensation from the Department of Labor.[16]

Daily Premium. The Fair Labor Standards Act, however, deals only with the workweek, not the workday. It requires overtime pay for hours worked over forty in any week, but does not concern itself with how those hours are distributed during the week. Thus, a work schedule consisting of four ten-hour days followed by three days off gives rise to no overtime differential under Fair Labor Standards. On the other hand, under Walsh-Healey prior to the 1985 amendments such a schedule would have required paying eight of the forty hours (two per day) at time and one-half, increasing the total labor cost for the week by 10 percent. The net result was that employers and employees in government contracting were denied the flexibility in scheduling assignments that were available to other employers who were not doing such work.

Contract Work Hours. It is hard to rationalize this restriction as a benefit to employees, but such as it is, it was the principal reason that the Walsh-Healey Act continued to exist after 1964. (As will be explained below, the wage provisions of Walsh-Healey have had no effect since 1964.) Even for this purpose, Walsh-Healey is needed only because the Contract Work Hours and Safety Standards Act does not apply to Walsh-Healey contracts.[17] The work hours statute was passed in 1962 for the sole purpose of expanding the overtime requirements of the Fair Labor Standards Act for premium pay after forty hours per week to include also premium pay after eight hours per day. This act applies to all laborers or mechanics employed by contractors or subcontractors on any public work, but there is a specific exception for work required to be done in accordance with the provisions of the Walsh-Healey Act.

The Davis-Bacon Act has no similar provision for maximum work hours, although contracts under it have been covered by the Fair Labor Standards Act since 1938. It might be tempting to speculate on why Davis-Bacon originally had no such provision, but the most likely reason is that the construction industry has always been dependent on the weather and oriented to hours of daylight. A certain amount of scheduling flexibility to make up for rain delays, for example, is therefore necessary to the industry. Thus, until the Contract Work Hours and Safety Standards Act was passed in 1962, the only limitations on Davis-Bacon contractors beyond those imposed by the Fair Labor Standards Act had been ones negotiated privately.

---

[16] Proviso added by Pub. L. No. 552, 77th Cong., 2d Sess., 56 Stat. 277 (1942).
[17] The Contract Work Hours and Safety Standards Act, Pub. L. No. 87-581 (1962).

Situation After January 1, 1986. In the spring of 1985, during the course of general debate on the federal budget, Senate Concurrent Resolution 32, sponsored by Senators Nickels and Armstrong and approved by a vote of 86–5, expressed a "sense of the Senate" that special work hours provisions of Walsh-Healey should be dropped.[18] This resolution was carried through into separate bills introduced to committees of both houses of Congress, but before they were reported out, another situation arose which made them unnecessary.

In preparing the defense authorization bill for fiscal 1986, the Senate had left standing an amendment that would have exempted military construction contracts of $1 million or less from the prevailing wage requirements of the Davis-Bacon Act.[19] The final House bill passed did not contain this measure, so a House-Senate conference was necessary to reconcile the differences before the $302.5 billion authorization bill could be sent to the President. After two weeks of closed-door negotiations, Senate conferees agreed to drop the Davis-Bacon modification, but only in exchange for the House conferees agreeing to accept an amendment adopting the language of the Senate version of the Walsh-Healey reform bill that had been approved by the Senate Labor and Human Resources Committee on July 17, 1985.[20] That bill amended the Walsh-Healey Act to permit employees of *all* federal contractors, not just defense contractors, to work any combination of hours in a forty-hour week without requiring overtime.[21] Thus, the final appropriations bill dropped Davis-Bacon reform, but added Walsh-Healey reform.

The new language added to the defense bill is scheduled to take effect January 1, 1986, a year earlier than called for in the Senate Labor Committee bill. After that time, the special overtime provisions of Walsh-Healey will no longer be effective.

---

[18] *Senate Passes Walsh-Healey Resolution,* GOV'T UNION CRITIQUE 2 (May 31, 1985). The purpose of this resolution, which extends also to the equivalent provisions of the Contract Work Hours and Safety Standards Act, is to eliminate the overtime premium requirement for hours over eight in a given day and allow employers and employees alike to take advantage of the concept of flextime in scheduling. Overtime premium pay would still be required for hours worked over forty in a given week. The Congressional Budget Office had recently estimated that, if enacted, such a resolution could lead to annual savings of $550 million, the majority of which would result from savings in industries covered by Contract Work Hours rather than Walsh-Healey. Although this particular resolution did not lead to legislation, the daily overtime provisions of both acts have been eliminated. See below.
[19] *See* Ch. III, *supra,* at note 3.
[20] S. 1105.
[21] *House-Senate Conferees Drop Davis-Bacon, Add Walsh-Healey Amendments to Defense Bill,* 145 DAILY LAB. REP. A-10–A-11 (July 29, 1985).

Other Stipulations. Other stipulations of Walsh-Healey prohibit employing boys under sixteen or girls under eighteen years of age, prohibit convict labor, and require working conditions that are not "unsanitary or hazardous or dangerous to the health and safety of employees." Two years after Walsh-Healey was passed, the Fair Labor Standards Act included a similar prohibition of child labor (differing only in that girls also could be employed at age sixteen), so this is not considered an important Walsh-Healey provision. Nor has convict labor been a major issue.

With respect to safe and sanitary working conditions, the secretary of labor passed responsibility on to individual states, by specifying that compliance with state-level factory inspection laws would be taken as *prima facie* evidence of compliance with the Walsh-Healey requirement. The only federal stipulation that remained in the regulations was a requirement that records of workplace injuries be maintained. Thus, none of these other stipulations has proven significant in itself. Walsh-Healey did serve as a conduit, however, for testing precepts on a control group of "volunteers" (firms that choose to try to do business with the government) before applying them across the board. For example, when the federal government decided to involve itself in workplace safety and health conditions of all employees, as it did in the Occupational Safety and Health Act, it used the Walsh-Healey experience as a guide.

Exemptions from Coverage. The scope of Walsh-Healey is limited in various ways. It does not apply, for example, to government purchases of perishables, agricultural or farm products, any contracts made by the secretary of agriculture for the purchase of commodities, or the carriage of freight or personnel by common carriers or where published tariff rates are in effect.[22] Also excluded by the secretary of labor, using his discretionary clause, were contracts for public utility services, contracts to construct merchant vessels (but not naval vessels), contracts for tire and tube repairing (but not tire recapping), contracts for the delivery of newspapers, magazines, or periodicals, and others.[23]

Open-Market Purchases. One area of controversy was the statutory exemption of open-market purchases. The Walsh-Healey Act

---

[22] Presumably, since the deregulation of most transportation systems during the late 1970s eliminated the requirement for published tarriffs in several areas where they had previously been required, the scope of Walsh-Healey expanded somewhat. There is no record of this point being raised as an issue.

[23] U.S. DEPARTMENT OF LABOR, 2 WALSH-HEALEY PUBLIC CONTRACTS ACT, RULINGS AND INTERPRETATIONS, 13 (1939); and U.S. DEPARTMENT OF LABOR, 3 WALSH-HEALEY PUBLIC CONTRACTS ACT, RULINGS AND INTERPRETATIONS, 3–7 (1963) [hereinafter cited as INTERPRETATIONS, No. 3].

specifies that it does not apply to "purchases of such materials, supplies, articles, or equipment as may usually be bought in the open market."[24] This exemption was added to the original Walsh bill just before it was reported out, apparently at the behest of the National Retail Dry Goods Association. This association drew attention to the difficulties of applying the original bill to purchases from retailers, since the wage requirements associated with such purchases would have to be enforced by the retailer on the manufacturer, over whose wage rates the retailer has no control.[25] As late as 1963, however, the secretary of labor still chose to place a narrow interpretation on the open-market exemption, specifying that it would only apply "where the public exigency requires immediate delivery of the goods" or where the purchase authorization contains the "express language" of the statute to buy "in the open market." Except in these two cases, even if goods are bought without competitive bidding, the Walsh-Healey act applies.[26]

WALSH-HEALEY ADMINISTRATION

Record keeping and reporting requirements under Walsh-Healey are minimal for this type of legislation, and much less onerous than those under Davis-Bacon. No weekly submission of payroll records or signing of affidavits of compliance are required. In fact, aside from the posting of a generic "official Walsh-Healey poster," nothing is required with respect to wages and hours beyond that required by the Fair Labor Standards Act.[27]

Violation of the act can entail a variety of punishments, including liquidated damages (for example, $10 a day for every day a minor below the permitted age or a convict is knowingly employed in the performance of a covered contract, or the amount of back pay that should have been paid to workers under minimum wage and overtime pay rules). Other punishments might involve contract termination at the discretion of the contracting agency, with charge backs to the original contractor for any additional costs; withholding of contract funds due to the United States as a result of violations; or

---

[24] 49 Stat. 2039, § 9 (1936).
[25] CHRISTENSON & MYREN, *supra* note 6, at 25.
[26] INTERPRETATIONS No. 3, *supra* note 23, at 6.
[27] There are a few special record keeping requirements in the safety and health area for such things as injury frequency rates or exposure levels for employees who enter radiation areas, the posting of radiation caution symbols, and a few other things, but these are not major and are far exceeded by the requirements of the Occupational Safety and Health Act. They are not considered to be a significant cost matter to Walsh-Healey contractors.

a three-year blacklisting. These are roughly similar to the provisions of the Davis-Bacon Act, although under the latter, employees themselves have greater access to recover wage underpayments.

Rate Setting

The secretary of labor adopted a completely different method of establishing prevailing rates under Walsh-Healey than under Davis-Bacon. Perhaps because the Walsh-Healey Act was an outgrowth of the failed NIRA, the secretary apparently thought it important to gain consent from those covered by it, or at least to involve them actively in the rate-setting process. A fairly elaborate procedure was developed, under which was created a Public Contracts Board in the Division of Public Contracts of the Department of Labor. Before a determination was made, this three-member board held public hearings attended by representatives of employers and employees of the industry, examined the wage studies made by the Bureau of Labor Statistics or private organizations, and performed independent studies of its own. The board then made its recommendations to the secretary. All interested parties had a period of time in which to file objections, after which the secretary made a final determination, and published the results in the Federal Register.[28]

According to one reviewer, the Department of Labor began by bringing people from the industry together to discuss the "need" for standards. "Responsible employers—that is, unionized employers—generally urged that standards be imposed in order to discipline 'unscrupulous,' low-cost competitors."[29] Regardless of the reason, the procedure was slow and cumbersome. During the entire active history of Walsh-Healey rate setting, from 1937 to 1964, only sixty-one original prevailing rate decisions were made, most of them containing only two or three individual rates. Many of the rates set were already obsolete when put into effect because of their old data, and were kept without change for as long as ten years, even in times of rapidly rising market wages. Much of this was attributable to the cumbersome wage-setting process rather than to any lack of interest on the part of the Department of Labor in getting rates set.

"No-Minimum" Contracts. It is curious, however, that the rate-setting process evolved so differently under Walsh-Healey than un-

---

[28] Dadian, *Comparison of Davis-Bacon and Walsh-Healey Acts*, 53 MONTHLY LAB. REV. 132 (July 1941).

[29] Reynolds, *Understanding Political Pricing of Labor Services: The Davis-Bacon Act* 3 J. LAB. RESEARCH 305 (Summer, 1982).

der Davis-Bacon. In contrast to the Walsh-Healey output of sixty-one determinations in twenty-six years, Davis-Bacon generates more than 14,000 determinations in any single year, some of which may encompass 125 individual rates, plus varying fringe benefits of several types. Obviously, some key factor separates the two laws. Surprisingly, however, it is not in the statutory language, but entirely in the administrative decisions made by the secretary of labor. Essentially, the secretary decided that the minimum wage provisions of Walsh-Healey would not apply to contracts for which one had not been determined, whereas under Davis-Bacon, no contract can be effective unless it contains a schedule of prevailing rates.[30]

Defining Prevailing

As was also true under Davis-Bacon, although responsibility for administering the Walsh-Healey Act was put on the secretary of labor, Congress did not encumber him with excess definitions. In fact, a case can be made that the secretary was given insufficient direction under either piece of legislation to carry out his statutory responsibilities in a fair and reasonable manner. There is no definition of prevailing provided in either act, or any indication of how Congress intended it to be determined.

Under Davis-Bacon, the secretary early on devised a formula to identify the rates which were said to prevail among those found by survey. The formula used has always been the subject of controversy, but at least it did provide a methodology, usually called "the 30 percent rule." Using it, if at least a 30 percent plurality of the rates in the survey are the same, that rate is taken as the prevailing one, but if fewer than 30 percent receive the same rate, then the "prevailing" rate is taken as the weighted average of all the rates in the survey. (In 1985, under new administrative rules for Davis-Bacon, a 50 percent plurality was substituted.)

Under Walsh-Healey, however, no similar algorithm was developed. In the early history of the act, when the Public Contracts Board still existed (it was abandoned in 1942 "for the duration of the war" and never reinstated) wage setting was less controversial, simply because there was little variation between minimum and maximum rates in most industrial jobs, or between the different wage rates offered by different employers in different locations. Thus, in the paper and pulp industry determination in 1939, the

---

[30] Under Davis-Bacon, the secretary has no option to decide, for example, that insufficient data exist upon which to base a prevailing rate. This forces a certain amount of arbitrariness upon the decisions made under that act.

Public Contracts Board could recommend 35 cents per hour in the southern states because, although base rates ranged from 25 to 52 cents per hour, "a substantial concentration was found clustered around the 35-cent rate."[31] Similarly for the northern states, with base rates from 25 to 64 cents, "the outstanding concentration took place at 40 cents an hour."[32] Each case was handled individually, in the apparent hope that an appropriate rate would present itself.

After the war, as prosperity increased and wage rates began to spread out, "naturally prevailing" rates occurred less frequently, requiring the development of some sort of a selection mechanism. Different approaches were tried. An example is provided by the 1953 redetermination of the prevailing minimum for employees in the paper bag branch of the paper and pulp industry.

> The newly separated paper-bag branch of the industry appears to be made up of 80 establishments with "approximately 15,000 workers." One half of the 80 establishments employed 78.8 per cent of the workers and paid base rates of 85 cents or over, while "less than a third of the plants employing a little more than a third of the workers had base rates of 90 cents or over." Of more importance perhaps was the observation that "A total of 7.5 per cent of the workers in this branch received less than 85 cents at the time of the survey, and 3.9 per cent received between 85 and 90 cents at that time." It was on the basis of this observation that the Secretary of Labor stated that the prevailing minimum wage appeared to be between 85.1 and 89.9 cents and concluded that the midpoint of this interval, "namely 87.5 cents was the prevailing minimum wage rate in the paper bag branch of the industry as of the date of the survey."[33]

That the arithmetic in this example does not add up is incidental to the main point; as of this time (1953) no particular calculating methodology seems to have been employed similar to the "30 percent rule" of Davis-Bacon. If anything, it seems that the rate picked as prevailing was chosen so that fewer than 10 percent of the establishments in the industry would have to adjust their rates to conform with it.

Records of the redetermination of rates for the same industry in 1959, however, show that the secretary had come to reject this concept. Employer representatives recommended that the new prevailing minimum be declared $1.25 per hour, on the ground that 10 percent of the establishments in the industry paid such a rate or less, but the secretary contended that this claim relied erroneously on the concept of the prevailing minimum as being "the

---

[31] CHRISTENSON & MYREN, *supra* note 6, at 81.
[32] *Id.*
[33] *Id.* at 85.

base on which the wage structure builds up."[34] (Unfortunately, we have no explanation of why the secretary felt that such a concept would be erroneous.) The secretary also rejected the notion of using the median wage (which was $1.90), noting simply that "it is too high to be considered the 'prevailing minimum' wage." He then produced, through marvelously involuted logic, a prevailing minimum of $1.60, which coincidentally was the rate suggested by the unions.

> [I]t appears that no single minimum wage is paid by any substantial portion of the industry so as to clearly emerge as "prevailing" in its own right. It is therefore necessary to choose... that minimum wage which is most representative... of practices of the industry as a whole, and the one most accurately reflecting the industry standard which I am directed to find and determine as the prevailing minimum wage for persons employed in the industry. As higher minimum wages and the majority of covered employment distinguish the plants in the *top half* of the industry from those in the remainder, the lowest minimum wage paid in this half fulfills these requirements.
>
> The specific identification of this particular rate is dependent on whether each of the several plants in the industry is regarded as equal. If this approach is used, a minimum wage of $1.58 per hour is indicated since 50.8 per cent of all plants pay none of their covered workers less than such a minimum rate. If the plants are weighted in accordance with their employment, a minimum wage of $1.64 is reflected in that 52 percent of the covered employees in the industry are employed in plants paying no such employee a lesser minimum wage.
>
> The recommendation of the Unions... falls fairly within this limited area between both rates. It is $1.60 per hour. More than 58 per cent of the covered workers in the industry are employed in more than 47 per cent of the establishments which pay no covered worker less than $1.60 per hour. This rate also corresponds closely to the one suggested by the statistical approach recommended by the employer's representative when that approach is related to the table in the wage survey to which it is truly pertinent. Upon the basis of the entire record before me, therefore, this tentative decision finds and determines that $1.60 per hour is the minimum wage prevailing in this industry as of the date of the wage survey.[35]

Thus, with the passage of time and the increasing complexity of the task at hand, the secretary came to develop a methodology that was subsequently applied more or less consistently. It consisted of: 1) arraying plants in order of increasing minimum wages paid, dividing the industry into two halves around the median plant, and taking as the prevailing minimum rate the minimum rate paid by

---

[34] 24 F.R. 1841, cited in CHRISTENSON & MYREN, *supra* note 6, at 88.
[35] *Id.* at 1842, quoted in CHRISTENSON & MYREN, *supra* note 6, at 89.

the employer whose plant was next above the median; 2) arraying plants in order of increasing minimum wages paid, weighting each plant by its employment size, dividing the industry into two halves around the median employee, and taking as the prevailing minimum rate the minimum rate paid to the employee whose plant was next above the median; and 3) taking as the prevailing rate a figure somewhere between these two.[36] On the record, the rate so calculated was sometimes modified to meet the recommendations put forth by the unions.

This is hardly a simple procedure, although it may be easier to do than to describe. It has no known relationship to any statistical or logical definition of prevailing, and was never formulated in any precise way by the secretary or made part of the administrative regulations of Walsh-Healey. It has also been shown to produce questionable results when regional geographic differences in wage rates were introduced. The $1.60 rate for the paper and pulp industry in the example discussed above was found to exceed the minimum paid to employees of over half the establishments in the Northeast, about a quarter of those in the South or North Central regions, and almost none of those in the Far West.[37]

Additional rate-setting examples from Walsh-Healey's history will not be reviewed, since rate setting is no longer a function of the law. The example already presented is sufficient to demonstrate the very different paths taken in developing definitions and administrative procedures to implement the similar statutory language and requirements of the Davis-Bacon and Walsh-Healey laws.

By the time this working definition had evolved, the Walsh-Healey Act had come to searching not so much for an actual prevailing wage rate as for some central tendency wage—that is, a wage based on the statistical mean or median—in much the same way that Davis-Bacon uses a central tendency rate when a 30 percent or 50 percent plurality does not exist. In applying a central rate as the minimum, Walsh-Healey thus began to create wage inflation. In any case where the middle rate found in surveys is used as the minimum rate applying to future work, an undeniable

---

[36] This procedure has a rough parallel in one of the stranger of the state prevailing wage laws, that of Delaware. In Delaware, the method used to establish the prevailing rate for state public works is to take "the average of the majority" of survey rates. Like the Walsh-Healey procedure, from which it may have been derived, the Delaware method arrays establishments by size of employment but takes as prevailing the average of all rates above the median. (*See* Ch. IV, *supra.*) The principal benefit of this procedure may be that it appears to be objective, but defies easy comprehension, and therefore is not much subject to challenge.

[37] CHRISTENSON & MYREN, *supra* note 6, at 94.

upward pressure is created simply because about half of the firms in the industry will have to adjust their basic wage rate higher when working on government contracts, and the other half, which had been higher in the first place, is unaffected.

Three factors saved Walsh-Healey from causing as much of a problem in this regard as the Davis-Bacon Act. First, the rate determined by Walsh-Healey was applied only to the lowest-paid industrial laborers, so management had some flexibility in wage rate assignments for the more highly skilled workers. Second, Walsh-Healey's cumbersome rate-setting procedures resulted in prevailing wages based on survey data as much as three years old. In times of rising wage rates, employers could often comply with Walsh-Healey requirements without having to change existing wage scales. Third, Walsh-Healey rates were applicable to an industry only when they had been issued for that particular industry. This is not true under Davis-Bacon, where a determination must accompany every contract.

The Locality Issue

The problem of determining the geographic area over which a given Walsh-Healey minimum wage determination should apply was discussed when the original bills were introduced, but no clear congressional intent emerged. Some who saw the bill primarily as a partial substitute for the NIRA preferred a broad application—preferably nationwide—as a means of regularizing competition throughout the marketplace. Others saw it primarily as an extension of the Davis-Bacon Act and preferred a narrow geographic application so as to create minimal disruption in local labor markets. The compromise language included in the legislation, calling for application by industry or related groups of industries "in the locality in which the materials, supplies, articles, or equipment are to be manufactured or furnished," satisfied both sides but at the expense of logic. A single rate set for an industry or groups of similar industries could not also reflect local differences.

One early commentator on the act expressed it well:

> It is possible that the language with respect to locality in the Public Contracts Act resulted from opposing forces, one of which preferred the standard of the Davis-Bacon Act (city, town, village), and another which wished to eliminate or greatly reduce existing minimum wage differentials within individual industries. As an act of compromise, language which could be interpreted in one way or the other may have been adopted to resolve the political difficulty. Or, after holding hearings before Congressional committees, contradictory testimony and conflicting views may have so evenly divided the minds of the

legislative body that, not having before it specific information derived from experience, ambiguous or cloudy language appeared the better means of passing to the administrative agency the task of exploring the field under a non-restrictive delegation of power. Conceivably, both of these alternative difficulties may have perplexed the Congressional managers of the legislation.[38]

Regardless of what might have been originally intended, almost all of the wage determinations under Walsh-Healey adopted broad areas of coverage. One of the first rate determinations for a major industry, begun in July 1938, concerned the steel industry. The determination issued the following year set separate rates for four geographic regions of the country. The rates were immediately protested because of the broadness of their application, and the United States Court of Appeals declared the four-area view an inappropriate interpretation of locality. In the court's opinion, "the determination in this case goes so far beyond any possible proper application of the word [locality] as to defeat its meaning and to constitute an attempt arbitrarily to disregard the statutory mandate."[39]

On appeal to the Supreme Court, the case was dismissed on the ground that Congress had not granted standing to those affected by the statute. This had the effect of leaving the secretary broad discretionary powers in interpreting the statute, and in effect sanctioned the nonlocal approach the secretary had already taken.

The fact that such a nonlocal approach was detrimental to the competitive advantages of firms located in low-wage areas of the country was not lost on politicians who represented such areas, such as Senator William Fulbright of Arkansas. Fulbright took issue with a number of administrative interpretations in which he felt that "the Secretary of Labor has misapplied the Walsh-Healey Act in such a way as to erect artificial obstructions to the development of industry in the small communities throughout the country."[40] He proposed amendments to the act which would correct those interpretations and which would also bring administration of the act within the review provisions of the Administrative Procedure Act.

In the ensuing floor action, the specific corrections Fulbright had sought were opposed by senators from more populous and higher-wage states, as well as by the secretary of labor, but as a compromise,

---

[38] O. STRACKBEIN, THE PREVAILING MINIMUM WAGE STANDARD: A STUDY OF THE WAGE STANDARD ESTABLISHED BY THE UNITED STATES GOVERNMENT FOR THE PURCHASE OF ITS SUPPLIES, 35 (1939), quoted in CHRISTENSON & MYREN, *supra* note 6, at 18.

[39] Lukens Steel Co. v. Perkins, 107 F.2d 627, 630 (D.C. Cir. 1939).

[40] 98 CONG. REC. 6529 (1952), quoted in CHRISTENSON & MYREN, *supra* note 6, at 21.

the administrative procedures provisions were left in. Apparently, all concerned were willing to bounce the ball to the courts. The added provision said:

> All wage determinations under ... this Act shall be made on the record after opportunity for a hearing. Review of any such wage determination, or of the applicability of any such wage determination, may be had within ninety days after such determination is made in the manner provided in section 10 of the Administrative Procedure Act by any person adversely affected or aggrieved thereby....
>
> Notwithstanding the inclusion of any stipulations required by any provision of this Act in any contract subject to this Act, any interested person shall have the right of judicial review of any legal question which might otherwise be raised, including, but not limited to, wage determinations and the interpretation of the terms "locality," "regular dealer," "manufacturer," and "open market."[41]

End of Wage Determinations Under Walsh-Healey

Given the way in which the Fulbright amendments arose, it is clear that their primary purpose was to allow judical review of the secretary's interpretations of such terms as "locality" or "open market." In this regard, the amendments were a failure. A case brought in 1955[42] on substantially the same locality question as that involved in *Lukens Steel*, described above, and another brought in 1957 on the open market question[43] produced identical results: in both, the courts contented themselves with bouncing the ball back to Congress. In the words of one:

> The Secretary's interpretation of the Act as permitting industry-wide determinations of minimum wages is not new.... His practice in this respect has repeatedly been called to the attention of committees of Congress. Attempts have been made to write his interpretation expressly into the Act. Attempts have also been made to write it expressly out of the Act. Both have failed. Congress has chosen to leave the interpretation of the Act to the Secretary and the courts. As the Supreme Court said in regard to a different but somewhat related statute ... "We decline to repudiate an administrative interpretation of the Act which Congress refused to repudiate after being repeatedly urged to do so...."[44]

---

[41] The Walsh-Healey Public Contracts Act, Pub. L. No. 846, 74th Cong., 2d Sess. (1936) § 10, amended by § 301 of the Defense Production Act Amendments of 1952, approved June 30, 1952 (66 Stat. 308).

[42] Mitchell v. Covington Mills, 229 F.2d 506, 508 (D.C. Cir. 1955), *cert. denied*, 350 U.S. 1002 (1956), *reh'g denied,* 351 U.S. 934 (1956).

[43] Ruth Elkhorn Coals v. Mitchell, 248 F.2d 635, 638-9 (D.C. Cir. 1957).

[44] Covington Mills, 229 F.2d at 509, quoted in CHRISTENSON & MYREN, at 29-30.

Thus, although aggrieved parties now had standing to sue for judicial review of the secretary's interpretations, that standing was valueless because it had not existed when the interpretations were new. Only Congress, apparently, could force the issue.

In 1964, however, in *Wirtz v. Baldor*,[45] the first portion of the Fulbright amendments, requiring rate hearings to take place pursuant to the Administrative Procedure Act, was tried. That act specifies in part that "the proponent of a rule or order shall have the burden of proof," and gives every party the right to present his case or defense, to submit rebuttal evidence, and to "conduct such cross-examination as may be required for a full and true disclosure of the facts."[46] The case concerned the procedures used by the secretary in fixing minimum rates for the electric motors and generators industry.

In arriving at a rate determination for the electric motors and generators industry, the secretary used a questionnaire distributed by the Bureau of Labor Statistics (BLS) which contained a pledge of confidentiality to the respondents. A table summarizing the wage data of 216 firms was compiled, a copy of which was furnished to the National Electrical Manufacturers Association (NEMA) a few weeks before the rate hearing. Based on its own investigations, the NEMA concluded that discrepancies existed in the wage data reported to the BLS. At the hearing, the NEMA contended that there was a substantial possibility that the BLS questionnaire had been widely misunderstood and might contain substantial errors, but that without access to the original documents it could not properly evaluate the BLS summary. It therefore attempted to subpoena the original documents.

The secretary of labor, fearful that disclosure of information provided confidentially to the BLS would destroy its credibility and harm its ability to gather statistics in the future, refused the subpoena. The court found that without it, the NEMA did not have an adequate opportunity for rebuttal and cross-examination, and that the NEMA had demonstrated that the likelihood for error in the BLS summary was substantial. The court therefore struck down the determination, although it made clear that it was not striking down all rate determinations, and would evaluate the evidence independently in each case brought to it. Furthermore, the Court solicited suggestions from the Department of Labor as to how surveys might be conducted in the future to avoid repetition of the problem. The secretary's responses, however, all involved main-

---

[45] Wirtz v. Baldor Electric, 337 F.2d 518 (D.C. Cir. 1964).
[46] Administrative Procedure Act, 60 Stat. 241, 5 U.S.C. § 1006(c).

taining the confidentiality of details of the surveys, and so were unacceptable.

The only unimpeachable, nonconfidential data available for rate setting were the statutory minimum rates required by the Fair Labor Standards Act. Because there was no point to issuing these as prevailing rates, new Walsh-Healey determinations ceased to be made. Determinations that had been issued before *Wirtz v. Baldor* were unaffected, and continued to be in force, but as the increasing Fair Labor Standards minimum wage overtook them, they ceased to be meaningful. No new determinations have been issued under Walsh-Healey since 1964.

CURRENT STATUS OF THE WALSH-HEALEY ACT

The Walsh-Healey Act covers four major topics: 1) prevailing minimum wage rates; 2) limitations on work hours; 3) prohibition of child and convict labor; and 4) safe and sanitary working conditions. The provisions of the act setting prevailing minimum wage rates are moribund, as explained above. Limitations on work hours have historically had the greatest impact (albeit for a questionable benefit), but these work hours provisions were entirely duplicated by the Contract Work Hours and Safety Standards Act of 1962, and the daily overtime provisions of both acts were repealed in 1985. The prohibition of child and convict labor has been almost completely replaced by the Fair Labor Standards Act. And the safe and sanitary workplace provisions have been superseded by the Occupational Safety and Health Act. In sum, it is extremely difficult to find any cause for the continued existence of Walsh-Healey. The law should be repealed simply as a matter of good housekeeping.

CHAPTER VI

The Service Contract Act[1]

The Service Contract Act is officially the O'Hara-McNamara Services Act,[2] although, unlike the Davis-Bacon or Walsh-Healey Acts, no one seems to call it by its sponsors' names. It was passed in 1965, so that except for one or two of the state laws, it is the most recent statement of a prevailing wage law in the country. In the drafting of it, unfortunately, Congress showed no evidence of having learned from the experiences of its predecessors, thus further increasing the amount of administrative confusion and controversy associated with prevailing wage laws.

Dissatisfaction with the Service Contract Act, centering not as much on wage rate determinations as on coverage questions, arose immediately after the law took effect. This resulted in two major amendments—one in 1972 and the other in 1976—but in large measure, the amendments added as many problems as they solved. Another attempt at correction was launched in 1981 during the early days of the first Reagan administration, when proposals were introduced for changes to twenty-six specific regulatory aspects of the act, all but one of which withstood court challenges and finally became effective by 1985. Nevertheless, relatively few observers feel that the Service Contract Act is capable either of fulfilling the original intent of its framers or of achieving any societal purpose which could not be handled better by other means.

As originally proposed, the Service Contract Act was to extend prevailing wage coverage to the last remaining stratum of non-professional employees who might be employed to work under contracts for the federal government and who were not yet covered by

---

[1] Sections of this chapter rely heavily on "The Service Contract Act of 1965: Time to Revise or Repeal" written by Beverly Hall Burns, and published in the *Villanova Law Review,* Vol. 29, No. 2, 1983-84, pp. 435-75, by permission of the author and publisher. Beverly Hall Burns was Assistant Professor, Glassboro State College in New Jersey and Research Specialist, Industrial Research Unit, the Wharton School, University of Pennsylvania. The manuscript was prepared at the Industrial Research Unit with inclusion in this volume in mind. Ms. Burns has since rejoined the law firm, Miller, Canfield, Paddock & Stone, in Detroit, Michigan.

[2] Service Contract Act of 1965, Pub. L. No. 89-286, 79 Stat. 1034 [codified as amended at 41 U.S.C. 351 (1976)].

some other prevailing wage law. Specifically, it was intended to apply to those "poorest and least skilled" workers in America who washed the laundry, prepared and served the meals, and did the janitorial work for government facilities.

Curiously, it was enacted at a time when the earlier prevailing wage laws were already showing signs of having outlived their usefulness. The wage provisions of the 1936 Walsh-Healey Act (covering employees of supply contractors), were in a court-induced limbo and had been determined to be unenforceable by the Department of Labor (DOL).[3] The 1931 Davis-Bacon Act (covering employees of construction contractors) was struggling to retain public favor. Furthermore, despite recurring problems under both Davis-Bacon and Walsh-Healey arising from the ambiguity of the prevailing wage concept, no greater precision of definition was applied to the new act.

In its favor, the Service Contract Act did finally identify and make provisions for the one group of employees who were at once the least organized and the most likely to benefit from whatever protection a prevailing wage law could offer. At the time the legislation was introduced, many classes of service employees were still not covered by the Fair Labor Standards Act, and so had no federal minimum wage provisions. Therefore, like earlier prevailing wage laws—both Davis-Bacon and Walsh-Healey preceded the Fair Labor Standards Act by several years—the Service Contract Act was intended to provide a wage floor for employees who otherwise did not have one.

But as it evolved, the Service Contract Act came to embrace and cover skilled technicians of various sorts, including clerical workers, key punchers, computer programmers and repairmen, and even lumberjacks. These are employees from an entirely different class than those forgotten, unprotected service workers originally envisioned, and have been the source of many of the administrative problems occasioned by the act.[4] The most recent regulatory changes to the act eliminated only some of these administrative problems.

HISTORY AND OVERVIEW
OF THE SERVICE CONTRACT ACT

The contention that employees of private contractors who provided services to the federal government deserved wage and benefit protections was hardly new in 1965. Bills designed to confront the

---

[3] See Ch. V, *supra*.
[4] GENERAL ACCOUNTING OFFICE, PROPRIETY OF MINIMUM WAGE DETERMINATIONS FOR CLERICAL AND OTHER OFFICE EMPLOYEES UNDER THE SERVICE CONTRACT ACT 2 (1973) [hereafter cited as 1973 PROPRIETY FOR CLERICAL EMPLOYEES].

same issue had been introduced earlier in the decade, and it was well known that employees of other types of contractors working for the federal government had enjoyed such wage protection for about thirty years. Specifically, in 1931, the Davis-Bacon Act had set up a statutory structure to require and enforce wage determinations on federal construction jobs exceeding a cost of $2,000.[5] Then, in 1936, the Walsh-Healey Public Contracts Act provided a minimum wage requirement for employees of manufacturing and supply companies who did business with the federal government on contracts in excess of $10,000.[6]

To some, therefore, a statute that protected employees of service contractors simply closed the last gap in remedial labor legislation applicable to federal contractors. Indeed, many "traditional" service employees, being on the bottom rung of the wage ladder, were poorly paid prior to the adoption of the act, a fact for which the federal government decided to assume responsibility. For example, in recommendations of the House Committee on Education and Labor,[7] the government cited itself as largely responsible for low pay in contract cleaning and other services, because many such employees were performing work for the government.

Furthermore, federal contracting rules required the government to accept the lowest bid of any responsible bidder.[8] In such labor-intensive areas as services, the potential effect of the low bid requirement was criticized as tolerance, if not actual encouragement, of "wage busting." According to the House Committee recommendations:

> The Federal Government has added responsibility in this area because of the legal requirement that contracts be awarded to the lowest responsible bidder. Since labor costs are the predominant factor in most service contracts, the odds on making a successful low bid for a contract are heavily stacked in favor of the contractor paying the lowest wage.... When a government contract is awarded to a service contractor with low wage standards, the government is in effect subsidizing subminimum wages.[9]

In addition, unlike construction contracts, service contracts were often rebid annually, so the possibility of downward wage pressures could recur regularly.

---

[5] The Davis-Bacon Act, 40 U.S.C. 276(a) (1931).

[6] The Walsh-Healey Public Contracts Act, 41 U.S.C. 34–45 (1936).

[7] H.R. Rep. No. 948, Senate Report No. 798, 89th Cong., 1st Sess., as cited in *Oversight Hearings on the Service Contract Act Before the Subcommittee on Labor-Management Relations of the House Committee on Education and Labor*, 97th Cong., 1st Sess. 4 (1981) [hereinafter cited as *1981 Oversight Hearings*].

[8] *Id.*

[9] *Id.* The process by which "low wage standards" produce "subminimum" wages was not explained in the text.

Protecting blue-collar service workers from such alleged exploitation was one of the principal purposes for which the Service Contract Act was adopted.[10] In this stated purpose, the statute is not significantly different from the Davis-Bacon and Walsh-Healey Acts. All of them were intended to protect the wage structure in the private sector from the impact of the federal government's highly regulated procurement process. This is the principal rationale of the act. The degree to which it is a valid foundation for legislation depends on whether the perceived problem is real, whether it continues to be a problem despite other legislation having been passed since it was introduced (in this case, the extension of the Fair Labor Standards Act to service employees) and the degree to which it is a reasonable substitute for modification to procurement regulations.

Other Possible Rationales

Legislation placed on the books of the United States, however nobly intentioned, is often vague as to the details of its purposes, leaving to the courts and later analysts to impute the original congressional intent. The Service Contract Act is no exception. There are, in fact, many possible rationales for the act and for the particular provisions that it contains which are not expressly stated either in the act itself, or in the hearings that led up to it. One recent economic analysis identified eight plausible rationales.[11]

Prevention of Average-Wage Busting. As discussed above, one of the major rationales for all prevailing wage laws is that they shield employees of government contractors from the competitive struggles among their employers brought on by the government procurement process. Basically, the argument is that since federal contracts are awarded to the lowest bidder, and since labor costs are an important factor in many contracts, absent the protection of a prevailing wage law the contract will tend to go to the bidder with the lowest labor cost. To achieve low labor costs in order to obtain the work, bidders will offer only low wage rates, and "bust" the locality's private wage scale.

Prevention of Individual-Wage Busting. Union representatives have argued that without the protection of a prevailing wage law, when unions succeed in organizing low-paid service employees such as guards or contract cleaning personnel, the resulting higher labor

---

[10] 1973 PROPRIETY FOR CLERICAL EMPLOYEES, *supra* note 4, at 1.

[11] Goldfarb & Heywood, *An Economic Evaluation of the Service Contract Act,* 36 INDUST. & LAB. REL. REV. 63–68 (1982).

costs provide the opportunity for nonunion firms to underbid union firms in the next round of negotiations,[12] taking away the contract. Having won the contract, the nonunion firms might offer jobs back to the same individuals who had performed them before, but at lower wage rates. Thus the wage gains to the individual from unionization would be thwarted. This line of argument was an important one in establishing the successorship provisions of the Service Contract Act, which were adopted with the 1972 amendments.

Encouragement of Collective Bargaining. If a prevailing wage law can effectively eliminate the wage advantage of nonunion firms (or the disadvantage of unionized firms) in seeking low-bid contracts, it will encourage the maintenance and growth of unions. The provisions of this and other prevailing wage laws that require either a union wage or some other superminimum wage undoubtedly reflect the fact that an ordinary wage floor, such as the minimum provided by the Fair Labor Standards Act, is not as effective in forcing wage parity between union and nonunion firms.

Establishing the Federal Government as a "Model Employer." This rationale holds that the federal government should act as a model employer (by paying attractive wages to prevent, for example, poverty among the employed), and also force its contractors to do likewise.

Protection of Government Workers. With respect to many of its service needs (cleaning and maintenance of federal office buildings, for example), the government has the choice of hiring and using its own employees (sometimes called "force account" employees), or of contracting the work out to private contractors.[13] A prevailing wage law such as the Service Contract Act can make contracting out relatively more expensive, thus reducing the incentive for the government to do it, and protecting the jobs of service workers on the government payroll.[14] As it is sometimes stated, cost savings from contracting out should not be at the expense of federal workers.[15]

---

[12] It had been, and to a lesser extent remains, the tradition in services contracting for the government to rebid such work as contract cleaning annually.

[13] The current policy on contracting out has been in effect since 1966, the year after the Service Contract Act was adopted. [OFFICE OF MANAGEMENT AND BUDGET, CIRCULAR A-76.] It requires that federal agencies conduct reviews to determine whether any of their services that are "not inherently governmental" could be performed at less expense by the private sector.

[14] Even with the prevailing wage laws in effect, the Office of Management and Budget estimates that when a service is turned over to a private contractor, the government saves an average of 20 percent of the service's cost. [See *Federal Unions Oppose Contracting-Out at Congressional Hearings,* GOV'T UNION CRITIQUE 6 (October 5, 1984).]

[15] *Congressional Oversight Hearings: The Plight of the Service Worker Revisited,*

This rationale was important to the 1972 amendments requiring that the DOL give due consideration to federal wage levels for comparable jobs when setting rates for a new contract.

Encouragement of Geographic Balance in Contracts. Although many service contracts are location specific, others are for services such as data processing or report writing which can be performed almost anywhere. A prevailing wage law applying a uniform level of wages can prevent the largess of government contracting from flowing to one particular area of the country just because it might have a generally lower scale of wages for the relevant occupations. Thus, geographic balance in the distribution of government work is encouraged.[16]

Preventing the Importation of Labor. The rationale here is similar to the principal ones used in support of the Davis-Bacon Act in 1931. The fear expressed then was that without the impediment of a prevailing wage law, contractors on federal jobs might import low-wage itinerant ("Gypsy") workers who would take work opportunities away from the locals, or who might remain in the community at the termination of the contract, disrupting and lowering the local wage scale. A prevailing wage law that enforced local wage levels can be used to prevent this phenomenon.[17]

Improving the Quality of Services Performed. Basically, the quality of service rationale reflects the old and well-understood adage, "You get what you pay for." By its logic, if the government wants first-class cleaning services, for example, it will have to pay a first-class price. Since government contracts are mandated to go to the lowest bidder, they will be performed by the lowest cost, and therefore putatively by the lowest quality level employees, unless a prevailing wage law ensures that wage costs are kept at a uniformly high level. Because union wages tend to be generally higher than free market ones, this argument equating cost and quality is frequently raised by union officials in hearings on prevailing wage legislation.[18]

94th Cong., 1st Sess. 6 (1975) as cited in Goldfarb and Heywood, *supra* note 11, at 66.

[16] To ensure geographic balance, wages set by the Service Contract Act should presumably be established nationally. But because the rates are also supposed to reflect, and not to interfere with, local labor market conditions, definition of what constitutes the proper locality has been a thorny problem for both framers and administrators of the act, and for the courts.

[17] The degree to which itinerant workers have been an actual presence in the labor market since the Great Depression, however, has never been documented.

[18] Goldfarb and Heywood, *supra* note 11, at 68. The authors cite examples from three union officials testifying in the 1964 oversight hearings that nonunion contractors pay subminimal wages resulting in the destruction of decent work and

THE ACT IN ITS ORIGINAL FORM

When it was adopted in 1965, the Service Contract Act applied to every federal contract in excess of $2,500 for services to be performed by service employees. Seven types of contracts were specifically exempted: 1) construction contracts, where the Davis-Bacon Act would apply; 2) manufacturing or supply contracts where the work required would be subject to the Walsh-Healey Act; 3) certain contracts for the carriage of freight or personnel where published tariff rates were in effect; 4) contracts for furnishing broadcast services subject to the Communications Act of 1934; 5) contracts for utility services; 6) employment contracts for direct services to a federal agency by an individual or individuals (essentially, consulting contracts); and 7) contracts for the operation of a postal contract station.[19]

All other service contracts covered by the original statute were required to contain the following:

1) provisions for minimum wages for the various classes of service employees in the performance of the contract or any subcontract, to be set by the secretary of labor in accord with "prevailing rates for such employees in the locality."[20]
2) provisions for fringe benefits to be furnished to the various classes of service employees, also to be determined by the secretary of labor in accord with the benefits "prevailing for such employees in the locality." The statute required that at bare minimum,

> such fringe benefits shall include medical or hospital care, pensions on retirement or death, compensation for injuries or illness resulting from occupational activity, or insurance to provide any of the foregoing, unemployment benefits, life insurance, disability and sickness insurance, accident insurance, vacation and holiday pay, costs of apprenticeship or other similar programs and other bona fide fringe benefits not otherwise required by Federal, State or local law to be provided by the contractor or subcontractor.[21]

The contracting concern did, however, have an alternative to providing all of these benefits, as the benefits obligation could be discharged "by furnishing any equivalent combinations of

---

salary standards and the lowering of the quality of the work performed. Similar statements from union spokesmen can be found in almost all of the recorded hearings on prevailing wage laws before or since.

[19] 41 U.S.C. 351 § 7.
[20] *Id.* § 2(a)(1).
[21] *Id.* § 2(a)(2).

fringe benefits or by making equivalent or differential payments in cash."[22]
3) provision that the contract would be performed under safe and sanitary conditions.[23]
4) assurance that employees of the successful bidder would be given notice of the compensation required under the act.[24]
5) provision that in no case could service employees under contracts subject to the act be paid less than the minimum wage specified by the Fair Labor Standards Act.[25]

The DOL was charged with administration of the new statute, and was given significant latitude in its activity with respect to enforcement. It could make "rules and regulations allowing reasonable variations, tolerances and exemptions to and from any or all provisions of this act."[26]

Contractors who violated the act were liable, and could be sued by the government, for compensation due employees.[27] If a violation was found, the contract involved was subject to cancellation and the violators to being debarred from further federal contracts for a period of three years.[28] No other remedies were suggested.

In establishing the regulations for the Service Contract Act, the secretary of labor was subject to a different set of pressures than had been the case at the time of Davis-Bacon's inception. The desire to protect the wage gains won by construction unions in the 1930s undoubtedly influenced Davis-Bacon's choice of the "30-percent rule" for selecting the prevailing rate, since this improved the opportunity for the union rate to be selected and therefore decreased the likelihood that a competitively important wage differential would exist between union and nonunion firms seeking government contracts. The groups to whom the new act were envisioned to apply were not highly unionized, however, and therefore the secretary of labor could more freely adopt a method for calculating the prevailing rate that did not have to consider the relative competitive positions of union or nonunion firms. The method selected was that of taking the median rate found in surveys of the relevant locality.

Although the median rate bears no better relationship to the concept of prevailing than does Davis-Bacon's 30-percent rule, the use of this method leaves the DOL open to fewer charges of favor-

---

[22] *Id.*
[23] *Id.* § 2(a)(3).
[24] *Id.* § 2(a)(4).
[25] *Id.* § 2(b)(1), citing the Fair Labor Standards Act, 29 U.S.C. 201 *et seq.*
[26] 41 U.S.C. 31 *et seq*, § 4(b).
[27] *Id.* §§ 3(c) and 5(b).
[28] *Id.* § 5(a).

itism in establishing the level of rates. As a result, the level of rates set by the Service Contract Act has not been a primary focus of discontent, except insofar as it is associated with the successorship provisions, covered below.[29] Where the major controversies surrounding the Service Contract Act arose were in the areas of defining the locality on which the rates would be based, and the types of employees to whom they would apply. Also, like the Walsh-Healey Act, the Service Contract Act did not impose wage requirements on contractors if the secretary of labor had not issued a wage determination covering them. This, too, became a source of controversy.

THE 1972 AMENDMENTS

The original statement of the Service Contract Act did not stand for long. Within eight months of its adoption, the DOL's Wage and Hour Administration had proposed amendments to some of the original regulations because they were already "unnecessary and outdated."[30] Moreover, within a few years, supporters of the act were promoting amendments to force the DOL to make more wage determinations and to eliminate what was seen as the "rapid turnover of government service contracts through underbidding on wages and working conditions."[31]

Hearings were scheduled in 1972, which revealed that the DOL had, in fact, failed to make wage determinations in more than two-thirds of all federal service contracts.[32] It also heard testimony to the effect that the turnover of service contracts was frequent. As a result of these concerns, the statute was amended in late 1972. Most of the new provisions extended coverage and fortified rather than softened the act. Among them were provisions to:

1) require successor contractors to pay service employees wages and fringe benefits no lower than those to which the predecessor contractor was committed by a collective bargaining agreement (including future increases) unless the secretary of labor, after a hearing, found those rates to be substantially at variance with the prevailing rates in the locality;

---

[29] Findings by the General Accounting Office that the Department of Labor makes inaccurate determinations by this method, however, are discussed later in the chapter.

[30] *Proposed Revision of Service Contract Act Regulation Published by W.H. Administrator,* 187 DAILY LAB. REP. A-8 (Sept. 26, 1966).

[31] *House Labor Committee Report on Service Contract Act Amendments Draws No Dissents,* 150 DAILY LAB. REP. A-3 (Aug. 2, 1972).

[32] H.R. Rep. No. 1251, 92d Cong., 2d Sess. 3 (1972).

2) allow multi-year service contracts of up to five years, if approved by the secretary of labor and if wages and fringe benefits were adjusted every two years;
3) require that in establishing prevailing rates, due consideration be given to the federal wage board rate applicable for similar work under civil service regulations (federal wage board employees correspond generally to blue-collar workers in the private sector);
4) mandate that wage determinations for all government service contracts subject to the act be issued as soon as administratively feasible, according to a time schedule specified in the amendments.

Clearly, the sponsors of these amendments hoped that by mandating wage determinations and insisting on closer administration and enforcement of the act it would become manageable, efficient, and effective. That, however, was not to be the case. Contracts ranging from laundry service to high technology continued to be let without wage determinations even in the 1980s; furthermore, the successor contractor provisions of the 1972 amendments have been under constant challenge for forcing wage rates upon a contractor which he did not negotiate, even though the rates might never actually have been paid by the predecessor.[33]

The successor provision, in effect, permitted the predecessor contractor and its unions to establish the wage rates for a successor, although to some this outcome appeared to conflict with a U.S. Supreme Court ruling. In *Burns International Security Service, Inc. v. NLRB*,[34] which was issued in 1972 prior to the passage of the act's amendments, the Court had said that although a successor employer was required under the National Labor Relations Act to bargain with a union certified as representative of employees who had also been employed by the predecessor, the successor was not required to assume obligations of the labor agreement negotiated by the predecessor. Although the Armed Services Board of Contract Appeals had ruled that the *Burns* decision would also apply to administration of the Service Contract Act, Congress appeared to reject that argument in adopting the successor provision later in 1972.[35] Problems with successor contractors remain even subsequent

---

[33]GENERAL ACCOUNTING OFFICE, ASSESSMENT OF FEDERAL AGENCY COMPLIANCE WITH THE SERVICE CONTRACT ACT 7 (1982). See also, with regard to the "due consideration" provision in the amendments, Government Employees v. Donovan, 95 LC par. 34, 177 (D.C. Dist. Ct., November, 1982).

[34] 406 U.S. S276 (1972).

[35] *Space Age Engineering,* Armed Services Board of Contract Appeals No. 16588, August 10, 1972.

to the administrative rule changes made in 1983, as will be discussed below.

THE 1976 AMENDMENTS

In 1976, it was evident that the law, unwieldy and still subject to *ad hoc* enforcement, continued to have serious administrative and enforcement problems. For example, although the DOL seemed to have taken its legislatively mandated responsibility to make wage determinations to heart, procuring agencies sometimes failed to notify the DOL that determinations were needed, and were letting contracts without ever asking for the determinations to be made.[36]

A second issue had also arisen by 1976: the question of what kind of employee was entitled to the protection of the statute. The DOL had vacillated since the beginning on the question of whether clerical employees of service contractors were to be covered by wage determinations. Although "the legislative history of the act strongly suggests that clerical and other office employees and non-service employees not be included,"[37] Congress reacted to a judicial decision in support of that legislative history by amending the statute to cover all employees of service firms except bona fide executive, administrative, and professional employees.[38]

In the judicial decision,[39] the U.S. District Court for the Middle District of Florida had found that Congress had meant the act to be limited in its coverage to blue-collar workers doing jobs similar to "wage board" classifications defined for federal service. A similar issue involving classification had arisen in a 1974 case in which the U.S. District Court for Delaware held that keypunch operators were not service employees according to the meaning of the Service Contract Act.[40]

The amendments as finally passed in 1976 were seen as a necessary clarification of legislative intent. Contrary to the federal court rulings, they defined service employees as any persons working on a government service contract other than bona fide executives, administrators, and professionals, and reiterated that services include any operations, other than those specifically exempted in the original act, that do not result in a physical product. Never-

---

[36] The problem continues today. *See* GENERAL ACCOUNTING OFFICE, *supra* note 33, at 7–10.

[37] 1973 PROPRIETY OF CLERICAL EMPLOYEES, *supra* note 4, at 1.

[38] U.S. COMPTROLLER GENERAL, REVIEW OF COMPLIANCE WITH LABOR STANDARDS FOR SERVICE CONTRACTS BY DEFENSE AND LABOR DEPARTMENTS 2 (1978).

[39] Federal Electric Corp. v. Dunlop, 419 F. Supp. 221 (1976).

[40] Descomp, Inc. v. Sampson, 377 F. Supp. 254 (D. Del. 1974).

theless, just as the 1972 amendments failed to resolve problems and in fact created their own, the definitional clarification in 1976 created still more problems, especially in the service industries associated with automatic data processing and research and development.

PROBLEMS WITH ADMINISTRATION AND INTERPRETATION OF THE ACT

The pragmatic and interpretive problems associated with the Service Contract Act that developed before 1981, when the DOL instituted regulatory changes in the hopes of correcting some of them, concern four major questions: 1) What is the proper interpretation of the locality from which rates will be drawn in making wage determinations? 2) What classifications of employees will be considered to be service employees on what types of contracts? 3) What rules should govern successor contractors, that is, those firms who take over performance of a long-term service need from a different contractor who had been doing it before? and 4) How can the act be enforced consistently when some federal agencies feel helped and others hindered by it? In addition to these major problem areas, there are others of more narrow application that will be grouped together and discussed subsequently.

The Locality Issue

The provision of the Service Contract Act that makes definition of locality a problem is that which requires specification of the minimum wage to be paid various classes of service employees. Such wages are to be paid:

> in accordance with prevailing rates for such employees *in the locality,* or, where a collective bargaining agreement covers any such service employees, in accordance with the rates for such employees provided for in such agreement, including prospective wage increases provided for in such agreement as a result of arms length negotiation.[41]

The fringe benefit requirement contains a similar locality provision. Although the 1976 amendments were intended to answer

---

[41] 41 U.S.C. 351(a)(1) (emphasis added). The collective bargaining agreements mentioned in this section refer to those that might be in effect for the particular group of employees employed on the government contract, not to those that might generally exist in the locality. It would seem to be a redundant requirement to impose on a firm already unionized, but it was considered important to deny contractors the (unlikely) option of locking out their union employees and hiring new ones to complete a government contract. Its principal impact is on the successorship issue, which is reviewed below.

the locality question, they did not resolve it. The issue is one which not only makes rates specified by the act seem at times arbitrary and capricious, but also calls into question whether the act as it exists is true to its own philosophy.

Some service contracts are location specific and others can be performed anywhere. For those that are location specific, prevailing rates for service employees in the locality of the specific location are easy enough to conceptualize, and are not a problem. But for the others, locality might logically mean the location of the contracting facility (the buyer), the location of the principal place of business of the contractor (the seller), or the location where the work is to be done. For simplification, this will be called the locus question.

No matter how the locus question is answered, the definition of locality requires further interpretation of the extent of geography over which wage equivalence should prevail, and therefore the geography from which existing wage data should be sought. The Davis-Bacon Act had specified that the geographic extent for prevailing rates would be the "city, town, village, or other civil subdivision" where the work was to take place, but was usually interpreted by the DOL as being a geographic area no smaller than a county.[42] By the time the Service Contract Act was passed, many of the determinations being made under Davis-Bacon were "area" determinations, covering whole states, or even the entire country. The logic of doing this, however, was that the calculating method employed by Davis-Bacon (the 30-percent rule, at that time) ensured that the union rate would be chosen as prevailing in all smaller polities within the territory covered by the area determinations. This same logic could not apply under the calculating method of the Service Contract Act, which took the median rate rather than the plurality rate as prevailing.

In addition to the locus questions, therefore, the Service Contract Act also had to answer an extent question similar to that of Davis-Bacon, but for which the Davis-Bacon experience was not useful. Should it be taken to mean the surrounding town, the county, the metropolitan area, or perhaps some arbitrary geographic area that reflects the labor market drawing area or even the ready availability of input data? Could locality be interpreted to mean the entire country? The locus questions will be discussed first.

Contractor Locus. Assume first an application of locality to mean the place where the contracting facility is located. For example, the

---

[42] See discussion of the Davis-Bacon Act in Ch. III, *supra*.

government might wish to contract for printing services. The locus of the contracting agency may very well be in Washington, D.C. Potential bidders, on the other hand, could be anywhere in the United States. Wages paid to printers in one part of the country may differ significantly from those paid in another, and further, will almost certainly differ from wages paid to printers in Washington, D.C. Using the locus of the contracting facility as the locality, all bidders would be required to agree to pay wages equivalent to the wage determination for Washington, D.C., as a condition of obtaining the federal work. This would probably involve considerable variation from the actual wage rates prevailing in the area where the printers themselves might be located.

If this hypothetical contract were bid on and won by a printer in Mississippi, where wage scales are much lower than those in Washington, D.C., the higher rates that the Mississippi printer would have to pay under the Service Contract Act would have an inflationary impact on wage and benefit rates in the actual labor market from which the employees would be drawn. This would pervert one of the basic tenets argued by supporters of prevailing wage legislation, that because wage rates already prevailing in a community are used as the basis for enforcement of such legislation, in application there is no impact on local wage scales.

This scenario would be in keeping with one of the rationales for the act—that of promoting broad geographic distribution of contracts by eliminating the competitive wage advantage of low-wage regions of the country. On the other hand, however, if the situation were reversed and the contracting agency was located in Mississippi, the low rates determined for the job might result in below poverty level wages being paid to service employees in Washington, D.C. (or San Francisco, New York City, or other places with high costs of living). Moreover, if another of the rationales—that involving the importation of labor—is realistic and low wage rates do result in itinerant low-wage workmen coming into an area and taking jobs away from the locals, here is the place it would actually happen and be encouraged to happen by the very act allegedly designed to prevent it.

Bidder Locus. A second interpretation would take locality to mean the principal place of business of the contracting employer. This resolution might be just as artificial, for the work would not necessarily be done in the same place for which the rates were set. It has the further disadvantage that each bidder would have to have a wage determination made for the locus of his own principal place of business before he could submit an informed bid.

Consider, for example, two large chemical companies seeking a contract to do certain research for the government. One is headquartered in Georgia and the other in Massachusetts. By happenstance, both plan to accomplish the work at research installations each has in northern New Jersey. Before bidding for the work, each company should have the right to know what minimum wage rates it will have to pay, so two determinations would have to be made by the DOL, one for Georgia and one for Massachusetts. This would, at the very least, complicate the bidding process, since the DOL would not know in advance who the bidders might be; furthermore, it would require twice as much work for the government as would using the contractor locus. It would give an arbitrary advantage to the firm headquartered in Georgia, and would produce unrealistic wage requirements for application in New Jersey regardless of who won the bidding.

Work Site Locus. In view of the intended protective purposes of the act, the only logical interpretation of locality would be the locus of the facility where the work is actually to be performed. Obviously, if the intent is to protect the wage scale of service workers who might be drawn upon to work on a particular government contract by ensuring that their earnings will be similar to those of comparable workers in private employment, the only relevant comparison base is the labor pool from which workers would be drawn for both types of work. Only an area in some proximity to the locus of the work site would meet this criterion.

Unfortunately, despite its better conceptual underpinnings, a system based on rates prevailing in the locus of the workplace creates awkward technical and administrative problems of its own. First, the bidding process is again made complex by the necessity of providing multiple determinations. Furthermore, in the event of a contract for data processing, or some other service which is not location specific, a large firm might contemplate doing various portions of it in several different locations, each one of which would now require its own wage determination. In such circumstances, wage determinations included in the contract would have to specify not only the various rates prevailing for each location, but also the proportion of the work that would have to be accomplished at each place. Second, the rationale for the act suggesting that its use might improve geographic dispersion of contracts would be obviated. Third, the successorship issue (discussed below) is made more complex by the requirement that the minimum wages paid by a predecessor also be paid by the successor, even though the location may be different. Which of the various rates on the hypothetical contract discussed above should be carried through?

The Extent Question. None of the logical alternatives for locus is completely acceptable, and the question of the extent of the geographic area that should be surveyed for existing rates to find those which actually prevail in the locality suffers from want of a satisfactory answer as well. It has been suggested that a possible solution to both problems might be to define locality in its broadest terms by taking national average prevailing rates as the basis for determinations. This solution does have the advantage that it would be easily implemented by the DOL, but it would also make a mockery of the basic concepts of prevailing wage legislation and expose the Service Contract Act as no more than a superminimum wage statute, in which the national median wage for covered service workers would become the minimum wage applicable to government contract work, regardless of local labor market or cost of living considerations. And even under this solution, unionized contractors or those operating in high-wage areas would still find themselves at relatively the same disadvantage as they would face if the act did not exist, unless the rules were further modified to take the union rate as prevailing, which would be a fundamental change in the act's philosophy. Furthermore, local wage structures in low-wage areas would be disrupted and pressured upwards, and the government would pay needlessly more than it should for the services it wished to contract out.

Unless the principal purpose of the act is construed to be its social one of paying more than the market rate for services so that the providers of services will not receive "subminimal wages ... with the consequent ... destruction of decent work and salary standards, and the lowering of quality of ... work performed,"[43] such a construction of locality flies in the face of logic. And if the principal purpose of the act is indeed the social one, then a more reasonable approach might be through modification of the Fair Labor Standards Act.

Legal Reaction to the Locality Question

The question of what constitutes a locality was raised in the earliest of the cases under the Service Contract Act, and it continues to be a problem in the most recent ones as well, although there have been no tests as yet of the administrative changes applied in

---

[43] Special Subcommittee on Labor, *Hearings on H.R. 1678 and H.H. 6088,* 88th Cong., 2d Sess. 8–12 (1964) (statement of James McGaney).

1985. In *Descomp, Inc. v. Sampson*,⁴⁴ the district court grappled with the statutory meaning of wages and fringe benefits being paid "in accordance with prevailing rates for such employees in the locality."⁴⁵

In *Descomp*, the bidder on a government keypunch contract sued for declaratory relief that the wage determination affecting its contract should have been for Wilmington, Delaware, the location of the contractor's principal place of business, instead of Washington, D.C., the location of the contracting federal agency. The government had four reasons for making the location of the contracting facility the locality for purposes of the act. The court considered those reasons one by one and raised counterpoint arguments which it found more persuasive, leading to its conclusion that the place of performance, not the place of the contracting facility, was to serve as the appropriate locus.

Specifically, the arguments for and against were:

1) that the use of the singular "locality" in the statute suggests that the contracting facility should be the locality because Congress must have known that there would be multiple bids from multiple bidders, and so would have used the word "localities," instead.⁴⁶ But the court found that "Congress was just as likely laying down a requirement that each and every contractor was to observe the prevailing wage rate in the locality where the work was to be performed.";⁴⁷

2) that Congress could not have meant locality of the place of performance because it would have known that the DOL does not have the manpower to do so many wage determinations. But the court reasoned that the inability of the DOL to do the requisite number of wage determinations had not been proved, and that such an unproved argument would be a weak basis for a decision in favor of the contracting facility as the locality;⁴⁸

3) that Congress meant to give the DOL more flexibility in determining locality than it had given under the Davis-Bacon Act, because it had been less specific in defining the term. Here the court's counterargument was that irrespec-

---
⁴⁴ 377 F. Supp. 254.
⁴⁵ 41 U.S.C. §§ 351(a)(1) and (2).
⁴⁶ 377 F. Supp. 254 at 264.
⁴⁷ *Id.*
⁴⁸ *Id.* at 265.

tive of that congressional intent, the question of defining locality remained unanswered;[49]

4) that the court should base its decision on the principle that where a duty to act rests on terms of doubtful meaning, the court should defer to the agency's expertise. To this the court responded that it was in no doubt that the legislative history supported location as "the place where the work was to be performed."[50]

Six years after *Descomp,* another court was called upon to consider the locality issue. It wrestled with the question, but ultimately refused to answer it. In *Midwest Maintenance and Construction Co. v. Vela,*[51] Midwest had bid on and received a contract to do maintenance and repair work on certain government equipment. The company's principal place of business was in Oklahoma City, Oklahoma; the wage determination provided in the government bid specifications was for Bexar and Guadalupe counties, Texas, the location of the government facilities; in fact, Midwest performed the work contracted for in Poteet, Atascose County, Texas, adjacent to Bexar County.

Midwest did not pay the wage as set forth in the bid specifications, but did pay at least the government minimum wage, which is the minimum acceptable under the statute.[52] Midwest was found in violation, had payments of more than $60,000 withheld, and was barred from further federal service contracts for three years.[53]

The appellate court determined that the government had failed to meet its burden with respect to the meaning of locality. Noting that the proper standard for that burden was the "preponderance of the evidence,"[54] the court tersely denied that the government had met the standard, stating that it had not even met the burden of establishing its claim that Bexar County was the location of the contracting facility.[55] The contract itself, made up of an ambiguous invitation to bid and a number of handwritten notes, was simply unclear to the court, and it therefore remanded to the district court with instructions for a further remand to the DOL to take steps consistent with the appeals court opinion.[56] There was one indirect

---

[49] *Id.*
[50] *Id.*
[51] Midwest Maintenance and Construction Co. v. Vela, 621 F.2d 1046 (10th Cir. 1980).
[52] 41 U.S.C. 351(b).
[53] 621 F.2d 1046, at 1048.
[54] 41 U.S.C., at 353-4; *see also* U.S. v. Powers Building and Maintenance Co., 336 F. Supp. 819 (Dist. Ct. Okla., 1972).
[55] 621 F.2d 1046, at 1049-50.
[56] *Id.* at 1051.

conclusion drawn by the court with respect to locality, namely that the locality was one of two places: "place of performance or place of the federal installation furnishing the equipment to be serviced."[57]

The other locality question, that of extent, was the subject of *Southern Packaging*,[58] a case decided at about the same time as *Midwest*. In *Southern Packaging*, the DOL contended that the correct extent of locality for establishing the prevailing rate was nationwide. The Southern Packaging Company had packaged meal-combat-individual rations ("c" rations) under government contracts for more than thirty-five years and, until passage of the Service Contract Act, its contracts had been governed by the Walsh-Healey Act. That act had been interpreted to mandate payment of the (Fair Labor Standard) minimum wage to employees of federal supply contractors. After the Service Contract Act was adopted, however, the DOL Employment Standards Administration decided to subject the "c" ration contracts to the new statute. Further, it decided that the locality for this case would be nationwide.

The DOL defended its position on locality on the basis of convenience, and stated that the alternative would have to be some kind of composite approach which would be less fair than the nationwide locality determination when a bidding agency neither knew nor cared where the contract work would be performed. Rejecting the government's arguments, the court concluded that it would not be an undue burden to require the Employment Standards Administration to provide wage determinations based on some more narrow geographic extent for the 0.5 percent of the cases for which it felt the DOL might wish to use a composite.

The court would not accept the "nationwide" theory. The dictionary, stated the court, defines locality as a "particular spot, situation or location," a definition that could not be compatible with so general a concept as "nationwide."[59] In affirming the lower court's finding, the appeals court found that locality for cases of this sort should be based on "the standard metropolitan statistical area, if applicable, or the specific county where the bidding party's plant or facility is located."[60]

---

[57] *Id.*

[58] Southern Packaging and Storage Co. v. U.S., 618 F.2d 1088 (4th Cir. 1980).

[59] *Id.* With respect to the applicability of the Service Contract over the Walsh-Healey Act, the court affirmed the lower court's finding that the Service Contract Act applied because the company was not a "manufacturer" or "assembler," even though providing "c" rations for the government seems, at least on the surface, to be more a supply than a service task.

[60] *Id.*

Summary, Locality Issue

It is clear that in drafting the Service Contract Act the Congress failed to contemplate situations in which the contracted work would not be location specific, but could be performed with equal ease in many different locations. The DOL, faced with the alternative of making a large number of wage determinations for the different locations of each individual bidder or of bending the purposes of the act and using determinations that were more easily produced, chose the latter alternative.

When its practices of issuing determinations based on the site of the contracting agency were challenged in *Descomp* (even though the judge there issued no order for the DOL to take remedial action), the DOL seemed to agree with this interpretation of the appropriate locus for determinations, but adopted as a fallback position the issuance of some of them based on regional composites or the average for the whole country. This compromise was challenged as encompassing too broad a geographic extent by the court in the *Southern Packaging* case, which suggested the metropolitan statistical area as the proper basis.

Lacking the manpower to make perhaps dozens of wage determinations for each contract bid or the prescience of who might be interested in bidding, the DOL still had developed no reasonable and consistent way of dealing with this problem by 1981. New regulations proposed in 1981, and finally cleared for implementation by a federal appeals court in 1985,[61] contain an attempt at a solution which entails a cumbersome two-step process. The new procedure will be implemented in cases where the geographic place of performance is unknown. First, the contracting agency will issue an initial qualifying solicitation with no wage determination, to identify potential bidders and their locations of performance. Second, wage determinations will be provided for all possible places of performance, and a money bid will be sought from the initial bidders. The winner will be required to pay the wage determination for the location specified in step one, regardless of whether he later changes the place of performance to an area in which the wage determination is lower.

This two-step approach offers a solution to the "nationwide locale" problem seen in the *Southern Packaging* case, and it seems to accept the theory that place of performance, not place of contracting agency or principal place of business of the contractor, should be the locus for determinations. It leaves unresolved, however, the

---

[61] AFL-CIO v. Donovan; CA DC, No. 84-5072.

geographic extent (short of the nationwide one) over which surveys will be conducted to find wage rates for the specified locations. Furthermore, it makes the procurement process more cumbersome and time consuming and fails to offer any insight into how the purportedly beleaguered DOL could promptly and efficiently provide such a large number of wage and benefit determinations. Finally, it does nothing to resolve the artificiality of the successor requirements, described below.

Contract and Employee Classification Issues

Issues involving the classification of contracts or of employees have already arisen in the *Southern Packaging* and *Descomp* cases, discussed above. In original concept, the Service Contract Act was aimed to protect the lowly service worker from exploitation when working under service contracts to the federal government. Because the service employee was typically seen as a building maintenance person, a laundry worker, a window washer, or a server of some sort, and the service contract was typically seen as a contract in which wages to such persons formed the bulk of the contract amount, little attention was devoted to defining either of these areas carefully. In practice, however, it is often difficult to distinguish between a supply contract and a service contract, or between a service worker and a technician.

The two questions are closely related. As illustrated in the *Southern Packing* case, a contract for supplying the government with a product, specifically packaged "c" rations, was considered by the DOL to be covered by the Service Contract Act, perhaps because the product is associated with food service and the employees in question were generally unskilled and low paid. In other words, the classification of the employees probably took precedence over the classification of the contract type.

On the other hand, in *Descomp,* a contract for keypunching data processing cards was also considered by the DOL to be covered, even though the bulk of the contract amount went to clerical workers and technicians, very few of whom were in classical service-type jobs. In this case, the classification of the contract seemed to take precedence over the classification of the employees.

There is also a third problem area, which arises from contracts involving research and development or data collection and analysis, in which a small portion of the employees of the contractor have actual service-type jobs. Here, the question is whether the actual service employees on such contracts should receive the protection of the act even though the bulk of the employees of the contractor are exempt.

Legal Reaction to the Classification Question

Throughout the history of the act, the DOL has had difficulty categorizing service employees. Clerical workers and technicians became a particular problem. Clearly, these are not traditional service workers, and as a General Accounting Office report concluded in 1973, there was little evidence suggesting that they were ever intended to be included.[62] Nevertheless, the DOL was issuing determinations for them.

In *Descomp*,[63] a 1974 case, the DOL had concluded that the contract for keypunching data processing cards was a service contract. Therefore, the DOL had made a wage determination and issued rates for the keypunch operators. The court first concluded that the contract was not one for services,[64] but the question of whether keypunch operators were service employees still remained. If they were not, then even if a service contract were involved, the act would not apply to them.

The court then found that the keypunch operators were not service employees under the terms of the statute. It applied a criterion which was to become the topic of much of the discussion surrounding the 1976 amendments,[65] namely that the status of a service employee is determined, for the purposes of the statute, according to how the employee's counterpart in the federal service would be classified. If the federal service counterpart were not a wage board (blue-collar) employee, but rather a general schedule (GS) employee (corresponding to the white-collar worker in the private sector), then the private contractor's employee in question would not be a service employee for the purpose of the statute.[66]

Similarly, in *Federal Electric Corp. v. Dunlop*,[67] a 1976 case determined without application of the amendments adopted that year, the contractor sued for a declaratory judgment on the question of whether ten different classifications of his employees, ranging from keypunch operators to senior computer operators, were "service employees." The parties had agreed that all of the ten classifications would be general schedule occupations in the federal civil service,

---

[62] *See supra* note 38 and accompanying text.
[63] 377 F. Supp. 254.
[64] *Id.* at 262, 265.
[65] *See supra* notes 36–40 and accompanying text.
[66] 377 F. Supp. 254, at 263.
[67] 49 F. Supp. 221.

The Service Contract Act 251

and that none would be even arguably blue-collar or wage board occupations.

In his arguments, the contractor contended that "the act was never intended to cover persons providing services who fell within the traditional 'white collar' classifications,"[68] and the court agreed that the *Descomp* precedent certainly supported that contention. The government argued that despite their white-collar status, the Federal Electric employees and others like them in the private sector were deserving of the protection of the statute. But the court, while sympathetic to the government's argument, noted:

> While this court must accord due deference to the expertise of the Secretary of Labor, this Court is also under a higher duty to [hold] when necessary, that the Secretary's determination has exceeded the boundaries set by Congress.[69]

These boundaries, the court found, incorporated only the blue-collar definition for service employees. The court's ruling, however, had little impact. In the same year it was handed down, Congress decided to insist on its own interpretation of who should be covered by the act. In the 1976 amendments, all employees of federal service contractors except those who were bona fide executives, administrators, or professionals were brought under the act's umbrella.[70]

Continuing Problems with Classification

Armed with the 1976 amendments, the DOL applied the Service Contract Act to all employees (other than executives, administrators, or professionals) working under contracts that had as a "principal purpose" the provision of service to the government. Many high technology and research firms therefore found themselves subject to the statute when they contracted with the federal government, and it was not a position all of them enjoyed.

In 1979, for example, the DOL announced that it would consider maintenance and repair-service specifications of all federal contracts for the purchase or rental of supplies or equipment, including high-tech items such as computers, subject to the Service Contract Act.[71] (Also included, obviously as a result of some special-interest

---

[68] *Id.* at 223.
[69] *Id.* at 224.
[70] See note 38, *supra*, and accompanying text.
[71] These proposals were contained in 44 Fed. Reg. 77,036 (December 28, 1979), but were never implemented. Subsequent to an often-extended comment period, revised final regulations were published by the Carter administration in the *Federal Register* on January 16, 1981 (46 Fed. Reg. 4320), but were withdrawn by the Reagan administration before they were scheduled to become effective on February 17, 1981.

lobbying, were timber sales contracts, thus bringing lumberjacks and mill sawyers under coverage.) Previously, the General Services Administration and other federal contracting agencies had not considered such contracts subject to the act. At stake was $5.4 billion in government computers which, in the opinion of a 1980 report of the comptroller general, might not be properly maintained or repaired if the act were held applicable because of the number of firms that refused to seek the work.[72] Several major firms, including the Digital Equipment Corporation and the Hewlett Packard Company, felt strongly enough about the situation to reject bid solicitations for government contracts rather than subject themselves to the terms of the act. In the words of one company official, "Why apply a cure when there is no disease?"[73]

The Computer and Business Equipment Manufacturers Association, in presentations to the 1981 Congressional Oversight Hearings on the act, made a plea for exemption from coverage, noting:

> The characteristics of our industry make SCA coverage unnecessary. The SCA was passed to prevent the procurement policy of awarding contracts to the lowest bidder, from inducing bidders on labor contracts to reduce wages to get government contracts, i.e., "wage bust." There is no such pattern of abuse in our industry, and one would not expect to find such a pattern. In general, our service workers are skilled and highly trained employees whose services are in demand in a highly-competitive labor market. They are well-compensated, possess a high degree of job mobility, and thus are not susceptible to wage busting.[74]

The association went on to point out that the concept of prevailing wages was incompatible with the industry's merit pay wage policy:

> In order to comply, an industry member could abolish its merit pay system, but such an action would diminish innovation and productivity within the company and not be wise. Or the company could set up a separate workforce to handle government business. This would cause a deterioration in service support to federal agencies and would adversely affect the job mobility of those employees. Since [our] typical member company does only about 5 to 10 percent of its business with the federal government, when faced with these alternatives it may find that the continued servicing of government equipment is uneconomical. In short, applying the SCA could result in increased costs

---

[72] GENERAL ACCOUNTING OFFICE, SERVICE CONTRACT ACT SHOULD NOT APPLY TO SERVICE EMPLOYEES OF ADP AND HIGH-TECHNOLOGY COMPANIES, September 16, 1980, pp. 4, 56.

[73] *Business Machine Firms Rap U.S. Contract Rules,* Washington Post, August 8, 1979, at 5.

[74] *1981 Oversight Hearings on the Service Contract Act,* 97th Cong., 1st Sess. (1981), at 501.

to the government and serious disruption to our business relationships.⁷⁵

Associated with this issue is the more general one of coverage for service employees under contracts that involve some service employees but a larger number of professionals. An example might be a contract requiring ten systems analysts and two keypunchers. Existing DOL regulations specified that "while the incidental employment of service employees will not render a contract for professional services subject to the act, a contract which requires the use of service employees to a substantial extent would be covered even though there is some use of professional employees in performance of the contract."⁷⁶

Summary of the Classification Issue

Classifications of employees and of contracts that broadened the definitions of each in terms of coverage under the Service Contract Act were responsible for extension of the act to areas far beyond those expressly contemplated when it was first passed. In summarizing the impact on the computer and automatic data processing industries alone, the comptroller general noted: 1) there was little incentive in the computer and high-technology industries to exploit workers, and therefore the act was not needed; 2) the practice of "wage busting" had never been a problem in these industries; 3) including automatic data processing and related service employees in the act's coverage was costly and destructive of morale; and 4) one large company estimated that the inflationary impact on its technicians' wages might be as much as $100 million in the first year alone.⁷⁷

Prior to 1981, despite these arguments and the continuing pragmatic difficulties, the 1976 amendments appeared to have settled the issue. Indeed, in the only case to raise the question of classifying service employees since that time, the court simply reiterated the broad inclusion resulting from the 1976 amendments and found the employee in question to be covered.⁷⁸ When the revised regulations

---

⁷⁵ *Id.* at 501–2.

⁷⁶ C.F.R. 4.1113(a)(2) (1980), in Goldfarb & Heywood, *supra* note 11, at 63. Goldfarb and Heywood go on to point out that the criteria used by the DOL for determining "substantial extent," in effect since 1981, are these: if service employees are less than 10 percent of the total projected employment, the act will not be applied; if they are 20 percent or more of total projected employment, the act will apply; if they are between 10 and 20 percent, the DOL will determine coverage on a case-by-case basis.

⁷⁷ GENERAL ACCOUNTING OFFICE, *supra* note 72, at 9, 40, 74, and 90.

⁷⁸ Nichols v. Mower's News Service Inc., 492 F. Supp. 258, 260 (Vt. Dist. Ct., 1980).

proposed in 1979 by the Carter administration were withdrawn, however, and replaced by the new regulations proposed in 1981 by the Reagan administration, some reversal of the applicability of the act to these extended groups occurred.

The Reagan revisions excluded services performed as part of contracts whose principal purpose was not provision of services, such as equipment supply contracts which include agreements to maintain the equipment after delivery, and generally any coverage by the Service Contract Act of contracts which included service as "a purpose" rather than as "the principal purpose" of the contract. Furthermore, the new regulations exempted certain automated data processing equipment contracts from coverage on the ground that the DOL, responding to the findings of the 1981 hearings, found such exemptions necessary to prevent impairment of government business.

Although challenged in the courts, these proposed regulations survived, and were cleared for implementation in March 1985.[79] With them in place, most of the problems of the act applying to technical service personnel have been eliminated, but the problems of the act applying to the clerical and nonexempt technical personnel of service firms remain.

The Successor Contractor Issue

A counterpart of extending the coverage of the act is increasing the level of protection that its wage determinations offer. Here, too, the Congress has favored expanding the original coverage in later amendments, even at the price of unmanageable administration. The successorship provision of the 1972 amendments, like the employee classification coverage provisions of the 1976 amendments, was the result of congressional reaction to adverse court decisions.[80] But unlike the latter which, for better or worse, seem to have clarified the legal issue, the successorship provision raised more conceptual and legal problems than it settled. Several court cases have dealt with the question, one of them as recently as 1981.[81]

---

[79] The changes and the ruling are discussed in *Court Holds that Revised Regulations Are Consistent With Service Contract Act,* 61 DAILY LAB. REP. A-6–A-9 (March 29, 1985).

[80] *See supra* note 33, and accompanying text.

[81] Clark v. Unified Services, 659 F.2d 49 (5th Cir. 1981). Cases which raised the successorship issue on fact situations which preceded the effective date of the 1972 amendments include Kentron Hawaii v. Warner, 480 F.2d 1166 (D.C. Cir. 1973); and Boeing Co. v. International Ass'n of Machinists and Aerospace Workers, 504 F.2d 307 (5th Cir. 1974), *cert. denied,* 421 U.S. 913 (1975).

The 1972 amendments required that successor contractors pay service employees wages and fringe benefits no lower than those to which the predecessor contractor was committed by a collective bargaining agreement (including future increases) unless the secretary of labor, after a hearing, found those rates to be substantially at variance with the prevailing rates in the locality. This is true even though the successor might be a nonunion firm located in an entirely different locality and using none of the former employees of the predecessor.

The rationale behind this provision is that it prevents individual-wage busting—that is, the rehiring of a predecessor's employees to perform the same job for the successor, but at lower wage rates. Clearly, it accomplishes that task, but at the cost of drastically altering the prevailing wage concept for those cases where it applies. It turns the Service Contract Act into a vehicle for mandating the perpetuation of union wage rates once they have been established on any continuing contract, regardless of local labor market conditions. Understandably, there have been a number of court cases involving the successorship provision.

Legal Reaction to the Successorship Question

In a 1977 case, *Service Employees' International Union Local 36 v. General Services Administration,*[82] the court was required to decide just when a successor contractor would be obligated to follow the predecessor's collective bargaining agreement for arbitration purposes, and the extent of the successor's obligation to hire employees of the predecessor. Here, the union sued to compel the successor (a maintenance service contractor) to hire the predecessor's employees and to use the predecessor's negotiated arbitration provisions for resolution of disputes.

The contract, a one-year agreement under which Ken-Rich Services, Inc., would take over the cleaning chores at the Philadelphia Social Security Building, had previously been performed by Prudential Building Maintenance. When the predecessor contended to Ken-Rich that Ken-Rich would have to hire the predecessor's employees, Ken-Rich sought official government advice, and was told that it "could hire its own employees so long as the new employees were paid at levels established by the Secretary of Labor and set out in the contract."[83]

---

[82] Service Employees' International Union Local 36 v. General Services Administration, 443 F. Supp. 575 (E.D. Pa., 1977).
[83] *Id.* at 576.

Subsequently, Ken-Rich hired forty employees, none of whom had worked for Prudential. It paid all forty at the Prudential pay scale, and engaged one former Prudential employee as a replacement worker on an as-needed basis. The court, in a careful and detailed opinion, considered both existing case law and the 1972 amendments to the act for sources that might possibly have required Ken-Rich to hire the predecessor employees or to comply with the arbitration procedure of the predecessor contract, but could find no basis for either. Specifically, it noted that "while [the 1972] amendment modified existing successorship law, it did so only to the extent that a successor employer is required to adopt the wage and benefit levels of his predecessor's collective bargaining agreement."[84]

The next case on successorship, however, took the wage and benefit question a step farther. In *Trinity Services Inc. v. Marshall*,[85] the court had to determine whether severance and seniority provisions were fringe benefits which a successor would be required to adopt from the predecessor's collective bargaining agreement. Here, the court built upon the successorship opinion of the *Local 36* court, adding these limitations:

> [T]he successor employer must give an employee it hires credit for similar work performed at the federal facility. . . . Seniority is not a form of compensation that the employer can pay. It is not specifically listed as a Section 351(a)(2) fringe benefit, and it is not in the same class as the other benefits listed there. Seniority is but a means of determining how wages and fringe benefits are to be allocated.[86]
>
> [There is no] obligation . . . to adhere to a provision in a collective bargaining agreement that requires the successor to make a payment to the predecessor's employees if that work force is not hired by the successor.[87]

Another case in accord with the doctrine of limiting the successor's obligations was *Clark v. Unified Services*,[88] a suit by former service employees to require a successor contractor to hire them and to grant them seniority rights because they had been employees of the predecessor. In this case, the successor had hired seventy-eight of the predecessor's ninety-eight employees, and had hired several at lower pay, because they were hired in at lower grade levels. The successor, however, recognized the union as bargaining agent since it had hired so many of the predecessor's employees, and the successor negotiated new seniority provisions with the union

---

[84] *Id.* at 380.
[85] Trinity Services Inc. v. Marshall, 493 F.2d 1250 (S.C. Cir. 1978).
[86] *Id.* at 1262.
[87] *Id.*
[88] 659 F.2d 49.

similar to those under the predecessor's contract.[89] Nevertheless, the employees argued that failure to hire all interested employees and give them all seniority equal to that under the predecessor's contract was in violation of the Service Contract Act. In its brief opinion, the court rejected the employees' argument, stating that "seniority ... rights are not included within [the amendment's] provision of fringe benefits."[90]

Summary of Successorship Question

Litigation on the successorship provision of the 1972 amendments has centered not on the question itself, but on how much more beyond wages and fringe benefits a successor must adopt from whomever held the contract before him. The fact that he must adopt any labor policies at all from his predecessor is a new notion in contracting, and this inclusion in the Service Contract Act sets it apart from all of the other prevailing wage laws.

Many contracts for services are of an obviously continuing nature, such as successive contracts for cleaning a government office complex. Even for these, there is a question about the validity of mandating wage levels and fringe benefits for successors that are negotiated between parties who are no longer, in fact, involved with the contract in any way; there is a larger question when the wages and fringes mandated were never even paid by the predecessor (which is possible);[91] there is an even larger one when one realizes that, as negotiated rates, these wages and benefits are almost inevitably higher than the wage rates for similar work that actually prevail in the community where the work is performed.

Prior to 1985, there was the additional problem that successors on contracts which are not location specific had the same obligations to continue the union rates of a predecessor. A new contractor for a data processing job may have been on the far side of the country and in an entirely different labor market from the previous contract holder. Nevertheless, if the contract was deemed a continuing one, the new contractor was bound by the successor provisions. This is the only aspect of the successor problem able to be corrected by the new DOL regulations, because the other aspects of it are part of the legislation and therefore beyond the reach of administrative redress.

---

[89] *Id.* at 50.
[90] *Id.* at 50, 51.
[91] *See, e.g.,* Brooks, *Service Contract Act Amendments of 1972,* 66 MIL. L. REV. 67–103 (Fall, 1974).

Administrative and Other Questions

Other administrative problems with the Service Contract Act show that it is at least as controversial as the Davis-Bacon Act in regard to administration. One recent case, *Collins International Service Co. v. United States*,[92] illustrates how an employer can be trapped by the Service Contract Act even when trying hard to comply with all of the act's provisions. In *Collins*, the Navy Department had issued a solicitation for operation and maintenance of Naval Space Surveillance System facilities which at that time were still subject to the act. Collins International Service Company felt that the DOL's wage determinations were ambiguous as to the classifications for certain workers, and tried repeatedly before the bid opening, although without success, to get clarification from the Navy Department and the DOL.

During the subsequent performance of the contract, several of Collins's employees complained to the DOL that their wages were too low, which led to enforcement action by the DOL and payments to these employees totalling $127,000. Collins sought to recover the additional costs from the Navy on the ground that the wage determination had been ambiguous. The court decided, however, that Collins had no right to recover from the Navy, because the Navy had no authority to make wage determinations, so any dispute Collins might have had about a determination would have to have been taken up with the DOL; but the DOL was not a party to the contract.

Thus, the bidder was faced with the prospect of having to second-guess the DOL when it cannot obtain prompt clarification of a wage determination, and will foot the bill if it guesses low and employees later successfully contest their classification. The judge conceded: "Application of this peculiar statutory scheme results in the business person bearing the burden of ... DOL's imprecision."[93]

Not all of the administrative problems of the Service Contract Act involve employers. A good number derive from the relationship between the DOL and other agencies or the Congress. For example, a number of the amendments to the act have been directed not to compel specific performance from contractors, but rather to force the DOL and the various governmental agencies which let contracts for services to make wage determinations or to include the requirements of the act in their contracts. In fact, compliance with the

---

[92] Collins International Service Co. v. U.S., 744 F.2d 812 (Fed. Cir. 1984).
[93] *Id.*, cited in *DOL Has Sole Power to Clarify Wage Determination, Court Says* 193 DAILY LAB. REP. A-4, A-5 (October 4, 1984).

statute has been inconsistent both by the DOL in executing its administrative and enforcement responsibilities, and by federal agencies in subjecting their service contracts to the act's provisions.

In a 1978 compliance review of both defense and labor departments, the comptroller general found that defense offices were failing to ask for wage determinations or to include them in many of their service contracts. In many cases, procurement personnel did not even know if the act's requirements and their procurement activities were or were not monitored for compliance.[94] Furthermore, the DOL had no idea, since it had no effective system for monitoring compliance, whether or to what extent contractors themselves might be violating the law.[95]

According to DOL regulations, contracting agencies must file a "Notice of Intention to Make a Service Contract" at least thirty days before making an invitation to bid on a service contract exceeding $2,500. Obviously, this requirement leaves the initial determination as to whether the procuring agency is dealing with a service contract to the agency itself. In nearly one-half (205 of 425) of the service contracts reviewed for the 1978 compliance study, the Department of Defense had failed to make wage determination requests as required,[96] and in some additional cases determinations had not been requested on a timely basis, leaving the DOL insufficient time to issue them.

The study indicated that whatever enforcement there was, was limited essentially to investigating complaints, and that the DOL initiated few reviews.[97] The DOL's explanation for this focused largely on lack of funds and staff. One California official stated, "There are an estimated 1,000 [Service Contract Act] contractors in our area. It is estimated that 80 percent of them are in violation. We can only get to those in which we receive a complaint."[98]

With respect to the mandated penalty of barring a contractor in violation of the act under certain circumstances, the compliance review found enforcement uneven. "[The review] at seven area offices identified four contractors in two area offices whose violations exceeded the ... criteria and should have been referred to the regional office for debarment consideration."[99]

---

[94] GENERAL ACCOUNTING OFFICE, REVIEW OF COMPLIANCE WITH LABOR STANDARDS FOR SERVICE CONTRACTS BY DEFENSE AND LABOR DEPARTMENTS (January 19, 1978).
[95] Id.
[96] Id. at 9.
[97] Id. at 19.
[98] Id. at 20.
[99] Id. at 22.

At one office, the director lacked knowledge of the conditions requiring debarment. Another said the government policy had not been followed recently in his office; rather, he would recommend for debarment only those cases involving intentional violations.[100] In both the agency and the DOL cases, the compliance review closed with statements of promises to improve performance. But four years later, in mid-1982, another General Accounting Office study found that procurement officers at twenty of twenty-two federal installations reviewed had failed to request required wage determinations from the DOL, and that wage determinations had not been included in fully one-third of the nearly 1,000 procurements reviewed that were actually subject to the act.[101]

Although the courts have been disinclined to extend application of the Service Contract Act by allowing it to be used as a private right of action by individuals affected by the procurement process,[102] they have been willing to extend coverage through liberal interpretation of its applicability, and have gone so far as to suggest that contracts let without wage determinations might be subject to annulment.

In one case, for example, the court required the Board of Governors of the Federal Reserve System to apply Service Contract Act provisions in its contracts. Despite the fact that the Federal Reserve Board is an independent agency, the court felt that it was closely enough related to the federal government to place reliance on the general remedial nature of the Service Contract Act, which suggests inclusion rather than exclusion, in order to protect as many workers as possible. The court suggested that definitions "must be liberally construed to effectuate the act's humanitarian purposes."[103]

---

[100] *Id.*

[101] GENERAL ACCOUNTING OFFICE, *supra* note 33 at 7.

[102] In two cases, Machinists v. Hodgson, 515 F.2d 373 (D.C. Cir. 1975) and Miscellaneous Service Workers, Drivers & Helpers, Teamsters Local 427 v. Philco Ford Corp., 661 F.2d 776 (9th Cir. 1981), union members sought damages from a contractor in the face of a DOL failure to issue wage determinations; in two others, American Federation of Government Employees v. Stetson, 640 F.2d 642 (5th Cir. 1981) and American Federation of Government Employees Local 1668 v. Dunn, 561 F.2d 1310 (9th Cir. 1977), former civil service employees sought to have outside contracts which had displaced them from their jobs set aside. In all four cases, the courts found that the Service Contract Act does not sustain a private right of action, and denied standing. These rulings were affirmed in Locals 666 and 780 of the International Alliance of Theatrical Stage Employees v. U.S. Department of Labor, 760 F.2d 141 (CA 7, 1985), *cert. denied*, __ U.S. __ (October 14, 1985), in which it was ruled that displaced contractors, employees, and unions are not within interests protected by the act; therefore, neither the union nor its members have standing to sue either the DOL or the contracting federal agency for violation of the act.

[103] Brinks v. Board of Governors of Federal Reserve System, 466 F. Supp. 117 (D.C. Dist. Ct., 1979), at 120.

In another case, involving the overhaul, repair, and rebuilding of jet engines, where an unsuccessful bidder sued for annulment of the contract because it did not require payment of determined wages and fringe benefits, the court allowed the contract to stand, but only because it felt that there was an open question as to whether the act applied to jet engine overhaul contracts.[104] It left open the possibility that in another case, annulment could be required. Inconvenience due to annulment, the court said, would not alone be enough to justify allowing a noncomplying contract to stand. In the face of a sheaf of affidavits from high-ranking officials regarding the inconveniences which would be suffered if the contract were annulled, the court stated, "these considerations, however important, cannot be a focus for this Court in determining" issues before it.[105]

This particular case, of jet engine overhaul contracts, was reflected in the 1985 administrative rule changes, which attempt to clarify whether overhaul contracts should be covered by the Service Contract Act or by the Walsh-Healey Act by providing guidelines for applicability. The guidelines, however, appear conclusory, because without explicitly defining the differences between "remanufacturing" and "repair," they state that a contract for the former would be subject to the Walsh-Healey Act, whereas a contract for the latter would be covered by the Service Contract Act. Some specific illustrations are offered for both cases, but the basic question of when, in a circumstance not illustrated, one act or the other would apply is left unanswered.[106]

Other 1985 Rule Changes

In addition to the items already discussed, the DOL's rule changes made effective in 1985 deal with rather specific situations. Research and development contracts, for example, are specifically exempted

---

[104] Curtiss-Wright Corp. v. McLucas, 381 F. Supp. 657 (N.J. Dist. Ct., 1974).
[105] *Id.* at 664.
[106] 46 Fed. Reg., No. 1571, August 14, 1981, "Proposed Rules," 29 C.F.R., Part 4. There is a third possible differentiation, as well, that between "remanufactured" and "overhauled" items. This is essentially a question of degree, and sometimes only of industry custom. In the general aviation industry, for example, where engines are life-rated and must be overhauled, rebuilt, or replaced after a set number of hours of use, the only difference between a new-limits "overhauled" engine and a "rebuilt" engine is that in the case of the latter the work is typically performed by the original manufacturer rather than by an engine shop. Both will carry the same new life rating after the work. The proposed regulations devote the equivalent of about two text pages to defining the terms "repaired," "overhauled," and "rebuilt," but the distinctions hinge on fine points and minute differences, which would certainly be subject to interpretation.

from coverage under the act. Since these are very likely to be performed mainly by professionals rather than by traditional service employees, they would be excluded in any event, but they are now also specifically exempted. Similarly, contracts for maintenance and repair of automated data processing equipment, including office information systems, related scientific and medical apparatus, and office machines, are specifically exempted. Finally, the previous practice requiring Service Contract Act compliance for contracts for the sale of timber was dropped. The DOL purportedly reviewed relevant statutes and found "no indication that timber sales contracts were predominantly service oriented."[107] Timber sales contracts had been covered informally since 1968, and formally since 1979, but have always been an anomaly in the act. This provision puts them back under Walsh-Healey coverage.

Even with all of these administrative changes in place, only a small portion of the problems resulting from the act have been obviated, and serious questions remain as to whether the Service Contract Act serves a valid procurement or societal purpose. The General Accounting Office, among others, having reviewed the act after the proposed changes had been introduced but before they were implemented, recommended repeal rather than modification.

1983 GENERAL ACCOUNTING OFFICE RECOMMENDATIONS

Early in 1983, having reviewed application of the Service Contract Act in both 1978 and 1982 and gone over approximately a thousand federal procurements under it,[108] the General Accounting Office recommended repeal of the act on several grounds:

- Inherent problems exist in its administration.
- Wage rates and fringe benefits set under it are generally inflationary to the Government.
- Accurate determinations of actual prevailing wage rates and fringe benefits cannot be made using existing data sources.
- The data needed to accurately determine prevailing wage rates and fringe benefits would be very costly to develop.
- The Fair Labor Standards Act and the administrative procedures implemented through the Federal procurement process could provide a measure of wage and benefit protection for employees the act now covers.[109]

---

[107] *Id.*, introductory comments.
[108] *See supra,* notes 94 and 101, and accompanying text.
[109] *Digest of GAO Report Recommending Repeal of Service Contract Act,* 26 DAILY LAB. REP. 9, D1. (February 7, 1983).

In its recommendation for repeal, the General Accounting Office noted that were the act to be eliminated, wage and benefit protection would be available under the Fair Labor Standards Act for service employees, who had not had such protection when the Service Contract Act was introduced. It also reiterated concerns over administration of the act which had been reported in both its 1978 and 1982 compliance reviews. One of these was over the failure of federal procuring agencies to ask for wage determinations even in cases where they were obviously required. It avoided suggesting that agencies were attempting deliberately to circumvent the statute, blaming instead broad ignorance of the act in 1978 and misinterpretation of where it fit into the system of prevailing wage and procurement laws in 1982. The General Accounting Office felt that the uneven application, administration, and enforcement of the law was a serious problem, and suggested that the DOL was remiss in not promoting better support for the contracting agencies so as to improve compliance.[110]

Since the General Accounting Office recommendations were issued after the DOL's regulatory proposals were made in 1981, it is clear that the General Accounting Office felt the act's problems were more than could be handled by tinkering with its provisions. Even if administration and enforcement problems could be overcome, it found that the basic requirements for determining and mandating wage rates and fringe benefits prevailing in the locality were undefined and ambiguous, and that such determinations as resulted were often inaccurate.

COSTS OF THE ACT

In 1981, the DOL, as part of its preliminary regulatory impact analysis, estimated the cost savings associated with the administrative changes implemented in 1985 to be $240 million a year,[111] and as we have seen, those changes corrected only a small portion of the identified problems with the act. Clearly, the savings that could be obtained by repealing the act in its entirety would be substantially greater.

The General Accounting Office review, discussed above, had surveyed twenty-five DOL wage determinations to evaluate their ac-

---

[110] GENERAL ACCOUNTING OFFICE, *supra* note 33, at 17–19.

[111] Goldfarb & Heywood, *supra* note 11, at 71. Goldfarb and Heywood's independent analysis of the savings possible from eliminating coverage of research and development contracts alone was $113 million—more than twice the amount of the $46 million estimate for this single element by the DOL.

curacy. It found that the stipulated wage and fringe benefits were generally higher than those which actually prevailed in the localities where the service work was performed. It estimated that for fourteen of the nineteen service contracts for which direct labor hour data were available, total contract costs were about 11 percent higher than they might have been had the actual rate figures been used.[112] If this same proportionality existed on all of the estimated $5.7 billion worth of work covered by the Service Contract Act each year,[113] total excess costs to the government would be approximately $462 million.

An independent economic analysis of a sample of sixty-six wage determinations issued in 1978 found similar, although not identical, results. Of the sixty-six determinations, twenty-seven varied by at least 5 percent from the basic Bureau of Labor Statistics data, and the overall average variation was just under 6 percent, whether corrected for inflation or not.[114] These figures and those in the previous paragraph are for variation in issued determinations both above and below what Bureau of Labor Statistics figures suggest they should have been, had the act been properly followed. Thus, they are indications not of the cost of the act, but of its arbitrary nature. As is true for the other prevailing wage laws, since the rates set by the Service Contract Act are applied as minimum rates, only those that are arbitrarily high have any effect. If a wage is set below the true market rate in an area, it has no effect on wages actually paid.

Furthermore, for the Service Contract Act, the measured variations use the median wage rate in the area as the comparison base. The actual impact of the act, in terms of what might be saved by its repeal, is not measured by the difference between the Service Contract Act rate and the median wage, but by the difference between the Service Contract Act rate and the best competitive rate in the marketplace. Neither this figure nor a reasonable substitute

---

[112] *Id.* Unlike the method used for Davis-Bacon determinations (where "majority or average" rates will prevail), the Service Contract Act calculates the median to set the prevailing rate, although due consideration of federal civil service rates and other factors do affect them. What is being measured here is the difference between the median rate for each job classification in the locality taken by the GAO based on Bureau of Labor Statistics data and that specified by the DOL. The 11 percent number, therefore, is a measure of the accuracy of the DOL, and not of the cost difference between having or not having a Service Contract Act on the books.

[113] The total amount of work covered by the Service Contract Act is not known. Goldfarb & Heywood [*supra* note 11, at 59] report estimates by "knowledgeable government officials" that the volume of contracts and associated employment covered in 1979 was "five to ten billion dollars." The figure used here, $5.7 billion, derives from GENERAL ACCOUNTING OFFICE, *supra,* note 33.

[114] Goldfarb & Heywood, *supra* note 11, at 61.

for it have been definitively estimated for the Service Contract Act, but it is certain that the amounts are nontrivial.

CONCLUSIONS AND RECOMMENDATIONS

From relatively modest beginnings, the Service Contract Act has grown in coverage and impact to affect spectrums of contracts and employees well beyond those contemplated by its authors. Administrative changes instituted in 1985 ease but do not eliminate the effects of this expansion. Are the burdens added since 1964 more than the original philosophical supports can reasonably bear? The total cost of the act, although not known precisely, is substantial— on the order of a half-billion dollars a year. For this cost, is the act accomplishing what it set out to accomplish, and if so, is the money well spent?

Towards the beginning of this chapter, a number of rationales, or purposes, for the Service Contract Act were presented. In light of the way the act and its administration have developed and the way problems under it have been solved by the DOL, Congress, and the courts, it appears that few of those rationales continue to be persuasive. Regrouped slightly from the earlier presentation, they are discussed below.

Providing Wage Protection for Unskilled, Low-Paid Service Workers

The principal purpose of the Service Contract Act was to provide a wage floor for the last group of employees who might work under contracts for the federal government who did not already have one—the low-paid, unskilled service workers. Although the act does, indeed, provide a wage floor, for the following reasons this function is no longer needed:

1) The act has been expanded to apply to skilled technicians, to clerical employees, and in some cases to any blue-collar or white-collar employees other than executives, managers, or professionals working for a service contractor. The need for special wage protection for these categories of employees is not manifest.

2) For the original group of low-paid, unskilled service workers contemplated, wage floor protection is now available from other sources. In the late 1960s, the Fair Labor Standards Act (the minimum wage law) was extended to service employees, who did not have such coverage at the time the Service Contract Act was introduced. The introduction of

full minimum wage protection should supersede a prevailing wage provision. To workers so covered, payment of "subminimum wages" is illegal.

Prevent Wage Busting and Maintain the Quality Level of Work

A second set of rationales for the act has to do with the federal procurement process, under which contracts must be awarded to the lowest bidder. It is hypothesized that prevailing wage requirements prevent bidders from debasing wage rates in order to achieve the lowest bid, and, by keeping wage rates up, also ensure high quality work.

The fact that government contracts go to the lowest bidder has been used in many forums to suggest that the procurement process thereby places unusual pressures on contractors to underpay their employees, thus reducing their labor costs and allowing them to underbid their competitors. There are elements of truth in this assertion, just as there are elements of truth in the assertion that an F-18 is nothing more than a bunch of parts flying in close formation, every one of which was supplied by the lowest bidder. But in essence, the argument is a false one, for several reasons:

1) It assumes that a government contractor, as a buyer of labor services, has monopsonistic powers—the ability to buy labor for whatever wages are offered, regardless of market conditions—because the only alternative to accepting the offer is unemployment. This hypothesis does not stand to reality. Employers who happen to be government contractors must compete with those who are not, in the same labor market for the same employees. As long as there are alternative employment opportunities for the low-level service employees (janitors, window washers, laundry workers, office cleaners, etc.) for whom the act is said to be intended, government contractors have no monopsonistic powers, and no particular ability to compel other than market wage rates.[115]

---

[115] In the normal situation, the addition of a government contract for services will increase the demand for, and therefore the price of, service labor in the community from which that labor will be drawn. The Service Contract Act, therefore, has no valid application in such situations. Even if it is argued that the act is predicated upon the abnormal situation of a new contractor taking over an old contract in the same location (the so-called successor contractor problem), since the total quantity of service labor demanded is unchanged, the market should be expected to clear at the same price (wage rate) as before. No excess supply of service labor is created when one contractor succeeds another, even if all of the employees of the predecessor are dismissed. Only if a government service contract is terminated and not replaced

2) It assumes that if contractors had the opportunity to offer "substandard" wages and get employees to work for them, that they would do so. This presupposes an antithetical relationship between contractors and their employees, which is far from universal, and overlooks the fact that certainly a majority of contractors have enough experience with employees to know that underpaid labor is seldom either happy or cost effective. So long as the contracts do not specify a set number of man-hours of time—and most do not—a contractor in a free market has the option of satisfying the same contract requirement by using various proportions of administration, machinery, and labor of differing skills. If mandated wage rates actually reflect (or are lower than) local market conditions, they have no impact on the decision-making involved, but they also serve no purpose. On the other hand, if they are higher than the local market, they influence decisionmaking in favor of higher proportions of administration and machinery, thus restricting employment opportunities for the very class they were intended to protect.

3) It assumes that by controlling the input price of labor at a high level, the output quality of government contracts will be high. Not only is this untrue, it is unreasonable. First, the best way to control output quality in a contract is to specify the desired level in the contract itself and leave it for the contractor to achieve it or pay the penalty. Second, although it is almost invariably said that government contracts go to the lowest bidder, they do not; rather, they go to the lowest *qualified* bidder. If output quality is important, bidders can be qualified based on their ability to provide it. Third, in many service contracts, high quality is not an important consideration, and so should not have to be purchased where it is not needed. (In most situations, what quality control attempts to effect is not the highest quality level, but rather an acceptable level of quality consistent with its price.) Finally, the prevailing wage law requirement, which usually results in paying higher than market rates for given labor input, is substantively different from being willing to pay more for demonstrably superior labor input. It is the difference between "having to spend more"

---

will an excess supply of service labor in the local market be created, along with the likelihood of lower prices (wage rates) for such labor, but this situation is not covered by the Service Contract Act, nor can it be.

and "having more to spend." The former has no impact on quality; the latter, does.

Geographic Balance and Protection of Local Contractors from Itinerants

As has been noted several times in discussing the problems of defining locality and establishing the rules for successor contractors, under the Service Contract Act in operation, prevailing rates specified are frequently those drawn from some other part of the country or those worked out by a predecessor in negotiations with the employees who performed the contract previously. They bear no necessary relationship to the local conditions where the new contract will be performed. In a substantial number of instances, therefore, wage determinations are completely independent of local conditions. If it is indeed a purpose of the Service Contract Act to preserve the structure and relationships of the local wage market, that purpose is poorly fulfilled, at least in these instances.

A second geographic consideration ascribed to the act is that it ensures geographic balance in the award of contracts, so that those of a given type will not all gravitate to some particular section of the country where relevant labor rates might be low. This consideration has no validity other than as a means of encouraging broad-based political support in Congress. If, absent a prevailing wage law, government contracts tended to go to a particular locale because of favorable, low wage rates, the demand for employees to perform them there would increase, which would require higher wage rates to increase the supply. Then, in the next round of bidding, contractors in that area would lose their competitive edge, and contracts would no longer gravitate to them. In other words, the problem, if it is one, solves itself, with or without the Service Contract Act.

That local contractors need protection from "itinerants" is also open to question. Fifty years ago, perhaps, itinerant contractors tended to be low-wage, low-skill, low-quality gypsies; in the current environment, however, itinerants are more likely to be the high-skill specialists. If the government needs cleaning services for a leaking nuclear reactor, to take an extreme case as an example, it needs to hire "glow boys," who would be very unlikely to be found in the employ of a local service contractor. Even when only ordinary services are needed, there is no reason to give preference to local contractors unless their location near the federal facility can be turned into a competitive advantage.

Other Rationales: Government as Model Employer, Protection of Government Workers, Encouragement of Labor Unions

Finally, several rationales for the act involve discretionary matters of federal labor policy that are not directly related to wage rates. A reasonably objective look at the Service Contract Act reveals that these are the only purposes which it serves well. The questions remain, however, of whether these labor policies are valid for the government to pursue, and whether the Service Contract Act is the appropriate vehicle for them.

Should government employees be protected against the possibility that their jobs might be lost to outside contractors who could do their work at lower cost? If so, should the protection take the form of making the outsider's wage rates arbitrarily higher to reduce the economic benefit of contracting out? Should the federal government be promoting and encouraging unionism by perpetuating negotiated wage rates, once established, in all successive iterations of a contract in the same location, regardless of who performs it? Should the government in its desire to set an example for private employers arbitrarily pay more for its service needs than it would on the open market?

These policy questions are normative. Answers to them must be found in debate rather than analysis. But since they seem to be the only rationales that are effectively served by the act, the answers should take cognizance of the administrative problems and high economic costs that are necessary to support them. One should also consider the propriety of using a prevailing wage law as a front for such purposes.

Recommendations

The changes in administrative regulations of the Service Contract Act implemented in 1985 have been salutary, at least to the degree that they do not expand the act and they remove or confine some of the more egregious earlier interpretations. But this attempt to shore up the act seeks by administrative process to fix once again a statute which has seen two significant amendments since its inception and still does not work.

The Service Contract Act does not adequately express its own intent. Since its adoption, it has been used to bring under federal wage setting requirements workers who do not need, and industries which do not require, its regulation. It has raised legal issues of statutory interpretation which cannot be answered by the courts in light of the ambiguity of the statute and the lack of guidance by the Congress. It suffers from pragmatic problems, including violations by contractors, noncompliance by federal agencies, arbitrary requirements, and capricious enforcement.

The problems with this statute are significant enough that the resolution must come from the source of the burden: Congress. The act, a "cure without an illness," must either be repealed, as suggested most recently by the General Accounting Office, or it must be completely overhauled to deal with the multitude of problems it has created. If total repeal is not politically possible, the contract threshold for coverage should be raised from $2,500 to $100,000, the successorship clause should be deleted, and methods for wage determinations should be tightened.

Repeal would save the government perhaps half a billion dollars per year in unnecessary expenditures without making a measurable impact on the quantity or quality of services it receives from its contractors. It would also cut back on government interference in private business activities and relieve some of the pressure on a number of government agencies, many of which have never fully supported or understood the act in the first place.

CHAPTER VII

Conclusion

This study reviewed the prevailing wage laws of the United States that affect private employers, including three at the federal level, thirty-five at the state level, and several more at the local level. Many of these laws have been on the books for a half-century or more, and the concepts and premises on which they depend are among the oldest that can be found reflected in labor policy or labor law. The persistence of laws, however, is often independent of their utility or their value to society, and with respect to the prevailing wage laws, there is considerable evidence that they may have outlived whatever usefulness they may once have had.

REVIEW

Among the federal prevailing wage laws, the Davis-Bacon Act is the most important, the most intrusive, and the most expensive. The $1 billion per year that it adds to the costs of government construction appears not to have increased the volume or quality of work performed, but simply its expense. It has also helped create artificially high levels of wage rates in the construction industry. In the face of studies by the General Accounting Office and others showing the act to be maladministered, changes have been carried out in recent years, but their effect has been that of fine-tuning a system that needs much more fundamental and substantive reform.

The Walsh-Healey Act, although probably intended as the major prevailing wage law (since it applied the concept to manufacturing and supply industries that employed the greatest number of employees, and applied it to contract amounts that were typically double those covered by Davis-Bacon) contained slight differences in verbiage that resulted in different and less significant consequences, as well as much lower costs, even before the *Baldor Electric* case in 1964 caused new rates to stop being issued under the act. For the next twenty years, the impact of Walsh-Healey was reduced to that of requiring differential pay for daily overtime work, but now even that requirement is gone, and the Walsh-Healey Act exists in name only.

To some extent, the Davis-Bacon Act and Walsh-Healey Act can be understood as products of their times. They were spawned by the Great Depression and offered what was considered to be a modicum of wage protection in advance of the more substantial protection provided subsequently by the minimum wage law. Logically, they should have been phased out after the Fair Labor Standards Act was passed in 1938. This makes the Service Contract Act, introduced twenty-five years later, even more of an anomaly, although many of the persons intended to be covered by the Service Contract Act were not covered by minimum wage laws at the time it was passed in 1965. As a relatively young act, the Service Contract Act has gone through an unusual number of major amendments that have changed its direction of application and its potential degree of impact. The act nevertheless remains the least understood by federal agencies required to enforce prevailing wage laws, and as a consequence has been the most inconsistently and arbitrarily applied. Its costs currently are estimated to be on the order of $500 million per year, and it has the potential to exceed the Davis-Bacon Act in both complexity and total costs in years to come.

RECOMMENDATIONS

The separate chapters on the individual federal prevailing wage laws have consistently recommended their repeal, and not only because they are administratively messy and economically costly. The fundamental objection to all of the prevailing wage laws—those of the states as well as the federal ones—is that they are intended to achieve a purpose that is in itself questionable through means that are imperfectly understood. At heart, the prevailing wage laws seek to protect wage rates from downward pressures allegedly brought on by price competition among government contractors in bidding for government work. It is reasonable to question whether the wage rates for direct labor involved in such work should be so protected when wage rates for indirect labor, the return to capital, and the price of materials are not similarly protected. Without having to answer that policy question, it must be noted that the entire prevailing wage concept presupposes that in the absence of regulation government contractors will lower wage rates in order to secure work (but presumably will be unable to lower the prices they pay for materials and supplies, the rents they pay, the interest on the money they borrow, or the amount they spend for any input other than direct labor). This supposition that there exists a monopsonistic market for direct labor, and that an employer can arbi-

Conclusion

trarily lower labor rates at will is fallacious. Furthermore, even if it were the case that employers could control wage rates in this manner, they could as easily do so for private as for government work, rendering the need for any special protection in the case of government contracting unnecessary.

The examples provided by the state prevailing wage laws are very helpful in sorting out the difference between the claimed consequences of repeal of prevailing wage laws and actuality. First, several states have never had operational laws, and yet have not seemed to suffer from low wage rates, unwillingness of contractors to do business in the state, or low quality level of buildings, supplies, or services compared to those in neighboring states. Second, a number of states that had previously enacted prevailing wage laws repealed them in the years following Florida's repeal in 1979. No credible evidence of deleterious consequences has surfaced in any of these states, and despite reviews in several cases, none of the states that repealed their laws have reinstated them.

If the prevailing wage laws were ever appropriate or useful, that time is past. On the basis of all available evidence, it can be safely said that repeal of all federal and state prevailing wage laws would produce considerable savings but would have no deleterious impact. It would result simply in the shift of some demand from higher-priced to lower-priced labor. Since this is what economic efficiency is all about, it is a desirable as well as a valid pursuit.

Index

Abrams, Philip, 50, 60
Administrative Procedure Act, 224, 226
AFL-CIO, 64, 83, 94, 102
Alabama, 139, 150–51, 159, 202, 205
  prevailing wage repeal, 201
Alaska, 139, 151–54, 188, 190
  wage determinations in, 148, 149
Allen, Steven G., 100, 109–13
American Road Builders Association, 107
Anderson, John, 109
Apprentices and helpers, 132
  rates for under Davis-Bacon Act, 141
Area determinations, 70, 111. *See also* locality
Arizona, 138–39, 154–56, 159, 177, 205
  prevailing wage law in, 27
  prevailing wage repeal, 201
Arkansas, 144, 156–57
  wage determinations in, 148–49
Armed Services Board of Contract Appeals, 238
Armstrong, Senator, 215
Associated Builders and Contractors, 107
Associated General Contractors of America, 97, 107
Associated Independent Electrical Contractors, 107
Average rate
  as determinant of prevailing rate, 15, 17, 18, 102
Bacon, Robert L., 29
BLS. *See* U.S. Bureau of Labor Statistics
Bond sales
  and public works funding, 144
Bourdon and Levitt study, 113, 116
Branstad, Terry, 169
Brown & Root, Inc., 58–59, 62
Building and Construction Trades Department of the AFL-CIO, 4
Building and Construction Trades Dept., AFL-CIO, v. Donovan, 86n, 87n
Bureau of Building Management of the Office of General Services, 187
Bureau of Public Roads of the U.S. Department of Agriculture, 168
Burns International Security Service, Inc., v. NLRB, 238
California, 62, 72, 144, 157–59, 170, 179, 190, 203
  and Service Contract Act, 259
  wage determinations in, 149

Canada, 8
Carter administration
  and Service Contract Act, 254
Central tendency
  as determinant of prevailing rate, 17–19
Christian Labor Association, 179
Clark v. Unified Services, 256
Collective bargaining
  and prevailing wage rates, 184, 190
  and Service Contract Act, 233
Collins Construction Co. *See D.A. Collins Construction Co.*
Collins Service Co. v. United States, 258
Colorado, 139, 159–60, 205
  prevailing wage repeal, 201
Commission on Government Procurement, 97
Communications Act of 1934, 235
Competition, 6–7, 13, 28
Comptroller General, 52–57, 61, 65, 75, 79, 91
Computer and Business Equipment Manufacturers Association, 252
Congressional Budget Office, 38, 85, 95–98, 101, 119, 131
Congressional Research Service, 23, 36
Connecticut, 144, 160–61
  threshold amounts in, 142
  wage determinations in, 148, 149
Construction, 28–29, 38–39, 43, 75, 89, 97, 104–13, 129
  commercial, 68, 103–4, 120
  and Davis-Bacon Act, 21, 33, 35, 68, 85
  DOL classifications of, 63–64
  earnings in, 126
  and prevailing wage laws, 6, 7, 8, 23
  public, 39–40, 48
  residential, 68, 102–3, 120
Construction Industry Stabilization Commission, 47
Construction Wage Determinations Branch of the Wage and Hour Division of the Employment Standards Administration, 47
Contractors' associations, 11, 28, 87
Contract threshold
  under Davis-Bacon Act, 33, 130–31
  purpose of, 142
  under Walsh-Healey Act, 211
Contract Work Hours and Safety Standards Act of 1962, 37, 130, 214, 227

275

Convicts, 167, 216, 227
Copeland (Anti-Kickback) Act of 1934, 33, 130
Council on Wage and Price Stability, 75, 95, 102
D.A. Collins Construction Co., 65n
Davis-Bacon Act, 1–2, 4, 6, 8–13, 16–17, 21
  amendments and reforms of, 3, 8, 24, 25, 32–33, 34, 35, 69–70, 84–93, 130–35
  classifications under, 44, 57, 61–63, 85, 88
  costs of, 22, 85–86, 89, 93–120, 123
  coverage of, 7, 21–24, 137
  definitions of, 141
  in District of Columbia, 162–63
  enforcement of, 47, 87
  and Florida law, 164
  history of, 25–40
  and "little Davis-Bacon" acts, 24, 137
  and Maine law, 173
  and Minnesota law, 178–79
  and New Mexico law, 186
  and Ohio law, 190
  and Oklahoma law, 191
  and Oregon law, 192, 193
  rates under, 202
  repeal efforts against, 5, 130, 204
  and Service Contract Act, 230–32, 236–37, 241
  and state-funded projects, 150
  suspension of in 1970s, 47, 104–7
  and Walsh-Healey Act, 43, 72, 77, 132–33, 134, 207–15, 217–20, 222–23
  work rule restrictions under, 127
Davis, James J., 29
Delaware, 161–62
  and Service Contract Act, 239, 245
  wage determinations in, 149
Department of Labor. *See* U.S. Department of Labor
Descomp, Inc., v. Sampson, 245, 246, 248–51
Digital Equipment Corporation, 252
District of Columbia, 137, 139, 142, 162–63, 204
  and Service Contract Act, 242, 245
  wage determinations in, 148, 149
  and Walsh-Healey Act, 210
Division of Public Contracts of the U.S. Department of Labor, 218
Dodge Construction Reports, 73
DOL. *See* U.S. Department of Labor
Donovan, Raymond, 84
Economic Development Authority, 185
Econometric analyses of Davis-Bacon Act, 109–13

Edwards, Edwin, 173
Eight-hour day, 27, 38
  and prevailing wage legislation, 138
  and Walsh-Healey Act, 213–14
  in Wisconsin, 200
Employment Standards Administration, 45, 47, 49, 90, 247
Evans, John, 165, 166
Fair Labor Standards Act of 1938, 12, 37, 272
  and Service Contract Act, 230, 232–33, 236, 262–63, 265
  and Walsh-Healey Act, 210, 214, 216–17, 227
False Statement Act of 1934, 33
Federal-aid contracts, 36, 44
Federal-Aid Highway Act of 1956, 36
Federal Electric Corp. v. Dunlop, 250
"Federal" formula, 148
Federal Register, 85, 218
Federal Reserve Board, 260
Federal Reserve System, 260
50-percent rule, 14, 17, 41–42, 70, 90–91
Flexibility, 58
Florida, 117, 139, 151, 163–64, 202, 205
  prevailing wage repeal, 7, 9, 129, 201, 273
  and Service Contract Act, 239
France, 8
Fringe benefits
  and prevailing wage concept, 34–35
  and rate determinations, 48, 191
  and Service Contract Act, 235, 257, 264
Fulbright, William, 224
Fulbright amendments, 224–25, 226
GAO. *See* General Accounting Office
General Accounting Office (GAO), 23, 40, 48, 52, 54–57, 62–63, 66–67, 71, 75, 77–84, 92, 95, 98–101, 103–4, 121, 134, 250, 260, 262, 263, 270, 271
General Services Administration, 252
Georgia, 90, 164, 243
Georgine, Robert, 4–5
Goldfarb, Robert, 102–3
Gould, John, 106, 109
Government, monopsonistic powers of, 266
Great Britain, 4, 8
Great Depression, 7, 8, 23, 25, 28, 157, 160, 168, 208, 210, 272
Greene, Harold, 86–89
Gujarathi, Damodar, 66
Harvard University, 113
Hawaii, 139, 164–65, 190
  wage determinations in, 149
Healey, Arthur D., 209, 211
Hewlett Packard Company, 252
Hoover administration, 27

Index

Hoover, Herbert R., 31, 32, 42
House Committee on Education and Labor, 231
Houston Gulf Coast Building and Trades Council, 196
Idaho, 27, 138, 139, 165-67
  prevailing wage repeal, 201, 205
Illinois, 167-68
  wage determinations in, 149
Indiana, 144, 168-69
  contract threshold in, 143
  wage determinations in, 148
International Brotherhood of Electrical Workers (IBEW), 61
Iowa, 169, 202
Itinerant workers, 5, 13, 29, 30, 35, 120-21, 129, 131-32
  and Service Contract Act, 234, 268
James Construction Co. *See T.L. James Construction Co.*
Job titles, 63
Johnson administration, 52
Kansas, 27, 138, 169-71
  wage determinations in, 149
Ken-Rich Services, Inc., 255-56
Kentucky, 17, 144, 171-72, 203
  contract threshold in, 142
  wage determinations in, 149
Kunin, Madelaine, 198
Lamm, Richard, 160
League of Oregon Cities, 193
Local contracts
  and Davis-Bacon Act, 144-45
Locality, definitions of
  in Massachusetts, 175
  in Oregon, 192
  under Service Contract Act, 240-49, 264
  under Walsh-Healey Act, 212-13, 223-25
Louisiana, 144, 172-73
  prevailing wage repeal, 201
  wage determinations in, 149
Maine, 144, 173
  wage determinations in, 149
"Majority or average" formula, 85
"Majority, 30-percent, or average" formula, 41, 148, 162-63, 174, 186
Manufacturing
  earnings in, 126
Marshall, Ray, 5, 78, 84, 122-25
Maryland, 67-68, 72, 142, 144, 149, 174, 184, 202, 203
Massachusetts, 27, 50, 138, 175-77, 182, 203, 243
  wage determinations in, 150
Massachusetts Institute of Technology, 113

Mean rate, 17
Mechanical Contractors Association, 107
Median rate, 15, 17
Metropolitan Transit Authority (D.C.), 198
Michigan, 144, 177-78, 203
  wage determinations in, 150
Midwest Maintenance and Construction Co. v. Vela, 246, 247
Miller Act of 1935, 36-37
Minimum wages, 2, 7, 12, 13, 19, 20, 26, 37, 69
  and prevailing wage laws, 272
  and Service Contract Act, 235
  and Walsh-Healey Act, 211-13
Minnesota, 145, 158, 178-79, 182
  contract threshold in, 142
  wage determinations in, 149
Minority employment, 30, 127-28
Mississippi, 151, 179
  and Service Contract Act, 242
Missouri, 144, 179-80
  wage determinations in, 149
Modal rate, 15, 17, 18, 19
Montana, 180-81
  wage determinations in, 149
Morrall, John, 102-3
National Association of Home Builders, 58
National Electrical Contractors Association, 107
National Electrical Manufacturers Association (NEMA), 226
National Industrial Recovery Act (NIRA), 12, 208, 210, 218, 223
National Labor Relations Act, 238
National Retail Dry Goods Association, 217
"Nationwide locale," 247-48
Naval Space Surveillance System, 258
Navy. *See* U.S. Navy
Nebraska, 27, 139, 144, 181-82, 202
  wage determinations in, 149
Nevada, 182-84
  wage determinations in, 149
New Deal, 12, 25, 26
New federal formula, 148
New Hampshire, 139, 184
  prevailing wage repeal, 201, 205
New Jersey, 27, 138, 177, 184-85, 202, 203, 243
  wage determinations in, 150
New Mexico
  prevailing wage repeal, 201
  wage determinations in, 149
New York, 27, 138, 144, 145, 154, 174, 186-89, 190, 198, 202, 203
  wage determinations in, 150

Nickels, Senator, 215
Nixon, Richard M., 47, 104
North Carolina, 189
North Carolina State University, 100
North Dakota, 190
"Notice of intention," 259
Occupational Safety and Health Act, 216, 227
Ogle County (IL), 167
O'Hara-McNamara Services Act. *See* Service Contract Act
Ohio, 144, 154, 188, 190–91, 203
  wage determinations in, 150
Oklahoma, 27, 144, 191–92, 246
  wage determinations in, 149
"Old federal" formula, 148, 164, 186
Oregon, 192–93
  wage determinations in, 148, 149
Oregon State University, 100, 117, 118–19, 121, 126–27
Overtime, 37, 38
Pennsylvania, 144, 145, 158, 193–94, 196
  contract threshold in, 143
  wage determinations in, 148–49
Perkins, Frances, 148, 209
Plurality rate, 15, 19
Prevailing, definitions of, 14–19, 40–43, 131–32
  with fringe benefits, 34–35, 48
  under Walsh-Healey Act, 219–23
Prevailing wage laws
  costs of, 2, 8, 18, 20
  in Great Britain, 4
  rationale for, 3, 120–24
  in states, 12, 15, 27
Prevailing wage rates. *See also* rate determinations
  accuracy of, 76, 133
  arbitrariness of, 76, 133
  and collective bargaining, 184, 190
  under Service Contract Act, 229–30
  under Walsh-Healey Act, 218–19, 225–27
Private sector
  prevailing wage effects on, 3
Procurement, 3, 6, 26, 28, 53, 126
Productivity, 113–20
Prudential Building Maintenance, 255–56
Public Affairs Research Council of Louisiana, 172
Public Contracts Board, 218, 219, 220
Public Roads Administration, 36
Public works, 1, 137, 139–41
Public Works Administration, 36
rate classification
  under Davis-Bacon Act, 44, 57, 61–62, 85, 87–88

  in Navy, 258
  under Service Contract Act, 249–54
  under Walsh-Healey Act, 218–19
Rate determinations, 45–47, 48, 141, 148
  costs created by, 93
  by DOL, 47, 77
  error rate, 84
  and fringe benefits, 191
  methods of, 2, 11, 15
  protests against, 49–52
  and rate importation, 66–68, 87–89
  under Service Contract Act, 260
  in states, 148–50
  by survey, 43, 48, 49, 62–63, 71–76, 85, 87–88, 90–92
  under Walsh-Healey Act, 218–19, 225–27
Rate importation, 66–68, 87–89
Reagan administration
  and Service Contract Act, 229, 254
Reagan, Ronald, 84–85
Reorganization Plan No. 14, 47
Reporting requirement, 85–87
Reynolds, Morgan, 6, 7
Rhode Island, 145, 194–95
  wage determinations in, 149
Roosevelt, Franklin Delano, 209
Rural Electrification Administration, 36
Sample size, problems of, 70, 71–73
Senate Committee on Commerce, 32
Senate Labor and Human Resources Committee, 38, 215
Senate Subcommittee on Education and Labor, 32
Service Contract Act, 1, 2, 6, 8–11, 13, 15, 17, 22, 25, 35, 272
  and collective bargaining, 233
  costs of 263–65
  and Davis-Bacon Act, 230–32, 236–37, 241
  and itinerant workers, 234, 268
  locality, definitions of, 240–49
  "notice of intention," 259
  prevailing rates under, 229–30
  rationales for, 4
  and Reagan administration, 229, 254
  reform of, 3
  and state acts, 137
  and successor contractors, 254–57
  and superminimum wage, 244
  and wage busting, 232–33, 253, 255, 266
  wage classifications under, 249–54
  wage determinations under, 260
  and Walsh-Healey, 230–32, 237, 261
Service Employees' International Union Local 36 v. General Services Administration, 255
South Carolina, 195

Index

South Dakota, 195
Southern Packaging and Storage Co. v. United States, 247–49
Staats, Elmer, 52, 78
Subcommittee on Labor of the Senate Committee on Labor and Human Resources, 95
Successor contractors
  and Service Contract Act, 254–57
Sununu, John, 184
Surveys, 80, 134
  to determine area, 70
  to determine prevailing rate, 43, 48, 49, 62–63, 71–76, 77, 85, 87–88, 90–92, 148
Teamsters, 199
Tennessee, 144, 151, 195–96, 202
  prevailing wage laws in, 17
  rate determinations in, 67, 149
Tenth amendment, 137
Texas, 80, 144, 196–97, 246
  wage determinations in, 149
Texas A & M University, 196–97
"30-percent or average" formula, 148
30-percent rule, 14, 18, 41–42, 56, 67, 69, 72, 81, 85–91, 102, 117, 148, 219, 236, 241
Thousand Islands Bridge Authority, 186
T.L. James Construction Co., 61
Tree trimmers, 167
Trinity Services, Inc., v. Marshall, 256
Tower, John, 66
Unemployment insurance, 26
Unionization, 96, 105, 110–11
Unions, 4, 26, 30, 31–32, 138
  in construction industry, 44
  and Davis-Bacon Act, 35
  v. nonunion, 2, 4, 125
  and rate determinations, 15, 19, 68–71, 90–91, 180
  support prevailing rates, 28
  work practices of, 62, 95
U.S. Bureau of Labor Statistics, 75–76, 102, 128, 218, 226, 264
U.S. Department of Defense, 259
U.S. Department of Housing and Urban Development, 48
U.S. Department of Labor, 11, 14, 21, 24, 34, 41, 42, 47–51, 55–57, 65–67, 71, 75, 77–84, 86, 92, 97–99, 111–13, 120, 131, 134, 145, 157, 161, 185, 188, 218, 230, 234, 236, 237, 239, 241, 244–48, 250, 251, 253, 257, 258–60, 263
United States Housing Act of 1937, 36
U.S. Housing Authority, 36
U.S. Navy, 258

University of California, 157
University of Chicago, 106
Utah, 139, 197
  prevailing wage repeal, 201, 205
Vermont, 198
Virginia, 66, 151, 198
Wage Appeals Board, 51–53, 64–65, 79, 134
Wage busting, 5
  and Service Contract Act, 231, 232–33, 253, 266
Wage classification. *See* rate classification
Wage determinations. *See* rate determinations
Wage and Hour Administration, 237
Wages, 6, 13
  exploitation, 8
  differentials, 94–104
Wagner Act, 208. *See also* National Labor Relations Act
Walsh-Healey Public Contracts Act, 1, 2, 8–12, 14, 17, 22, 25, 35, 38, 129, 134, 271
  contract thresholds under, 211
  and Davis-Bacon Act, 42, 72, 77, 132–33, 207–15, 217–20, 222–23
  and Delaware law, 161
  exemptions from, 216–17
  and locality, definitions of, 223–25
  minimum wage and, 211–13
  prevailing, definitions of, 219–23
  and "projects of a character similar," 212
  rates under, 218–19
  rationales for, 4
  reform of, 3, 38
  and Service Contract Act, 230–32, 237, 261
  and state acts, 137
Walsh, David, 209
Washington, 198–99
  wage determinations in, 149
Webb, Beatrice and Sidney, 4
Weighted average rate, 15, 17, 72
West Virginia, 199
  wage determinations in, 149
Williams, Walter, E., 128
Wirtz v. Baldor, 226, 227, 271
Wisconsin, 144, 145, 199–200
  contract threshold in, 142
  wage determinations in, 149
Workmen's compensation, 26
Wyoming, 144, 200–1
  wage determinations in, 149

STUDIES OF NEGRO EMPLOYMENT

Vol. I. *Negro Employment in Basic Industry: A Study of Racial Policies in Six Industries (Automobile, Aerospace, Steel, Rubber Tire, Petroleum, and Chemicals),* by Herbert R. Northrup, Richard L. Rowan, et al. 1970.

Vol. II. *Negro Employment in Finance: A Study of Racial Policies in Banking and Insurance,* by Armand J. Thieblot, Jr., and Linda Pickthorne Fletcher. 1970.

Vol. III. *Negro Employment in Public Utilities: A Study of Racial Policies in the Electric Power, Gas, and Telephone Industries,* by Bernard E. Anderson. 1970.

Vol. IV. *Negro Employment in Southern Industry: A Study of Racial Policies in the Paper, Lumber, Tobacco, Coal Mining, and Textile Industries,* by Herbert R. Northrup, Richard L. Rowan, et al. 1971.

Vol. V. *Negro Employment in Land and Air Transport: A Study of Racial Policies in the Railroad, Airline, Trucking, and Urban Transit Industries,* by Herbert R. Northrup, Howard W. Risher, Jr., Richard D. Leone, and Philip W. Jeffress. 1971. $13.50*

Vol. VI. *Negro Employment in Retail Trade: A Study of Racial Policies in the Department Store, Drugstore, and Supermarket Industries,* by Gordon F. Bloom, F. Marion Fletcher, and Charles R. Perry. 1972.

Vol. VII. *Negro Employment in the Maritime Industries: A Study of Racial Policies in the Shipbuilding, Longshore, and Offshore Maritime Industries,* by Lester Rubin, William S. Swift, and Herbert R. Northrup. 1974.

Vol. VIII. *Black and Other Minority Participation in the All-Volunteer Navy and Marine Corps,* by Herbert R. Northrup, Steven M. DiAntonio, John A. Brinker, and Dale F. Daniel. 1979.

Order from University Microfilms, Inc.
Attn: Books Editorial Department
300 North Zeeb Road
Ann Arbor, Michigan 48106

* Order this book from the Industrial Research Unit, The Wharton School, University of Pennsylvania, Philadelphia, Pennsylvania 19104.

Racial Policies of American Industry Series

1. *The Negro in the Automobile Industry,* by Herbert R. Northrup. 1968
2. *The Negro in the Aerospace Industry,* by Herbert R. Northrup. 1968
3. *The Negro in the Steel Industry,* by Richard L. Rowan. 1968
4. *The Negro in the Hotel Industry,* by Edward C. Koziara and Karen S. Koziara. 1968
5. *The Negro in the Petroleum Industry,* by Carl B. King and Howard W. Risher, Jr. 1969
6. *The Negro in the Rubber Tire Industry,* by Herbert R. Northrup and Alan B. Batchelder. 1969
7. *The Negro in the Chemical Industry,* by William Howard Quay, Jr. 1969
8. *The Negro in the Paper Industry,* by Herbert R. Northrup. 1969
9. *The Negro in the Banking Industry,* by Armand J. Thieblot, Jr. 1970
10. *The Negro in the Public Utility Industries,* by Bernard E. Anderson. 1970
11. *The Negro in the Insurance Industry,* by Linda P. Fletcher. 1970
12. *The Negro in the Meat Industry,* by Walter A. Fogel. 1970
13. *The Negro in the Tobacco Industry,* by Herbert R. Northrup. 1970
14. *The Negro in the Bituminous Coal Mining Industry,* by Darold T. Barnum. 1970
15. *The Negro in the Trucking Industry,* by Richard D. Leone. 1970
16. *The Negro in the Railroad Industry,* by Howard W. Risher, Jr. 1971
17. *The Negro in the Shipbuilding Industry,* by Lester Rubin. 1970
18. *The Negro in the Urban Transit Industry,* by Philip W. Jeffress. 1970
19. *The Negro in the Lumber Industry,* by John C. Howard 1970
20. *The Negro in the Textile Industry,* by Richard L. Rowan. 1970
21. *The Negro in the Drug Manufacturing Industry,* by F. Marion Fletcher. 1970
22. *The Negro in the Department Store Industry,* by Charles R. Perry. 1971
23. *The Negro in the Air Transport Industry,* by Herbert R. Northrup et al. 1971
24. *The Negro in the Drugstore Industry,* by F. Marion Fletcher. 1971
25. *The Negro in the Supermarket Industry,* by Gordon F. Bloom and F. Marion Fletcher. 1972
26. *The Negro in the Farm Equipment and Construction Machinery Industry,* by Robert Ozanne. 1972
27. *The Negro in the Electrical Manufacturing Industry,* by Theodore V. Purcell and Daniel P. Mulvey. 1971
28. *The Negro in the Furniture Industry,* by William E. Fulmer. 1973
29. *The Negro in the Longshore Industry,* by Lester Rubin and William S. Swift. 1974
30. *The Negro in the Offshore Maritime Industry,* by William S. Swift. 1974
31. *The Negro in the Apparel Industry,* by Elaine Gale Wrong. 1974

Order from: Kraus Reprint Co., Route 100, Millwood, New York 10546